Incidental and Dance Music in the American Theatre from 1786 to 1923

by John Franceschina

Volume 1

Introduction and Chronology

BearManor Media
2018

Incidental and Dance Music in the American Theatre from 1786 to 1923:
Volume 1, Introduction and Chronology

© 2018 John Franceschina

All Rights Reserved.

No part of this book may be reproduced in any form or by any means, electronic, mechanical, digital, photocopying, or recording, except for in the inclusion of a review, without permission in writing from the publisher

For information, address:

BearManor Media
P. O. Box 71426
Albany, GA 31708

bearmanormedia.com

Typesetting and layout by John Teehan

Published in the USA by BearManor Media

ISBN—978-1-62933-239-0

For John Berkman,
in memory of *The Coldest War of All*

Table of Contents

Preface ix

Introduction 1

Chronology 23

Alphabetical Checklist of Choreographers
    and Stage Managers 267

Highlights of Future Volumes 295

Bibliography 319

Index 349

Preface

THE IMPULSE TO EXPLORE the dance music in the American musical theatre was probably planted during my second grade production of the school Christmas pageant for which I supplied the songs and dance music and conducted an orchestra of two accordions. I did not act upon the impulse at the time because I was in the seond grade and the thought of writing books had not yet occurred to me. Writing music, however, was already a familiar pursuit and, I composed scores of musical entertainments for my grammar school convinced that the composer of a show was necessarily the orchestrator, dance arranger, and conductor as well. I continued in that belief through college, regularly pumping out scores of songs, dance music, and orchestrations for shows I conducted—*This I What It's Like*, *The Dollmaker's Dilemma*, *The Day the Senate Fell in Love, Man Alive!*—that is, until the production of *The Coldest War of All* (libretto by Leo Brady), one of the first rock musicals to be professionally (though unsuccessfully) produced. After a summer production at the Olney Theatre in Maryland (for which I provided the score, dance music, and orchestrations, as well as the musical direction), the musical moved to the City Island Theatre in New York. For that iteration of the show, the celebrated Jerome Robbins dancer and teacher, Jay Norman, acted as choreographer, and John Berkman, son of the dean of the music school I attended, functioned as musical director. John had composed the dance music for *Hellza-Poppin* and *Come Summer* but hd yet to become the renowned dance arranger of *Follies*, *The Grass Harp*, and *Pippin*, and he and I collaborated on the dance music, adapting what I had written for the Olney production. It was here that I first experienced a separation of functions. No longer was the composer of a musical show *required* to serve as musical director (even though, subsequently, as musical director of various LORT theatres around the country, I often acted in both capacities). Since I was unable to be present for the dance rehearsals, someone on site had to be responsible for any necessary alterations to the original dance music, which I soon discovered included discarding whole dance breaks in favor of new music that enabled the choreographer to maximize the strengths of a cast that differed from the original production.

In the 1970s and 1980s my work as a LORT (and sometimes New York City) musical director resulted in my needing to provide a fair amount of incidental music for non-musical productions that included source music (coming from a radio or other onstage devices or instruments), overtures, entr'actes, and *melos* (music designed to support onstage action and stimulate an emotion in the audience). As Michael V. Pisani explained, in his excellent and ground-breaking study, *Music for the Melodramatic Theatre in Nineteenth-Century London and New York* (2014), melos communicated "some affect or sentiment . . . through the relationship of melody, key, harmony, and tempo and even an allusion to a known text" (7). For twenty-first century audiences, perhaps the best way to appreciate stage melos is to associate it with film music. Theatre scholars, such as Katherine K. Preston (2012) have argued convincingly that there was a clear connection between incidental music for the theatre and that for film (10); and Herbert Stothart, longtime Broadway dance arranger and incidental composer and Oscar-winning film composer, writing about film music in *The New York Times* (7 December 1941), furthers Pisani's interpretation of melos:

> The composer, through experience, learns what elements generate certain moods. Anger can be generated by what I call "red" tones, which slightly clash in orchestration and so mentally irritate. A tranquil mood can be inspired by quiet, gently flowing melody. Alarm can be created by clashing harmonies; unrest by the monotonous beat of tom-toms, and by effects strange in musical principle, and hence played to unaccustomed ears. Sonorous bells and deep tones of the organ inspire reverence. These are all matters of elemental psychology. By deciding to what extent to use them, one gets the shades in between the basic classifications.

It was Trude Rittman who suggested that I add the incidental music component to this study. Her experience as a dance arranger and composer of "continuity" music for Broadway musicals demonstrated a close association between dance and incidental music throughout her career; and the music she provided for Agnes DeMille's "story" ballets (for example, Louise's "Ballet" in *Carousel* and the "Civil War Ballet" in *Bloomer Girl*) certainly involved the use of melos to communicate affect and sentiment. Subsequent research seemed to verify my decision to follow Ms. Rittman's directive since nearly all of the incidental music I had located had been composed by men and women known to have also been dance arrangers.

Initially titled *The Music that Made Them Dance*, the original plan for this book began as a neat, genre-classified study that began in 1866 and continued through 2010, as you can read below:

> *The Music that Made Them Dance* is a critical survey of dance arrangers on Broadway: what they did and how they did it in the 150 years since *The Black Crook* initiated the role of dance arranger in American musicals. Since no book currently exists that chronicles the art of dance arranging, it is the aim of this text to fill an important gap in musical theatre scholarship in language that is easily accessible yet rich in descriptive analysis. Since many successful dance arrangers were women and African-American artists, it is also the hope that this book might appeal to a readership that extends beyond libraries, musical theatre aficionados and students. *The Music that Made Them Dance* cannot presume to include every dance arrangement for every show on Broadway since 1866. Instead, the most representative arrangers and musicals are the focus of the book—taking into account only the significance of the dance arrangements rather than the significance of the show (*Show Boat*, for example, is nowhere to be found here). To aid in the analysis the author hopes to include many musical examples, some bars from published scores but most material from manuscript sources.
>
> *(In the outline below there are numerous references to dance arrangers and their shows without explanation. Whenever a dance arranger is listed—or initially listed, if he or she has multiple references—there will be a brief biography and analysis of the distinctive features of the arranger's work. Then follows a more in-depth analysis of the arranger's*

contribution to the particular shows listed beside him or her. The shows were chosen as representative of the artist's work not because of the success or failure of the project. Other shows and dance arrangers may also be mentioned throughout the book in passing. Where there are multiple listings such as "Trude Rittman with Richard Rodgers and Agnes de Mille," the first name is always the dance arranger, the second the principal composer of the show, and the third the choreographer.)

PART ONE: THE EARLY DAYS OF DANCE COMPOSITION

1. Bringing on the Dancing Girls.

(Not only did The Black Crook's *combination of musical melodrama with ballerinas wearing skimpy and exotic costumes create a long-run sensation in New York, it defined the office of the "dance arranger" in American musical theatre.)* The Black Crook established the paradigm for dance composition: music to contextualize dance as extension of song; as spectacular divertissement; as virtuosic display; and as plot development. Analysis of how dance music in *The Black Crook* exemplifies the paradigm, combining folk structures and social dances like the hornpipe, waltz, jig, and quadrille into extended dance pieces. A Definition of "dance arranger" and the requirements of the office. A brief examination of the careers of our earliest dance arrangers and how they created music for the choreographers with whom they worked: Thomas Baker, composer of *The Black Crook,* with choreographer Davide Costa; David Braham, composer of *Aladdin the Second,* with choreographer Antonio Grossi; Michael Connelly, composer of *The Black Crook* revivals, with Davide Costa; Howard Glover, composer of *The White Fawn,* with Davide Costa; Giuseppe Operti, composer of *The Black Crook* revivals, with Davide Costa; A. Reiff, Jr., composer of Humpty Dumpty, with choreographer Michele Jambone; Henry Tissington, composer of *The Twelve Temptations,* with Davide Costa; Analysis of dance arrangements in later spectacle shows: *Mr. Bluebeard, A Yankee Circus on Mars, The White Cat,* and *The Soul Kiss.*

2. Hoofing It.

(While Extravaganzas traded on the exotic and spectacular, early Musical Comedies relied on settings familiar to the audience with dances that emphasized clogging, tap dancing, and ballroom styles instead of ballet. As a result, dance composers relied heavily on a simplified use of folk structures and social dances to establish characterization and plot development.) An examination of composer David Braham and his dance arrangements for Harrigan and Hart, with an emphasis on the dance music in *The Mulligan Guards' Ball* and *Reilly and the Four Hundred*. An examiniation of the George M. Cohan style: Analysis of dance music (by Charles J. Gebest) in *Little Johnny Jones* and *George Washington, Jr.*; An investigation into the "anonymous" dance arrangements for the Princess Shows and the Ragtime and Jazz musicals choreographed by Edward Royce, Sammy Lee, Bobby Connolly, and Robert Alton, with an emphasis on the dance music in *Oh, Boy!*, *Sally*, *Lady, Be Good!*, *No, No, Nanette*, *Good News*, *The Cocoanuts*, and *Anything Goes*.

3. Going Back to the Waltz: Dance Arrangements in American Operettas.

(While the dance compositions in early musical comedies tended to be little more than an extended chorus of a tune, dance music in the early operettas relied on motivic development and pantomimic underscore to assist the choreographer. The fact that most operettas traded on exotic locales also enabled the dance music—typically assembled by the composer of the songs—to be more lavish and complex than that of the musical comedies.) A study of the characteristics of Reginald deKoven's dance compositions, with an emphasis on *Robin Hood* and *The Fencing Master;* A study of Victor Herbert's dance music, with particular interest in *The Fortune Teller*, *Little Nemo* and the ballet music he composed for other composers' musicals; A study of Rudolf Friml's dance styles, comparing his operetta dance music (in *Rose-Marie* and *The Vagabond King*) to that of his musical comedies (*Some Time*, *You're in Love*); A study of Sigmund Romberg's dance compositions with special focus on *Maytime*, *The Desert Song*, and *Nina Rosa*.

Part Two: The "Modern" Age of Dance Music

4. Accompanying Dreams with a Corps de Ballet.

(*The return of ballet choreographers to the musical theatre at the same time composers and librettists were aiming for the tightest possible integration among the elements of music, words, and movement led not only to a golden age of the American Musical, but to a golden age of dance arrangers as well. This chapter chronicles those dance arrangers who developed the musical's tunes into throughcomposed accompaniments for musical theatre ballets.*) Exploration of the careers of dance composers writing ballets in musicals: Leonard Bernstein and choreographer Jerome Robbins: Analysis of dance music in *On the Town* and *West Side Story*; Genevieve Pitot with Hanya Holm, Jerome Robbins, and Michael Kidd: Dance music in *Kiss Me Kate, Miss Liberty, Call Me Madam, Out of This World, Can-Can, Li'l Abner,* and *Destry Rides Again*; Trude Rittman with Agnes de Mille, Michael Kidd, Jerome Robbins, and Hanya Holm: Dance music in *Carousel, Finian's Rainbow, Look Ma, I'm Dancin', Brigadoon, Paint Your Wagon, My Fair Lady,* and *Camelot*; Richard Rodgers and choreographer George Balanchine: Analysis of dance music in *On Your Toes* and *Babes in Arms*; Laurence Rosenthal and choreographer Onna White: *The Music Man*; Jule Styne and Jerome Robbins' "Mack Sennett Ballet" in *High Button Shoes*.

5. Syncopating Sex: 40s and 50s "Jazz" Musicals.

(*The integration of music, words, and movement in a musical was not limited to ballet choreography. The development of different styles of dance required the creation of different kinds of dance music by arrangers who were adept at transforming Broadway tunes into brassy and rhythmical accompaniments, often more angular than lyrical with asymmetrical construction.*) An exploration into the careers of dance arrangers known principally for their work with choreographers of "jazz" or "modern" styles of dance: Roger Adams with choreographer Eugene Loring in *Buttrio Square*; with Bob Fosse in *Pajama Game, Damn Yankees,* and *New Girl in Town*; Irma Jurist with Michael Kidd: *Hold It!*; with choreographer Jack Cole: *Alive and Kicking*; John Kander with Betty Walberg, Jule Styne and Jerome Robbins: *Gypsy*; Oscar Kosarin, Jule Styne, and choreographer Robert Alton with *Hazel Flagg*; Hugh Martin with choreographer Hermes Pan: *As*

The Girls Go; Alan Morand with choreographer Nick Castle: *Heaven on Earth*; Hal Schaefer with choreographer Jack Cole: *Kismet* and *Foxy*; Billy Strayhorn with Duke Ellington and choreographer Valerie Bettis: *Beggar's Holiday*.

6. Exotic Dancing.

(Although all dance music is, in its own way, atmospheric, certain projects require the dance arranger to explore musical styles beyond what could be called "ethnic sweetening" of the traditional musical theatre sound. In such cases, the dance arranger may succeed even better than the composer of the songs in establishing the atmosphere and environment of the show.) An exploration into representative musicals with exotic dance arrangements: Roger Adams, Manos Hadjidakis, and Onna White with *Illya Darling*; Bob Atwood with Eaton Magoon, Jr. and choreographer Rod Alexander: *13 Daughters*; Richard DeBenedictis with Walter Marks and choreographer Peter Gennaro: *Bajour*; Dorothea Freitag with John Kander and choreographer Ron Field: *Zorba*; Peter Matz with Harold Arlen and Jack Cole in *Jamaica*; with Moose Charlap and Onna White on *Whoop Up*; John Morris with Richard Adler and Agnes de Mille: *Kwamina*; Trude Rittman, Richard Rodgers, Jerome Robbins and *The King and I*; Betty Walberg with Jerry Bock, and Jerome Robbins: *A Fiddler on the Roof*; Neil Warner with Mitch Leigh and Jack Cole: *Man of La Mancha*.

7. Amalgamating Styles and Composing for Runways: Blockbuster Musicals of the 60s and 70s.

*(As the book musical matured into a form that liberally blended all types of sounds within a single show—*110 in the Shade, *for example, demonstrates the wide range of musical styles—dance arrangers became associated less with a single style and an eclectic musical ability to develop songs into a variety of dance patterns began to develop.)* An investigation of the primary dance arrangers of the 60s and 70s: Jack Elliot with Jerry Bock and Peter Gennaro on *Fiorello!*; with Jerry Bock and choreographer Joe Layton on *Tenderloin*; Dorothy Freitag with Stanley Lebowsky and Onna White on *Gantry*; with John Kander and Onna White on *70, Girls, 70*; with Peter Link and Ron Field on *King of Hearts*; Billy Goldenberg with

Harvey Schmidt and Agnes de Mille on *110 in the Shade*; with Noel Coward and Danny Daniels on *High Spirits*; with Marvin Hamlisch, Bob Merrill, and Michael Bennett on *Henry, Sweet Henry*; with Michael Bennett on *Ballroom*; Peter Howard with Bob Merrill and Gower Champion on *Carnival*; with Jule Styne and Michael Kidd on *Subways Are For Sleeping*; with Meredith Willson and Michael Kidd on *Here's Love*; with Jerry Herman and Gower Champion on *Hello, Dolly!*; with Ervin Drake and choreographer Dania Krupska on *Her First Roman*; with Sherman Edwards and Onna White on *1776*; with Marvin Hamlisch, Larry Grossman, and Marc Breaux on *Minnie's Boys*; with John Kander and Bob Fosse on *Chicago*; with Charles Strouse and Peter Gennaro on *Annie*; John Morris with Charles Strouse and choreographer Gower Champion on *Bye Bye Birdie*; with Cy Coleman and Michael Kidd on *Wildcat*; with Charles Strouse and choreographer Danny Daniels on *All American*; with Jerry Herman and Gower Champion on *Mack and Mabel*; Harold Wheeler with Burt Bacharach and Michael Bennett on *Promises, Promises*; with Andre Previn and Michael Bennett on *Coco*; with Marvin Hamlisch and Michael Bennett on *A Chorus Line*; David Baker with John Kander and choreographer Ron Field on *Cabaret*; Fred Werner with Cy Coleman and Bob Fosse on *Sweet Charity*; Lee Holdridge with Oscar Brand, Paul Nassau, and choreographer Michael Bennett on *A Joyful Noise*.

PART THREE: POSTMODERN DANCE MUSIC

8. Dancing Sondheim.

(Although acknowledged as the master of the musical theatre form and arguably the most important composer-lyricist of the second half of the twentieth century, Stephen Sondheim has never been associated with "dance" even though many of his shows have a fair amount of dance music. How does dance figure into the fabric of a Sondheim piece, and how does a dance arranger contribute to a composer who already has all the notes written down? Please note that with the exception of Betty Walberg who came in to do patch work on Forum, *Sondheim never uses a dance arranger twice.)* A look at the experience of writing dance music for Stephen Sondheim: Hal Schaefer and Betty Walberg with Jack Cole (and Jerome Robbins): *A Funny Thing Happened on the Way to the Forum*; Betty Walberg with choreographer Herbert Ross: *Anyone Can Whistle*; Richard DeBenedictis

with Richard Rodgers and Herbert Ross: *Do I Hear a Waltz?*; Wally Harper with Michael Bennett: *Company*; John Berkman with Michael Bennett: *Follies*; Danny Troob with choreographer Patricia Birch: *Pacific Overtures*; Tom Fay with choreographer Larry Fuller: *Merrily We Roll Along*.

9. Dancing with African-Americanisms.

(Although African-American musicals have been in evidence since the beginning of the twentieth century, the African-American dance arranger—who is not the principal composer of the show and who is designing music specifically for African-American dance—is a much later phenomenon. An exploration of this category of dance music provides much insight into "funky" popular musical styles that have gradually worked their way into the Broadway musical theatre sound.) H.B. Barnum with Bert Keyes and Bob Larimer and choreographer Talley Beatty on *But Never Jam Today*; with Alex Bradford et al. and Talley Beatty on *Your Arms Too Short to Box with God*; Timothy Graphenreed with Charlie Smalls and choreographer George Faison on *The Wiz*; with Garry Sherman and choreographer Michael Peters on *Comin' Uptown*; Luther Henderson with Gary Geld and choreographer Louis Johnson on *Purlie*; with Buster Davis and choreographer Donald MacKayle on *Doctor Jazz*; with Bob Brush and choreographer Alan Johnson on *The First*; with Jelly Roll Morton and choreographers Hope Clarke and Gregory Hines on *Jelly's Last Jam*; Danny Holgate with Micki Grant and Vinnette Carroll on *Don't Bother Me, I Can't Cope*; Doug Katsaros with Cliff Jones and Gower Champion on *Rockabye Hamlet*; Harold Wheeler with Henry Krieger and Michael Bennett on *Dreamgirls*; Judd Woldin with Dorothea Freitag and Donald MacKayle on *Raisin*;

10. Reviving, Revising, and Revisiting Past Styles.

(As revivals and remakes became the rule on Broadway, dance arrangers had to adapt the show songs not only to the requirements of the choreography but also to the timbre of different musical styles—either transforming a contemporary-sounding score into a period piece, or modernizing a period piece into a contemporary-sounding score. More often than not, it is the dance arranger—and/or orchestrator—rather than the principal composer who is most challenged—and who deserves the majority of the credit—

when a transfer of period is required.) Wally Harper with Harry Tierney, Charles Gaynor and Otis Clements, and Peter Gennaro on *Irene*; with George Gershwin and choreographers Thommie Walsh and Tommy Tune on *My One and Only*; with Rudolf Friml and choreographer Lester Wilson on *The Three Musketeers*; Russell Warner with Bert Kalmar, Harry Ruby, and choreographer Dan Siretta on *The Five O'Clock Girl*; with George M. Cohan and Dan Siretta on *Little Johnny Jones*; Louis St. Louis with Jim Jacobs, Warren Casey, and Patricia Birch on *Grease*; with Richard M. and Robert B. Sherman and Patricia Birch on *Over Here!*; Luther Henderson with Vincent Youmans and choreographer Donald Saddler on *No, No, Nanette*; Donald Johnson with Harry Warren and Gower Champion on *Forty-Second Street*; James Raitt with Hugh Martin and Ralph Blaine and choreographer Joan Brickhill: *Meet Me in St. Louis*.

11. Dancing to a Different Beat: the New Wave of Dance Arrangers

David Chase with Henry Krieger and choreographer Robert Longbottom: *Side Show*; with Frank Wildhorn and Robert Longbottom: *The Scarlet Pimpernel*; with James Van Heusen, Jeanine Tesori and choreographer Rob Ashford: *Thoroughly Modern Millie*; with Matthew Sklar and Rob Ashford: *The Wedding Singer*; with John Kander and Rob Ashford: *Curtains*; with Alan Menken and choreographer Stephen Mear: *The Little Mermaid*; David Krane with Michael Valenti and choreographer Ernest O. Flatt on *Honky Tonk Nights*; with John Kander and choreographer Rob Marshall: *Kiss of the Spider Woman*; with Henry Mancini and Rob Marshall: *Victoria/Victoria*; with David Shire and choreographer Susan Stroman: *Big*; with Stephen Flaherty and Graciela Daniele: *Ragtime*; Glen Kelly with Alan Menken and choreographer Matt West: *Beauty and the Beast*; with John Kander and Susan Stroman: *Steel Pier*; with Cole Porter and Lar Lubovitch: *High Society*; with Mel Brooks and Susan Stroman: *The Producers*; Henry Aronson with Barry Keating and choreographer Michele Asaf: *Starmites*; Stephen Flaherty with choreographer Graciela Daniele: *Once On This Island*; Jeanine Levenson with Lucy Simon and choreographer Michael Lichtefeld: *The Secret Garden*; Mark Hummel with Marvin Hamlisch and Graciela Daniele: *The Goodbye Girl*; Gordon Harrell with Jule Styne and choreographer Lar Lubovitch: The *Red Shoes*; Phil Edwards with the Bee Gees and choreographer Arlene Phillips: *Saturday Night Fever*; Bob Gustafson with Elton John and choreographer Wayne Cilento:

Aida; Zane Mark with David Yazbek and choreographer Jerry Mitchell: *The Full Monty*; James Lynn Abbott with Stephen Schwartz and Wayne Cilento: *Wicked*.

Although admittedly many readers might have preferred that heavily illustrated coffee-table book dealing with familiar titles and songwriters, the original approach was deeply flawed on several accounts. Why begin, for example, with *The Black Crook* (1866) when there was ample evidence of music composed for ballets and pantomimes on the American stage seventy-five years earlier? Why restrict the subject to dance music only in New York when other cities (such as Philadelphia, Boston, Baltimore, Chicago, San Francisco) had thriving theatrical scenes that produced interesting dance-focused shows that never appeared on Broadway? Why use genre divisions based on stereotypical production styles such as "operetta" or "African-American musicals" when varying styles of music found their way into many dramatic forms. African-American musicals, for example, were not entirely filled with syncopated ragtime music and operettas often made use of popular musical forms such as ragtime and foxtrot. Moreover, how could *The Black Crook* be viewed as the defining moment for the position of dance music arranger when the first actual program credit for dance music arrangements was assigned to Henry Tissington for his work on Hervé's *Le Petit Faust* (26 September 1870).

The biggest obstacle to sustaining the original plan, however, was the carrying into the past an assumption that was true during the golden age of American musicals: that dance arrangers worked side-by-side with choreographers and directors in the creation of dance numbers. Although that may have been the case for some arrangers—those who served as musical director and/or rehearsal accompanist—there was ample evidence of dance music connected with theatre productions that was published prior to or simultaneous with performance, composed in multiples of eights (eight beats, or two measures of 4/4 or common time) without any accommodation of accents that might suggest a fit to specific choreography. When a particular dance form was required—waltz, minuet, mazurka, bolero, march, gavotte, hornpipe, fandango, or jig—the composer simply provided music according to form, and the stage manager (the individual who stages the production) or choreographer staged the dance to the music he or she was given. Melville Ellis (1875–1917) was perhaps the most significant dance music arranger of the early twentieth century because he actually shaped dance music during dance rehearsals, though even he was heavily reliant on traditional structures.

As research progressed it also became clear that there were more similarities than differences among dance compositions (and incidental music) written at various periods in the history of the American musical theatre. From 1786 through 1923, dance music relied on traditional dance structures; incidental music sought to support dramatic action and establish mood, character, and atmosphere; and music for ballets was composed either as an extended dance or suite of dances. What differentiated one piece of dance or incidental music from another was the musical language used (i.e., a Western European influence; an African-American influence; popular versus serious music, etc.). Depending on the nationality of the composer, serious dance music (i.e., ballet music) was modelled after Italian, German, or French romantic operas and ballets; and popular dance music typically relied either on comic operas / burlesques (borrowing heavily from Offenbach, von Suppé. Strauss, and Sullivan) or on the light popular music of the day (minstrel songs; parlor songs; instrumental dance music; ragtime). What appeared to be novel forms—the cakewalk, foxtrot, "Charleston," for example—were more of an issue about the musical language used (syncopation versus square, for example) than anything completely original. As you will read over and over in this text, originality was hardly a positive attribute when it came to incidental and dance music in the American musical theatre. To support a theatrical action and communicate a mood or atmosphere, the music the audience heard had to be familiar enough to evoke the proper response. Of course there were adverse reactions to whatever novelties were added to the musical language, but, as in any language, changes gradually became part of the musical fabric. I recall a time when split-infinitives were condemned in every writing class and Leonard Bernstein's brilliant music for *West Side Story* was actually considered noise. Now, we no longer fault *Star Trek*'s five-year mission, "to boldly go where no man has gone before," and *West Side Story* is canonized as a musical theatre classic.

Each publisher that expressed interest in the project advised me on possible directions the book might take. Having long admired Kurt Gänzl's *Encyclopedia of the Musical Theatre* (1994; second edition, 2001) and Larry Billman's *Film Choreographers and Dance Directors: An Illustrated Biographical Encyclopedia, with a History and Filmographies 1893 through 1995* (1997), I chose to recast the project as a series of short critical biographies of the men and women who composed dance and incidental music for American productions between the years 1786 (when the first extant piece of dance music was produced) and 2015 (ending with a study of the dance music in *Hamilton*). The first series would cover the period from 1786 ("Durang's Horn-Pipe") to1923 (*Kid Boots*); the second series would begin in 1924 (*Lady, Be Good!*) and extend through 1966 (*Cabaret*); the third (and last) would begin with *Hair* (1967) and continue through *Hamilton* (2015). Each series would contain a chronology of significant (or simply interesting) dance productions as well as critical biographies of the damce music arrangers and musical examples. In addition, the second and third series would contain interviews with dance arrangers and analyses of the collaboration between arranger and choreographer—an aspect of this project made possible by the video records of contemporary productions.

For the present series, I am indebted to the groundbreaking studies conducted by Ken Bloom (*American Song: The Complete Musical Theatre Companion*); Gerald Bordman (*American Musical Theatre: A Chronicle*); Lynn Matluck Brooks (*John Durang: Man of the American Stage*); Kurt Gänzl (*Encyclopedia of the Musical Theatre*); Lincoln Kirstein (*Dance: A Short History of Classic Theatrical Dancing*); Richard C. Norton (*A Chronology of Americn Musical Theater*); Julian Mates (*The American Musical Stage before 1800*); George C.D. Odell (*Annals of the New York Stage*); Bernard L. Peterson, Jr. (*A Century of Musicals in Black and White*); Michael V. Pisani (*Music for the Melodramatic Theatre in Nineteenth-Century London and New York*); Susan L. Porter (*With an Air Debonair: Musical Theatre in America 1785–1815*); Thomas L. Riis (*Just Before Jazz: Black Musical Theater in New York, 1890 to 1915*); Oscar G. Sonneck (*Early Opera in America*); and Donald Stubblebine (*Early Broadway Sheet Music: A Comprehensive Listing of Published Sheet Music from Broadway and Other Stage Shows, 1843–1918*). I am also grateful to the librarians for their helpful advice and courteous assistance at the Library of Congress, the New York Public Library, the Free Library of Philadelphia, the Sheridan Libraries Special Collections at Johns Hopkins University, the College of Music Allen Library at Florida State University, and the music division of Patee Library at The Pennsylvania State University. I am also grateful to Trude Rittman for her kind suggestions; to composer and dance arranger John Morris for his encouragement and support of this project; to Eberle Thomas, Sue Lawless, and Howard Millman for their continued belief in my work; to John Teehan for his expert layout and typesetting; and to Ben Ohmart who agreed to publish this ungainly project simply because it spoke about men and women who need to be remembered.

Introduction

AT THE STAGE DOOR of a Broadway theatre, the dance arranger and conductor of the musical being performed bumps into the choreographer of the production. After a convivial greeting and small talk, the arranger begins to make his way into the orchestra pit. Before disappearing beneath the stage, he turns and shouts to the choreographer, "What tempo would you like for the dances tonight? Too fast or too slow?" I do not recall when I first heard that joke, or in which of its many permutations, but it must have been early in my career as a dance arranger, and told to me by a witty though wizened trumpet player in the pickup orchestra I found myself conducting.

In the late twentieth and early twenty-first centuries, much has been written about the association between music and dance and the composers and choreographers whose collaborations assisted in the creation of the American musical theatre as we know it. Articles in dance magazines discussing the activities of "dance arrangers" and their mediant relationship between the composer of the musical numbers and the choreographer and/or director of the production have brought forward the important function they serve, that often exceeds what audiences might consider dance music. In an interview with Jonathan Mandell in *TDF Stages: A Theatre Magazine* (July 2011), veteran dance arranger David Chase explained: "The dance arranger is the go-between between the songs and the choreography. I address whatever needs the composer has, and the choreographer has, and I literally arrange the music in a way that both honors the music and helps the dancing." For Chase, the concept of musical arrangement involved everything but the actual melody of the number: "All other elements of a piece of music are what might be termed its arrangement—the accompaniment, the tempo, the melodic variations, the key, the style, the length and context of the intro, the harmonies, the number of verses and choruses, etc." In an earlier article in *Ask Playbill. Com: The Dance Arranger* (8 May 2008), Chase added: "On a larger level a dance arranger has to look at the song as a whole. When should the dance breaks happen? When do the dancers need a short bit of background music to play as a transition, while they make their way up the stairs, for instance? What kind of music should that be? A dance arranger then has to write those dance breaks and those transitions, using music that the composer has written for that song or for other songs in the show, or from other songs from that time period. While making these decisions, a dance arranger has to make sure that these decisions fit the style of music the composer is trying to evoke, and the story that the director wants the song to tell."

Chase's comments certainly ring true for the American musical theatre as far back as the 1940s when seminal dance arrangers Trude Rittman and Genevieve Pitot were creating ballet music and "continuity" for Broadway musicals. "Continuity" was a term that involved much of what Chase described as part of the musical arrangement. It generally consisted of introductions to songs; music for playoffs, scene changes, and underscores; and any other incidental music that was not specifically dance related. Rittman and Pitot were exceptional pianists, experienced rehearsal pianists, and ballet accompanists; and they could well be considered the originators of modern dance arranging. However, since it is an accepted fact that dance existed in the American theatre in America during the eighteenth century, the function of dance arranger must certainly have existed in some form 200 years prior to Rittman and Pitot. In his *Dance: A Short History of Classic Theatrical Dancing*, Lincoln Kirstein (1987) noted:

> The harlequinade, the English descendant of the commedia dell'arte, was a particularly popular form in early America. In 1767, *Harlequin's Vagaries* was given in New York "by command of His Excellence the Governor, for the entertainment of Ten Indian Warriors that arrived here ... from South Carolina." From 1782 on, a series of "pantomimes," extravaganzas with frequent songs and dance numbers, was the rage. ... In 1783, New York saw *The Witches, or, Birth, Vagaries and Death of Harlequin*, concluding with a grand "Dance of Shepherds and Shepherdesses," and in the same year *Columbus, or, the Discov-*

ery of America with *Harlequin's Revels*, concluding with a double hornpipe. (335)

A clue to the identities of the earliest dance arrangers in America comes from a remark made by Michael O'Flaherty, veteran musical director and dance arranger at the Goodspeed Opera House in East Haddam, Connecticut. According to O'Flaherty in *Dance Magazine* (1 January 2010), "Almost all dance arrangers come from the ranks of music directors."

It is now generally accepted that theatres in eighteenth-century America employed musical directors to lead an orchestra of varying sizes and to provide musical "continuity" that held together the evening's entertainment. Writing in *Musical Theatre in America*, William Brooks reported that such continuity involved the composition and/or arrangement of overtures and entr'acte music; incidental music to support plays of various genres (tragedies, melodramas, comedies, farces); and songs and dance music interpolated in the production of a comic opera, pantomime, or ballet. Brooks continued with a probable description of the incidental music used in the early days of the American theatre:

> Most incidental music probably displayed dancelike rhythms and employed a consistent family of evocative gestures. Thus certain thematic types served for battles, others for rejoicing, others for despair. ... Themes with similarly evocative contours appear with some frequency in short keyboard works by theatre composers; it may be that parts of these were originally used in stage productions. ... Care must be taken, however, to avoid works of special merit. Like its modern counterpart [i.e., music for television or film] eighteenth-century incidental music masked stylistic distinction with an agreeable veneer of conventionality. (39)

The concept of conventionality is important in regard to theatre music. Designed to produce a particular effect in the minds of the audience, the early musical directors/dance arrangers/composers had to rely on an accepted convention of sound signs that were familiar to everyone in the theatre (from the most discerning listener to the near tone-deaf). As Benjamin Deane remarked in *The New York Times* (6 October 1878), "[Musical directors'] work is rather arranging than composing, although there are few if any who do not write some original music, and some of them write a great deal. Having the power to get his creations before the public is a great temptation to any musician, and few are able to withstand it. But, for the music of the theatre of the present day, familiarity with the music which has been written, a good knowledge of where to reach readily for what is wanted, and facility of working it in, are more important essentials to a leader than the divine inspiration for the construction of more music. ... The leader's object must be to please the public, and so long as he does that, it doesn't make much odds where he gets his material. His precise contract duty is to supply the theatre with overtures and entr'actes, and to write and arrange the music necessary for any piece that may be gotten up in the theatre with which he is connected. But anything he writes for star or author, to be used outside the theatre, he must be paid for separately. For his regular duty he gets from $25 to $75, and perhaps even $100 a week, according to his popularity and ability, and for the outside work he gets—what he can."

Versatility was another important factor. The theatrical event might involve a classical ballet, a rope dancer, an animal act, a pantomime, tumbling acrobats, a high-wire dancer, a melodrama, and a farce—each of which required music that had to match the onstage activity. It should come as no surprise, then, that familiar-sounding music that was immediately accessible to the audience was the preferred idiom. When composer and musical director Thomas Baker went to Niblo's Garden to rehearse his music for *The Black Crook* (1866), for example, he heard members of the orchestra mumbling the names of familiar composers as they played through Baker's music. "Rossini," "Meyerbeer," "Mendelssohn," "Verdi," were uttered by various players until they came to the music for the incantation scene. Then in one loud voice, the orchestra shouted "Weber!" Baker good-naturedly admitted to borrowing motifs and sometimes large sections of music from the composers mentioned, saying "You have to admit that it is good music" (*The New York Times* 6 October 1878). The issue of authorship was further compounded in the early American musical theatre when foreign scores were produced. Invariably the musical director was responsible for adjusting the music to the capabilities of the performers on stage, the size of the orchestra, and the requirements of the choreographer. Keys were changed, the order of musical numbers was often rearranged, new songs were interpolated, and new "continuity" was added, all (more often than not) without input from the original composer.

The earliest extant example of original dance music from the eighteenth-century American musical theatre was composed by William Hoffmaster, a violinist in the orchestra of the John Street Theatre in New York City. Hoffmaster was also a violin instructor and among his pupils was John Durang, the American stage dancer who also worked at the theatre. For Durang, Hoffmaster composed the music for the hornpipe which the dancer performed as entr'acte entertainment. George C.D. Odell (1927) described the event in detail:

> The first appearance [at the John Street Theatre] of Hallam and Allen's company was in a "lecture" advertised for that evening … as beginning with a Monody to the Memory of the Chiefs who have fallen in the Cause of American Liberty. The lecture was "in two parts—each part preceded by a Poetical Introduction to a display of characters *comic* and *satiric*"; between the parts figured a hornpipe, probably by Durang. At the end of the lectures was danced an Alamande, also doubtless with Durang. Then followed Garrick's Ode on Shakespeare, and two scenes from Loutherbourg's *Eidophusicon* [scenes from nature that appeared to be moving pictures through the use of mirrors and other devices]. (1: 232)

It is believed that Durang choreographed his hornpipe and a "Dwarf Dance" for which Hoffmaster provided music as well. Other early dancers and choreographers on the American stage included Alexander Placide who Durang considered "the best tight rope dancer that ever was in America" (Durang 1966, 31); William Francis, and James Byrne, both specialists in ballet-pantomime.

The earliest composers of incidental and dance music in America were European musicians who found employment in America as composers, musical directors, orchestra members, music educators, and music publishers—some of whom served all of those functions. Since the early theatre in America had been imported from England, it should come as no surprise that a majority of composers and musical directors were also English (and Irish or Scottish) in origin and that the American musical theatre adhered to patterns established in London during the eighteenth century. Musicians also arrived in America from France and Germany and imported musical trends from their homelands, particularly in styles of dance and incidental music. Characteristic social dances of the eighteenth century provided musical models in the New World. These included the allemande, contra dance, fandango, gavotte, hornpipe, jig, march, minuet, quadrille, and (in the 1780s) the waltz. According to Lincoln Kirstein, even the music for early ballets in America was based on social dance models since ballet masters often taught social dancing and "their choreographic patterns for the stage were frequently theatricalized social dances" (337). Originality and innovation was significantly less important than the appropriateness of incidental music to the dramatic situation and the adherence of dance music to eight-beat units. Even triple meters were grouped in eight-measure phrases and counted "1–and–a–2–and–a" up to "8–and–a" before returning to "1–and–a." Popular dance music arrangers during the earliest period (1786–1825) included John Bray, Benjamin Carr, James Hewitt, Victor Pelissier, Alexander Reinagle and Raynor Taylor; though, perhaps, the most original composer of the period was the Bohemian-born Anthony Philip Heinrich, who was also an exponent of the nineteenth-century Romantic view of art as self-expression. Even though his music was heavily influenced by eighteenth-century dance music, it was far too advanced for theatrical consumption and found a happier home in concert halls. A small number of popular incidental and dance music arrangers during this period never even stepped foot on American soil: Michael Kelly, William Reeve, James Sanderson, and William Ware who had composed incidental and dance music for British productions were also published in the United States when their music was performed here.

A second wave of dance and incidental arrangers occurred between 1826 and 1867, roughly bookended by dance arranger Charles Gilfert's management of the Bowery Theatre in the late 1820s and the year-long production of *The Black Crook* that began in 1866. In between, theatrical dancing exhibited the influence of new social dances—the galop and the polka—that vied for dominance over the waltz; and dance music, which displayed a debt to Rossini at the beginning of the period, became undeniably Offenbachian by the end of the term. During this period the schottische also became a favored dance with music characterized by dotted rhythms and triplets as if it were a waltz in duple, rather than triple time. Dance music employing schottische rhythms would remain a favorite with dance music arrangers well into the twentieth century. The second wave also witnessed the rise and flowering of American minstrelsy and its music, an amalgamation of African-American culture with Western musical traditions under the influence of Irish and Scottish folk music, which would also have a profound impact on American popular dance music into the twentieth century. As suggested by Clayton W. Henderson, "the animated rhythmic element of the banjo tunes or jigs composed for the minstrel shows between 1840 and 1890 greatly influenced American popular music. Some of the jigs rely heavily on British dance types; others illustrate irregular rhythmic accentuations achieved through phrasing, rests, textures, ornamentations and metrical shifts. These patterns of syncopation served as rhythmic models for ragtime, blues and early jazz" (Stanley Sadie [1980] 12: 352).

The second wave reached its climax with the production at Niblo's Garden of *The Black Crook*, the show which, according to George C.D. Odell, "revolutionized ballet spectacle in America, and caused boys of 1867–1868 to sneak off—with a sense of being very wicked—to gaze at female pulchritude their mammas wot not of" (1936, 8:153). A famous and often quoted descriptive review of the production appeared in the New York *Tribune* on 17 September 1866:

> Niblo's Garden opened in a literal blaze of glory on Wednesday evening. The audience assembled on that occasion was so large that filled the house in every part, overflowed into the lobbies, and, in the shape of frequent and large detachments, extended to the street and pervaded the neighborhood. Great enthusiasm prevailed before the curtain, and great excitement behind it. A livelier scene than was thus presented could not well be imagined. *The Black Crook* was played by easy stages, from 7:45 o'clock until 1:15. Most of the auditors remained until the gorgeous end. ... By dint of great energy on the part of [producer William] Wheatley and the mechanics, *The Black Crook* was at length played through; and a patient multitude, dazed and delighted, went to brief dreams of fairyland. It takes time to digest so much radiance, and we have not, therefore, been in haste to describe this extraordinary drama. Having swallowed the rainbows, however, it is now our pleasant duty to say that they are very good to take. The scenery is magnificent; the ballet is beautiful; the drama is—rubbish. ... To call *The Black Crook* "original" is merely to trifle with intelligence. Herein, for

example, we encounter our venerable and decrepit friend the Alchymist [Hertzog] who wants to live forever, and is perfectly willing to give, not only his own soul to the Devil, but every other soul that he can possibly send to Avernus. Here, too, is the humble youth [Rodolphe], torn from his peasant maid and shut up in "the lowest cell," ha! ha! by the Baron [Wolfenstein], cruel and bold. And then the Fiend's Minister, the Alchymist, surnamed "the Black Crook," is on hand to release him and send him on the road to avarice, vengeance, and perdition. Here are the old manorial or baronial servitors, the red-nosed steward and the high-capped dame; and along with them comes the arch and piquant little village-maid [Amina], who sings a song, and smiles, and shows her pretty ankles to the sheepish swains. There are fairies, too, and demons; and, in the upshot, of course, the former conquer the latter, and the parted lovers are joined in happiness, and the Baron bold is run through his bold body, and the Fiend is cheated of his prey, and the Black Crook is removed, through a dreadful hole in the earth, to a region of great heat and many dragons. ... There was, in fact, no pretense of a drama in this instance; or, if there was, almost any old spectacle would have been preferable to *The Black Crook*. All that was needed was a medium for the presentation of several gorgeous scenes, and a large number of female legs; and it was only necessary that the medium should not be tedious. And this brings us to the real merits of the entertainment . ... Some of the most perfect and admirable pieces of scenery that have ever been exhibited upon the stage are employed in the exhibition of this piece. The best one . . . is that which closes the second act. A vast grotto is herein presented, extending into an almost measureless perspective. Stalactites descend from the arched roof. A tranquil and lovely lake reflects the golden glories that span it like a vast sky. In every direction one sees the bright sheen or dull richness of massy gold. Beautiful fairies, too, are herein assembled—the sprites of the ballet, who make the scene luxuriant with their beauty. There is not so much stormy power in this scene as there is in [designer] R. Smith's *Der Freischütz* combination of horrors, which closes the first act; but it is a successful work in a higher region of art. Both these scenes . . . evince rare poetic sensibility and even imagination. Everybody should see them. The last scene in the play, however, will dazzle and impress to even a greater degree, by its lavish-richness and barbaric splendor. All that gold, and silver, and gems, and light, and woman's beauty can contribute to fascinate the eye and charm the senses is gathered up in this gorgeous spectacle. Its luster grows as we gaze, and deepens and widens, till the effect is almost painful. One by one curtains of mist ascend and drift away. Silver couches, on which the fairies loll in negligent grace, ascend and descend amid a silver rain. Columns of living splendor whirl, and dazzle as they whirl. From the clouds droop gilded chariots and the white forms of angels. It is a very beautiful pageant . . . and though we cannot say that anything has been done for the dramatic art, by the production of *The Black Crook*, we can heartily testify that Scenic Art has never, within our knowledge, been so amply and splendidly exemplified. In respect to the Ballet, it is the most complete troupe of the kind that has been seen in the country. To discriminate between the dancers would be as difficult as to distinguish one rose from another amid a wilderness of roses. But if either be more fascinating than another it is Mlle. [Betty] Rigl [from the Grand Opera, Paris]. The greater share of applause, on Wednesday, fell to the lot of Mlle. [Rita] Sangalli [from the Grand Opera, Berlin, and Her Majesty's Theatre, London]. Marie Bonfanti [from the Grand Opera, Paris, and the Theatre Royal, Covent Garden, London], too, was welcomed with cordial enthusiasm. ... Mr. [Davide] Costa, however, is to be especially congratulated on his directorship of the Ballet.

The New York Times (13 September 1866) added that, while the *Pas de Fleurs*, the *Pas de Sabot*, and the *Pas de Naiad* were noteworthy and beautiful, the "ballet success of the night" was the witching *Pas de Demons*, "in which the demons, who wear no clothes to speak of, so gracefully and prettily disported as to draw forth thunders of applause. No similar exhibition has been made on an American stage that we remember, certainly none where such a combination of youth, grace, beauty, and *élan* was found." It is noteworthy that in their lengthy description of the merits (and faults) of *The Black Crook*, neither the *Tribune* nor *The New York Times* made mention of the incidental and ballet music composed and arranged by Thomas Baker.

The Black Crook ultimately became the longest-running production on the New York stage to date with a run of four hundred and seventy-five performances, aided and abetted by the producers' decision to refurbish and refresh the show at regular intervals. New cast members, new scenery, and new ballets were added, including "The Bouquet," "The Water Lily" (both on 27 May 1867), and a "Pas de Militaire," an intricate military march, introduced on 21 October 1867, performed by more than a hundred children, ranging in height between thirty-five to forty-five inches and led by four-year-old Le Petit Ravel, the youngest member of the Ravel family of French dancers who had debuted in New York City in 1832.

Notable examples of dance music during the second wave included William Michael Rooke's ballet music from the opera *Amilie* (1838); Thomas Comer's "Aladdin's Quick Step" from *Aladdin, or, the Wonderful Lamp* (1847); George Loder's "Captain Cuttle's Quick Step" from *Dombey and Son* (1848); Howard Glover's orchestral incidental music from *Tom O'Shanter* (1855); Roert Stoepel's "Lester Wallack Polka" (1861–1862); Thomas Baker's "Military Galop" from *The Seven Sons!* (1861), "The Transformation Polka" from *The Black Crook* (1866), and "The Emperor's March" from *The Christian Martyrs* (1867); and W.D.C. Böteführ's "Pas de Demons" from *The Black Crook* (1867).

A third wave extending between 1868 and 1890 began with two productions that seemed destined to continue the traditions of *The Black Crook*: *The White Fawn* (17 January 1868), for which Davide Costa choreographed the ballets and Edward Mollenhauer functioned as musical director and arranger of ballet music; and *Ixion!, or, The Man at the Wheel* (28 September 1868), the first appearance in New York City of Lydia Thompson and her company of British blondes, for which Michael Connelly served as musical director and arranger of dance music. Unveiling the story of a princess who is changed into a fawn by day (and back to a woman at night) by the requisite evil fairy, *The White Fawn* attempted to combine spectacle, ballet, burlesque, pantomime, fairy extravaganza, and opera into a cohesive entertainment and failed. *The New York Times* (18 January 1868), however, had this to say about the dances:

> The ballets are exquisite as ballets, but as exhibitions of sedate figuration are, as Davy Crockett was in the habit of saying, "nowhere." The dance of the "Fire Flys" is a ballet of striking originality; the fairy creatures caper about with torches on their heads, which they agitate in such a manner as, notwithstanding the gracefulness of the action, makes one tremble lest they should set themselves on fire, and thus offer their fair bodies as a holocaust to the inconceivable horror of enraptured thousands. There is a march of the little fishes in act third which might be omitted with profit. It is not funny, and takes up too much time. The tableau that brings the first act to an end is an adaptation of the principal effect of a London pantomime called *The House that Jack Built*. An army of juvenile masons, carpenters, etc., with all the necessary tools and materials, enter and go through the mimic action of erecting the dark tower for the princess, who is condemned to be kept from the light of day for seventeen years. ... The first transformation scene was not given last evening. At 1:50, after the Harliquinade (which had been unkindly hissed), Mr. Wheatly appeared and apologized for not permitting the transformation to be given. Eighty carpenters and twenty gasmen could not work it perfectly, and he preferred not to have it imperfectly rendered. The audience dispersed quietly.

Of the British Blondes, whom Lincoln Kirstein called "hefty, sexy," and "prophetic of Gypsy Rose Lee and Ann Corio" (347), and their burlesque of *Ixion*, *The New York Times* (1 October 1868) provided the following descriptive review:

> The story of *Ixion* can be as easily remembered as related. Ixion (Miss Thompson), scouted by his wife and people, is invited to dinner by Jupiter (Miss Harland), goes, accompanied by Mercury (Miss Weber), flirts with Venus (Miss Markham), deserts her for Juno (Miss Logan), and is doomed by the jealous Jupiter, whose hospitality he has outraged, to speak a tag to the audience behind a wheel. This is not brilliant *per se*, but a company of dash-

ing strangers lends it vigor and it becomes enjoyable. The whole success of the piece depends upon dressing up all the above named good looking young ladies as immortals, lavish in display of person—and setting them to dance and sing in the most reckless burlesque manner.

The music of *Ixion* has been, for the most part, culled from that eccentric collection which just now fills the popular album, and "The Sabre," "Captain Jinks," "Through the Park," and "Barbe Bleu" exhibit the susceptibility of burlesque to be burlesqued. The height of absurdity seems to be reached in a treatment, after the most approved operatic rules, of the nursery rhyme about *Tuffy the Welshman*; and Miss Harland, Miss Markham, Miss Weber, Mr. Harry Beckett (as Minerva), and Mr. Sol Smith, Jr. (as Ganymede), who have the leading share in this concerted parody, to use the common phrase, "literally bring down the house." ... No great expense has been lavished on the scenery which illustrates *Ixion*, although some clever conceits, such as "Bacchus's Beer Brewery" in the clouds, and "Cupid's Bower," were deserving of better treatment, and certainly suggested burlesques as telling as any of the uttered localisms of the piece. ... Miss Thompson is a blonde of the purest type, saucy, blue-eyed, golden-haired and of elegant figure. She seems to be a sort of Prometheus in ardor and ambition, and breathes the breath of life into everything she does, whether it be in making wicked advances on the wives of the gods, or singing local songs, or in beating [blackface comic and minstrel] Dan Bryant at his own trade. ... Miss Thompson's voice is quite sufficient for the duty required in a burlesque of this character, where distinctness is one of the first requisites. She sings correctly and very pleasingly. Miss Ada Harland is a much better dancer—the cleverest and most graceful of the troupe, indeed—and Miss Weber's vocalism is better, but in the possession of that "general spicy way"—which Miss Thompson carries into everything she does, she is ... "equaled by few and surpassed by none." Her versatility is displayed in a clever solo upon a tiny cornet, which had a furious encore.

In mid-May 1869, Hungarian folk dancers Imre and Bolossy Kiralfy arrived in New York City with their family dance troupe to provide dance specialties for the George L. Fox vehicle, *Hiccory Diccory Dock* (18 May). Billed as "The Dancers of the Age," the Kiralfys were featured in a scene entitled "The Palace of Dazzling Light" where they performed their world-famous "Magyar Czardas" to the delight of American audiences and critics. For ballets that did not involve the Kiralfy troupe, Davide Costa provided choreography and Frederic Strebinger, composed, selected, and arranged the music. As time passed the brothers transformed from performers into producers, choreographers, and stage managers of many of the grandest spectacles ever witnessed on the American stage. They purchased exclusive production rights to *The Black Crook* in 1873 and controlled touring companies and New York City revivals through the 1880s, using music originally composed by Thomas Baker and others, rearranged, recomposed, and revised at various times by musical directors Michael Connelly, Charles Puerner, and A.W. Hoffman. Subsequent ballet-spectacles produced by Imre and Bollosy Kiralfy (either together or individually) included *The Deluge, or, Paradise Lost* (7 September 1874), with ballet music arranged by William Withers, Jr.; *Around the World in 80 Days* (28 August 1875), originally staged at the Théâtre de la Porte-Saint Martin in Paris, with music by Jean-Jacques Debillemont; *Azurine, or A Voyage to the Earth* (25 December 1876), originally staged in Italy at the Teatro San Carlo; *A Trip to the Moon* (14 March 1877); *Enchantment* (4 September 1879), with music selected, composed, and arranged by Charles Puerner; *The Black Venus* (12 January 1881), originally produced at the Châtelet in Paris, with music composed by Charles Puerner and drawn from the works of Arthur Sullivan, Richard Eilenberg, and Enrique Granados; *Michael Strogoff* (3 September 1881); *Excelsior* (22 August 1883), originally staged at La Scala in Milan, with choreography by Luigi Manzotti, and ballet music by Romualdo Marenco; *Sieba and the Seven Ravens* (18 August 1884), ballets by Ettore Coppini, with music by Marenco and Adolph Neuendorf; *The Ratcatcher, or, The Pied Piper of Hamelin* (30 November 1885), music by Selli Simonson; *Dolores* (1 September 1887), with the "Dresdina Ballet" imported from the Alhambra Theatre in London (music by Georges Jacobi), and a new ballet, "The Wild Gypsies," choreographed by Bolossy Kiralfy to music by Jules Massenet; *Mathias Sandorf* (3 September 1888); *The Water Queen* (11 February 1889), music selected and composed by Georges Jacobi; and *Antiope* (17 August 1889), originally staged at the Alhambra Theatre, London, with choreography by E. Casati and music by Georges Jacobi.

The third wave of dance and incidental music in the American musical theatre was not, however, given entirely to clones of *The Black Crook*, burlesques, spectacular entertainments, and female choruses in various stages of undress, though such things certainly thrived during the period. Vaudeville and variety acts also flourished and with them their various dances. As Lincoln Kirstein (1987) explained:

> Vaudevile or the variety show contained mixtures of minstrelsy and burleycue. Its dances involved all manner of technical innovation; ninety per cent of the two-a-day performers danced. Charlie Dimond did his softshoe number while he played the harp. Fine sand was spread on the stage and the dancer, in 4/4 "ballroom schottische" tempo, traced a pattern in it with thin hard soles, sliding and shuffling, to accent an accompaniment with double or triple taps. Douglas Gilbert in his compendious *American Vaudeville; its Life and Times* (1941), tells us that Kitty O'Neill was the outstanding sand-jigger during the seventies and eighties. In the egg dance, a dozen raw eggs were deftly avoided. In the spade dance, the shovel was used like a pogo stick. Bottles and lighted candles served as hurdles, and here dancing overlapped into circus. The "mirror" dance was good for a sister act, the "cane" dance was natural for the dandy or city slicker, and later on came roller skates and stilts. (348)

Significant examples of incidental and dance music during the third wave included Edward Mollenhauer's "March d'Aika Amazonian," J. Hood McKever's "Fire-Fly Waltz," and A. Jannotta's "Fire Fly Galop," all from *The White Fawn* (1868); Jesse Williams's polka dance music in "All among the Hay" (1869); Michael Connelly's "Galop" from *The Forty Thieves* (1869); Giuseppe Operti's "Galop Diabolique" and "Bolero Diabolique" from *The Black Crook* (1871 revival); E.N. Catlin's dance in "Sweet Louisa," and John J. Braham's dance in "Steady Company," both from *The Little Frauds* (1871); Charles Schultz's "The Palace of Truth Polka-Mazurka" from *The Palace of Truth* (1872); Charles Koppitz's "Cardinal's March" and "Minuet" from Henry VIII (1872); Jean-Jacques Debillemont's "Solemn March of the Rajahs" from *Around the World in 80 Days* (1875); Edward E. Rice's "Heifer Dance" from *Evangeline* (1875); William H. Brinkworth's dance in "Happy Little Flip-Flaps" (1875); Alfred B. Sedgwick's incidental music from *Gambrinus, King of Lager Beer* (1875) and his "March of the Hash Brigade" from *The Charge of the Hash Brigade* (1876); Charles Puerner's "Egypian March" from *Enchantment* (1879); Fred Perkins's dances in "Perplexity" and "The 'Fauncy Dauncers'" from *Our Goblins* (1880); Francis T.S. Darley's "Matapa March" and "Transformation Music" from *Fortunio and his Seven Gifted Servants* (1883); Operti's "The Sea" from *The Stranglers of Paris* (1883); Romualdo Marenco's ballet score for *Excelsior* (1883); Rice's "Adonis Gavotte" from *Adonis* (1884); Napier Lothian's "March" from *Zanita* (1884); George Schleiffarth's "Valse Lente" and "Castanet Dance" from *Rosita* (1884); Florian Pascal's "March of the Janissaries" from *Little Jack Sheppard* (1886); Joseph Meinrath's "Phaeton Galop" from *The Crystal Slipper* (1888); Adolph Nowak's "March of the Epori" from *The Lady or The Tiger?* (1888); Meyer Lutz's "The Fight" and "Pas de Quatre" from *Faust Up To Date* (1889); W.S. Mullaly's dance in "The Hebrew Fancy Ball," and Ted Peiper's "Amazonian March," both from *Bluebeard, Jr.* (1890).

The fourth wave of dance and incidental music extends from 1891 through 1923, the end date for the present series, and serves as the highpoint of the musical language that had been developing since the series began. Within its parameters, we find ragtime music in full flower, infecting even serious-minded composers with its syncopations and accented rhythms designed to accompany dances, such as the "Cake Walk," the "Turkey Trot," "The Camel Walk," and other animal-christened turns; we hear music subtitled the "Argentine Tango," the "Hesitation Waltz," the "Maxixe" (a Brazilian Tango), the "Castle Walk" (Vernon and Irene Castle's distinctive version of the "One-Step"), the "Half-and-Half" (an interesting amalgam of duple and triple rhythms, typically composed in 5/4), the "Fox-Trot," and the "Charleston," all designed to accompany and support the dances for which they were named. In addition, we continue to find allemandes, waltzes, polkas, marches, schottisches, hornpipes, galops (cancans), and concerted ballet music evoking that of the finest European Romantic composers. In short, the fourth wave marked the assimilation of all that came before into a musical language that audiences in the twentieth century recognized as the "modern musical theatre sound."

Noteworthy examples of evocative incidental music include André Wormser's pantomime score for *The Prodigal Son* (1891); Edgar Stillman Kelley's "Entrance of Elizabeth" and "Melodrama" from *Puritania* (1892); Max S. Witt's "Danse Antique" from *Henry V* (1900); Paul Tietjens's "Dance of Beauties" from *A Kiss for Cinderella* (1916); Frank Howson's "March and Two-Step" from *The King's Musketeer* (1899); Julian Edwards's "Melodrame" from *When Johnny Comes Marching Home* (1902). Although some of these titles are also labeled "dances," their function was to provide the ambiance of the time period in which the play was set, or to evoke a fairyland or dream world in which the characters find themselves.

Notable examples of ethnic dances, designed to create a special atmosphere or to assist in the establishment of the setting of a scene or the entire play, include Rudolph Aronson's "Syrian Dance" and "Military March" from *The Rainmaker of Syria* (1893); Aberano Colon's "Spanish Dance" from *1492, Up to Date or Very Near It* (1893); De Koven's Japanese Ballet" in *From Broadway to Tokio* (1900); Isidore Witmark's dance in "Egyptland" from *The Chaperons* (1902); Karl Hoschna's "Indian Dance" from *The Belle of the West* (1905); Max Hoffmann's Irish dances in "Killarney" from *The Rogers Brothers in Ireland* (1905); Dan Sullivan's "The Ghost Dance" and "Dance of the Woodland Sprites" from *Miss Pocahontas* (1907); Melville Ellis's "The Tango Dance" from *The Merry Countess* (1912); Manuel Klein's "The Hippodrome Tango" from *America* (1913); Silvio Hein's "Santley Tango" from *When Dreams Come True* (1913). These dances display the active association between dance and incidental music. Both provide atmosphere, create mood, and support the onstage movements. The dance music, however, appears in musical theatre works whereas the incidental music is given to plays, in the production of which, music is not a primary focus.

Noteworthy examples of dances based on traditional forms—marches, waltzes, polkas, galops, schottisches, hornpipes, mazurkas, etc.—include Richard Stahl's galop in "The Bounding Brothers of Barbary" from *The Lion Tamer* (1891); William Furst's hornpipe in "The North Pole" from *The Isle of Champagne* (1892); Jesse Williams's "Eulalie Schottische" (1894); Percy Gaunt's "The Milk-White Flag March" from *A Milk White Flag* (1894); Oscar Hammerstein's "Santa Maria March" from *Santa Maria* (1896); Walter Slaughter's "Can-Can" from *The French Maid* (1897); Maurice Levi's "Gay Coney Island March and Two-Step" from At Gay Coney Island (1897); Reginald De Koven's "Hornpipe" from *The Highwayman* (1897); John Philip Sousa's "Tarantella" from *The Bride-Elect* (1897) and "Mazurka" from *The Charlatan* (1898); Paolo Giorza's "Skirt Dance" from *Monte Carlo* (1898); W.T. Francis's schottische dance in the "Golf Song" from The Little Host (1898); Alfred Norman's dance in "The French Danseuse," and Edward W. Corliss's pantomime and dance in "Three Little

Lambs," both from *Queen of the Ballet* (1898); De Koven's "Galop" from *The Man in the Moon* (1899); Robert G. Morse's schottische in the "Ballet of the Flowers" from *Miladi and the Musketeer* (1901); Frederic Solomon "Witches Dance" and "Galop" from *The Sleeping Beauty and the Beast* (1901); Nat D. Mann's waltz in "It Happens Ev'ry Day" from *The Wizard of Oz* (1903); J. Rosamond Johnson's schottische dance in "Cupid's Ramble" and Henry K. Hadley's schottische dance in "Strange, Odd, Queer" both from *Nancy Brown* (1903); Ben M. Jerome's schottische in "We Are a Band of Gentlemen," and hornpipe in "An Admirable Admiral," both from *The Royal Chef* (1904); Melville Ellis's "School Boy and Girl Dance" from *The Earl and the Girl* (1905);); Henry L. Sanford's "Dance Duet," and John S. Zamecnik's Aragonese jota, schottische, and can-can in "The Dancing Lesson" both from *The Hermits in Dixie* (1908); Rudolf Friml's schottische dance in "Call Me Uncle" from *The Firefly* (1912); Malvin Franklin's "Waltz Ballet" in *Snapshots of 1921* (1921); and Gustave Kerker's "Mazurka" in "Burning to Sing, or, Singing to Burn" from *Some Party* (1922). During a period marked for its innovations in dance and dance music, it is significant that older formulas continued to thrive.

Significant examples of ragtime dance music, characterized by syncopations and rhythmic variety, include Bert Williams's "Jig," and Harry Von Tilzer's "Chocolate Drops," both from *In Dahomey* (1903); Gustav Luders's cakewalk in "The American Girl" from *The Prince of Pilsen* (1903); Lewis F. Muir's dance in "Play That Fandango Rag," and "Mexatexa," both from *Follies of 1909* (1909); Raymond Hubble's "Cake Walk" from the *Ziegfeld Follies of 1911* (1911); Scott Joplin's "Frolic of the Bears" from *Treemonisha* (1911); James Reese Europe's "Castle Doggy Fox Trot" (1913); Silvio Hein's "The Parisian Trot," from *All over Town* (1915); Otto Motzan's "Nobody Home Cake Walk" from *Nobody Home* (1915); Victor Herbert's foxtrot in "Throwing the Bull" from *The Velvet Lady* (1919); Harry Tierney's dance in "The Talk of the Town" from *Irene* (1919); James P. Johnson's "Charleston" from *Runnin' Wild* (1923). The characteristics of ragtime music, which were introduced at the beginning of the fourth wave, had been absorbed into the standard musical vocabulary by the early 1920s. Even the most classically-trained composers, such as Victor Herbert, employed ragtime syncopations and rhythmic structures late in the nineteen-teens.

Noteworthy examples of music for eccentric or specialty dances include Watty Hydes's dance in "The Possum Chase" from *Sister Mary* (1899);); Jean Schwartz's "Radium Dance" from *Piff! Paff!! Pouf!!!* (1904), and "Pony Galop: Skipping Rope Dance" from *Miss Dolly Dollars* (1905); Manuel Klein's "Eccentric Dance" from *Top o' th' World* (1907); Reginald De Koven's "Coconut Dance" from *The Beauty Spot* (1909); Silvio Hein's "Eccentric Dance," and "Pierrette Dances" from *All over Town* (1915); Sigmund Romberg's "Danse Excentrique" from *A World of Pleasure* (1915); Hugo Felix's "Apache Dance Parody" from *Pom-Pom* (1916). Eccentric dance music was often ironic, a satirical comment on traditional dance music formulas; but it also supported novel dance effects such as the glowing dancers in the "Radium Dance" or the Pony Ballet skipping rope while dancing in *Miss Dolly Dollars*. Onstage props may also have been involved, such as cocoanuts in De Koven's *The Beauty Spot* or a stuffed possum-look-alike in *Sister Mary*.

Important examples of ballet music during the final wave include Carl Pflueger's "Ballet Music" from *1492, Up to Date or Very Near It* (1893); Angelo Venanzi's ballet score for *America* (1893); Carl Kiefert's "Pantomimic Scene" and "Dance" from *The Ballet Girl* (1897); William Devin's "Ballet" from *The Casino Girl* (1900); Victor Herbert's "The Birth of the Butterfly" from *Babes in Toyland* (1903); Louis F. Gottschalk's "Ballet Music and Finale" from *Cinderella and the Prince* (1904); C.J.M. Glaser's ballet score for *The Silver Star* (1909); Klein's "Niagara Ballet" from *The International Cup* (1910); Edmond Diet's ballet score for *Temptations* (1911); Thomé's "Sous la feuillée" from *The Passing Show of 1914* (1914); John Adam Hugo's "Dance of Temptation" from *The Temple Dancer* (1919); Victor Herbert's ballet music from *Sally* (1920); Percy E. Fletcher's "Bacchanale" from *Mecca* (1920); and Leopold Godowsky's "Rendezvous" in *Snapshots of 1921* (1921). The ballet music of the period continued to draw inspiration from famous European ballets, the music of which had become well known in America. Ballet music invariably included polkas, galops, waltzes, hornpipes, and other standard dances; but the music was presented in an elevated style designed to raise it above the dance music being arranged for standard musical comedies. By the end of the fourth wave, however, ragtime had infiltrated even ballet music's uplifted nineteenth-century Romantic style and modern rhythms and harmonies were added to refresh the musical palette.

The fourth wave of dance and incidental music was one of great variety that served as a culmination of everything that came before. Even though the music of the old minstrel shows had blossomed into ragtime, an example of the older style could be found in Watty Hyde's The Possum Chase"; and even the music for dances in the earliest period—Pelissier's "Fandango" from *Gil Blas,* for example—found a modern analogue—Lewis F. Muir's dance in "Play That Fandango Rag." The study of dance and incidental music from 1786 to 1923 offers a musical history of the American Musical Theatre exhibiting a reliance on European and African-American forms as well as European and African-American composers. There is much talk nowadays about multiculturism in the arts (*Hamilton* is a huge hit based on that very principle) but few histories have capitalized on the profound multiculturism present in the development of what we now think of as the American musical. Perhaps these pages will stimulate discussion in that area.

To determine who composed or arranged dance and/or incidental music for a particular production, several sources were used: theatre programs; published scores; unpublished manuscripts; published reviews; theatrical contracts; composer biographies; memoirs; and related newspaper articles. Unlike the composer of the songs in a musical show, the composer (or arranger) of dance and incidental music was not always named in the program; and if credit was given to a specific individual, sometimes published scores and reviews provided other names that may also have been involved. During the earliest periods of this study, when it was typically left to the musical director to satisfy all the musical requirements of a production, it was accepted that the same person functioned as dance arranger when evidence of dance music specifically attributed to him (or her) could be found. Moreover, if the resident musical director at a particular theatre was also credited as the composer of the production, there was some degree of certainty that he (she) was the arranger of dance music if no other name was found in other documents relating to the show. Early scores displayed a fondness for attributing authorship at the beginning of a song title even in complete scores for musical plays and much incidental and dance music was published independently invariably with a composer's name attached. Admittedly there would always be cases like that of "I Wonder Who's Kissing Her Now" where Joe Howard purchased the music for the song from composer Harold Orlob and claimed the right of authorship; but that is where a study of contracts, newspaper articles, and memoirs aids in the attribution. Some composers—particularly those who composed primarily in an elevated comic opera style—consistently provided their own dance music arrangements and orchestrations. Victor Herbert, for example, invariably composed the ballet music for his own shows (and for those of other composers); Reginald De Koven provided dance music and orchestrations as well; as did John Philip Sousa, Gustave

Kerker, Gustav Luders, and Ludwig Englander (although his name appears as Engländer in his European shows, he consciously dropped the umlaut when he came to America). Other composers, such as Rudolf Friml, made use of their published piano music as dance or incidental music; that list includes Harry Von Tilzer whose ragtime "Chocolate Drops" was interpolated as dance music for *In Dahomey*; Francis Thomé, whose "Sous la feuillée" was borrowed for Marilyn Miller's dance music in *The Passing Show of 1914*; and Charles Puerner, whose "Ethiopian Serenade," a piece designed to suggest the sound of a banjo, was used as an entr'acte in an 1883 production of *Romeo and Juliet*. Moreover, a great many composers of the more popular styled musical comedies also provided their own dance arrangements, though quite often such arrangements were simply instrumental reiterations of the sung number that preceded the dance. The instruction "Repeat for dance" was common in late nineteenth and early twentieth-century scores, particularly when the accompaniment included the melody. This is not to suggest that all composers writing in the popular idiom did no more than repeat their melodies. Manuscripts, for example, of composers George Gershwin, Jerome Kern, Cole Porter, and Richard Rodgers displayed original dance music as well.

When composer authentication was difficult, contracts, reviews, and supporting newspaper articles were extremely helpful. Actor, singer, pianist, costume designer Melville Ellis is a case in point. Rarely were Ellis's dance arrangements attributed, but the fact that he had contracted with the Shubert Brothers to serve as their general musical director during a twelve-year period helped narrow the focus and several attributable titles appeared. Ellis was often taxed with providing costumes as well as musical support for productions—responsibilities that led to his mental and physical breakdown at the end of his association with the Shuberts. Double duties such as his were not uncommon, however. Incidental and dance composer Charles E. Horn was also a prominent actor on the American stage; A.W. Maflin and Joseph Kline Emmet were noted pantomimists; Jesse Williams was a respected stage director; Max Maretzek, Oscar Hammerstein, and Rudolph Aronson were famous impresarios; and ragtime pianist and composer Ned Wayburn was also an important and influential choreographer.

Given the great number of possible contributors to the dance and incidental music in American musical theatre a practice of exclusion had to be established. Since the primary focus of this study had been on the creation of dance and incidental music for productions in America,

American composers and immigrant musicians who worked on American soil were first to be included. Foreign composers who collaborated with American librettists on productions for American audiences were also included if they produced a significant body of dance music. Invariably excluded were big-name foreign composers of musical theatre works produced without change in America: Michael William Balfe, Franz von Suppé, Johann Strauss, Jr., Jacques Offenbach, and Arthur Sullivan, for example, are mentioned throughout but do not receive critical biographies. The same is the case for composers such as Gioachino Rossini, Pyotr Ilyich Tchaikovsky, Nikolai Rimsky-Korsakov, and others, from whose works American or immigrant dance arrangers drew themes and inspiration. Lesser known ballet composers, such as Edmond Diet, C.J.M. Glaser, Romualdo Marenco, and Angelo Venanzi, for example, whose work was associated with significant dance productions on American soil (and who often participated in the American productions) were, however, included in the critical biographies. It was also decided to postpone discussion of Gershwin, Kern, Rodgers, and Porter to the next series that covers the period from 1924 through 1966 (*Lady, Be Good!* to *Cabaret*), when their most significant work was represented.

As in the determination of the arrangers of incidental and dance music, musical examples cited and exhibited in these volumes were culled from published and manuscript scores in the author's possession and from the Library of Congress, the New York Public Library, the Free Library of Philadelphia, the Sheridan Libraries Special Collections at Johns Hopkins University, the College of Music Allen Library at Florida State University, and the music division of Patee Library at The Pennsylvania State University. Most of the excerpts exhibited are piano/vocal score reductions of orchestrated music used in the theatre. Several dance arrangements actually began as solo piano pieces and they are so labelled in their discussion. When full scores are used as examples, they have been published at concert pitch to facilitate the reading of individual parts which would normally have been written in transposing keys.

On the pages that follow, the reader will find a chronology of productions in America for which the arrangers of dance and incidental music are known. Variations in titles, credits, and dates are addressed in the commentaries in volumes two and three. Following the chronology can be found an alphabetical survey of the principal choreographers found in this series, and an alphabetical listing of dance music arrangers included in forthcoming volumes.

Undoubtedly there will be quibbles about the choices made. Having been limited to the shows for which there was a credible identification of the arranger of dance and/or incidental music, I will almost certainly have neglected some of the productions that the readership finds significant and necessary in a study such as this. It is my hope that this survey will inspire further study of the subject and lead to a fuller if not exhaustive appreciation of the work of the dance and incidental music arranger in the American musical theatre.

Selected Chronology: 1786–1923

THE ENTRIES ARE ORGANIZED IN THE FOLLOWING MANNER:

- The name of the theatrical event.
- The date of performance in New York City. When the theatrical piece did not perform in New York, the date reflects the earliest known performance.
- The name of the composer of the music for the theatrical event.
- The name(s) of the composer(s) of additional music, if any.
- The name of the musical director and/or orchestra conductor, if known.
- The name(s) of the musical arranger(s) or orchestrator(s), if known.
- The name of the composer(s) and/or arranger(s) of the dance music. In the case of American adaptations of earlier works, the name of the original creator of the dance music is given first; the designation "uncredited" is used when the name of the dance music composer/arranger is not specifically given in the credits.
- The name of the person(s) responsible for choreography or the staging of musical numbers, if known.

"Durang's Horn-Pipe"
    Spring 1786
    Music by William Hoffmaster
    Dance staged by John Durang

"Dwarf Dance"
    13 July 1786
    Music by William Hoffmaster
    Dance staged by John Durang

Love in a Camp, or Patrick in Prussia
    9 April 1787
    Music by William Shield
    Additional music by Alexander Reinagle
    Original dance music by William Shield
    Dance music arranged by Alexander Reinagle (uncredited)

Capocchio and Dorinna
    20 January 1793
    Music by Raynor Taylor
    Musical director, Raynor Taylor
    Incidental and dance music arranged by Raynor Taylor (uncredited)

Fair Luna
    28 February 1793
    Music by Raynor Taylor
    Musical director, Raynor Taylor
    Incidental and dance music arranged by Raynor Taylor (uncredited)

Caledonian Frolic
    2 November 1793
    Music by Benjamin Carr
    Incidental and dance music arranged by Benjamin Carr (uncredited)
    Ballet by William Francis

Olio
    28 January 1794
    Music by Raynor Taylor
    Orchestrations by Raynor Taylor
    Incidental and dance music arranged by Raynor Taylor (uncredited)

Tammany, or, The Indian Chief
    3 March 1794
    Music by James Hewitt
    Dance music by James Hewitt (uncredited)
    Indian dance by John Durang and Mrs. Miller

La Forêt Noire
    26 April 1794
    Music by Alexander Reinagle
    Musical director, Alexander Reinagle
    Orchestrations by Alexander Reinagle
    Incidental and ballet music arranged by Alexander Reinagle (uncredited)
    Ballet by William Francis

The Patriot, or, Liberty Asserted
    5 June 1794
    Incidental and dance music by James Hewitt and Benjamin Carr
    Orchestrations by James Hewitt

Robin Hood, or, Sherwood Forest
    6 November 1794
    Music by William Shield
    Overture composed by Karl Baumgarten
    Music for additional numbers composed by Alexander Reinagle
    Original dance music composed by William Shield (uncredited)
    New dance music adapted and arranged by Alexander Reinagle (uncredited)

Harlequin Pastry Cook
    21 November 1894
    Music by Victor Pelissier

Incidental and ballet music arranged by Victor Pelissier (uncredited)

The Children in the Wood
24 November 1794
Music by Samuel Arnold
Music for additional numbers composed by Benjamin Carr, Mrs. Melmoth, Stephen Storace, and William Shield
Musical director, Benjamin Carr
Orchestrations by Benjamin Carr
Incidental and dance music arranged by Benjamin Carr (uncredited)
Dance by John Durang

Sophia of Brabant, or, the False Friend
29 December 1794
Music by Victor Pelissier
Orchestrations by Victor Pelissier
Incidental and ballet music arranged by Victor Pelissier (uncredited)
Dance by John Durang

Harlequin Shipwreck'd, or, the Grateful Lion
2 January 1795
Music selected by Mr. DeMarque from Pleyel, Grétry, Giordani, Shield, Reeve, and others
New music by Alexander Reinagle
Musical director, Alexander Reinagle
Orchestrations by Alexander Reinagle
Incidental and ballet music arranged by Alexander Reinagle (uncredited)
Ballet by James Byrne

The Haunted Tower
7 January 1795
Music by Stephen Storace
Musical director, Victor Pelissier
Musical arrangements by Victor Pelissier

Original incidental and dance music by Stephen Storace (uncredited)
Incidental and dance music adapted and arranged by Victor Pelissier (uncredited)

The Purse, or, Benevolent Tar
7 January 1795
Original music by William Reeve
New music composed by Alexander Reinagle
Orchestrations by Alexander Reinagle
Original incidental and dance music by William Reeve (uncredited)
Incidental and dance music adapted and arranged by Alexander Reinagle (uncredited)

The Volunteers
21 January 1795
Music by Alexander Reinagle
Incidental music composed and arranged by Alexander Reinagle (uncredited)

La Forêt Noire
30 March 1795
Music by Alexander Reinagle
Music for additional numbers composed by Victor Pelissier
Musical director, Victor Pelissier
New orchestrations by Victor Pelissier
New incidental and ballet music arranged by Victor Pelissier (uncredited)
Ballet by William Francis

Macbeth
5 April 1795
Incidental music by Matthew Locke
Incidental Scottish music adapted by Benjamin Carr

Poor Jack, or, the Sailor's Landlady
7 April 1795
New music by Benjamin Carr

New overture, "The Sailor's Medley," compiled by Benjamin Carr

Orchestrations by Benjamin Carr

New incidental and dance music arranged by Benjamin Carr (uncredited)

Rural Revels, or, the Easter Holiday
10 April 1795
Music selected and composed by Mr. DeMarque
Incidental and dance music arranged by Mr. DeMarque (uncredited)
Ballet by William Francis

The Little Yankee Sailor
27 May 1895
Music selected from Shield, Hook, Dibdin, Raynor Taylor, and others
Orchestrations by George Gillingham
Dance music arranged by George Gillingham (uncredited)

Harlequin's Invasion
12 June 1795
Original music by William Boyce
Orchestrations by George Gillingham
Dance music arranged by George Gillingham (uncredited)
New overture arranged by Alexander Reinagle

The Miraculous Mill, or, The Old Ground Young
26 June 1795
Music selected and composed by Louis Boullay
Dance music arranged by Louis Boullay (uncredited)
Ballet by William Francis

The Miraculous Mill, or, The Old Ground Young
21 November 1795
Music by Mr. DeMarque
Incidental and dance music arranged by Mr. DeMarque (uncredited)
Ballet by William Francis

The Warrior's Welcome Home
    10 February 1796
    Music by Alexander Reinagle
    Incidental and dance music arranged by Alexander Reinagle (uncredited)
    Ballet by William Francis

Rosina
    17 February 1796
    Music by William Shield
    New Orchestrations by Victor Pelissier
    Original incidental and dance music composed by William Shield (uncredited)
    Dance music arranged by Victor Pelissier (uncredited)

A Flitch of Bacon, or, the Matrimonial Prize
    7 March 1796
    Music by William Shield
    Musical director, Victor Pelissier
    Orchestrations by Victor Pelissier
    Incidental and dance arrangements by Victor Pelissier (uncredited)

Poor Vulcan
    16 March 1796
    Original music by Charles Dibdin
    Orchestrations by Victor Pelissier
    New incidental and dance music arranged by Victor Pelissier (uncredited)

The Irish Tailor, or, the Humours of the Thimble
    7 April 1796
    Music by Raynor Taylor
    Musical director, Raynor Taylor
    Orchestrations by Raynor Taylor
    Incidental and dance music arranged by Raynor Taylor (uncredited)

The Milliners, or, The Wooden Block
    13 April 1796
    Music by Victor Pelissier
    Incidental and dance music arranged by Victor Pelissier (uncredited)

The Archers, or, The Mountaineers of Switzerland
    18 April 1796
    Music by Benjamin Carr
    Musical director (conductor), James Hewitt
    Ballet music composed by Benjamin Carr (uncredited)

The Sicilian Romance, or, The Spectre of the Cliffs
    27 April 1796
    Music by William Reeve
    Music for "Kind zephyr waft my passing sighs" by Victor Pelissier
    Musical director, Victor Pelissier
    Incidental and dance music by Victor Pelissier (uncredited)

Pierre de Province and La Belle Magulone
    2 May 1796
    Music by Alexander Reinagle
    Orchestrations by Alexander Reinagle
    Incidental and ballet music arranged by Alexander Reinagle (uncredited)

Robinson Crusoe, or, the Genius of Columbia
    15 June 1796
    Music by Victor Pelissier
    Orchestrations by Victor Pelissier
    Incidental and dance music composed and arranged by Victor Pelissier (uncredited)

American Tar, or, The Press Gang Defeated
    17 June 1796
    Music by Raynor Taylor
    Incidental and dance music arranged by Raynor Taylor (uncredited)
    Ballet by William Francis

The Lucky Escape, or, the Ploughman Turned Sailor
    29 July 1796
    Music selected from Charles Dibdin
    Musical director, Alexander Reinagle
    Orchestrations by Alexander Reinagle
    New overture composed by Alexander Reinagle
    Ballet by William Francis

The Quaker
    28 September 1796
    Music by Charles Dibdin
    New overture composed by Raynor Taylor
    Orchestrations by Raynor Taylor
    Incidental and dance music adapted and arranged by Raynor Taylor (uncredited)

The Mysterious Monk
    31 October 1796
    Music by Victor Pelissier
    Orchestrations by Victor Pelissier
    Incidental music composed by Victor Pelissier

Edwin and Angelina, or, The Banditti
    19 December 1796
    Music by Victor Pelissier
    Dance music by Victor Pelissier (uncredited)

Bourville Castle, or, The Gallic Orphans
    16 January 1797
    Music by Benjamin Carr
    Musical director, Victor Pellissier
    Orchestrations by Victor Pelissier
    Incidental and dance music arranged by Victor Pelissier (uncredited)

Columbus, or, The Discovery of America
    30 January 1797
    Incidental and dance music composed by Alexander Reinagle

Richard Coeur de Lion, or, The Triumph of Love
    23 January 1797
    Music by A.E.M. Grétry
    Musical director, Trille Labarre
    Musical arrangements by Trille Labarre
    Music for "Pastoral Dance, Incidental to the Piece" arranged by Trille Labarre

The Lock and Key
    8 March 1797
    Music by William Shield
    Orchestrations by Victor Pelissier
    Dance music adapted and arranged by Victor Pelissier (uncredited)

The Iron Chest
    2 June 1797
    Original music by Stephen Storace
    Music by Raynor Taylor
    Musical director, Raynor Taylor
    Orchestrations by Raynor Taylor
    Incidental and dance music arranged by Raynor Taylor (uncredited)

The Launch, or, Huzza for the Constellation
    20 September 1797
    Music selected "from the best composers" by Victor Pelissier
    Musical director, Victor Pelissier
    Orchestrations by Victor Pelissier
    Incidental and dance music selected and arranged by Victor Pelissier (uncredited)

The Son in Law
    7 February 1798
    Music by Samuel Arnold
    Orchestrations by Victor Pelissier
    Original incidental and dance music by Samuel Arnold (uncredited)
    Incidental and dance music arranged by Victor Pelissier (uncredited)

The Italian Monk
    25 April 1798
    Music by Samuel Arnold
    Musical director, Alexander Reinagle
    Orchestrations by Alexander Reinagle
    Original incidental and dance music by Samuel Arnold (uncredited)
    Incidental and dance music arranged by Alexander Reinagle (uncredited)

Columbus, or, The Discovery of America
    15 May 1799
    Incidental music composed by James Hewitt

The Mysterious Marriage, or, the Heirship of Roselva
    5 June 1799
    Music by James Hewitt
    Orchestrations by James Hewitt
    Incidental and ballet music arranged by James Hewitt (uncredited)

Blue Beard
    10 June 1799
    Music by Michael Kelly
    Musical director, Alexander Reinagle
    Orchestrations by Alexander Reinagle
    Original incidental and dance music composed by Michael Kelly (uncredited)
    Incidental and dance music arranged by Alexander Reinagle (uncredited)

Fourth of July, or, Temple of American Independence
    4 July 1799
    Music by Victor Pelissier
    Orchestrations by Victor Pelissier
    Incidental and ballet music by Victor Pelissier uncredited)

The Secret, or, Partnership Dissolved
    30 December 1799

Music by Alexander Reinagle
Incidental and dance music by Alexander Reinagle (uncredited)

Pizarro, or, The Spaniards in Peru
19 May 1800
Music selected and composed by Michael Kelly
Music arranged by Alexander Reinagle and Raynor Taylor
Original incidental and dance music composed by Michael Kelly (uncredited)
Dance music arranged by Alexander Reinagle and Raynor Taylor (uncredited)

The Castle of Otranto
7November 1800
Music by Victor Pelissier
Musical director, Victor Pelissier
Orchestrations by Victor Pelissier
Incidental and dance music arranged by Victor Pelissier (uncredited)

Speed the Plough
1 December 1800
Incidental and dance music composed by Alexander Reinagle

Robin Hood, or, Sherwood Forest
24 December 1800
Music by James Hewitt
Orchestrations by James Hewitt
Incidental and dance music composed and arranged by James Hewitt (uncredited)

Paul and Virginia
18 March 1801
Music by William Reeve and Joseph Mazzinghi
Music arranged by Alexander Reinagle
Original dance music composed by William Reeve (uncredited)
Incidental and dance music arranged by Alexander Reinagle (uncredited)

Macbeth
> 11 May 1801
> Music by Matthew Locke
> Musical director, Gottlieb Graupner
> Vocal and dance music arranged by Gottlieb Graupner

Adelmorn, the Outlaw
> 25 February 1802
> Music by Michael Kelly
> Additional music by Victor Pelissier
> Music arranged by Frederick Granger
> Original dance music composed by Michael Kelly (uncredited)
> Dance music arranged by Victor Pellissier and Frederick Granger (uncredited)

Raymond and Agnes, or, The Bleeding Nun
> 7 May 1802
> Music by William Reeve
> Additional music composed by Frederick Granger, Alexander Reinagle, and Victor Pelissier
> Original ballet music composed by William Reeve (uncredited)
> Dance music arranged by Frederick Granger (uncredited)

Gil Blas, or, The Cavern
> 10 December 1802
> Music by William Reeve
> Additional music by Victor Pelissier
> Incidental and dance music composed by William Reeve (uncredited)
> New incidental and dance music arranged by Victor Pelissier (uncredited)
> Ballet by Mr. Bates.

The Voice of Nature
> 4 February 1803
> Incidental and dance music by Victor Pelissier

A Tale of Mystery, or, The Dumb Man of Arpenay
> 16 March 1803

Music by Thomas Busby
Music adapted by Victor Pelissier
Additional music composed by James Hewitt
Orchestrations by Alexander Reinagle
Incidental and dance music arranged by Victor Pelissier (uncredited)

Harlequin's Almanac, or, The Four Seasons
2 April 1803
Music by William Reeve, William Henry Ware, and Alexander Reinagle
Incidental and dance music arranged by Alexander Reinagle (uncredited)

Black Beard, or, The Genovese Pirate
2 April 1804
Music by James Sanderson
Additional music composed by James Hewitt
Original dance and incidental music by James Sanderson
Dance music adapted and arranged by James Hewitt (uncredited)

Cinderella
1 January 1806
Music by Michael Kelly
Music arranged by James Hewitt
Original ballet music composed by Michael Kelly
New dance music arranged by James Hewitt (uncredited)

The Tars from Tripoli
24 February 1806
Music by James Hewitt
Incidental and dance music composed and arranged by James Hewitt (uncredited)

Lodoiska, or, The Rescue of the Princess of Poland
3 March 1806
Music by Stephen Storace, Rodolphe Kreutzer, and Luigi Cherubini

Music arranged by Frederick Mumler and Frederick Granger
Ballet music composed by Stephen Storace
Ballet music arranged by Frederick Granger (uncredited)

Black Castle, or, Specter of the Forest
20 March 1807
Music by James Hewitt and Alexander Reinagle
Incidental and dance music arranged by James Hewitt and Alexander Reinagle (uncredited)

The Indian Princess, or, La Belle Sauvage
6 April 1808
Music by John Bray
Incidental and ballet music composed and arranged by John Bray (uncredited)

The Spanish Patriots, or, Royal Restoration
4 January 1809
Music by Charles Gilfert
Ballet music composed and arranged by Charles Gilfert (uncredited)

Mother Goose, or, The Golden Egg
3 March 1809
Music by William Henry Ware
Additional music by Victor Pelissier
Dance music arranged by Victor Pelissier (uncredited)

Feudal Times, or, The Banquet Gallery
20 March 1809
Music by Michael Kelly
Music arranged by Frederick Granger
Original ballet music composed by Michael Kelly
Ballet music arranged by Frederick Granger (uncredited)

Harlequin's Triumph in War and in Love
21 January 1810
Music by Phil Trajetta
Musical arrangements by Phil Trajetta

Incidental and ballet music composed and arranged by Phil Trajetta (uncredited)

Bee Hive, or, Industry Must Prosper
23 October 1811
Music by Charles E. Horn
Music adapted and arranged by Charles Gilfert
Dance music adapted and arranged by Charles Gilfert (uncredited)

Lady of the Lake
1 January 1812
Music by James Sanderson
Additional music by Victor Pelissier
Original dance and incidental music by James Sanderson
Additional dance and incidental music arranged by Victor Pelissier (uncredited)
Ballet by William Francis

The Bridal Ring
10 February 1812
Music by Henry Condell
New music by Victor Pelissier
Dance music arranged by Victor Pelissier (uncredited)
Ballet by William Francis

Peasant Boy, or Innocence Protected
11 March 1812
Music by Michael Kelly
Music arranged by Victor Pelissier
Ballet by William Francis

Virgin of the Sun
15 November 1813
Music by Henry Rowley Bishop
Additional music by Charles Gilfert
Ballet music arranged by Charles Gilfert (uncredited)

The Ethiop, or, Child of the Desert
1 January 1814
Music by Raynor Taylor
Dance music by Raynor Taylor (uncredited)

Macbeth
5 November 1814
"Scotch Medley Overture" composed by Alexander Reinagle

For Freedom Ho
5 April 1815
Music by Henry Rowley Bishop
Music adapted and arranged by Charles Gilfert
Ballet music arranged by Charles Gilfert (uncredited)

Macbeth
18 December 1815
Overture composed by William Henry Ware

The Enterprise, or, Love and Pleasure
25 May 1822
Music by Arthur Clifton (Philip Antony Corri)
Dance music by Arthur Clifton (uncredited)

The Forty Thieves
4 February 1824
Original music by Michael Kelly
Incidental and dance music composed by Michael Kelly
Dance music arranged by Gottlieb Graupner (uncredited)

A Trip to Niagara, or, Travelers in America
28 November 1828
Incidental and dance music composed by Charles Gilfert

The Tempest
8 December 1828
Incidental music composed by Charles E. Horn

Cinderella
    29 August 1831
    Music adapted from Rossini's *La Cenerentola* by Rophino Lacy
    Dance music composed and arranged by Monsieur Pons (uncredited)

The Deep, Deep Sea, or, The Sea Serpent
    15 November 1834
    "Musical yarns strung together and dedicated nauti-cally disposed and Amphitrite in particular, (some of them being handed Over-to-her), by way of Overture, by Mr. William Penson"
    Dance and incidental music arranged by William Penson (uncredited)

The Saw Mill, or, A Yankee Trick
    29 November 1834
    Written and composed by Micah Hawkins
    Orchestra accompaniments by James Hewitt
    Dance music arranged by James Hewitt (uncredited)

Norman Leslie
    11 January 1836
    Music by St. Luke
    Ballet music selected and arranged by St. Luke (uncredited)
    Dances by Mr. Parker

Cinderella
    15 November 1837
    Incidental and dance music composed by J. Sprake

Mazeppa and the Wild Horse
    2 April 1838
    Incidental and dance music composed and arranged by J. Sprake

Amilie, or, The Love Test
    15 October 1838
    Music by William Michael Rooke
    Musical director, William Penson

Incidental and dance music composed by William Michael Rooke (uncredited)

La Musquitoe
21 May 1840
"Music has been begged, borrowed and stolen from all sorts of Operas and Ballets, in the most imprudent and free and easy style" by George Loder
Musical director, George Loder
Incidental and dance music arranged by George Loder (uncredited)

Ahmed al Kamel
12 October 1840
Music by Charles E. Horn
Incidental and ballet music arranged by Charles E. Horn (uncredited)

The Cat's in the Larder, or, The Maid with a Parasol
23 December 1840
Music arranged [from the operas of Rossini] by George Loder
Incidental and ballet music selected from Rossini by George Loder (uncredited)
Staging by William Mitchell

The Naiad Queen, or, The Mysteries of the Lurlie Berg!
21 April 1841
Original music by Edward Woolf
Musical director, Mr. Duggan
Ballet music arranged by Edward Woolf (uncredited)
Dances by Madame Petit and Mr. Oakey

The Bohea-man's Girl
11 March 1845
Music arranged [from *The Bohemian Girl* by Michael William Balfe] by George Loder
Dance music selected from Balfe and arranged by George Loder (uncredited)
Staging by William Mitchell

Leonora
>4 June 1845
>Music composed by William Henry Fry
>Ballet music arranged by William Henry Fry (uncredited)

The Naiad Queen
>5 April 1847
>Ballet music arranged and partly composed by Sidney Pearson (uncredited)

Aladdin, or, The Wonderful Lamp
>1847
>Music composed and selected by Thomas Comer
>Musical director, Thomas Comer
>Incidental and dance music composed by Thomas Comer (uncredited)

A Glance at New York in 1848
>15 February 1848
>Music arranged by Edward Woolf
>Incidental and dance music arranged by Edward Woolf (uncredited)
>Staging by William Mitchell

Dombey and Son
>24 July 1848
>Musical director, George Loder
>Incidental and dance music arranged by George Loder (uncredited)

The Enchanted Beauty, or, the Dream of 100 Years
>1850
>Music composed and selected by Thomas Comer
>Musical director, Thomas Comer
>Incidental and dance music composed by Thomas Comer (uncredited)

Faustus, or, The Demon of the Drachenfels
>13 January 1851

Music by Sir Henry Bishop
"Melo-dramatic music composed, selected and arranged" by Mons. Perot
Ballet and incidental dances by Monsieur Schmidt

The Andalusian, or, The Young Guard
15 January 1851
Music by Edward Loder
Musical director, George Loder
Music "arranged for this establishment" by George Loder
Staging by Harry Lynne

The World's Fair, or, Columbia in the Clouds
10 February 1851
Musical director, George Loder
Dance music selected and arranged by George Loder (uncredited)
Staging by Harry Lynne

The Spirit of the Air, or, The Enchanted Star
7 April 1851
"New and original music" composed by George Loder
Musical director, George Loder
Dance music arranged by George Loder (uncredited)
Staging by Harry Lynne

Azael, the Prodigal
21 July 1851
Music by Daniel Auber
Music under the supervision of W.T. Peterschen
Original ballet music composed by Daniel Auber
Incidental and ballet music arranged by W.T. Peterschen (uncredited)
Ballet and incidental dances by Monsieur Schmidt

Paul Clifford
19 January 1852
Musical director, Mr. Roberts
Ballet and incidental music selected and arranged by Mr. Rob-

erts (uncredited)
Ballets by Signor Neri

The Corsican Brothers
24 February 1852
Play by Dion Boucicault
Incidental music by Pierre Joseph Alphonse Varney
Incidental music adapted and arranged by Robert Stöpel (Stoepel)

The Peri, or, The Enchanted Fountain
13 December 1852
Music by James Gaspard Maeder
Musical director, James Gaspard Maeder
Orchestra leader (and chorus master), Mr. Roberts
Dance music arranged by James Gaspard Maeder (uncredited)
Staging by Mr. Barry

Uncle Tom's Cabin
1852
Music composed and selected by Thomas Comer
Musical director, Thomas Comer
Incidental and dance music composed by Thomas Comer (uncredited)

Valeria
1852
Music composed and selected by Thomas Comer
Musical director, Thomas Comer
Incidental and dance music composed by Thomas Comer (uncredited)

Shylock: A Jerusalem Hearty Joke
29 October 1853
Musical director, John Cooke
Incidental and ballet music selected and arranged by John Cooke (uncredited)
Staging by John Moore

Apollo in New York
    11 December 1854
    Music arranged by John Cooke
    Ballet music selected and arranged by John Cooke (uncredited)

Rip Van Winkle
    27 September 1855
    Music by George F. Bristow
    Musical director, George F. Bristow
    Incidental and dance music by George F. Bristow (uncredited)

King Charming, or, The Blue Bird of Paradise
    24 December 1855
    Music by John Cooke
    Musical director, John Cooke
    Ballet music selected and arranged by John Cooke (uncredited)
    Dances and ensembles by Monsieur Monplaisir

Po-Ca-Hon-Tas, or, The Gentle Savage
    24 December 1855
    "Music entirely dislocated and re-set" by James Gaspard Maeder
    Musical director (conductor), Signor La Manna
    Ballet music selected and arranged by James Gaspard Maeder (uncredited)
    Indian dances and marches by B. Yates

Novelty
    22 February 1856
    Music composed by Thomas Baker
    Musical director, Thomas Baker
    Incidental and dance music arranged by Thomas Baker (uncredited)
    Ballets by Monsieur Monplaisir

Hiawatha, or, Ardent Spirits and Laughing Waters
    25 December 1856
    Music arranged by Signor La Manna
    Ballet music selected and arranged by Signor La Manna (uncredited)

Young Baccus, or, Spirits and Water
  5 January 1857
  Music composed, adapted and arranged by Thomas Baker
  Ballet music selected and arranged by Thomas Baker (uncredited)

The Elves, or, The Statue Bride
  16 March 1857
  Music composed and arranged by Thomas Baker
  Ballet music selected and arranged by Thomas Baker (uncredited)
  Dances by B. Yates

Variety, or, The Picture Gallery
  11 May 1857
  Music arranged by Thomas Baker
  Ballet music selected and arranged by Thomas Baker (uncredited)
  Ballets by Monsieur Monplaisir

Olympiana, or, A Night with Mitchell
  13 June 1857
  Music composed and arranged by Anthony Reiff
  Incidental and dance music selected and arranged by Anthony Reiff (uncredited)

The King of Coney Island
  30 June 1857
  Music arranged by Anthony Reiff
  Incidental and dance music selected and arranged by Anthony Reiff (uncredited)

Cinderella
  15 June 1859
  Music arranged by Thomas Baker
  Ballet music selected and arranged by Thomas Baker (uncredited)
  Ballets by Monsieur Monplaisir

Massaniello, Hero and Martyr of Italian Liberty
27 June 1859
Inspired by the opera by Daniel Auber
Music arranged by Thomas Baker
Musical director (conductor), Thomas Baker
Ballet music selected from the work of Daniel Auber and arranged by Thomas Baker (uncredited)

The Invisible Prince, or, The Island of Tranquil Delights
11 July 1859
Music arranged by Thomas Baker
Musical director (conductor), Thomas Baker
Ballet music selected and arranged by Thomas Baker (uncredited)

Lalla Rookh, or, The Fire Worshippers
18 July 1859
Music, new and selected by John Cooke
Ballet music selected and arranged by John Cooke (uncredited)
Staging by W.J. Florence

Blue Beard, or, The Punishment of Curiosity
7 May 1860
Music arranged by John Cooke
Musical director, John Cooke
Ballet music selected and arranged by John Cooke (uncredited)

The Tycoon, or, Young American in Japan
2 July 1860
Music composed and arranged by Thomas Baker
Ballet music selected and arranged by Thomas Baker (uncredited)

The Seven Sisters!
26 November 1860
New music by Thomas Baker
Musical director, Thomas Baker
Ballet music selected and arranged by Thomas Baker (uncredited)
Marches and military drills by Frederick Cook

Harlequin Jack, The Giant Killer
    4 February 1861
    Written and composed by George L. Fox
    Musical director (conductor), Henry D. Beissenherz
    Incidental and ballet music arranged by Henry D. Beissenherz (uncredited)

Cinderella
    9 September 1861
    New music composed and arranged by Charles Koppitz
    Ballet music selected and arranged by Charles Koppitz (uncredited)

The Seven Sons!
    23 September 1861
    Music composed and arranged by Thomas Baker
    Ballet music selected and arranged by Thomas Baker (uncredited)

Ondina!, or, The Spirit of the Waters
    23 December 1861
    Music, choruses and marches composed and arranged by W.T. Peterschen
    Ballet music selected and arranged by W.T. Peterschen (uncredited)
    Dances by Mlle. Deulin
    Marches by Frederick Cook

Sadak and Kalasgrade!, or, The Waters of Oblivion
    3 March 1862
    Music composed and arranged by W.T. Peterschen
    Ballet music selected and arranged by W.T. Peterschen (uncredited)
    Dances by Mlle. Deulin

Hop O' My Thumb, or, The Ogre and the Dwarf!
    7 April 1862
    Original music by W.T. Peterschen
    Ballet music selected and arranged by W.T. Peterschen (uncredited)

Selected Chronology: 1786–1923 | 49

The Doctor of Alcantara
    7 April 1862
    Music by Julius Eichberg
    Musical director (conductor), Julius Eichberg
    Incidental music composed and arranged by Julius Eichberg (uncredited)

King Cotton, or, The Exiled Prince
    21 July 1862
    Musical director, Edward Mollenhauer
    Ballet music selected and arranged by Edward Mollenhauer (uncredited)

Blondette, or, The Naughty Prince and the Pretty Peasant
    25 November 1862
    "Music composed and arranged from the works of Meyerbeer, Weber, Mendelssohn, Rossini, Verbi, Auber, etc. by Thomas Baker."
    Musical director, Thomas Baker
    Ballet music selected and arranged by Thomas Baker (uncredited)

The Pet of the Petticoats!
    26 January 1863
    Musical director, Thomas Baker
    Ballet music selected and arranged by Thomas Baker (uncredited)

The Loan of a Lover
    30 January 1863
    Musical director, Thomas Baker
    Incidental music selected and arranged by Thomas Baker (uncredited)

The Fair One with the Golden Locks
    9 February 1863
    New music compiled and arranged by James Gaspard Maeder and Thomas Baker
    Musical director, Thomas Baker
    Ballet music selected and arranged by Thomas Baker (uncredited)

King Linkum the First
    23 February 1863
    Music arranged by John Hill Hewitt
    Incidental and dance music selected and arranged by John Hill Hewitt (uncredited)

Tib, or, The Cat in Crinoline
    4 May 1863
    Music by Thomas Baker
    Musical director, Thomas Baker
    Ballet music selected and arranged by Thomas Baker (uncredited)

The Duke's Motto
    1 June 1863
    Music composed by Harvey B. Dodworth
    Incidental and ballet music arranged by Harvey B. Dodworth (uncredited)

The Devil in the Bowery
    28 September 1863
    Music arranged by Henry D. Beissenherz
    Musical director (conductor), Henry D. Beissenherz
    Incidental and ballet music arranged by Henry D. Beissenherz (uncredited)

Brother and Sister
    8 October 1863
    Music by Sir Henry Bishop
    Musical director, Thomas Baker
    Ballet music selected and arranged by Thomas Baker (uncredited)
    Staging by Charles M. Walcot

Po-Ca-Hon-Tas, or, Ye Gentle Savage
    19 October 1863
    Music selected and arranged by Thomas Baker
    Musical director, Thomas Baker
    Orchestra leader, Signor La Manna

Ballet music selected and arranged by Thomas Baker (uncredited)

The House that Jack Built, or, Harlequin and the Fairy Generous
11 January 1864
Musical director, Ferdinand Von Olker
Ballet music and incidental music selected and arranged by Ferdinand Von Olker (uncredited)
Ballet by Paul Brillant

Mazeppa, or, the Untamed Rocking Horse
18 January 1864
Music by Thomas Baker
Musical director, Thomas Baker
Ballet music selected and arranged by Thomas Baker (uncredited)
Staging by Charles M. Walcot

The House that Jack Built
25 January 1864
Music and arranged by Alexander Tyte
Ballet music selected and arranged by Alexander Tyte (uncredited)
Staging by George L. Fox

Ill Treated Il Travadatore!, or, The Mother, The Maiden and the Musicianer
8 February 1864
"New music, including all the principal Gems from the Real Opera," arranged by Thomas Baker
Musical director, Thomas Baker
Ballet music selected and arranged by Thomas Baker (uncredited)

Loyalina, or, Brigadier-General Fortunio, and His Seven Gifted Aides-de-Camp
11 April 1864
Music, selected and original, composed and arranged by Thomas Baker

Ballet music selected and arranged by Thomas Baker (uncredited)

Staging by J.H. Selwyn

Fra Diavolo, or, The Beauty and the Brigands / Thrice Married

23 May 1864

New music by John Cooke

Additional music by Michael William Balfe and Charles Gounod

Spanish dances selected and arranged by John Cooke (uncredited)

Aladdin, or, The Wonderful Lamp

2 June 1864

"Music, Real, Descriptive and Pantomimical, composed and arranged on sound principles, expressly for the piece," by Thomas Baker

Musical director, Thomas Baker

Ballet music selected and arranged by Thomas Baker (uncredited)

The Ring of Fate, or, Fire, Air, Earth and Water

26 December 1864

New and original music composed by W.T. Peterschen

Ballet music selected and arranged by W.T. Peterschen (uncredited)

Staging by E.F. Taylor

Harlequin Bluebeard, or, The Good Fairy Preciosa and the Bad Demon Rustifusti

26 December 1864

Musical director (conductor), H. Wayrauch

Ballet music selected and arranged by H. Wayrauch (uncredited)

Staging by James M. Nixon

Mother Goose! And the Fairy Legend of the Golden Egg

13 February 1865

Musical director (conductor), H. Wayrauch

Ballet music selected and arranged by H. Wayrauch (uncredited)

Petroliamania, or, Oil on the Brain
6 March 1865
Musical director (conductor), Edward Mollenhauer
Incidental and dance music selected and arranged by Edward Mollenhauer (uncredited)

The Fairy Prince O'Donoughue, or, the White Horse of Killarney
3 April 1865
Musical composed and arranged by H. Wayrauch
Incidental, gymnastic, and equestrian music selected and arranged by H. Wayrauch (uncredited)
Dances and marches by Signor Ronzani

The Green Monster, or, The White Knight and the Giant Warrior
10 July 1865
Musical director (conductor), W.T. Peterschen
Ballet music selected and arranged by W.T. Peterschen (uncredited)
Staging by Monsieur A. Grossi

Arrah-Na-Pogue, or, The Wicklow Wedding
12 July 1865
Original music composed by C. Levy
Additional music composed by Benjamin Edward Woolf and John P Cooke
Musical director, Harvey B. Dodworth
Musical supervisor, Benjamin J. Deane
Incidental and melodramatic music arranged by Harvey B. Dodworth (uncredited)

Sinbad the Sailor
27 November 1865
Music, new and selected, by Alexander Tyte
Incidental and dance music selected and arranged by Alexander Tyte (uncredited)
Staging by George L. Fox

The Black Domino / Between You and Me and the Post
29 January 1866
Music arranged and composed by Jonathan P. Cooke
Musical director, Henry Tissington
Incidental and dance music arranged by Henry Tissington (uncredited)

Jack and Gill Went Up the Hill
29 February 1866
New music, original and selected, by Alexander Tyte
Incidental and ballet music selected and arranged by Alexander Tyte (uncredited)
Ballets by Monsieur A. Grossi

Cinderella e la Comare, or, The Lover, The Lackey, and the Little Glass Slipper
26 February 1866
Music, new and selected, by Thomas Baker
Incidental and dance music selected and arranged by Thomas Baker (uncredited)

Valiant Valentine
27 March 1866
Music by Henry Tissington
Musical director (conductor), Henry Tissington
Music for ballet specialties selected and arranged by Henry Tissington (uncreditd)
Ballets by Monsieur A. Grossi

The Elves, or, The Statue Bride
30 April 1866
Original music by Count Nicolo Gabrielli
Musical director (conductor), Henry D. Beissenherz
Incidental and ballet music adapted and arranged by Henry D. Beissenherz (uncredited)

The Sheep's Foot!
18 June 1866
New music by Charles Schultz

Musical director (conductor), Charles Schultz
Ballet music selected and arranged by Charles Schultz (uncredited)
Ballets by Monsieur A. Grossi

Po-Ca-Hon-Tas
18 June 1866
"Music entirely dislocated and re-set" by James Gaspard Maeder
Musical director (conductor), Robert Stoepel
Ballet music selected and arranged by James Gaspard Maeder (uncredited)

The Three Sisters!
18 June 1866
Music selected, composed, and arranged by Henry D. Beissenherz (uncredited)
Musical director (conductor), Henry D. Beissenherz
Dance music selected and arranged by Henry D. Beissenherz (uncredited)

A Night in Rome
25 June 1866
Libretto and music by Julius Eichberg
Musical director (conductor), Julius Eichberg
Incidental and dance music composed and arranged by Julius Eichberg (uncredited)

Fra Diavolo
2 July 1866
Original music by Daniel Auber
Music adapted by Henry D. Beissenherz (uncredited)
Musical director (conductor), Henry D. Beissenherz
Original ballet music composed by Daniel Auber
Ballet music selected, adapted, and arranged by Henry D. Beissenherz (uncredited)
Staging by Benjamin A. Baker

Columbus Reconstructed
9 July 1866

Music by Robert Stoepel
Incidental and pyrotechnic music selected and arranged by Robert Stoepel (uncredited)

The Black Crook
12 September 1866
Music by Thomas Baker
Additional music by George Bicknell, C.T. de Coeniel, and V.B. Aubert
Musical director (conductor), Harvey B. Dodworth
Ballet music selected, composed, and arranged by Thomas Baker (uncredited)
Ballets by Davide Costa

Lady Audley's Secret
12 September 1866
Music by Henry Tissington
Musical director (conductor), Julius Eichberg
Incidental and dance music composed and arranged by Henry Tissington (uncredited)

Cinderella, or, The Lover, the Lackey, and the Little Glass Slipper
24 September 1866
"The music, original, incidental, operatic and otherwise has been taken (honestly, of course) from any ancient or modern source, and re-arranged, re-constructed and elaborated with a view to unison and harmony by Chas. Koppitz and N. Lothian"
Musical director, Napier Lothian
Incidental and ballet music arranged by Charles Koppitz and Napier Lothian

Tom-Tom, The Piper's Son Stole a Pig and Away He Run
3 December 1866
Music composed and arranged by Benjamin Deane
Ballet music selected and arranged by Benjamin Deane (uncredited)
Ballets and incidental dances by W. Stanton

Cendrillon
> 17 December 1866
> "New and appropriate music" composed and arranged by Henry Tissington
> Ballet music selected and arranged by Henry Tissington (uncredited)
> Ballets by Monsieur A. Grossi

A Bird of Paradise
> 29 January 1867
> "New and appropriate music" composed and arranged by Henry Tissington
> Music for ballet specialties selected and arranged by Henry Tissington (uncredited)
> Ballets by Monsieur A. Grossi

The Christian Martyrs
> 18 February 1867
> Music by Thomas Baker
> Musical director, Thomas Baker
> Incidental and spectacular music selected and arranged by Thomas Baker (uncredited)

Little Boy Blue, or, Hush-A-Bye Baby and Patty and Her Pitcher
> 1 April 1867
> "New overture and appropriate music composed, arranged and selected" by Alexander Tyte
> Music for ballet specialties selected and arranged by Alexander Tyte (uncredited)
> Ballets by Monsieur A. Grossi

The Black Crook
> May 1867
> Incidental and dance music composed by W.D.C. Böteführ

Faust, or, The Demon, the Doctor and the Devil's Draught
> 10 June 1867
> Musical director, Henry Tissington

Incidental and dance music selected and arranged by Henry Tissington (uncredited)

The Devil's Auction, or, The Golden Branch
3 October 1867
New music by Auguste Predigan
Ballet music selected and arranged by Auguste Predigan (uncredited)
Ballets by Monsieur Ronzani

Shylock, or, The Merchant of Venice Preserved
28 October 1867
Musical director, Napoleon Gilles
Incidental and descriptive music arranged by Charles Koppitz

Medea!, or, The Best of Mothers with a Brute of a Husband
18 November 1867
New music arranged by Napoleon Gilles
Musical director, Napoleon Gilles
Incidental and dance music selected and arranged by Napoleon Gilles (uncredited)

Little Dew Drop, or, The Fairies' Home in the Palace of Neptune
23 December 1867
New and original music by Prof. Krakaner
Music for dance and transformation music arranged by Prof. Krakaner (uncredited)

The White Fawn
17 January 1868
Music by Edward Mollenhauer and Howard Glover
Additional music composed by E.G.B Holder and Jacques Offenbach
Musical director, Edward Mollenhauer
Ballet music composed by A. Jannota, J. Hood McKever, and Edward Mollenhauer
Additional dance music selected and arranged by Howard Glover (uncredited)
Ballets by Davide Costa

The Two Cadis
    5 March 1868
    Music by Julius Eichberg
    Musical director, Julius Eichberg
    Incidental and dance music composed and arranged by Julius Eichberg (uncredited)

Humpty Dumpty
    10 March 1868
    Music composed and arranged by Anthony Reiff
    Musical director, Anthony Reiff
    Ballet music selected and arranged by Anthony Reiff (uncredited)
    Ballets by Michele Jambone

Fire Fly, or, The Friend of the Flag
    10 August 1868
    Original music by Thomas Baker
    Musical director (conductor), Thomas Baker
    Music for dance specialties selected and arranged by Thomas Baker (uncredited)

Ixion!, or, The Man at the Wheel
    28 September 1868
    "New music arranged and composed" by Michael Connelly
    Musical director, Michael Connelly
    Incidental and dance music selected and arranged by Michael Connelly (uncredited)

Ernani, or, The Horn of a Dilemma
    28 December 1868
    "New music arranged and composed" by Michael Connelly
    Musical director, Michael Connelly
    Incidental and dance music selected and arranged by Michael Connelly (uncredited)

The Page's Revel, or, the Summer Night's Bivouac/Nicodemus
    4 January 1869
    Musical director, Giuseppe Operti

Incidental music composed, and arranged by Giuseppe Operti
Ballet music selected and arranged by Giuseppe Operti (uncredited)
Ballets by Carlo Carle

The Forty Thieves, or Striking Oil in Family Jars!
1 February 1869
Music selected and arranged by Michael Connelly
Musical director, Michael Connelly
Incidental and dance music selected and arranged by Michael Connelly (uncredited)
Dances by Carlo Carle

Pluto
1 February 1869
Music by David Braham
Musical director, David Braham
Incidental and dance music selected, composed, and arranged by David Braham (uncredited)

The Field of the Cloth of Gold
1 February 1869
Music composed, selected and arranged by Howard Glover
Musical director (conductor), Henry Hahn
Incidental and dance music selected and arranged by Howard Glover (uncredited)

Lucretia Borgia, M.D., La Grande Doctresse
17 February 1869
Music by Gaetano Donizetti
Music arranged and adapted by Napier Lothian
Musical director (conductor), Fred W. Zaulig
Incidental and dance music arranged by Napier Lothian (uncredited)
Staging by Harry Wall

The Horse Marines / Nicodemus
1 March 1869
Musical director, Signor Giuseppe Operti

Musical arrangements by Giuseppe Operti
Incidental and ballet music selected, composed, and arranged by Giuseppe Operti (uncredited)

Ivanhoe
31 March 1869
Musical director (conductor), Howard Glover
Incidental and dance music selected and arranged by Howard Glover (uncredited)
Staging by Harry Wall

Robinson Crusoe, and His Man Friday!
26 April 1869
Musical director, Signor Giuseppe Operti
Incidental and ballet music selected, composed, and arranged by Giuseppe Operti (uncredited)
Staging by Benjamin A. Baker

Paris, or, The Judgement
28 April 1869
New music selected by Elise Holt
Music arranged and orchestrated by Howard Glover
Musical director (conductor), Howard Glover
Incidental and dance music selected and arranged by Howard Glover (uncredited)
Staging by Asa Cushman

Robinson Crusoe
8 May 1869
Music composed, selected and arranged by Fred W. Humphrey
Orchestra leader, H.W. Humphreys
Music for ballet specialties selected and arranged by Fred W. Humphrey (uncredited)

Pygmalion, or, The Peerless and Beautiful Statue
15 May 1869
Musical director, Howard Glover
Incidental and dance music selected and arranged by Howard Glover (uncredited)

Hiccory Diccory Dock, or, Harlequin Jack of the Beanstalk!
18 May 1869
Music selected and arranged by Frederic Strebinger
Musical director (conductor), Frederic Strebinger
Music for ballet specialties selected, composed, and arranged by Frederic Strebinger (uncredited)
Ballets by Davide Costa

Clorinda! The Girl of the Period / Peter Gray, or, Ding Dong Din
24 May 1869
Musical director, Giuseppe Operti
Incidental and dance music selected and arranged by Giuseppe Operti (uncredited)
Ballets by Alexander Zanfretta

Beppo
12 June 1869
Musical director, Giuseppe Operti
Music for musical and dance specialties arranged by Giuseppe Operti (uncredited)

The Queen of Hearts, or, Harlequin, the Knave of Hearts, who stole the Tarts, and the Old Woman that Lived in a Shoe
16 August 1869
Musical director (conductor), Richard Arnold
Ballet music arranged by Richard Arnold (uncredited)
Ballets by John Lauri

Formosa, or, The Railroad to Ruin
6 September 1869
Musical director, Giuseppe Operti
Incidental music composed by Giuseppe Operti

Flick Flock
18 October 1869
Music arranged by J. Aberle
Specialties composed by Paolo Giorza

Fire-Fly!
>22 November 1869
>Music composed by Giuseppe Operti
>Musical director, Giuseppe Operti
>New overture, incidental music, and music for specialties composed and arranged by Giuseppe Operti

Bad Dickey
>6 December 1869
>Music by Richard Arnold
>Musical director (conductor), Richard Arnold
>Incidental and dance music composed and arranged by Richard Arnold (uncredited)

The Glorious 7
>31 January 1870
>Music by Richard Arnold
>Musical director (conductor), Richard Arnold
>Incidental and ballet music composed and arranged by Richard Arnold (uncredited)
>Ballets by Davide Costa

The Twelve Temptations!
>7 February 1870
>Music arranged by Henry Tissington
>Ballet music selected and arranged by Henry Tissington (uncredited)
>Ballets by Davide Costa

Pippin, or, The King of the Gold Mines
>4 April 1870
>Music arranged and composed by Michael Connelly
>Musical director, Michael Connelly
>Music for specialties composed by Giuseppe Operti, selected and arranged by Michael Connelly (uncredited)

The Fair One with Blonde Wig
>16 May 1870
>"Selected gems (music) from all the popular operas."

Musical director (conductor) Frederic Strebinger
Incidental and dance music selected and arranged by Frederic Strebinger (uncredited)

The Daughter of the Regiment, or, The 800 Fathers
13 June 1870
"Music selected from popular operas."
Musical director (conductor) Frederic Strebinger
Incidental and dance music selected and arranged by Frederic Strebinger (uncredited)

The Golden Butterfly
5 September 1870
Music arranged by William H. Brinkworth
Musical director, William H. Brinkworth
Incidental and ballet music selected and arranged by William H. Brinkworth (uncredited)
Staging by James Barnes

Le Petit Faust
26 September 1870
Music composed by Hervé
Musical director, Carlo Patti
Ballet music composed by Henry Tissington (first actual credit for dance arrangements in a theatre program)
Ballets by Davide Costa

Humpty Dumpty Junior, or, The Fairy of the Diamond Mines and the Giant's Festival
3 October 1870
Musical director, William H. Brinkworth
Incidental, transformation, and dance music selected and arranged by William H. Brinkworth (uncredited)
Staging by Imre and Bolossy Kiralfy

Wee Willie Winkie
5 October 1870
Music composed and arranged by Frederic Strebinger
Incidental, dance, and military music arranged by Frederic

Strebinger (Uncredited)
Staging by George L. Fox

Lurline
17 October 1870
Music composed and arranged by Michael Connelly
Musical director, Michael Connelly
Music for ballet specialties arranged by Michael Connelly (uncredited)
Staging by Lydia Thompson

Paris, or, The Apple of Discord
14 November 1870
Music selected and arranged by Michael Connelly
Musical director, Michael Connelly
Incidental and dance music arranged by Michael Connelly (uncredited)
Staging by Lydia Thompson

The Black Crook
12 December 1870
Music by Thomas Baker
New music arranged and composed by Giuseppe Operti
Musical director (conductor), Giuseppe Operti
Ballet music arranged by Giuseppe Operti (uncredited)
Ballets by Davide Costa

St. George and the Dragon, or The 7 Champions of Christendom
9 January 1871
Music selected and arranged by Michael Connelly
Musical director, Michael Connelly
Incidental and dance music arranged by Michael Connelly (uncredited)
Staging by Lydia Thompson

Richelieu of the Period!
6 February 1871
Music composed and arranged by Frederic Strebinger "without respect to the Ancient Masters, but with great regard to the

Lays of the Last Minstrel"
Musical specialties arranged by Frederic Strebinger (uncredited)
Staging by E.S. Tarr

The Little Frauds
1 May 1871
Music by John Braham, E.N. Catlin, and Edward Harrigan
Musical director, John Braham
Dance music arranged by John Braham, and E.N. Catlin (uncredited)

The Three Hunchbacks!
22 May 1871
Musical Director, Henry Tissington
Ballet music arranged by Henry Tissington (uncredited)
Staging by A.S. Pennoyer

Three Blind Mice!, or, Harlequin Tell-Tale Tit
5 June 1871
Music composed by A.W. Maflin
Ballet music selected and arranged by A.W. Maflin (uncredited)

Paul Clifford!
12 June 1871
Musical director (conductor), Giuseppe Operti
Incidental and dance music selected and arranged by Giuseppe Operti (uncredited)

Blue Beard, or, the Mormon, the Maiden, and the Little Militaire
16 August 1871
"The latest musical novelties from Europe, specially imported, assorted and concerted" by Michael Connelly
Musical director, Michael Connelly
Ballet music selected and arranged by Michael Connelly (uncredited)
Staging by Harry Beckett

On the Track
    28 August 1871
    Music composed and arranged by E.N. Catlin
    Musical director, B.J. Deane
    Incidental and ballet music arranged by E.N. Catlin (uncredited)

Humpty Dumpty
    31 August 1871
    Music composed and selected by Frederic Strebinger
    Musical director, Frederic Strebinger
    Music for ballets and specialties selected and arranged by Frederic Strebinger (uncredited)
    Ballets by Imre Kiralfy

Carl, The Fiddler
    18 September 1871
    Incidental music composed by Giuseppe Operti

The Black Crook
    18 December 1871
    Music by Giuseppe Operti
    Musical director, Giuseppe Operti
    Music for ballets and specialties composed and arranged by Giuseppe Operti, and selected from the work of Stephen Foster and Arthur Sullivan (uncredited)
    Ballets by Davide Costa

Dick Whittington and His Cat
    5 February 1872
    Music by William H. Brinkworth
    Musical director, William H. Brinkworth
    Incidental and dance music arranged by William H. Brinkworth (uncredited
    Staging by James Barnes

Poll and Partner Joe
    19 February 1872
    Music by William H. Brinkworth

Musical director, William H. Brinkworth
Incidental and dance music arranged by William H. Brinkworth (uncredited)
Staging by James Barnes

Luna, the Little Boy who cried for the Moon
4 March 1872
Music by William H. Brinkworth
Musical director, William H. Brinkworth
Incidental and dance music arranged by William H. Brinkworth (uncredited)
Staging by James Barnes

Lalla Rookh, or The Pearl of India
18 March 1872
Music composed by Henry Tissington
Musical director (conductor), Henry Tissington
Ballet music arranged by Henry Tissington (uncredited)
Ballets by Monsieur Van Hamme

Poll and Partner Joe
1 April 1872
Music selected and arranged by Napier Lothian
Musical director, Napier Lothian
Incidental and dance music arranged by Napier Lothian (uncredited)

The Palace of Truth
10 April 1872
Incidental and dance music composed by Charles Schultz

Fortunio and His Gifted Servants!
3 June 1872
Musical director, Frank A. Howson
Incidental and dance music composed by Frank A. Howson (uncredited)

Robin Hood; or, The Maid That Was Arch, and the Youth That Was Archer
>22 July 1872
>Music by Vincent Davies
>Musical director, Michael Connelly
>Incidental and dance music arranged by Michael Connelly (uncredited)
>Staging by James Schonberg

Chow Chow, or, A Tale of Pekin
>9 September 1872
>Music selected and arranged by William H. Brinkworth
>Incidental, military, and dance music arranged by William H. Brinkworth (uncredited)
>Staging by James Barnes

Kenilworth, or, Ye Queen, Ye Knight and Ye Maiden
>21 September 1872
>Music by Michael Connelly
>Musical director, Michael Connelly
>Incidental and dance music arranged by Michael Connelly (uncredited)
>Staging by James Schonberg

Henry VIII
>19 October 1872
>Incidental music composed by Charles Koppitz

The Three Mus-Ke-Teers
>21 October 1872
>Musical director, William H. Brinkworth
>Overture composed and incidental music arranged by William H. Brinkworth
>Staging by James Barnes

Aladdin the Second
>November 1872
>Music composed and arranged by David Braham
>Ballet music arranged by David Braham (uncredited)

Ballets by John Lauri

Leo and Lotos
    30 November 1872
    Musical director (conductor), Michael Connelly
    Music for ballet specialties arranged by Michael Connelly (uncredited)
    Staging by L.J. Vincent

The Babes in the Wood
    16 December 1872
    Musical director, William H. Brinkworth
    Incidental and dance music arranged by William H. Brinkworth (uncredited)
    Staging by James Barnes

Jack, the Giant Killer
    30 December 1872
    Musical director, William H. Brinkworth
    Incidental and dance music arranged by William H. Brinkworth (uncredited)
    Staging by James Barnes

Roughing It!!
    18 February 1873
    Music by Auguste Predigam
    Music for "Dance of Passengers, Conductors, Porters and Breakmen" arranged by Auguste Predigam (uncredited)

Azrael, or The Magic Charm
    28 April 1873
    Music composed by Michael Connelly
    Ballet music arranged by Michael Connelly (uncredited)
    Pantomime by James S. Maffit

Mephisto and the Four Sensations
    25 August 1873
    Music composed, arranged and selected from the latest Parisian novelties by John Elliot Mallandaine

Musical director, William Withers, Jr.
Incidental and dance music selected and arranged by John Elliot Mallandaine (uncredited)
Staging by Alexander Henderson

Sinbad the Sailor
11 September 1873
Music by Michael Connelly and William Withers, Jr.
Musical director, William Withers, Jr.
Music for the "Dancing Quakers" arranged by Charles E. Pratt
Original music for ballet specialties selected and arranged by Michael Connelly
New music for ballet specialties selected and arranged by William Withers, Jr.(uncredited)
Staging by Alexander Henderson

Arrah-Na-Brogue!
13 October 1873
New music by David Braham
Musical director (conductor), David Braham
Music for dances and diversions arranged by David Braham (uncredited)
Staging by G.L. Stout

Humpty Dumpty Abroad!
24 November 1873
Music by Frederic Strebinger
Music for ballets arranged by Frederic Strebinger (uncredited)
Ballets by Imre Kiralfy

The Children in the Wood
8 December 1873
Songs composed and arranged by W.C. Levy
Musical Director, Michael Connelly
Overture and ballet music by Michael Connelly
Ballets and dances by Frederick and (Walter) Fawdon Vokes

Gabriel Grub; or, The Story of the Goblins Who Stole the Sexton!
22 December 1873
Music by David Braham
Musical director (conductor), F. Rochow
Incidental, eccentric, and dance music composed, selected, and arranged by David Braham (uncredited)

Aladdin
6 July 1874
Music by Giuseppe Operti
Musical director, Giuseppe Operti
Ballet music arranged by Giuseppe Operti (uncredited)

Evangeline, or The Belle of Arcadie
27 July 1874
Music by Edward Everett Rice
Musical director, William Withers, Jr.
Dance music composed by Edward Everett Rice (uncredited)

The Bride of Abydos, or, The Pirate of the Isles
24 August 1874
Music by William Withers, Jr.
Musical director, William Withers, Jr.
Ballet music arranged by William Withers, Jr. (uncredited)

The Deluge, or, Paradise Lost
7 September 1874
Music by Alexander Artus (of Paris), and William Withers, Jr. (of New York)
Musical director, William Withers, Jr.
Ballet music arranged by William Withers, Jr. (uncredited)
Ballets by Imre Kiralfy

The Shaughraun
14 November 1874
Incidental music composed by Thomas Baker

Round the Clock; or, New York by Dark
23 November 1874

Music by William H. Brinkworth
Musical director, William H. Brinkworth
Specialties music arranged by William H. Brinkworth (uncredited)
Staging by James Barnes

The Two Orphans
21 December 1874
Incidental and dance music composed by Henry Tissington

Jack and Jill
21 December 1874
Musical director, William Withers, Jr.
Music for ballet specialties arranged by William Withers, Jr. (uncredited)
Pantomime by James S. Maffit

Fee-G!
21 December 1874
Music by David Braham
Musical director (conductor), David Braham
Dance music composed and arranged by David Braham (uncredited)
Staging by G.L. Stout

Around the World in 80 Days
29 March 1875
Music by Benjamin J. Deane
Musical director, Benjamin J. Deane
Incidental and dance music arranged by Benjamin J. Deane (uncredited)
Staged by Maurice Pike

Ahmed!
30 March 1875
Music by William Withers, Jr.
Musical director, William Withers, Jr.
Music for ballet specialties arranged by William Withers, Jr. (uncredited)
Ballets by Mme. Kathi Lanner

The Donovans
   31 May 1875
   Incidental music composed and arranged by David Braham

Gambrinus, King of Lager Beer
   21 July 1875
   Music by Frank Dumont and Alfred B. Sedgwick
   Music arranged by Alfred B. Sedgwick
   Incidental and dance music arranged by Alfred B. Sedgwick (uncredited)

Around the World in 80 Days
   16 August 1875
   Incidental and dance music composed and arranged by E. Harrison
   Staging by Robert Johnston

Around the World in 80 Days
   28 August 1875
   Music composed and arranged by Jean-Jacques Debillemont
   Musical director (conductor), L. Conterno
   Music for spectacles and ballets arranged by Jean-Jacques Debillemont (uncredited)
   Staging by Imre and Bolossy Kiralfy
   Ballets by Monsieur Buisseret

Robinson Crusoe, His Man Friday, Monkey, and the King of Caribee Islands
   18 October 1875
   Musical director, David Braham
   Incidental and dance music selected and arranged by David Braham (uncredited)

Humpty Dumpty in Every Clime
   25 October 1875
   Music composed or adapted by Giuseppe Operti
   Dance and transformation music arranged by Giuseppe Operti (uncredited)

Nimble Nip!, or, Ogre Ugliphiz, Fairy Silvereyes and the Princess with the Strawberry Mark
    20 December 1875
    Musical director, Fred W. Zaulig
    Ballet music arranged by Fred W. Zaulig (uncredited)

Harlequin! Demon Statue, The Enchanted Pills and Magic Apple Tree; or, High Diddle Diddle, the Cat's in the Fiddle, the Cow Jumped over the Moon!
    27 December 1875
    Music by David Braham
    Musical director, David Braham
    Music for dances and transformations composed and arranged by David Braham (uncredited)

Palomita
    1875
    Music and lyrics by Howard Glover
    Incidental and dance music composed and arranged by Howard Glover (uncredited)

Rosemi-Shell!, or, My Daughter! Oh, My Daughter!
    24 January 1876
    Music by David Braham
    Musical director, David Braham
    Incidental and dance music arranged by David Braham (uncredited)

The Pique Family!, a Play on the Da-ly
    13 March 1876
    "Music incidental to the burlesque, and adapted to the author's original burlesque songs," selected, composed, and arranged by Fred Perkins
    Musical director, Fred Perkins
    Music for dances and transformations arranged by Fred Perkins (uncredited)

Humpty Dumpty
    17 April 1876

Music, original and selected by Fred W. Zaulig
Musical director, Fred W. Zaulig
Ballet music arranged by Fred W. Zaulig (uncredited)
Ballets by Julien Martinetti and Mlle. Adele Buimi

Frow-Frow
26 June 1876
New and original music by Prof. Vogel
Musical director, Prof. Vogel
Dance music, selected from Offenbach, arranged by Prof. Vogel

Amour, or, The Arabian Nights
24 July 1876
Musical director, George Loesch
Incidental and dance music arranged by George Loesch

The Blue and the Gray
7 August 1876
Music by David Braham
Musical director, David Braham
Dance music composed and arranged by David Braham (uncredited)

Sardanapalus
14 August 1876
Music "selected from the great composers" by Charles Calvert
Music arranged by Giuseppe Operti
Musical director, Giuseppe Operti
Ballet music arranged by Giuseppe Operti (uncredited)

Sir Dan O'Pallas, Chief of the Assyrian Jim Jams
2 September 1876
Musical director (conductor), Prof. Vogel
Incidental and ballet music arranged by Prof. Vogel (uncredited)
Staging by Edwin Kelly

Selected Chronology: 1786–1923 | 77

Baba!
    18 September 1876
    Marches by Max Maretzek
    Musical director, Max Maretzek
    Ballet music arranged by Max Maretzek (uncredited)
    Ballets by A. Blandowski

Down Broadway
    25 September 1876
    Music by David Braham
    Musical director, David Braham
    Incidental and dance music composed and arranged by David Braham (uncredited)

Sardine-Apples!, King of Ninnyvah and Astoria, L.I.
    9 October 1876
    Musical director (conductor), Henry Wannemacher
    Incidental music selected from great composers by Henry Wannemacher

Iascaire
    20 November 1876
    Music by David Braham
    Musical director, David Braham
    Incidental music composed and arranged by David Braham (uncredited)

Musette, or, The Secret of Guilde Court
    27 November 1876
    Musical director (conductor), William Withers
    Music for "Plantation Dance" arranged by William Withers (uncredited)
    Staging by E.A. Locke

Azurine, or, A Voyage to the Earth
    25 December 1876
    Music composed by Fred Perkins
    Ballet music arranged by Fred Perkins (uncredited)
    Staging by Imre and Bolossy Kiralfy

Santa Claus; or, Harlequin Bob Cratchet and Ding Dong Dell!
1 January 1877
Music by Henry Wannemacher
Musical director, Henry Wannemacher
Music for dances and transformations arranged by Henry Wannemacher (uncredited)

The Danicheffs
5 February 1877
Incidental and dance music composed by Henry Tissington

The Goats
12 March 1877
Music by David Braham
Musical director, David Braham
Incidental music composed and arranged by David Braham (uncredited)

The Wonder Child, or, The Follies of Earth, Air and Sea
30 April 1877
Music by George Loesch
Musical director, George Loesch
Incidental and dance music arranged by George Loesch (uncredited)

Oxygen!, or, Gas in Burlesque Metre
27 August 1877
Music by Offenbach, "others as selected" by Michael Connelly
Musical director, Michael Connelly
Dance music selected and arranged by Michael Connelly (uncredited)
Staging by Willie Edouin

Old Lavender
3 September 1877
Musical director, David Braham
Incidental music composed and arranged by David Braham
Staging by Edward Harrigan

Robinson Crusoe
    12 September 1877
    "Music, original and selected" by Michael Connelly
    Musical director, Michael Connelly
    Dance music selected and arranged by Michael Connelly (uncredited)
    Staging by Willie Edouin

Piff-Paff, or, The Magic Armory
    21 November 1877
    Music arranged by Michael Connelly
    And dance music selected and arranged by Michael Connelly (uncredited)

Babes in the Wood, or, Who Killed Cock Robin?
    24 December 1877
    Music by Charles Christrup
    Musical director, Charles Christrup
    Music for pantomimes, dances, and transformations arranged by Charles Christrup (uncredited)
    Staging by Willie Edouin

Christmas Joys and Sorrows
    14 January 1878
    Music by David Braham
    Musical director, David Braham
    Incidental and dance music composed and arranged by David Braham (uncredited)
    Staging by Edward Harrigan

A Celebrated Hard Case
    18 March 1878
    Music by David Braham
    Musical director, David Braham
    Incidental and dance music composed and arranged by David Braham (uncredited)
    Staging by Edward Harrigan

Diplomacy
    1 April 1878
    Musical director, Thomas Baker
    Incidental music composed and arranged by Thomas Baker

The New Fritz, Our Cousin German
    22 April 1878
    Play, music and lyrics by Joseph K. Emmet
    Musical director, Ernest Neyer
    Dance music composed and arranged by Joseph K. Emmet (uncredited)

Nia-For-Lica, In the Halls of Montezuma
    22 April 1878
    Musical director, Charles Puerner
    Dance music selected and arranged by Charles Puerner (uncredited)
    Staging by J.H. Browne

Humpty Dumpty's Dream
    21 May 1878
    Music by Frank Peterschen
    Incidental, pantomimic, and dance music arranged by Frank Peterschen (uncredited)

Alhambra
    Summer 1878
    Music by Woolson Morse
    Incidental and dance music arranged by Woolson Morse (uncredited)

The Mulligan Guard Pic-Nic
    23 September 1878
    Music by David Braham
    Musical director, David Braham
    Incidental and dance music composed and arranged by David Braham (uncredited)
    Staging by Edward Harrigan

The Banker's Daughter
    30 September 1878
    Musical director, Henry Tissington
    Incidental music arranged by Henry Tissington (uncredited)

Almost a Life
    9 November 1878
    Musical director, Ernest Neyer
    Incidental music composed by Ernest Neyer

The Lorgaire
    25 November 1878
    Music by David Braham
    Musical director, David Braham
    Incidental and dance music composed and arranged by David Braham (uncredited)
    Staging by Edward Harrigan

Babes in the Wood and The Good Little Fairy Birds; or, Who Killed Cock Robin?
    23 December 1878
    Music selected, arranged and composed by Henry Sator
    Musical director, Henry Sator
    Dance music arranged by Henry Sator (uncredited)
    Staging by William Gill

The Mulligan Guard Ball!
    13 January 1879
    Music by David Braham
    Musical director, David Braham
    Incidental and dance music composed and arranged by David Braham (uncredited)
    Staging by Edward Harrigan

The Black Crook
    5 March 1879
    Music by Thomas Baker and others
    Musical director (conductor), Charles Puerner
    Ballet music selected from Offenbach and arranged by Charles

Puerner (uncredited)
Staging by Imre and Bolossy Kiralfy

Joshua Whitcomb
28 April 1879
Incidental and dance music composed by Ferdinand Von Olker

The Brook
12 May 1879
Music selected and arranged by Frank Maeder
"Pretty as a Picture" composed by Brigham Bishop
Musical director (conductor), Frank Maeder
Incidental and dance music selected and arranged by Frank Maeder (uncredited)
Staging by Nate Salsbury

Horrors, or, The Marajah of Zogobad
28 May 1879
Music composed by Edward Everett Rice, John J. Braham, and Henry Woolson Morse
Musical director, Henry Sator
Dance music composed and arranged by Edward Everett Rice and Henry Sator (uncredited)
Staging by Willie Edouin

The Mulligan Guard's Chowder
11 August 1879
Music by David Braham
Musical director, David Braham
Incidental and dance music composed and arranged by David Braham (uncredited)
Staging by Edward Harrigan

The Magic Slipper
25 August 1879
Musical director, Jesse Williams
Incidental and dance music selected and arranged by Jesse Williams (uncredited)
Staging by Charles Colville

Enchantment
    4 September 1879
    Music composed and arranged by Charles Puerner
    Musical director (conductor), Charles Puerner
    Ballet music arranged by Charles Puerner (uncredited)
    Staging by Imre and Bolossy Kiralfy

Love's Young Dream
    17 September 1879
    Music, original and selected, by Edward Mollenhauer
    Musical director, Edward Mollenhauer
    Incidental and dance music arranged by Edward Mollenhauer (uncredited)
    Staging by Augustin Daly, with Fred Williams, and John Moore

Newport, or, The Swimmer, the Singer and the Cypher
    17 September 1879
    Music by Charles Lecoq, DeBrille, Meyer Lutz, and Edward Mollenhauer
    Musical director, Edward Mollenhauer
    Incidental and dance music arranged by Edward Mollenhauer (uncredited)
    Staging by Augustin Daly, with Fred Williams, and John Moore

Sleepy Hollow, or, The Headless Horseman
    25 September 1879
    Music by Max Maretzek
    Incidental and ballet music by Max Maretzek (uncredited)

Fritz in Ireland, or, The Bellringer of the Rhine
    3 November 1879
    Music by Joseph Kline Emmet
    Dance music composed and arranged by Joseph K. Emmet (uncredited)

The Tourists in a Pullman Palace Car
    3 November 1879
    Music by Arthur Sullivan, Robert Planquette, Stephen Foster, David Braham, Giuseppe Verdi, James Bland, and Franz

von Suppé
Musical director, Fred Perkins
Incidental and dance music selected and arranged by Fred Perkins (uncredited)

The Mayor
7 November 1879
Music by Frederick W. Mills
Musical director, Frederick W. Mills
Incidental and dance music composed by Frederick W. Mills (uncredited)

The Mulligan Guard's Christmas
17 November 1879
Music by David Braham
Musical direction by David Braham
Incidental and dance music composed and arranged by David Braham (uncredited)
Staging by Edward Harrigan

The Masked Ball
1879
Music by Edward Mollenhauer
Incidental and ballet music arranged by Edward Mollenhauer (uncredited)

Humpty Dumpty
3 February 1880
Musical director, Henry Wannemacher
Incidental and ballet music composed and arranged by Henry Wannemacher (uncredited)

The Black Crook
16 February 1880
Music by Charles Puerner
Musical director (conductor) Charles Puerner
Ballet music selected, composed, and arranged by Charles Puerner (uncredited)
Staging by Imre and Bolossy Kiralfy

The Mulligan Guard's Surprise
    16 February 1880
    Music by David Braham
    Musical direction by David Braham
    Incidental and dance music composed and arranged by David Braham (uncredited)
    Staging by Edward Harrigan

Hiawatha
    21 February 1880
    Original music by Edward Everett Rice
    Musical director, Henry Sator
    Incidental and dance music arranged by Edward Everett Rice and Henry Sator (uncredited)
    Staging by Willie Edouin

Robinson Crusoe, Esq. and His Man Friday
    8 March 1880
    Original music by Edward Everett Rice
    Musical director, Henry Sator
    Incidental and dance music arranged by Edward Everett Rice and Henry Sator (uncredited)
    Staging by Willie Edouin

Minnie Palmer's Boarding School
    14 May 1880
    Music and lyrics by William J. Scanlan
    Musical director (conductor), Christian Krause
    Incidental music composed and arranged by Christian Krause
    Staging by George C. Davenport

Our Goblins, or, Fun on the Rhine in Germany
    14 June 1880
    Music arranged and partly composed by George Loesch
    Incidental and dance music selected and arranged by George Loesch (uncredited)
    Staging by William Gill

Druessa
    2 August 1880
    Music by Ferdinand Von Olker
    Musical director, Ferdinand Von Olker
    Incidental and ballet music selected and arranged by Ferdinand Von Olker

The Grim Goblin
    5 August 1880
    Music arranged by Oscar Barrett
    Musical director (conductor), Herman Brode
    Incidental and dance music arranged by Oscar Barrett (uncredited)
    Staging by W.R. Floyd

Fun on the Bristol, or A Night on the Sound
    9 August 1880
    Music by Verdi, Donizetti, Bizet, Offenbach, Lecoq, Braham, et al.
    Musical director (conductor), George Loesch
    Music for divertissements arranged by George Loesch (uncreditd)
    Staging by John F. Sheridan

The Mulligan Guard Pic-Nic
    9 August 1880
    Music by David Braham
    Musical director, David Braham
    Incidental and dance music composed and arranged by David Braham (uncredited)
    Staging by Edward Harrigan

Edgewood Folks
    23 August 1880
    Incidental music by George Bowron
    Staging by J.W. Lanergan

Carmen, or, Soldiers and Seville-ians
    13 September 1880
    Music composed and selected from the most popular repertoires by Frank Musgrave

Musical director, Frank Musgrave
Ballet music assembled by Frank Musgrave (uncredited)
Ballets by Signor Arthur Novissimo

Lawn Tennis
20 September 1880
Music by Benjamin E. Woolf
Musical Director, Jesse Williams
Incidental and dance music arranged by Benjamin E. Woolf (uncredited)
Staging by John Howson

La Fille du Tambour Major
4 October 1880
Music by Jacques Offenbach
Musical director, Frank Musgrave
Ballet music arranged by Frank Musgrave
Ballets by Signor Arthur Novissimo

Cinderella, or, The Little Glass Slipper
12 October 1880
Music by Gioacchino Rossini
Musical director, Anthony Reiff
Dance music characteristic for foreign nations arranged by Anthony Reiff (uncredited)
Staging by Henry C. Jarrett

Revels, or Bon-Ton George, Jr.
25 October 1880
Original and selected music by Henry Sator
"Strolling in the Woodland" composed by Edward Everett Rice
Musical director, Henry Sator
Incidental and dance music arranged by Henry Sator (uncredited)
Staging by Edward E. Rice

The House-Warming
1 November 1880
Music by Fred R. Miller

Musical director, Fred R. Miller
Incidental and dance arrangements by Fred R. Miller (uncredited)

The Mulligan Guard's Nominee
22 November 1880
Music by David Braham
Musical director, David Braham
Incidental and dance music composed and arranged by David Braham (uncredited)
Staging by Edward Harrigan

Prince Achmet!
29 November 1880
New music selected and arranged by Henry Sator
Musical director, Henry Sator
Incidental and dance music arranged by Henry Sator (uncredited)

Black Venus
12 January 1881
Music by Charles Puerner
Ballet music by celebrated European composers
Staging by Imre and Bolossy Kiralfy

Zanina, or, The Rover of Cambaye
17 January 1881
Music by Richard Genée
Additional musical numbers by Edward Mollenhauer
Original ballet music by Richard Genée
Ballet music adapted and arranged by Edward Mollenhauer

Mulligan's Silver Wedding
21 February 1881
Music by David Braham
Musical director, David Braham
Incidental and dance music composed and arranged by David Braham (uncredited)
Staging by Edward Harrigan

Cinderella at School
5 March 1881
Book, music and lyrics by Henry Woolson Morse
Musical director, Edward R. Mollenhauer
Incidental and dance music arranged by Henry Woolson Morse (uncredited)
Dances and ensembles by Mme. Malvina

Voyagers in Southern Seas, or The Children of Captain Grant
21 March 1881
Music by Jean-Jacques de Debillemont
Musical director, Henry Widmer
Original ballet music composed by JeanJacques de Debillemont
Ballets by Mamert Bibeyran

Our Goblins; or, Fun on the Rhine
28 March 1881
Music "arranged and the greater part of it composed expressly for the Goblins" by Fred Perkins
Musical director, Fred Perkins
Dance music arranged by Fred Perkins (uncredited)

Castles in Spain
9 May 1881
Music selected "from the best numbers of the most popular Spanish Comic Operas"
Musical director (conductor), Charles Puerner
"Incidental music for the play and ballet" composed by Juan Goula
Ballet music composed by Ricardo Moragas
Ballets by Signor Giovanni Lepri

Smiff
22 August 1881
Music composed, selected and arranged by Frank Musgrave
Musical director (conductor) William Lloyd Bowron
Incidental and dance music selected and arranged by Frank Musgrave (uncredited)

My Sweetheart
> 27 August 1881
> Music by Robert Emmet Graham and Theodore Bendix
> Musical director, Theodore Bendix
> Incidental and dance music arranged by Theodore Bendix (uncredited)

The Major
> 29 August 1881
> Music by David Braham
> Musical director, David Braham
> Incidental and dance music composed and arranged by David Braham (uncredited)
> Staging by Edward Harrigan

Michael Strogoff
> 31 August 1881
> Musical director, Charles Puerner
> Conductor, William Withers
> Ballet music arranged by Charles Puerner (uncredited)
> Staging by Thomas B. MacDonough

Le Voyage en Suisse
> 12 September 1881
> Music composed and selected by Carl Neyder (London) and Henry Widmer (New York)
> Musical director, Henry Widmer
> Incidental and dance music arranged by Henry Widmer (uncredited)

Humpty-Dumpty
> 10 October 1881
> Music for "Dublin Bay" by George Barker
> Music for "Sally in Our Alley" by Henry Carey
> Music for "The Blue Alsatian Mountains" by Michael Maybrick
> Musical director, H.T. Dyring
> Music for dances and pantomimes arranged by H.T. Dyring (uncredited)
> Staging by Arthur Hernandez

Fun on the Bristol, or, A Night on Long Island Sound
    28 November 1881
    Music by Giuseppe Verdi, Gaetano Donizetti, Georges Bizet, Jacques Offenbach, Charles Lecoq
    Musical director, Christian Krause
    Incidental and dance music arranged by Christian Krause (uncredited)

Squatter Sovereignty
    9 January 1882
    Music by David Braham
    Musical director, David Braham
    Incidental and dance music composed and arranged by David Braham (uncredited)
    Staging by Edward Harrigan

Oedipus Tyrannus
    30 January 1882
    Musical director George W. Chadwick
    Incidental music composed by John Knowles Paine

Venus
    5 June 1882
    Music by Thomas W. Hindley
    Musical director, Thomas W. Hindley
    Incidental and dance music arranged by Thomas W. Hindley (uncredited)

The Blackbird
    26 August 1882
    Music by David Braham
    Musical director, David Braham
    Incidental and dance music composed and arranged by David Braham (uncredited)
    Staging by Edward Harrigan

Mordecai Lyons
    26 October 1882
    Music by David Braham

Musical director, David Braham
Incidental and dance music composed and arranged by David Braham (uncredited)
Staging by Edward Harrigan

McSorley's Inflation
27 November 1882
Music by David Braham
Musical director, David Braham
Incidental and dance music composed and arranged by David Braham (uncredited)
Staging by Edward Harrigan

The Silver King
28 January 1883
Incidental music by Herman Brode

M'Liss, Child of the Sierras
29 January 1883
Musical director, G.P. Bernard
Melodramatic and dance music arranged by G.P. Bernard (uncredited)

The Black Venus!
5 February 1883
New music arranged by Charles Christrup
Ballet music by celebrated European composers

Zara!
5 February 1883
Musical director, G.P. Bernard
Incidental and dance music arranged by G.P. Bernard (uncredited)

The Muddy Day
2 April 1883
Music by David Braham
Musical director, David Braham
Incidental and dance music composed and arranged by David

    Braham (uncredited)
    Staging by Edward Harrigan

Fortunio and His Seven Gifted Servants
    23 April 1883
    Music by Francis T.S. Darley
    Musical director, William J. Rostetter
    Incidental and dance music composed and arranged by Francis T.S. Darley (uncredited)
    Staging by William H. Fitzgerald

Romeo and Juliet
    30 April 1883
    Incidental music composed by Charles Puerner

Pop
    21 May 1883
    Play and music, original and selected by Edward Everett Rice
    Music for "For Goodness Sake, Don't Say I Told You" by Maggie Duggan
    Musical director (conductor), Fred J. Eustis
    Incidental and dance music arranged by Edward Everett Rice and Fred J. Eustis (uncredited)
    Staging by Edward E. Rice

The Mulligan Guard Ball
    6 August 1883
    Music by David Braham
    Musical director, David Braham
    Incidental and dance music composed and arranged by David Braham (uncredited)
    Staging by Edward Harrigan

The Devil's Auction, or, The Golden Branch
    18 August 1883
    Original music composed by Auguste Predigam
    Musical director, Francis Tamponi
    Ballet music adapted, selected and arranged by Francis Tamponi (uncredited)

Excelsior
    21 August 1883
    Music by Romualdo Marenco
    Musical director, A.W. Hoffman
    Ballet music composed and arranged by Romualdo Marenco (uncredited)
    Staging and ballets by Imre and Bolossy Kiralfy from the ballet created by Luigi Manzotti

Zenobia, Queen of Palmyra
    21 August 1883
    Libretto and music by S.G. Pratt
    Musical director, Antonio DeNovellis
    Incidental and ballet music arranged by S.G. Pratt (uncredited)

Jalma
    17 September 1883
    Musical director, Napier Lothian
    Incidental and ballet music arranged by Napier Lothian

The Mulligan Guard Pic-Nic
    24 September 1883
    Music by David Braham
    Musical director, David Braham
    Incidental and dance music composed and arranged by David Braham (uncredited)
    Staging by Edward Harrigan

Z-Seltzer!
    1 October 1883
    Music by W.S. Mullaly
    Musical director, W.S. Mullaly
    Incidental and dance music arranged by W.S. Mullaly

Cordelia's Aspirations
    5 November 1883
    Music by David Braham
    Musical director, David Braham
    Incidental and dance music composed and arranged by David

Braham (uncredited)
Staging by Edward Harrigan

The Stranglers of Paris
10 November 1883
Incidental music composed by Giuseppe Operti

On the Yellowstone
13 February 1884
Music composed by Giuseppe Operti
Ballet music selected, composed, and arranged by Giuseppe Operti (uncreditd)

Red Letter Nights!, or, Catching a Croesus
12 March 1884
New and original music by Louis Jacobson
Music arranged by Henry Widmer
Musical director, Henry Widmer
Dance music arranged by Henry Widmer (uncredited)
Dances by Mme. Malvina

Rosita, or, Cupid and Cupidity
1 April 1884
Music composed by George Schleiffarth
Ballet music composed and arranged by George Schleiffarth (uncredited)

Dan's Tribulations
7 April 1884
Music by David Braham
Musical director, David Braham
Incidental and dance music composed and arranged by David Braham (uncredited)
Staging by Edward Harrigan

A Rag Baby
17 March 1884
Music composed by Napier Lothian
Musical director, Harry Braham

Additional music by Carl Millöcker, David Braham, and Arthur Sullivan
Dance music assembled by Napier Lothian and Harry Braham (uncredited)
Staging by Charles H. Hoyt

Madam Piper
12 May 1884
"Music composed and play concocted" by Henry Woolson Morse
Musical director (conductor), Michael Connelly
Dance and incidental music arranged by Henry Woolson Morse (uncredited)

Well-Fed Dora
19 May 1884
Music for "The Rose's Greeting" by Julius J. Lyons
Musical director, Charles Puerner
Marches and dance music arranged by Charles Puerner (uncredited)
Marches and dances by A.W. Maflin

Penny-Ante, or, The Last of the Fairies
9 June 1884
Music by Fred J. Eustis
Musical director, Fred J. Eustis
Incidental and dance music by Fred J. Eustis (uncredited)

Sieba and the Seven Ravens
18 August 1884
Original music by Romualdo Marenco
Musical director (conductor), Herman Brode
"Dramatic music" composed by Adolph Neuendorf
Staging by Imre and Bolossy Kiralfy
Ballets by Ettore Coppini

The Little Primrose
18 August 1884
Music by Fred R. Miller

Musical director, Fred R. Miller
Incidental and dance music arranged by Fred R. Miller (uncredited)

Investigation
1 September 1884
Music by David Braham
Musical director, David Braham
Incidental and dance music composed and arranged by David Braham (uncredited)
Staging by Edward Harrigan

Adonis
4 September 1884
Original music by John Eller and Edward E. Rice
"Selected music cheerfully contributed by Beethoven, Audran, Suppé, Planquette, Offenbach, Strauss, Mozart, Haydn, Dave Braham, and many others too numerous to individualize."
Musical director, Henry Sator
Incidental and dance music arranged by Edward E. Rice and Henry Sator (uncredited)
Staging by Henry E. Dixey

Zanita
Music selected, composed, and arranged by Napier Lothian
16 September 1884
Musical director, Napier Lothian
Incidental and ballet music composed and arranged by Napier Lothian

Vassar Girls
27 December 1884
Musical director, Jesse Williams
Incidental and dance music selected and arranged by Jesse Williams (uncredited)

We, Us and Company at Mud Springs
29 December 1884
Music by Fred J. Eustis

Musical director, Fred J. Eustis
Incidental and dance music arranged by Fred J. Eustis (uncredited)

McAllister's Legacy
5 January 1885
Music by David Braham
Musical director, David Braham
Incidental and dance music composed and arranged by David Braham (uncredited)
Staging by Edward Harrigan

Pierrette
14 March 1885
Music by Robert Stoepel
Musical director, Jesse Williams
Incidental and dance music arranged by Robert Stoepel (uncredited)

The Major
16 March 1885
Music by David Braham
Musical director, David Braham
Incidental and dance music composed and arranged by David Braham (uncredited)
Staging by Edward Harrigan

Cordelia's Aspirations
20 April 1885
Music by David Braham
Musical director, David Braham
Incidental and dance music composed and arranged by David Braham (uncredited)
Staging by Edward Harrigan

Are You Insured?
11 May 1885
Music by George F. Braham
Musical director, George F. Braham

Dance music selected from Carl Millöcker's *Gasparone* by
George F. Braham (uncredited)
Staging by Edward Harrigan

Clio
17 August 1885
Original music composed and arranged by Giuseppe Operti
Musical director (conductor), Giuseppe Operti
Ballet music arranged by Giuseppe Operti (uncredited)
Ballets by Mamert Bibeyran

Old Lavender
31 August 1885
Music by David Braham
Musical director, David Braham
Incidental and dance music composed and arranged by David Braham (uncredited)
Staging by Edward Harrigan

Jack Sheppard
23 November 1885
Music by Adam Itzel, Jr.
Musical director, Adam Itzel, Jr.
Incidental and dance music composed and arranged by Adam Itzel, Jr. (uncredited)

The Ratcatcher, or, The Pied Piper of Hamelin
30 November 1885
Music by Selli Simonson
Musical director, W.H. Hoffmann
Ballet music composed, selected, and arranged by Selli Simonson (uncredited)
Staging by Imre and Bolossy Kiralfy

The Grip
30 November 1885
Music by David Braham
Musical director, David Braham
Incidental and dance music composed and arranged by David

Braham (uncredited)
Staging by Edward Harrigan

The Leather Patch
15 February 1886
Music by David Braham
Musical director, David Braham
Incidental and dance music composed and arranged by David Braham (uncredited)
Staging by Edward Harrigan

The Ivy Leaf
8 March 1886
Incidental music arranged by Prof. Spiel

The Little Tycoon
29 March 1886
Words and music by Willard Spenser
Musical director, Fred Perkins
Dance music composed by Willard Spenser (uncredited)
Staging by William H. Daly

The Black Crook
29 March 1886
Music composed and selected by Thomas Baker, Louis Baer, A.W. Hoffman
Musical director, A.W. Hoffman
Music for ballets selected and arranged by A.W. Hoffman (uncredited)
Staging and ballets by Imre and Bolossy Kiralfy

Arcadia
26 April 1886
Music composed and selected by John J. Braham
Musical director, John J. Braham
Music for "Sword Dance" and "Doleful Dance of Two" selected and arranged by John J. Braham (uncredited)
Staging by William Gill

A Tin Soldier
3 May 1886
Music composed by Charles Gounod, Charles H. Hoyt, and Charles Zimmerman
Musical director, Charles Zimmerman
Dance music composed and arranged by Charles Zimmerman
Staging by Charles H. Hoyt

Erminie
10 May 1886
Music by Edward Jakobowski
Additional music composed by Henry Hallam, Frederic Solomon, Ivan Caryll, Bernard Lolt, and Stephen Howard
Musical director, Jesse Williams
Original dance music composed by Edward Jakobowski (uncredited)
Staging by Edward Paulton

Little Jack Sheppard
13 September 1886
Music selected and arranged by W. Meyer Lutz, "with original contributions by Gustave Kerker, W. Meyer Lutz, Florian Pascal, R. Corney Grain, Arthur Cecil, Hamilton Clarke, Henry J. Leslie, Alfred Cellier."
Musical director, Gustave Kerker
Dance music composed by Florian Pascal and Alfred Cellier
Dances by Paul Veron

Marita
28 September 1886
Music by Theodore Bendix
Musical director, Theodore Bendix
Incidental and dance music arranged by Theodore Bendix (uncredited)
Staging by Thomas H. Burns

Mystic Isle
2 October 1886
Music by John B. Grant

Musical director, John B. Grant
Incidental and dance music composed by John B. Grant (uncredited)

The O'Reagans
11 October 1886
Music by David Braham
Musical director, David Braham
Incidental and dance music composed and arranged by David Braham (uncredited)
Staging by Edward Harrigan

Over the Garden Wall
27 December 1886
Music uncredited
Additional music composed by Theodore Bendix, George S. Knight, and Alfred Cellier
Musical director uncredited
Dance music arranged by Theodore Bendix (uncredited)

McNooney's Visit
31 January 1887
Music by David Braham
Musical director, David Braham
Incidental and dance music composed and arranged by David Braham (uncredited)
Staging by Edward Harrigan

Big Pony, The Gentlemanly Savage
31 March 1887
Music by Edward I. Darling
Musical director, Gustave Kerker
Orchestrations by Gustave Kerker
Incidental and dance music arranged by Gustave Kerker (uncredited)

The Pyramid
16 May 1887
Music by Charles Puerner and Caryl Florio

Musical director, Charles Puerner
Incidental and dance music composed and arranged by Charles Puerner (uncredited)

Lagardère; or, the Hunchback of Paris
17 August 1887
Musical director, A.W. Hoffman
Music for "The Seven Ages" ballet selected and arranged by A.W. Hoffman (uncredited)
Staging by Imre Kiralfy
Ballets by Ettore Coppini

A Hole in the Ground
12 September 1887
Music and lyrics, Charles Zimmerman
Music for additional numbers composed by Arthur Sullivan, Charles Gounod, and Robert Martin
Musical director, Charles Zimmerman
Incidental music by Charles Zimmerman
Staging by Julian Mitchell

A Circus in Town
12 September 1887
Music composed, selected and arranged by Richard Stahl
Music for additional numbers composed by Richard Golden
Musical director, Richard Stahl
Dance music selected and arranged by Richard Stahl (uncredited)

The Arabian Nights, or, Aladdin's Wonderful Lamp
12 September 1887
Musical director, Anthony Reiff
Music for ballets selected and arranged by Anthony Reiff (uncredited)
Ballets by Rose Beckett

The Corsair
18 October 1887
Music by Edward E. Rice and John J. Braham
Musical director, Gustave Kerker

Incidental and dance music arranged by John J. Braham (uncredited)
Staging by Henry E. Dixey

The Begum
21 November 1887
Music by Reginald De Koven
Musical director (conductor), Adolph Nowak
Orchestrations by Reginald De Koven
Incidental and dance music composed and arranged by Reginald De Koven (uncredited)
Staging by H.A. Cripps

Pete
22 November 1887
Music by David Braham
Musical director, David Braham
Incidental and dance music composed and arranged by David Braham (uncredited)
Staging by Edward Harrigan

Maggie, the Midget
12 March 1888
Music by David Braham
Musical director, Otto Vogler
Incidental and dance music arranged by David Braham (uncredited)
Dances by Signor Arthur Novissimo

The Pearl of Pekin
19 March 1888
Music by Charles Lecocq and Gustave Kerker
Musical director (conductor), Gustave Kerker
Dance music arranged by Gustave Kerker (uncredited)
Staging by Edward E. Rice

Monte Cristo, Jr.
2 April 1888
Original music by Meyer Lutz, Ivan Caryll, and Tito Mattei

    Music for additional numbers composed by Robert Martin and Edward Solomon
    Music arranged by Fred. A. Rothstein
    Musical director, Fred. A. Rothstein
    "Patrol March" arranged by Alexander Spencer
    Music for ballets composed by Tito Mattei (uncredited)
    Ballets and dances by Mme. Augusta Sohlke

The Lady or the Tiger?
    7 May 1888
    Music by Julius J. Lyons and Adolph Nowak
    Musical director, Adolph Nowak
    Music for dances composed and arranged by Adolph Nowak (uncredited)
    Staging by H.A. Cripps

Nadjy
    14 May 1888
    Music by Francis Chassaigne
    Musical director, Jesse Williams
    Music for "Czardas" composed by Francis Chassaigne (uncredited)
    Ballets by Mamert Bibeyran

Waddy Coogan
    3 September 1888
    Music by David Braham
    Musical director, David Braham
    Incidental and dance music composed and arranged by David Braham (uncredited)
    Staging by Edward Harrigan

A Brass Monkey
    15 October 1888
    Music by Thomas Casey
    Music arranged by Charles Zimmerman
    Musical director, Charles Zimmerman
    Incidental and dance music arranged by Charles Zimmerman (uncredited)
    Staging by Charles H. Hoyt

Penelope
>   15 October 1888
>   Music by Edward Solomon
>   Musical director (conductor), William Robinson
>   "Eccentric Dance" composed by Edward Solomon (uncredited)
>   Staging by Jay Rial

The Lorgaire!
>   10 December 1888
>   Music by David Braham
>   Musical director, David Braham
>   Incidental and dance music composed and arranged by David Braham (uncredited)
>   Staging by Edward Harrigan

Miss Esmeralda
>   17 December 1888
>   Original music by Meyer Lutz and Robert Martin
>   Musical director (conductor), Lovell Phillips
>   Ballet music composed by Meyer Lutz (uncredited)
>   Ballets by Fred Storey

The Kitty
>   31 December 1888
>   Music for the waltz, "My Last Thoughts," by Richard Stahl
>   Musical director, Professor Fleischer
>   Music for "The 'Nadjy' Dance" composed by Francis Chassaigne
>   Staging by William A. Mestayer

The Water Queen
>   11 February 1889
>   Music specially selected and composed by Georges Jacobi
>   Ballet music arranged by Georges Jacobi (uncredited)
>   Staging by Bolossy Kiralfy

A Midnight Bell
>   5 March 1889
>   Music by Percy Gaunt
>   Musical director, Percy Gaunt

Music for "The Village Dance" arranged by Percy Gaunt
Staging by Charles H. Hoyt

4-11-14
21 March 1889
Music by David Braham
Musical director, David Braham
Incidental and dance music composed and arranged by David Braham (uncredited)
Staging by Edward Harrigan

The White Elephant
15 July 1889
"Music selected, arranged and composed" by J. Clarence West
Musical director, J. Clarence West
Music for additional numbers composed by Richard Stahl
Incidental and dance music arranged by J. Clarence West (uncredited)
Staging by John Fowler

Antiope
17 August 1889
Music by Georges Jacobi
Music for ballets and processions arranged by Georges Jacobi (uncredited)
Ballets and spectacle by Bolossy Kiralfy

Paola, or, The First of the Vendettas
26 August 1889
Music by Edward Jakobowski
Musical director (conductor), Julian Edwards
Incidental and ballet music arranged by Edward Jakobowski (uncredited)
Staging by John Nash

Faust on Time
23 September 1889
Words and Music by Frederic Solomon
Ballet music composed by Francis Chassaigne

The Seven Ages
   7 October 1889
   Music by Edward E. Rice
   Musical director (conductor), John J. Braham
   Overture composed, and Rice's songs arranged, by Edgar Stillman Kelley (uncredited)
   "Grand March of the Continentals" composed by Edward E. Rice (uncredited)
   Staging by Henry E. Dixey

Kajanka
   2 December 1889
   Music by Sidney H. Horner
   Musical director, Sidney H. Horner
   Pantomimic and ballet music composed by Sidney H. Horner (uncredited)
   Staging by George D. Melville

Faust Up to Date
   10 December 1889
   Music by Meyer Lutz
   Music for additional numbers composed by Edward Solomon, and Frederick Bowyer
   Musical director, Lovell Phillips
   Dance music composed and arranged by Meyer Lutz (uncredited)
   Staging by Walter Raynham

Bluebeard, Jr., or, Fatima and the Fairy
   13 January 1890
   Music by Fred J. Eustis, Richard Maddern, and John Braham
   Additional music composed by Charles Warren and F. Coes
   Musical director, Fred J. Eustis
   Music for "Amazonian March" composed by Ted Peiper
   Music for "Dance of the Grasshoppers" composed by Walter Slaughter
   Dance music for "The Hebrew Fancy Ball" composed by W.S. Mullaly
   Music for "Grand Ballet Divertissement" and other characteristic dances arranged by Fred J. Eustis, Richard Maddern,

and John Braham (uncredited)
Staging by Richard Barker

Castles in the Air
5 May 1890
Music by Gustave Kerker
Music for additional numbers composed by Marion Manola
Musical director, Adolph Nowak
Incidental and dance music arranged by Gustave Kerker (uncredited)
Staging by Max Freeman

The Brazilian
2 June 1890
Music by Francis Chassaigne
Musical director, Gustave Kerker
Music for characteristic dances arranged by Francis Chassaigne (uncredited)
Ballets by Mamert Bibeyran

The Crystal Slipper
19 June 1890
Music by Fred J. Eustis
Additional music composed by F. David and John D. Gilbert
Musical director, W.H. Batchelor
Ballet music, "Phaeton Galop," composed by Joseph Meinrath
Ballet music, "La Carte d'Amour," composed by W.H. Batchelor

The Red Hussar
5 August 1890
Music composed by Edward Solomon
Musical director, Julian Edwards
Music for dances composed and arranged by Edward Solomon (uncredited)
Staging by John E. Nash

The Merry Monarch
18 August 1890
Music by Woolson Morse

Musical director (conductor), Antonio DeNovellis
Orchestrations by John Philip Sousa
Incidental and dance music composed and arranged by Woolson Morse (uncredited)
Staging by Richard Barker

Hendrik Hudson, or, The Discovery of Columbus
18 August 1890
"Music from all sources arranged and partly composed" by Fred Perkins
Incidental and dance music selected and arranged by Fred Perkins (uncredited)
Staging by William H. Daly

The Pupil in Magic
15 September 1890
Music selected and arranged by Carl Josef
Musical director, E. Christiani
Ballet music selected and arranged by Carl Josef (uncredited)
Staging by Charles Rosenfeld
Ballets by Mr. Leoni

Claudius Nero
21 October 1890
Musical director, Karl Broschi
Music for Ballets selected and arranged by Karl Broschi (uncredited)
Staging by Max Freeman
Ballets by Mamert Bibeyran

A Texas Steer, or, Money Makes the Mare Go
10 November 1890
Musical director, William Lloyd Bowron
Incidental music arranged by William Lloyd Bowron (uncredited)
Staging by Charles H. Hoyt

Pippins
26 November 1890

Music by John J. Braham
Musical director, John J. Braham
Music for ballets arranged by John J. Braham (uncredited)
Staging by Richard Barker

Ship Ahoy!
8 December 1890
Music by Fred Miller, Jr.
Musical director (conductor), Fred Miller, Jr.
Incidental and dance music arranged by Fred Miller, Jr. (uncredited)
Staging by I.W. Norcross, Jr.

Reilly and the 400
29 December 1890
Music by David Braham
Musical director, David Braham
Incidental and dance music composed and arranged by David Braham (uncredited)
Staging by Edward Harrigan

The Babes in the Wood, Robin Hood and His Merry, Merry Men, and Harlequin, Who Killed Cock Robin?
30 December 1890
Music by Walter Slaughter, Alfred Cellier, Edward Solomon, H.J. Leslie, Ivan Caryll, and Edward Jones
Musical director, Edward Jones
"Original and descriptive music" composed by Alfred Cellier
Ballets by A. Bertrand

A Straight Tip
26 January 1891
Music by Richard Stahl
Music for additional numbers composed by F.T. Ward and John Philip Sousa
Musical director, John Mullaly
Music for "Butterfly Dance" composed by Richard Stahl
Music for "Twilight Dance" composed by F.T. Ward

The Prodigal Son
    3 March 1891
    Music by André Wormser
    Musical director, Henry Widmer
    Ballet and pantomime music by André Wormser (uncredited)
    Staging by Augustin Daly

Wang
    4 May 1891
    Music by Woolson Morse
    Musical director (conductor), J. Sebastian Hiller
    Incidental and dance music arranged by Woolson Morse (uncredited)
    Staging by H.A. Cripps

The Tar and the Tartar
    11 May 1891
    Music by Adam Itzel, Jr.
    Music for additional numbers composed by Felix McGlennon
    Musical director, Adam Itzel, Jr.
    Incidental and dance music arranged by Adam Itzel, Jr. (uncredited)
    Staging by Napier Lothian, Jr.

Sinbad, or, The Maid of Balsora
    11 June 1891
    Music by W.H. Batchelor
    Musical director, W.H. Batchelor
    Incidental and dance music arranged by W.H. Batchelor (uncredited)

The Khedive
    27 August 1891
    Music by Louis Blake, Harry B. Edwards, and Micah Blake
    Musical director (conductor), Albert Krausse
    Dance music composed by Louis Blake
    Staging by Harry B. Edwards

The Cadi
    21 September 1891
    Music by David Braham
    Music for "T.Q. Seabrooke" arranged by Josephine Gro
    Musical director, David Braham
    Incidental and dance music arranged by David Braham (uncredited)
    Staging by Charles T. Parsloe

Mavourneen
    28 September 1891
    Songs by William J. Scanlan
    Musical director, George Loesch
    "Original dramatic music" composed by George Loesch
    Staging by Augustus Pitou

Robin Hood
    28 September 1891
    Music by Reginald De Koven
    Musical director (conductor), Samuel L. Studley
    Orchestrations by Reginald De Koven
    Incidental and dance music composed and arranged by Reginald De Koven (uncredited)
    Staging by Jerome Sykes

Beautiful Stars
    12 October 1891
    Music by Charles Puerner
    Ballet music arranged by Charles Puerner (uncredited)
    Staging by William H. Daly and John B. Day

La Cigale
    26 October 1891
    Music by Edmond Audran
    Music for additional numbers composed by Ivan Caryll and Jesse Williams
    Musical director, Jesse Williams
    Dance music composed by Ivan Caryll and Jesse Williams
    Staging by Richard Barker

A Trip to Chinatown
9 November 1891
Music by Percy Gaunt
Music for "The Chaperone" composed by W. Barton
Musical director, Percy Gaunt
Incidental and dance music arranged by Percy Gaunt (uncredited)
Staging by Julian Mitchell

The Hustler
23 November 1891
Principal composer uncredited
Additional music composed by Charles Graham
Musical director, George Bowron
Incidental and dance music arranged by George Bowron (uncredited)

Cinderella
24 November 1891
Original music composed by Alfred Cellier, Edward Solomon, Ivan Caryll, and Henry John Leslie.
Musical director, A.W. Hoffman
Ballet music arranged by Alfred Cellier (uncredited)
Ballets by Signora Vincenzina Chitten

New York City Directory
7 December 1891
Music by Thomas LeMack and Isidore Witmark
Musical director, W.S. Mullaly
"Musical interruptions" [incidental music] composed by W.S. Mullaly
Staging by Louis Harrison

The Last of the Hogans
22 December 1891
Music by David Braham
Musical director, David Braham
Incidental and dance music composed and arranged by David Braham (uncredited)
Staging by Edward Harrigan

The Lion Tamer
>30 December 1891
>Music by Richard Stahl
>Orchestrations by John Philip Sousa
>Ballet music arranged by Richard Stahl (uncredited)
>Staging by Richard Barker

The Foresters
>17 March 1892
>Music for the ballads and choruses composed by Arthur Sullivan
>Musical director, Henry Widmer
>Incidental and dance music composed by Henry Widmer
>Staging by Augustin Daly

Polly Middles
>18 April 1892
>Music by William W. Lowitz
>Musical director, A. Tomasi
>Orchestrations by William W. Lowitz and Charles Puerner
>Incidental and dance music arranged by William W. Lowitz (uncredited)
>Staging by Richard Barker

A Jolly Surprise
>18 April 1892
>Music selected from Arthur Sullivan and Franz Von Suppé
>Musical director, Watty Hydes
>Dance music selected and arranged by Watty Hydes (uncredited)
>Staging by Jesse Williams

Jupiter, or, The King and the Cobbler
>2 May 1892
>Music by Julian Edwards
>Musical director (conductor), Julian Edwards
>Incidental and dance music by Julian Edwards (uncredited)
>Staging by Napier Lothian, Jr.

Elysium
>16 May 1892
>Music by Jesse Williams
>Musical director (conductor), Mr. Davis
>Incidental and dance music composed by Jesse Williams (uncredited)
>Staging by William Fleron

The Robber of the Rhine
>28 May 1892
>Music by Charles Puerner
>Musical director (conductor) Charles Puerner
>Music for dance composed by Charles Puerner (uncredited)
>Staging by Richard Barker

Ali Baba, or, Morgiana and the Forty Thieves
>3 June 1892
>Music by W.H. Batchelor and John D. Gilbert
>Additional music by Willard Thompson and Henry Norman
>Musical director, W.H. Batchelor
>Incidental and dance music arranged by W.H. Batchelor (uncredited)

Puritania, or, The Earl and the Maid of Salem
>6 June 1892
>Music by Edgar Stillman Kelley
>Musical director, Adolph Neuendorff
>Incidental and dance music by Edgar Stillman Kelley (uncredited)
>Staging by Frederic Solomon

King Kaliko
>7 June 1892
>Music by Frederic Solomon
>Musical director, Jesse Williams
>Music for "The Coconut Dance" dance composed by Frederic Solomon (uncredited)
>Staging by Jesse Williams and Martin Hayden

Sinbad, or, The Maid of Balsora
>27 June 1892
>Music composed and arranged by W.H. Batchelor
>Additional music composed by John D. Gilbert, W.J. Melbourne, Dan Hart, Harry F. Carson, Henry Norman, and Roy L. Burtch
>Musical director, Jesse Williams
>Music for ballet sequences arranged by W.H. Batchelor (uncredited)
>Staging by Richard Barker
>Ballets by Mamert Bibeyran

Candy
>19 September 1892
>Music selected and arranged by Carl Josef
>Musical director, E. Christiani
>Ballet music selected and arranged by Carl Josef (uncredited)
>Staging and ballets by Carl Rosenfeld

Miss Blythe of Duluth
>26 September 1992
>Music by Harry Braham
>Musical director, D.S. Godfrey
>Dance music arranged by Harry Braham (uncredited)

The Fencing Master
>14 November 1892
>Music by Reginald De Koven
>Musical director, Gustave Kerker
>Orchestrations by Reginald De Koven
>Incidental and ballet music composed and arranged by Reginald De Koven (uncredited)
>Staging by Max Freeman

The Isle of Champagne
>5 December 1892
>Music by William Furst
>Additional music composed by Josephine Gro and Mrs. Louis Harrison
>Musical director, Paul Steindorff

Incidental and dance music arranged by William Furst
Ballets by Mamert Bibeyran

Superba
26 December 1892
Music composed, adapted, and arranged by Max Frehrmann
Pantomimic and dance music selected and arranged by Max Frehemann (uncredited)
Staging by the Hanlon Brothers

The Mountebanks
11 January 1893
Music by Alfred Cellier
Musical director, Charles Puerner
Incidental and dance music composed by Alfred Cellier, arranged by Charles Puerner (uncredited)
Dances by Mamert Bibeyran

Panjandrum
1 May 1893
Music by Woolson Morse
Musical director (conductor), J. Sebastian Hiller
Dance music arranged by Woolson Morse (uncredited)
Staging by H.A. Cripps

1492, Up to Date or Very Near It
15 May 1893
Music by Carl Pflueger
Additional music composed by Anton Rubenstein, Herman Perlet, Adam Itzel, Jr., George B. Seevers, Richard Stahl, Mercy Bateman, and Edward E. Rice
Musical director, Herman Perlet
Music for "Spanish Dance" composed by Aberano Colon
Ballet music composed by Carl Pflueger (uncredited)
Staging by Edward E. Rice

The Knickerbockers
29 May 1893
Music by Reginald De Koven

Musical director, Samuel L. Studley
Orchestrations by Reginald De Koven
Incidental and ballet music composed and arranged by Reginald De Koven (uncredited)
Staging by John E. Nash

The Black Crook
14 August 1893
Music composed and selected by Thomas Baker, Louis Baer, and A.W. Hoffman
Music for "Grand Ballet of the Birth of the Rainbow" composed by Georges Jacobi
Ballets by Monsieur A. Bertrand

A Trip to Mars
8 September 1893
Music composed and arranged by Fritz Krause
Musical director (conductor), Fritz Krause
Incidental and ballet music arranged by Fritz Krause (uncredited)
Staging and ballets by Carl Rosenfeld

The Rising Generation
11 September 1893
Music by Emil O. Wolff
Music for additional numbers composed by James Thornton, Charles Graham, Isidore Witmark, Wendell Tennant, and George M. Cohan
Musical director, Emil O. Wolff
Dance music arranged by Emil O. Wolff (uncredited)
Dances by James H. Manning and Joseph Davis

The Rainmaker of Syria, or, The Woman King
25 September 1893
Music by Rudolph Aronson
Musical director, Gustave Kerker
Incidental and dance music arranged by Rudolph Aronson (uncredited)
Dances by H. Fletcher Rivers

The Woolen Stocking
   9 October 1893
   Music by David Braham
   Musical director, David Braham
   Incidental and dance music composed and arranged by David Braham (uncredited)
   Staging by Edward Harrigan

Princess Nicotine
   25 October 1893
   Music by William Furst
   Music for additional numbers composed by Maurice Levi
   Musical director, Gustave Kerker
   Music for "Cuban Bull Fight Ballet" arranged by William Furst (uncredited)
   "Pickaninny Dance" by Lucy Daly
   Ballets by Signor Augusto Francioli

The Algerian
   26 October 1893
   Music by Reginald De Koven
   Musical director (conductor), Louis F. Cornu
   Orchestrations by Reginald De Koven
   Incidental and ballet music composed and arranged by Reginald De Koven (uncredited)
   Staging by Ben Teal

America
   5 December 1893
   Music by Angelo Venanzi
   Musical director, Fred J. Eustis
   Music for ballet sequences composed by Angelo Venanzi (uncredited)
   Staging and ballets by Imre Kiralfy

The Voyage of Suzette
   23 December 1893
   Original music by Jesse Williams and Charles Puerner
   Acrobatic, pantomimic, and ballet music arranged by Charles

Puerner (uncredited)
Ballets by Signor Augusto Francioli

Africa
25 December 1893
Music composed by Randolph Cruger
Music for additional numbers composed by D.L. White
Musical director (conductor), Randolph Cruger
Incidental and ballet music composed by Randolph Cruger (uncredited)
Staging by Napier Lothian, Jr.

The Maid of Plymouth
15 January 1894
Music by Thomas Pearsall Thorne
Musical director, Samuel L. Studley
Incidental and dance music arranged by Thomas Pearsall Thorne (uncredited)
Staging by John E. Nash

Prince Kam, or, A Trip to Venus
29 January 1894
Music by Gustave Kerker
Musical director, Gustave Kerker
Music for "Cupid's Dance" composed and arranged by Gustave Kerker (uncredited)

The Rainmakers
29 January 1894
Music by Frank Dumont, Richard Stahl, Thomas LeMack, May Irwin, and Fred Perkins
Music for additional numbers composed by George B. Seevers, John W. Bratton, Henry V. Donnelly, Girard, and J.A. Silberberg
Musical director, Fred Perkins
Dance music arranged by Fred Perkins (uncredited)

The Ocallallas
12 February 1894
Music by Henry Waller

Musical director, Samuel L. Studley
Incidental and dance music arranged by Henry Waller (uncredited)
Staging by John E. Nash

About Town
26 February 1894
Music selected and arranged by Alexander Haig
Musical director, Alexander Haig
Incidental and dance music arranged by Alexander Haig (uncredited)

Hendrick Hudson, or, The Discovery of Columbus
19 March 1894
Music compiled and arranged by Fred Perkins and Watty Hydes
Musical director, Watty Hydes
Dance music by Fred Perkins (uncredited)
New dance music by Watty Hydes (uncredited)

The Idea
9 April 1894
Music by W.T. Francis and Joseph Hart
Musical director, W.T. Francis
Dance music arranged by W.T. Francis (uncredited)

Mavourneen
7 May 1894
Music by Chauncey Olcott
Musical director, Albert Krausse
"Original dramatic music" composed by George Loesch
Staging by Augustus Pitou

The Passing Show (1894)
12 May 1894
Music composed by Ludwig Englander
Music for additional numbers composed by Dave Reed, Jr. and Barney Fagan
Musical director (conductor), Ludwig Englander
Ballet music arranged by Ludwig Englander (uncredited)

Dances and marches by Barney Fagan
   Ballets by Signor Augusto Francioli

Tabasco
   14 May 1894
   Music by George W. Chadwick
   Musical director, Ludwig Englander
   Orchestrations by George W. Chadwick
   Incidental and ballet music composed and arranged by George W. Chadwick (uncredited)
   Staging by C.D. Marius

Dr. Syntax
   23 June 1894
   Music by Woolson Morse
   Musical director (conductor), J. Sebastian Hiller
   Incidental and dance music arranged by Woolson Morse (uncredited)
   Staging by Joseph Humphreys and H.A. Cripps

Davy Jones
   2 July 1894
   Music by Fred R. Miller
   Musical director, Fred R. Miller
   Incidental and dance music arranged by Fred R. Miller (uncredited)

The Little Trooper
   30 August 1894
   Original music by Victor Roger
   New music by William Furst
   Additional music composed by Frederic Solomon, Phil Harmonic, and Sidney Jones
   Musical director, Adolph Bauer
   Original ballet music composed by Victor Roger
   Ballet music adapted and arranged by William Furst and Adolph Bauer (uncredited)
   Staging by Richard Barker

A Gaiety Girl
>18 September 1894
>Music by Sidney Jones
>Music for additional numbers by Harry Greenbank and S. Potter
>Musical director, Granville Bantock
>Incidental and dance music arranged by Sidney Jones (uncredited)
>Staging by George Edwardes

The Irish Artist
>1 October 1894
>Music by Chauncey Olcott
>Musical director, Albert Krausse
>Incidental and dance music arranged by Albert Krausse
>Staging by Augustus Pitou

A Milk White Flag, and Its Battle-Scarred Followers on the Field of Mars and in the Court of Venus
>8 October 1894
>Music by Percy Gaunt
>Music for additional numbers composed by Harry Kennedy
>Musical director, Percy Gaunt
>Incidental and dance music arranged by Percy Gaunt (uncredited)
>Staging by Julian Mitchell
>Dances by Frank Lawton

Little Christopher Columbus
>15 October 1894
>Music by Ivan Caryll and Gustave Kerker
>Musical director, Gustave Kerker
>Music for "The Marionette Dance" composed by Ivan Caryll
>Staging by Edward E. Rice, with George Walton and Thomas Terriss

Rob Roy
>29 October 1894
>Music by Reginald De Koven
>Musical director, Antonio DeNovellis

Orchestrations by Reginald De Koven
Incidental and dance music composed and arranged by Reginald DeKven (uncredited)
Staging by Max Freeman

The Brownies
12 November 1894
Music by Malcolm Douglas
Musical director, Fred Perkins
Orchestrations by Fred Perkins
Music for "The Oriental Ballet of Beautiful Women" composed by Fred Perkins
Staging by Ben Teal
Ballets by Carl Marwig

Prince Ananias
20 November 1894
Music by Victor Herbert
Musical director, Samuel L. Studley
Orchestrations by Victor Herbert
Incidental and dance music composed and arranged by Victor Herbert (uncredited)
Staging by Jerome Sykes

Jacinta, or, The Maid of Manzanillo
26 November 1894
Music by Alfred G. Robyn
Musical director, Herman Perlet
Ballet music composed by Alfred G. Robyn (uncredited)
Staging by Max Freeman
Manzanillo ballet by Signor Augusto Francioli

Notoriety
10 December 1894
Music by David Braham
Musical director, David Braham
Incidental and dance music composed and arranged by David Braham (uncredited)
Staging by Edward Harrigan

Westward Ho
>31 December 1894
>Music by Benjamin E. Woolf
>Incidental and dance music arranged by Benjamin E. Woolf (uncredited)

A Run on the Bank
>14 January 1895
>Music by Maurice Levi, David Marion, Sidney Jones and F. Osmond Carr
>Musical director, Maurice Levi
>Incidental music composed and arranged by Maurice Levi
>Staging by E.D. Stair

Off the Earth
>21 January 1895
>Words and music by John D. Gilbert
>Additional music composed by Ivan Caryll and F. Osmond Carr
>Music arranged and ensemble music composed by Fred J. Eustis
>Musical director, Fred J. Eustis
>Dance music arranged by Fred J. Eustis (uncredited)
>Dances by Harry Barnes

The 20th Century Girl
>25 January 1895
>Music by Ludwig Englander
>Music for additional numbers composed by Claude Perrier
>Musical director (conductor), Selli Simonson
>Incidental and dance music arranged by Ludwig Englander (uncredited)
>Staging by Richard Barker
>Ballets by Signor Augusto Francioli

Madeleine, or, The Magic Kiss
>25 February 1895
>Music by Julian Edwards
>Musical director, Julian Edwards
>Incidental and dance music arranged by Julian Edwards (uncredited)

Staging by Max Freeman

Aladdin, Jr.
8 April 1895
Music composed and arranged by W.H. Batchelor, W.F. Gloves, and Jesse Williams
Music for additional numbers composed by Hattie Starr
Musical director, Jesse Williams
Ballet music composed by Georges Jacobi
Staging by Richard Barker
Ballets by Carlo Coppe and Filiberto Marchetti

The Viking
9 May 1895
Music by Edward Irving Darling
Musical directors, Caryl Florio and Fred Perkins
Orchestrations by Max Maretzek
Incidental and dance music arranged by Fred Perkins (uncredited)

The Tzigane
16 May 1895
Music by Reginald De Koven
Musical director, Paul Steindorff
Orchestratations by Reginald De Koven
Incidental and ballet music composed and arranged by Reginald De Koven (uncredited)
Staging by Max Freeman

The Buccaneers
22 May 1895
Music by Frederick W. Mills
Musical director, Frederick W. Mills
Incidental and dance music arranged by Frederick W. Mills (uncredited)

Hamlet II
27 May 1895
Music by Homer Tourjée

Musical direction, Jesse Williams
Incidental and dance music arranged by Jesse Williams (uncredited)
Staging by James Barton Key
Ballets by Mme. Eloise Kruger

Daughter of the Revolution
27 May 1895
Music by Ludwig Englander
Musical director, Ludwig Englander
Dance music composed and arranged by Ludwig Englander (uncredited)
Staging by Richard Barker
Dances by Signor Augusto Francioli

Thrilby
3 June 1895
Music by Charles Puerner
Music for additional numbers composed by Nelson Kneass and Carl Keller
Musical director, W.T. Francis
Music for "New Defender Ballet" arranged by Charles Puerner (uncredited)
Staging by R.H. Burnside

The Merry World
8 June 1895
Music by Nicholas Biddle
Additional music composed by Francis Bryant
Musical director, Herman Perlet
Music for the cakewalk, "Aunt Jemima's Big Pound Cake" composed by John T. Kelly
Staging by Edgar Smith

Kismet, or, Two Tangled Turks
12 August 1895
Music by Gustave Kerker
Musical director, Selli Simonson
Incidental and dance music arranged by Gustave Kerker (un-

    credited)
    Staging by Max Freeman

Fleur-De-Lis
    29 August 1895
    Music by William Furst
    Musical director, Fred J. Eustis
    Incidental and dance music composed by William Furst (uncredited)
    Staging by Richard Barker

Princess Bonnie
    2 September 1895
    Words and music by Willard Spenser
    Musical director, William J. Rostetter
    Incidental and dance music arranged by Willard Spenser (uncredited)
    Staging by Richard Barker

The Widow Jones
    16 September 1895
    Music by George M. Cohan, Lewis S. Thompson, James Thornton, Fay Templeton, Charles E. Trevathan, and Reginald De Koven
    Music arranged by John C. Sorg
    Incidental and dance music arranged by John C. Sorg (uncredited)
    Staging by R.A. Roberts

Fortuna, or, The Princess Tough
    16 September 1895
    Music by John Stromberg
    Musical director, John Stromberg
    Incidental and dance music arranged by John Stromberg (uncredited)

His Excellency
    14 October 1895
    Music by Osmond Carr

Musical director, Gustave Howig
Incidental and dance music composed and arranged by Osmond Carr (uncredited)
Staging by John Gunn
Dances by John D'Auban

Leonardo
21 October 1895
Music by Thomas Pearsall Thorne
Musical director, Gustave Kerker
Incidental and dance music arranged by Thomas Pearsall Thorne (uncredited)
Staging by James C. Duff

The Shop Girl
28 October 1895
Music by Ivan Caryll
Additional songs by Adrian Ross and Lionel Monckton
Musical director, Barter Johns
Incidental and dance music composed and arranged by Ivan Caryll (uncredited)
Staging by A.E. Dodson

The Wizard of the Nile
4 November 1895
Music by Victor Herbert
Musical director, Frank Palma
Orchestrations by Victor Herbert
Incidental and dance music composed and arranged by Victor Herbert (uncredited)
Staging by Napier Lothian, Jr.

The Night Clerk
11 November 1895
Music selected and composed by Rene Stretti
Musical director, Rene Stretti
Dance music arranged by Rene Stretti (uncredited)
Staging by Frank Tannehill, Jr.

Excelsior, Jr.
25 November 1895
Music by George Lowell Tracy, A. Baldwin Sloane, and Edward E. Rice
Musical director (conductor), John J. Braham
Music for "Snow Ballet" composed by A. Baldwin Sloane

Stag Party, or, A Hero In Spite of Himself
17 December 1895
Music composed and arranged by Herman Perlet
Musical director, Herman Perlet
Incidental and dance music arranged by Herman Perlet (uncredited)
Staging by Richard Barker

An Artist's Model
23 December 1895
Music by Sidney Jones
Musical director (conductor), William Furst
Original incidental and dance music arranged by Sidney Jones
Incidental and dance music adapted by William Furst (uncredited)
Dances by John D'Auban and Mr. Lefranc

The School Girl
30 December 1895
Music by Albert Maurice
Musical director, Fred Perkins
Dance music arranged by Fred Perkins (uncredited)
Dances by Carl Marwig

A Black Sheep
6 January 1896
Music by Richard Stahl, Charles H. Hoyt, William Devere, Otis Harlan, Harry Conor, Reginald De Koven, and Herbert Dillea
Music for additional numbers composed by Andrew Mack, Ernest Hogan, Louis F. Gottschalk, John T. Kelly, and Mr. Thorton

Musical director, Richard Stahl
Incidental and dance music arranged by Richard Stahl (uncredited)
Staging by Julian Mitchell

Gentleman Joe, the Hansom Cabby
30 January 1896
Music by Walter Slaughter
Music for additional numbers composed by John W. Bratton, Frank J. Guerney, and Ella Chapman
Musical director, Herman Perlet
Dance music arranged by Herman Perlet (uncredited)
Staging by Richard Barker

The Lady Slavey
3 February 1896
Music by Gustave Kerker
Musical director, Gustave Kerker
Incidental and dance music arranged by Gustave Kerker (uncredited)
Dances by Rose Beckett

Marguerite
10 February 1896
Libretto and music by Oscar Hammerstein
Musical director, Fritz Scheel
Ballet music arranged by Oscar Hammerstein (uncredited)
Ballets by Signor Augusto Francioli

The Minstrel of Clare
2 March 1896
Music by Chauncey Olcott and Hope Temple
Musical director, Albert Krausse
Incidental and dance music arranged by Albert Krausse (uncredited)
Staging by Augustus Pitou

El Capitan
20 April 1896

Music by John Philip Sousa
Musical director, J. Sebastian Hiller
Orchestrations by John Philip Sousa
Incidental and dance music composed and arranged by John Philip Sousa (uncredited)
Staging by H.A. Cripps

The Sunshine of Paradise Alley
11 May 1896
Music by John W. Bratton, James Thornton, Walter A. Phillips, and Kerry Mills
Musical director, Thomas W. Hindley
Incidental music by Thomas W. Hindley
Staging by Ben Teal

In Gay New York
28 May 1896
Music by Gustave Kerker
Musical director (conductor), Gustave Kerker
Ballet music composed and arranged by Gustave Kerker (uncredited)
Ballet by Signor Augusto Francioli

Marty Malone
31 August 1896
Music by David Braham
Musical director, George F. Braham
Incidental and dance music arranged by George F. Braham (uncredited)
Staging by Edward Harrigan

The Caliph
3 September 1896
Music by Ludwig Englander
Musical director, Fred J. Eustis
Incidental and dance music arranged by Ludwig Englander (uncredited)
Staging by Richard Barker

The Art of Maryland
    5 September 1896
    Music by John Stromberg
    Musical director, John Stromberg
    Music for dances and ballets selected and arranged by John Stromberg (uncredited)
    Ballets by Leon Franchi

The Geisha
    9 September 1896
    Music composed by Sidney Jones.
    Music for additional numbers composed by Lionel Monckton, James Philip, Napoléon Lambelet, Frank E. Tours, and Lawrence Kellie
    Incidental and dance music arranged by Sidney Jones (uncredited)
    Staging by Augustin Daly

Half a King
    14 September 1896
    Music by Ludwig Englander
    Musical director, W.H. Batchelder
    Incidental and dance music arranged by Ludwig Englander (uncredited)
    Staging by Richard Barker

The Gold Bug
    21 September 1896
    Music by Victor Herbert
    Musical director (conductor), Gustave Kerker
    Orchestrations by Victor Herbert
    Incidental and dance music composed and arranged by Victor Herbert (uncredited)
    Staging by Max Freeman

A Parlor Match
    21 September 1896
    Music by John T. Kelly, Alfred Plumpton, Harry B. Morris, Arthur Sullivan, Ivan Caryll, Sidney Jones, Paul Lacome, and

    George B. Seevers
    Additional music composed by Herman Perlet
    Musical Director (conductor), William Potter Brown
    Staging by James T. Galloway

Santa Maria
    24 September 1896
    Libretto and music by Oscar Hammerstein
    Musical director, J. Luckstone
    Incidental and dance music arranged by Oscar Hammerstein (uncredited)
    Staging by Max Freeman

The Merry Tramps
    28 September 1896
    Music by Carl Pleininger
    Musical director, Carl Pleininger
    Ballet music arranged by Carl Pleininger (uncredited)
    Staging by Carl Rosenfeld

Hogan's Alley
    12 October 1896
    Music by John F. Leonard
    Musical director (conductor), David Braham
    Incidental and dance music arranged by David Braham (uncredited)
    Staging by Jack Gardiner

Brian Boru
    19 October 1896
    Music by Julian Edwards
    Musical director, Julian Edwards
    Incidental and dance music composed and arranged by Julian Edwards (uncredited)
    Staging by John E. Nash

The Strange Adventures of Jack and the Beanstalk
    2 November 1896
    Music composed by A. Baldwin Sloane

Musical director (conductor), Gustave Kerker
Incidental and dance music composed and arranged by A. Baldwin Sloane (uncredited)
Staging by Ben Teal
Ballets by Carl Marwig

The Mandarin
2 November 1896
Music by Reginald De Koven
Musical director, Antonio DeNovellis
Orchestrations by Reginald De Koven
Incidental and dance music composed and arranged by Reginld De Koven (uncredited)
Staging by Richard Barker
Dances by Samuel Marion

Oriental America, or, In the Isle of San Domingo
16 November 1896
Music by Fay Templeton, George M. Cohan, Robert Planquette, Charles Gounod, Reginald De Koven, Friedrich von Flotow, Giuseppi Verdi, and Gaetano Donizetti
Musical director, John Villers Stamford
Incidental music composed and arranged by John Villers Stamford
Staging by John W. Isham

The Girl from Paris
8 December 1896
Music by Ivan Caryll
Music for additional numbers composed by Nat D. Mann and Frank David
Musical director, Herman Perlet
Orchestrations by George Hayes
Original dance and incidental music composed by Ivan Caryll (uncredited)
Dance music arranged by Herman Perlet (uncredited)
Dances by H. Fletcher Rivers

A Contented Woman
> 4 January 1897
> Music by Richard Stahl
> Music for additional numbers composed by Eugene Ellsworth
> Musical director, Richard Stahl
> Incidental and dance music arranged by Richard Stahl (uncredited)
> Staging by Charles H. Hoyt

Kismet, or, Two Tangled Turks
> 4 January 1897
> Music by Gustave Kerker
> Musical director, Gustave Kerker
> Ballet music arranged by Gustave Kerker (uncredited)
> Dances by Signor Augusto Francioli

Shamus O'Brien
> 5 January 1897
> Music by Charles Villiers Stanford
> Musical director, Gustave A. Kerker
> Original dance and incidental music composed by Charles Villiers Stanford (uncredited)
> Dance music arranged by Gustave Kerker (uncredited)
> Dances by Edward Murphy

A Boy Wanted
> 18 January 1897
> Music by Harry James
> Music for additional numbers composed by Walter Hawley and George M. Cohan
> Musical director, Harry James
> Incidental and dance music arranged by Harry James (uncredited)
> Dances by Lillie Sutherland

Sweet Inniscarra
> 25 January 1897
> Music and lyrics by Chauncey Olcott
> Music for additional numbers composed by James Frederic Clay

Musical director, Albert Krausse
Dramatic music composed by David Braham
Staging by Augustus Pitou

At Gay Coney Island
1 February 1897
Music and lyrics by J. Sherrie Mathews and Harry Bulger
Music for additional numbers composed by Maurice Levi
Incidental and dance music arranged by Maurice Levi (uncredited)
Staging by Julian Mitchell
Dances by H. Fletcher Rivers

The Serenade
16 March 1897
Music by Victor Herbert
Musical director, Samuel L. Studley
Orchestrations by Victor Herbert
Incidental and dance music composed and arranged by Victor Herbert (uncredited)
Staging by William H. Fitzgerald

The Circus Girl
23 April 1897
Music by Ivan Caryll
Additional songs by Lionel Monckton
Musical director, Paul Steindorff
Incidental and dance music composed and arranged by Ivan Caryll (uncredited)
Additional dance music provided by Lionel Monckton (uncredited)
Dances by Carl Marwig

The Isle of Gold
26 April 1897
Music by Herman Perlet
Music for additional numbers composed by William B. Gottlieb
Musical director, Maurice Levi

Incidental and dance music arranged by Herman Perlet and Maurice Levi
Dances by H. Fletcher Rivers

A Round of Pleasure
24 May 1897
Music by Ludwig Englander
Music for additional numbers composed by James Thornton, Charles Trevathan, and Richard Carle
Musical director, Paul Schindler
Ballet music composed and arranged by Ludwig Englander (uncredited)
Staging by Ben Teal
Ballets by Carl Marwig

The Whirl of the Town
25 May 1897
Music composed by Gustave Kerker
Music for additional numbers composed by John W. Bratton
Musical director, Gustave Kerker
Incidental and ballet music composed and arranged by Gustave Kerker (uncredited)
Ballets by Signor Augusto Francioli

The Good Mr. Best
30 August 1897
Music by Henry J. Sayers
Music for additional numbers composed by Sidney Perrin, John H. Bratton, and Frederic Dana
Musical arrangements by Jesse Williams
Incidental and dance music arranged by Jesse Williams (uncredited)
Staging by R. A. Roberts
Dances by Samuel Marion

In Town
6 September 1897
Music by F. Osmond Carr
Musical director, Harold Vicars

Incidental and dance music composed and arranged by F. Osmond Carr (uncredited)
Staging by J.E.A. Malone
Dances by Willie Warde

A Stranger in New York
13 September 1897
Music by Richard Stahl
Additional music composed by Harry Conor, A. Baldwin Sloane, and Max Hoffman
Incidental and dance music arranged by Richard Stahl (uncredited)
Staging by Charles H. Hoyt

The French Maid
27 September 1897
Music by Walter Slaughter
Music for additional numbers composed by Donald MacGregor, Herman Perlet, and Edward E. Rice
Musical director, Herman Perlet
Original music for ballets arranged by Walter Slaughter (uncredited)
Additional ballet music arranged by Herman Perlet
Ballets by Augustus Sohlke

The Belle of New York
28 September 1897
Music by Gustave Kerker
Music for additional numbers composed by Richard Stahl
Musical director, Gustave Kerker
Incidental and dance music composed and arranged by Gustave Kerker (uncredited)
Staging by George W. Lederer
Ballets by Signor Augusto Francioli

The Idol's Eye
25 October 1897
Music by Victor Herbert
Musical director, Frank Palma

Orchestrations by Victor Herbert
Incidental and dance music composed and arranged by Victor Herbert (uncredited)
Staging by Julian Mitchell

An Irish Gentleman
29 November 1897
Music by Andrew Mack
Musical director, Louie Maurice
Incidental music by Louie Maurice
Staging by R.A. Roberts

Pousse Café / The Worst Born
2 December 1897
Music by John Stromberg
Musical director, John Stromberg
Incidental and dance music arranged by John Stromberg (uncredited)
Staging by Julian Mitchell

The Highwayman
13 December 1897
Music by Reginald De Koven
Musical director, A. DeNovellis
Orchestrations by Reginald De Koven
Incidental and dance music composed and arranged by Reginald De Koven (uncredited)
Staging by Max Freeman
Dances by Carl Marwig

The Ballet Girl
21 December 1897
Music by Carl Kiefert
Music for additional numbers composed by Edward E. Rice and Charles Graham
Musical director, Joseph Van Den Berg
Original dance and incidental music composed by Carl Kiefert
Additional dance music composed by Edward E. Rice
Ballets by Augustus Sohlke

The Telephone Girl
27 December 1897
Music by Gustave Kerker
Musical director, Gustave Kerker
Incidental and dance music composed and arranged by W.T. Francis and Gustave Kerker (uncredited)
Ballets by Signor Augusto Francioli

Miss Philadelphia
27 December 1897
Music by Herman Perlet and Frederick Gagel
Musical director, Frederick Arundel
Dance music composed by John Philip Sousa
Staging by Junius Howe

The Bride-Elect
28 December 1897
Music by John Philip Sousa
Musical director, Paul Steindorff
Orchestrations by John Philip Sousa
Incidental and dance music arranged by John Philip Sousa (uncredited)
Staging by Ben Teal
Ballets by Carl Marwig

A Hired Girl
10 January 1898
Music by Harry James
Musical director, Harry James
Incidental and dance music arranged by Harry James (uncredited)
Staging by James T. Kelly

Queen of the Ballet
7 February 1898
Music by Edward W. Corliss
Additional music composed by Alfred Norman, George Lowell Tracy, Harry Lawson Heartz, Walter Gould, and Hastings Weblyn

Ballet music arranged by Edward W. Corliss, Harry Lawson Heartz, and Alfred Norman
Dances by John Coleman

Monte Carlo
21 March 1898
Music by Howard Talbot
Additional music composed by Herman Perlet
Musical director, Herman Perlet
"Skirt Dance" composed by Paolo Giorza
Additional dance music composed by Edward E. Rice and arranged by Henry Marchetti
Staging by Frank Smithson
Ballets by Filiberto Marchetti

The Origin of the Cakewalk, or, Clorindy
18 June 1898
Music by Will Marion Cook
Musical director, Will Marion Cook
Dance music arranged by Will Marion Cook (uncredited)
Staged by Ernest Hogan

Yankee Doodle Dandy
25 July 1898
Music by Gustave Kerker
Additional songs by Henry Bauer and Jackson Gouraud
Musical director (conductor), Thomas H. Joyce
Music for "Frivolity Ballet" composed by Edward E. Rice
Incidental and dance music arranged by Gustave Kerker (uncredited)
Staging by George W. Lederer

A Runaway Girl
25 August 1898
Music by Ivan Caryll and Lionel Monckton
Music for additional numbers composed by Alfred D. Cammeyer
Musical director (conductor), J. Sebastian Hiller
Incidental and dance music arranged by Ivan Caryll (uncredited)

Additional dance music provided by Lionel Monckton (uncredited)
Staging and dances by Herbert Gresham

A Day and a Night in New York
30 August 1898
Music by Richard Stahl, Charles H. Hoyt, Edmund Vance Cooke, William Devere, Safford Waters, Henri Christiné, and Charles Zimmerman
Musical director, Charles Zimmerman
Dance music composed by Charles Zimmerman
Staging by Charles H. Hoyt
Dances by Thomas Evans

The Charlatan
5 September 1898
Libretto and music by John Philip Sousa
Musical director, Paul Steindorff
Conductor, William T. Francis
Orchestrations by John Philip Sousa
Incidental and dance music arranged by John Philip Sousa (uncredited)
Staging by H.A. Cripps

Hurly-Burly / Cyranose De Bric-a-Brac / The Heathen
8 September 1898
Music by John Stromberg
Olio music by John Crook
Musical director, John Stromberg
Incidental and dance music arranged by John Stromberg (uncredited)

Wine, Women and Song
19 September 1898
Music by Carl Schilling
Musical director, Carl Schilling
Conductor, Thomas H. Joyce
Music for characteristic dances arranged by Carl Schilling (uncredited)
Staging by George Paxton

In Gotham
19 September 1898
Music by Max Gabriel
Music for additional numbers composed by Alfred E. Aarons and Richard Carle
Musical director, Max Gabriel
Incidental and ballet music composed and arranged by Max Gabriel (uncredited)
Staging by John E. Nash
Dances by Signor Luigi Albertieri

The Marquis of Michigan
21 September 1898
Music by A. Baldwin Sloane
Music for additional numbers composed by John Crook and Edward E. Rice
Incidental music by Louie Maurice
Staging by J.K. Adams

The Fortune Teller
26 September 1898
Music by Victor Herbert
Musical director, Paul Steindorff
Orchestrations by Victor Herbert
Incidental and dance music composed and arranged by Victor Herbert (uncredited)
Staging by Julian Mitchell

Hotel Topsy Turvy
3 October 1898
Music by Victor Roger
Additional music by Lionel Monckton
Music for additional numbers composed by H. Fragson and A. Stanislaus, N. Lambelet, Eddie Foy, Aubrey Boucicault, John S. Ross, and Joseph E. Howard
Musical director (conductor), Herman Perlet
Dance music composed by Lionel Monckton, arranged by Herman Perlet (uncredited)
Staging by Frank Smithson

Ballets by John Wagner

Kate Kip, Buyer
    31 October 1898
    Music by A. Baldwin Sloane, Ignacio Martinetti, Cissie Loftus, Hattie Nevada, Ned Wayburn, Arthur Dunn, and John T. Kelly
    Musical director, Watty Hydes
    Incidental music composed by Watty Hydes
    Staging by May Irwin

The Jolly Musketeer
    14 November 1898
    Music by Julian Edwards
    Musical director, A. Krausse
    Incidental and dance music arranged by Julian Edwards (uncredited)
    Staging by Richard Barker

The Little Host
    26 December 1898
    Music by William T. Francis and Thomas Chilvers
    Music for additional numbers composed by Edwin S. Brill and Herman Perlet
    Musical director, William T. Francis
    Incidental and dance music arranged by William T. Francis and Thomas Chilvers (uncredited)
    Staging by Max Freeman
    Dances by John C. Slavin

A Romance of Athlone
    8 January 1899
    Music and lyrics by Chauncey Olcott
    Dramatic music composed and arranged by Gus Salzer
    Staging by Augustus Pitou

The Evil Eye, or the Many Merry Mishaps of Nid and the Weird Wonderful Wanderings of Nod
    16 January 1899
    Music composed and arranged by Alfred J. Kuttner

Music for "Sabot Dance of the Grape-Pickers" and "Electric Ballet" arranged by Alfred J. Kuttner (uncredited)
Staging by Sydney R. Ellis

The Three Dragoons
30 January 1899
Music by Reginald De Koven
Musical director, Antonio DeNovellis
Orchestrations by Reginald De Koven
Incidental and dance music composed and arranged by Reginald De Koven (uncredited)
Staging by Julian Mitchell

By the Sad Sea Waves
28 February 1899
Music by Gustav Luders
Music for additional numbers composed by Barney Fagan, Vinnie DeWitt, Harry Bulger, J. Sherrie Mathews, George A. Nichols, Leslie Stuart, Ernest Hogan, Al Trahern, and Charles Gebest
Musical director, Gustav Luders
Dance music arranged by Gustav Luders (uncredited)
Staging by Barney Fagan and Ned Wayburn

A Reign of Error
2 March 1899
Music by Maurice Levi
Music for additional numbers compose by André Messager, Harry Von Tilzer, M.M. Ellis, Jackson Gouraud, Billy Johnson, and A. Baldwin Sloane
Musical arrangements by Maurice Levi
Musical director (conductor), Maurice Levi
Dance music arranged by Maurice Levi (uncredited)
Staging by Ben Teal
Dances by Carl Marwig and the Rogers Brothers

The King's Musketeer
13 March 1899
Incidental music by Frank Howson

In Gay Paree
20 March 1899
Music by Ludwig Englander
Musical director, Herman Perlet
Music for "Grisette Two Step" by Alfred Newman
Ballet music composed and arranged by Ludwig Englander (uncredited)
Staging by Ben Teal
Ballets and dances by Carl Marwig

The Man in the Moon
24 April 1899
Music by Ludwig Englander, Gustave Kerker, and Reginald De Koven
Musical director, Gustave Kerker
Music for "When Our Ship Comes Home," song and dance for the Pony Ballet, composed by Frederic Solomon
Music for "The Orchid Ballet" and "Grand Pageant and Review (The Genius of Freedom)" composed by Reginald De Koven
Music for the "Animation of Diana," "The Bellamy Dance," and "Ballet of the Four Seasons" composed by Ludwig Englander
Staging by George W. Lederer
Ballets by Carl Marwig

An Arabian Girl and 40 Thieves
29 April 1899
Music by W.H. Batchelor, John J. Braham, Jesse Williams, and Meyer Lutz
Music for additional numbers composed by W.T. Francis and Louise Tunison
Musical director (conductor), John J. Braham
Music for "Grand Ballet Orientale," "Danse Egyptienne," "Danse Diabolique," and
"The Pickaninny Dance" composed by W.H. Batchelor (uncredited)
Staging by Julian Mitchell
Ballets by Filiberto Marchetti

The Rounders
    12 July 1899
    Music by Ludwig Englander
    Musical director, Antonio DeNovellis
    Incidental and dance music composed and arranged by Ludwig Englander (uncredited)
    Staging by Max Freeman

The Maid in the Moon
    31 July 1899
    Music by Frederic Solomon
    Music for the "Ballet of the Four Seasons" composed by Frederic Solomon (uncredited)
    Staging by Edward E. Rice
    Ballet by H. Fletcher Rivers

Sister Mary
    15 September 1899
    Music by Lionel Monckton, Gus Edwards, Napoleon Lambelet, Melville Ellis, Cissie Loftus, Albert H. Fitz, Billy Johnson, J. Rosamond Johnson, and Herbert Cawthorne
    Musical director, Watty Hydes
    Incidental and dance music arranged by Watty Hydes
    Staging by Herbert Gresham

Cyrano de Bergerac
    18 September 1899
    Music by Victor Herbert
    Musical director (conductor), John McGhie
    Orchestrations by Victor Herbert
    Incidental and dance music composed and arranged by Victor Herbert (uncredited)
    Staging by A. M. Holbrook

(The Rogers Brothers) In Wall Street
    18 September 1899
    Music Maurice Levi
    Additional songs by Richard Carle, Gus Edwards, Arthur Trevelyan, Arthur Dunn, and Gustav Luders

Musical director, Maurice Levi
Dance music arranged by Maurice Levi (uncredited)

(Isham's) Octoroons
2 October 1899
Original music for Act 1: "7-11-77" by William J. Accooe
Original music for Act 3: "Thirty Minutes Around the Operas" by Carl Schilling
Music for "Oh, Listen to the Band" composed by Lionel Monckton
Musical director, Carl Schilling
Ballet music for "Cavalleria Dance," "Cuba Girls," and "Porto Rico Girls" arranged by Carl Schilling (uncredited)
Ballets by H. Fletcher Rivers

The Policy Players
16 October 1899
Music and lyrics by Bert Williams
Additional songs by William J. Accooe, Cecil Mack, and Tom Lemonier
Musical director, Will Marion Cook
Dance music arranged by Will Marion Cook (uncredited)
Staging by Jesse A. Shipp

The Singing Girl
23 October 1899
Music by Victor Herbert
Musical director (conductor), Paul Steindorff
Orchestrations by Victor Herbert
Incidental and dance music composed and arranged by Victor Herbert (uncredited)
Staging by Julian Mitchell

Robespierre
30 October 1899
Incidental and dance music composed by Georges Jacobi

'Round New York in 80 Minutes
6 November 1899

Music original and selected by Edward E. Rice and John J. Braham
Music for additional numbers composed by Robert A. Keiser, Louis Weslyn Jones, Paul Cohn, and Fred J. Hamill
Musical director, John J. Braham
Dance music arranged by John J. Braham (uncredited)
Staging by William A. Brady

A Greek Slave
28 November 1899
Music by Sidney Jones
Additional music by Lionel Monckton
Incidental and dance music composed by Sidney Jones (uncredited)
Additional dance music provided by Lionel Monckton (uncredited)
Staging by Julian Mitchell

The Ameer
4 December 1899
Music by Victor Herbert
Musical director, L.F. Gottschalk
Orchestrations by Victor Herbert
Incidental and dance music composed and arranged by Victor Herbert (uncredited)
Dances by H. Fletcher Rivers

Chris and the Wonderful Lamp
1 January 1900
Libretto and music by John Philip Sousa
Musical director, Albert Krausse
Orchestrations by John Philip Sousa
Incidental and dance music composed and arranged by John Philip Sousa (uncredited)
Staging by Ben Teal
Dances by Mme. Malvina

Little Red Riding Hood
8 January 1900
Original and selected music by Edward E. Rice, Charles Dennée, Fred J. Eustis, T.W. Conner, Frank Perlet, and B. Gilbert

Musical director, Fred J. Eustis
Music for "Grand Toy Dances" and "Barnyard Ballet" composed and arranged by Fred J. Eustis
Music for "Maypole Dance" composed by Charles Dennée
Staging by William Seymour
Dances by Marquette

From Broadway to Tokio
23 January 1900
Music by A. Baldwin Sloane and Reginald De Koven
Musical director (conductor), Antonio DeNovellis
Music arranged by Karl L. Hoschna and Frank Sadler
Ballet music composed by Reginald De Koven
Staging by Max Freeman
Ballets by Carl Marwig

The Princess Chic
12 February 1900
Music by Julian Edwards
Musical director (conductor), William E. MacQuinn
Incidental and dance music arranged by Julian Edwards (uncredited)
Staging and dances by Julian Mitchell

The Regatta Girl
14 March 1900
Music by Harry McLellan
Musical director, Fred J. Eustis
Ballet music composed by Romualdo Marenco and John J. Braham
Ballet by Luigi Manzotti and Vincenzo Romeo

The Casino Girl
19 March 1900
Music by Ludwig Englander
Music for additional numbers composed by Harry T. MacConnell, Arthur Weld, Arthur Nevin, Reginald De Koven, Maurice Lecocq, and Will Marion Cook
Musical director, Antonio DeNovellis
Ballet music arranged by William Devin (uncredited)

Incidental dance music devised by Ludwig Englander, Harry T. MacConnell, Arthur Weld, and Arthur Nevin
Staging by George W. Lederer

The Sunken Bell
26 March 1900
Incidental music composed by Aimé Lachaume

Quo Vadis
9 April 1900
Incidental music composed by Julian Edwards

The Viceroy
9 April 1900
Music by Victor Herbert
Musical director (conductor), Samuel L. Studley
Orchestrations by Victor Herbert
Incidental and dance music composed and arranged by Victor Herbert (uncredited)
Staging by William H. Fitzgerald

The Cadet Girl
25 July 1900
Music by Louis Varney and Ludwig Englander
Musical director, Frederic Solomon
Dance music composed by Louis Varney, arranged by Ludwig Englander (uncredited)
Staging by George Marion

The Rebel
20 August 1900
Music and lyrics by Andrew Mack
Musical director, John C. Sorg
Incidental music arranged by John C. Sorg
Staging by Joseph Humphries

A Million Dollars
27 September 1900
Music by A. Baldwin Sloane

Musical director (conductor), Joseph Van Den Berg
Music for "The Ballet on the Beach at Coney Island" and "The Gold, Silver and Rose Ballet" composed by A. Baldwin Sloane (uncredited)
Staging by Frank Smithson
Ballets by Carl Marwig

Zaza
1 October 1900
Incidental music composed by William Frederick Peters

San Toy
1 October 1900
Music by Sidney Jones
Music for additional numbers composed by Lionel Monckton and L.S. Potter
Musical director, George P. Towle
Dance music arranged by Sidney Jones (uncredited)
Dances by Willie Warde

David Harum
1 October 1900
Incidental and dance music composed by William Furst

Henry V
3 October 1900
Incidental and dance music composed by Max S. Witt

Sons of Ham
15 October 1900
Music and lyrics by Bert Williams and George Walker
Additional music composed by Cecil Mack, W.S. Estren, J. Tim Brymn, and Will Accooe
Musical director, Will Accooe
Dance music arranged by Will Accooe (uncredited)
Staging by Jesse A. Shipp

In a Balcony
26 October 1900

Incidental music by Julian Edwards

The Belle of Bridgeport
  29 October 1900
  Music by J. Rosamond Johnson
  Music for additional numbers by William Jefferson, Cissie Loftus, and William J. Accooe
  Musical director, Watty Hydes
  Dance music arranged by William Jefferson and Watty Hydes
  Staging by George A. Beane

Foxy Quiller
  5 November 1900
  Music by Reginald De Koven
  Musical director, Antonio DeNovellis
  Orchestrations by Reginald De Koven
  Incidental and dance music composed and arranged by Reginald De Koven (uncredited)
  Staging by Ben Teal
  Dances by Mme. Malvina

Florodora
  10 November 1900
  Music by Leslie Stuart
  Music for additional numbers composed by Paul Rubens
  Musical director (conductor), Arthur Weld
  Music for "Barn Dance" arranged by Arthur Weld (uncredited)
  Staging by Lewis Hooper, under the supervision of Willie Edouin

The Burgomaster
  31 December 1900
  Music by Gustav Luders
  Musical director, Gustav Luders
  Dance music arranged by Gustav Luders (uncredited)
  Staging by Thomas Ricketts

Garrett O'Magh
  7 January 1901
  Music and lyrics by Chauncey Olcott

Musical director, Gus Salzer
Incidental music by Gus Salzer
Staging by Augustus Pitou

My Lady
11 February 1901
Music by Harry Lawson Heartz
Additional songs by Edward W. Corliss, Robert G. Morse, D.K. Stevens, and Clifton Crawford
Musical director, Paul Schindler
Music for "Pas de Fleur (Ballet)" composed by Harry Lawson Heartz, D.K. Stevens, and Robert G. Morse
Additional dance music composed by Harry Lawson Heartz (uncredited)
Staging by Will A. McCormick
Ballets by M.B. Gilbert

The Governor's Son
25 February 1901
Libretto and music by George M. Cohan
Musical director, Charles J. Gebest
Incidental and dance music arranged by Charles J. Gebest (uncredited)
Staging by R.A. Roberts and Ned Wayburn

The King's Carnival
13 May 1901
Music by A. Baldwin Sloane
Additional songs by Mae Anwenda Sloane and Jean Schwartz
Musical director (conductor), J. Sebastian Hiller
Dance music arranged by A. Baldwin Sloane (uncredited)
Staging by Frank Smithson

The Strollers
24 June 1901
Music by Ludwig Englander
Music for additional numbers composed by Fred Meyer, Jean Schwartz, Gus Edwards, Harry T. MacConnell, and Evans Lloyd

Musical director (conductor), A. DeNovellis
Incidental and ballet music composed and arranged by Ludwig Englander (uncredited)
Staging by A. M. Holbrook, under the supervision of George W. Lederer

The Explorers
30 June 1901
Music by Walter H. Lewis
Musical director, Walter H. Lewis
Incidental and dance music arranged by Walter H. Lewis

The Rogers Brothers in Washington
2 September 1901
Music by Maurice Levi
Musical director, Maurice Levi
Dance music arranged by Maurice Levi (uncredited)
Staging by Ben Teal

The Messenger Boy
16 September 1901
Music by Ivan Caryll and Lionel Monckton
Music for additional numbers composed by T.W. Conner, Paul Rubens, and Brent Brantford
Musical director (conductor), Louis F. Gottschalk
Original dance music composed by Ivan Caryll and Lionel Monckton (uncredited)
Dance music adapted and arranged by Louis F. Gottschalk (uncredited)
Staging by Herbert Gresham

The Hottest Coon in Dixie
16 September 1901
Music by Will Accooe
Musical director, Will Accooe
Dance music arranged by Will Accooe (uncredited)
Staging by Robert A. Kelly

The Liberty Belles
   30 September 1901
   Music by John W. Bratton, Clifton Crawford, Aimé Lachaume, Harry Von Tilzer, A. Baldwin Sloane, Mae Anweda Sloane, Louis F. Gottschalk, William J. Accooe, and Alfred E. Aarons
   Musical director (conductor), Aimé Lachaume
   Dance music composed by Clifton Crawford and Aimé Lachaume
   Staging by Herbert Gresham

The Little Duchess
   14 October 1901
   Music by Reginald De Koven
   Music for additional numbers composed by Leo LeBrunn, Ellen Wright, Herman Perlet, J. Rosamond Johnson, and A. Baldwin Sloane
   Musical director (conductor), Herman Perlet
   Incidental and dance music composed and arranged by Reginald De Koven (uncredited)
   Staging by George Marion

The Sleeping Beauty and the Beast
   4 November 1901
   Music by J.M. Glover and Frederic Solomon
   Music for additional numbers composed by J. Rosamond Johnson and Jean Schwartz
   Musical director, Frederic Solomon
   Music for Hengler Sisters' dance composed by Maurice Levi
   Ballet music composed and arranged by Frederic Solomon (uncredited)
   Staging by Ben Teal and Marshall Moore
   Ballets by Ernest D'Auban

The Toreador
   6 January 1902
   Music by Ivan Caryll and Lionel Monckton
   Additional music by Paul Rubens and John W. Bratton
   Musical director, Louis F. Gottschalk
   Original incidental and dance music composed by Ivan Caryll and Lionel Monckton (uncredited)

Dance music adapted and arranged by Louis F. Gottschalk
Staging by Herbert Gresham

Dolly Varden
27 January 1902
Music by Julian Edwards
Musical director and conductor, W.F. Macquinn
Incidental and dance music composed and arranged by Julian Edwards (uncredited)
Staging by A.M. Holbrook

Maid Marian
27 January 1902
Music by Reginald De Koven
Musical director, Samuel L. Studley
Orchestrations by Reginald De Koven
Incidental and dance music composed and arranged by Reginald De Koven (uncredited)
Staging by Herbert Gresham

The Hall of Fame
5 February 1902
Music by A. Baldwin Sloane
Music for additional numbers composed by Mae Anwerda Sloane, Raymond A. Brown, and Billy Johnson
Musical director, Genaro Saldierna
"Feather Ballet" composed by Henry Waller
Staging by Ned Wayburn
Ballet by Carl Marwig

Miss Simplicity
10 February 1902
Music by Harry Lawson Heartz
Additional music composed by E.W. Corliss, Benjamin Hapgood Burt, and Clifton Crawford
Musical director, Fred J. Eustis
Dance music composed by Harry Lawson Heartz (uncredited)
Dances by M.B. Gilbert and Signor Luigi Albertieri

Foxy Grandpa
>17 February 1902
>Music and lyrics by Joseph Hart
>Musical director (conductor), William H. Batchelor
>Orchestrations by William H. Batchelor
>Dance music arranged by William H. Batchelor (uncredited)
>Staging by R. Melville Baker

A Trip to Buffalo
>24 March 1902
>Music by William Loraine
>Musical director, William Loraine
>Music for "Oriental Ballet" arranged by William Loraine (uncredited)
>Staging by Eugene Rogers

The Show Girl, or The Cap of Fortune
>5 May 1902
>Music by Harry Lawson Heartz and Edward W. Corliss
>Additional music composed by L.S. Thompson, M.W. Daniels, William T. Francis, John W. Bratton, Jean Schwartz, C.E. Billings, Karl L. Horchus, Harry Linton, and Harry F. MacConnell
>Musical director (conductor), Edward E. Rice
>Dance music arranged by Edward W. Corliss and Edward E. Rice (uncredited)
>Dances by Joseph C. Smith

The Wild Rose
>5 May 1902
>Music by Ludwig Englander
>Music for additional numbers composed by Harry Linton, Ren Shields, Clifton Crawford, Will Marion Cook, Harry Von Tilzer, William H. Penn, Ben Jerome, Melville Ellis, and Jean Schwartz
>Musical director, Frederic Solomon
>Incidental and dance music composed by Melville Ellis (uncredited)
>Dances by Adolph Neuberger

A Chinese Honeymoon
2 June 1902
Music by Howard Talbot
Music for additional numbers composed by Jean Schwartz, Melville Ellis, Leo Edwards, Edward James Howe, Jr., Louis Tocaban, Ernie Woodville, George Dee, and Ivan Caryll
Musical director (conductor), Gustave Kerker
Orchestrations by Gustave Kerker
Dance music arranged by Gustave Kerker (uncredited)
Staging by Gerald Coventry

The Chaperons
5 June 1902
Music and lyrics by Isidore Witmark
Additional music by Ben M. Jerome
Musical director (conductor), Max Hirschfeld
Incidental and dance music composed by Isidore Witmark (uncredited)
Staging by George W. Lederer

Sally in Our Alley
29 August 1902
Music by Ludwig Englander
Interpolated music by Harry Von Tilzer, William H. Penn, Henry Carey, Bert Williams, J. Rosamond Johnson, and William Frederick Peters
Musical direction, Max Hirschfeld
Incidental and dance music arranged by Ludwig Englander (uncredited)
Staging by George W. Lederer

The Rogers Brothers in Harvard
1 September 1902
Music by Maurice Levi
Musical director, Maurice Levi
Dance music arranged by Maurice Levi (uncredited)
Staging by Ben Teal

King Highball
    6 September 1902
    Music by Frederick V. Bowers
    Musical director, Selli Simonson
    Ballet music composed, selected, and arranged by Frederick V. Bowers (uncredited)
    Staging by Edward E. Rice
    Ballets by Carl Marwig

Twirly-Whirly
    11 September 1902
    Music by W.T. Francis and John Stromberg
    Music for additional numbers by John T. Kelly, W.T. Travers
    Musical director, W.T. Francis
    Dance music arranged by W.T. Francis (uncredited)
    Staging by Julian Mitchell

A Country Girl
    22 September 1902
    Music by Lionel Monckton
    Music for additional numbers by Paul A. Rubens
    Musical director, J. Sebastian Hiller
    Original dance music arranged by Lionel Monckton
    Staging by Augustin Daly

The Silver Slipper
    27 October 1902
    Music by Leslie Stuart
    Additional music by Arthur Weld, Landon Ronald, and Ivan Caryll
    Musical director (conductor), Arthur Weld
    Music for "Dance (Slow Waltz)" by Arthur Weld
    Staging by James Francis, with Harry B. Burcher

The Mocking Bird
    10 November 1902
    Music by A. Baldwin Sloane
    Musical director (conductor), Max Knauer
    Dance music arranged by A. Baldwin Sloane (uncredited)
    Staging by R.H. Burnside

Mary of Magdala
    12 November 1902
    Incidental and dance music composed by Charles Puerner
    Dances by Carl Marwig

Fad and Folly
    27 November 1902
    Music and lyrics by Safford Waters
    Music for additional numbers composed by Henry Waller, George Evans, Jackson Gowraud, F. Chandler, John W. Bratton, and William FrederickPeters
    Musical director, William Frederick Peters
    Dance music composed by William Frederick Peters
    Staging by Lewis Hooper

The Darling of the Gods
    3 December 1902
    Incidental and dance music composed by William Furst

When Johnny Comes Marching Home
    16 December 1902
    Music by Julian Edwards
    Music for additional numbers by Stephen Foster
    Musical director (conductor), William MacQuinn
    Incidental and dance music composed by Julian Edwards (uncredited)
    Staging by A.M. Holbrook

The Billionaire
    29 December 1902
    Music by Gustave Kerker
    Music for additional numbers composed by Harry Armstrong and William E. Bock
    Musical director (conductor), Antonio DeNovellis
    Dance music arranged by Gustave Kerker (uncredited)
    Staging by Herbert Gresham
    Dances by Ned Wayburn

The Sultan of Sulu
>29 December 1902
>Music by Alfred G. Wathall
>Music for additional numbers composed by Nat. D. Mann, Maurice Pratt Dunlap, George L. Brun, and Anton Heindl
>Musical director, Alexander Spencer
>Incidental and dance music composed by Alfred G. Wathall
>Dances by Joseph C. Smith

Zig-Zag Alley
>19 January 1903
>Music for songs composed by Henry Carey, Andy Louis, Bob Cole, and J. Rosamond Johnson
>Incidental music composed by Karl Weixelbaum
>Staging by James Gorman

Mr. Pickwick
>19 January 1903
>Music by Manuel Klein
>Musical director, Manuel Klein
>"March" composed by George Spink
>Staging by George Marion

The Wizard of Oz
>20 January 1903
>Music by Paul Tietjens and A. Baldwin Sloane
>Music for additional numbers composed by Nat D. Mann, Bob Adams, Maurice Steinberg, Bruno Schilinski, Charles Albert, Gus Edwards, Edward Hutchison, Theodore Morse, George Spink, Edwin S. Brill, Frank Leo, and Bert Branford
>Musical director (conductor), Charles Zimmerman
>Original incidental and dance music composed by Paul Tietjens
>Music for "Ball of All Nations (Dance of All Nations)" composed by A. Baldwin Sloane
>Additional incidental music composed by Nat D. Mann
>Staging by Julian Mitchell

Mr. Bluebeard
>21 January 1903
>Music by Frederic Solomon
>Music for additional numbers composed by Matt Woodward, Harry Von Tilzer, Jean Schwartz, Theodore Morse, Gus Edwards, Dan McAvoy, Ben M. Jerome, J. Rosamond Johnson
>Musical director, Frederic Solomon
>Music for dance specialty composed by C. Herbert Kerr
>Music for Pony Ballet composed by Jean Schwartz
>Staging by Herbert Gresham and Ned Wayburn
>Ballets by Ernest D'Auban

Nancy Brown
>16 February 1903
>Music by Henry K. Hadley
>Additional music composed by J. Rosamond Johnson, Max S. Witte, Louis G. Munz, and Eugene Ellsworth
>Musical director, George P. Towle
>Dance music composed by Henry K. Hadley and J. Rosamond Johnson (uncredited)
>Staging by Frank Smithson

The Jewel of Asia
>16 February 1903
>Music by Ludwig Englander
>Music for additional numbers composed by Theodore F. Morse
>Musical director (conductor), Max Hirschfeld
>Incidental and dance music arranged by Ludwig Englander
>Staging by George W. Lederer

In Dahomey
>18 February 1903
>Music by Will Marion Cook
>Music for additional numbers composed by Benjamin L. Shook, James Vaughn, Tom Lemonier, Al Johns, Will Accooe, Alex Rogers, and John H. Cook
>Musical director, James Vaughn
>Dance music composed by Harry Von Tilzer, Benjamin L. Shook, James Vaughn, Bert Williams, and J. Leubrie Hill

(uncredited)
Staging by Jesse A. Shipp

The Prince of Pilsen
17 March 1903
Music by Gustav Luders
Musical director (conductor), Gustav Luders
Incidental and dance music arranged by Gustav Luders (uncredited)
Staging by George Marion

Running for Office
27 April 1903
Libretto and music by George M. Cohan
Musical director (conductor), Charles J. Gebest
Orchestrations by Charles J. Gebest
Incidental and dance music arranged by Charles J. Gebest (uncredited)
Staging by George M. Cohan and James Gorman

The Runaways
11 May 1903
Music by Raymond Hubbell
Music for additional numbers composed by Leo Friedman, Theodore F. Morse, William Gould, Ernest R. Ball, and Neil Moret
Musical director, Arthur Weld
Dance and incidental music composed by Raymond Hubbell
Staging by Gerald Coventry
Dances by Samuel Marion

The Blonde in Black
8 June 1903
Music by Gustave Kerker
Musical director (conductor), Gustave Kerker
Incidental and dance music arranged by Gustave Kerker (uncredited)
Staging by George W. Lederer
Dances by Carl Marwig

George W. Lederer's Mid-Summer Night Fancies
22 June 1903
Music by Ben M. Jerome
Music for additional numbers by A. Baldwin Sloane, Max Hoffmann, and Harry Morris
Musical director (conductor), Max Hoffmann
Ballet music arranged by Max Hoffman (uncredited)
Staging by George W. Lederer and Ned Wayburn
Dances by Pat Rooney and Ned Wayburn

A Son of Rest
17 August 1903
Music, book, and lyrics by George Weston
Additional music composed by Theodore F. Morse and Max S. Witt
Musical director, Max S. Witt
Incidental and dance music composed and arranged by Max S. Witt (uncredited)
Staging and dances by Samuel Marion

Three Little Maids
1 September 1903
Music by Paul Rubens
Music for additional numbers composed by Walter Rubens and Howard Talbot
Musical director (conductor), Frank E. Tours
Incidental and dance music arranged by Howard Talbot and Paul Rubens (uncredited)

The Rogers Brothers in London
7 September 1903
Music by Max Hoffmann and Melville Ellis
Music for additional numbers composed by Theodore F. Morse and Max and Gus Rogers
Musical director, Max Hoffmann
Dance music arranged by Melville Ellis (uncredited)
Staging by Herbert Gresham and Ned Wayburn

Peggy from Paris
>10 September 1903
>Music by William Loraine
>Additional music composed by W.C. Powell
>Incidental and dance music composed by William Loraine (uncredited)
>Staging by George Marion

Under Cover
>14 September 1903
>Music composed and arranged by George Braham
>Musical director, George Braham
>Incidental and dance music arranged by George Braham (uncredited)
>Staging by Edward Harrigan

The Jersey Lily
>14 September 1903
>Music by Reginald De Koven
>Additional music by Max Hoffmann, George W. Lederer, Ernest Hanegan, and Jean Schwartz
>Musical director (conductor), Daniel Dore
>Dance music arranged by Max Hoffmann
>Staging by George W. Lederer
>Dances by Joseph C. Smith

Whoop-Dee-Doo
>24 September 1903
>Music by W.T. Francis
>Music for additional numbers composed by Alfred Müller-Norden and J. Rosamond Johnson
>Musical director (conductor), W.T. Francis
>Incidental and dance music arranged by W.T. Francis (uncredited)
>Staging by Ben Teal

The Fisher Maiden
>5 October 1903
>Music by Harry Von Tilzer

Musical director (conductor), Fred Perkins
Incidental and dance music composed and arranged by Harry Von Tilzer and Fred Perkins
Staging by Harry Von Tilzer
Dances by Joseph C. Smith

The Proud Prince
12 October 1903
Incidental music composed by Manuel Klein

Babes in Toyland
13 October 1903
Music by Victor Herbert
Musical director (conductor), Max Hirschfeld
Orchestrations by Victor Herbert
Ballet music composed and arranged by Victor Herbert (uncredited)
Staging by Julian Mitchell

The Girl from Kay's
2 November 1903
Music by Ivan Caryll
Music for additional songs composed by Cecil Cook, Bernard Rolt, Ernest Bucalossi, W. Meyer Lutz, Howard Talbot, Clare Kummer, Maurice J. Stonehill, Paul Rubens, Julius Einödshofer, and A.D. Cammeyer
Musical director (conductor), Gus Salzer
Original dance music composed by Ivan Caryll and Howard Talbot (uncredited)
Incidental and dance music adapted by Gus Salzer (uncredited)

The Office Boy
2 November 1903
Music by Ludwig Englander
Music for additional numbers composed by R.G. Knowles, John W. Bratton, Theodore Morse, Bob Cole, and James Weldon Johnson
Musical director, Watty Hydes
Incidental and dance music arranged by Watty Hydes (uncred-

ited)
Staging by A.M. Holbrook

Red Feather
9 November 1903
Music by Reginald De Koven
Music for additional numbers composed by A. Baldwin Sloane
Musical director (conductor), Louis F. Gottschalk
Orchestrations by Reginald De Koven
Incidental and dance music composed and arranged by Reginald De Koven (uncredited)
Staging by Joseph W. Herbert and Max Figman
Dances by Joseph C. Smith

Babette
16 November 1903
Music by Victor Herbert
Musical director (conductor), John Lund
Orchestrations by Victor Herbert
Incidental and dance music composed and arranged by Victor Herbert
Staging by Fred G. Latham and A.M. Holbrook

Winsome Winnie
1 December 1903
Music by Harry Paulton
Music for additional numbers composed by Edward Jakobowski, Gustave Kerker, and Gus Edwards
Musical director (conductor), Gustave Kerker
Incidental and dance music arranged by Gustave Kerker (uncredited)
Staging by R.H. Burnside

Mother Goose
2 December 1903
Music by Frederic Solomon
Music for additional songs composed by Clifton Crawford, Will Heelan, J. Fred Helf, Paley and Kendis, T. Mannering, Bennett Scott, Bob Cole, Ben M. Jerome, Frederick W. Hager,

Billy Johnson, George M. Cohan, William H. Penn, J.M. Glover, Jean Schwartz, Bernard Rolt, Matthew Woodward, J. Rosamond Johnson, Albert H. Fitz, Benjamin Hapgood Burt, and James Reece Europe
Musical director, Frederic Solomon
Incidental and dance music arranged by Frederic Solomon (uncredited)
Staging by Herbert Gresham and Ned Wayburn
Ballets by Ernest D'Auban

Mam'selle Napoleon
8 December 1903
Music by Gustav Luders
Musical director (conductor), Herman Perlet
Incidental and dance music arranged by Gustav Luders (uncredited)
Staging by Joseph W. Herbert

The Medal and the Maid
11 January 1904
Music by Sidney Jones
Music for additional songs composed by Paul Rubens, Gus Edwards, S. Stenhammer, and Theodore H. Northrup
Musical director (conductor) Arthur Weld
Music for the "Shoeblack Dance" composed by Sidney Jones (uncredited)
Staging by Cyril Scott
Dances and musical numbers by Tom Terriss

An English Daisy
18 January 1904
Music by Walter Slaughter
Additional music by Alfred Müller-Norden, Gus Edwards, Jerome Kern, Jean Schwartz, Maud Nugent, and J. Rosamond Johnson
Incidental and dance music composed by Alfred Müller-Norden
Staging by Ben Teal

Sergeant Kitty
    18 January 1904
    Music by A. Baldwin Sloane
    Musical director, Carl Burton
    Orchestrations by Frank Saddler
    Dance music arranged by A. Baldwin Sloane (uncredited)
    Staging by R.H. Burnside

Cinderella and the Prince, or, The Castle of Heart's Desire
    1 February 1904
    Music by Louis F. Gottschalk and Edward W. Corliss
    Additional music composed by J.S. Chipman, Daniel J. Sullivan, and D.K. Stevens
    Ballet music composed by Louis F. Gottschalk
    Incidental and dance music arranged by Edward W. Corliss, J.S. Chipman, Daniel J. Sullivan, and D.K. Stevens
    Staging by R.A. Barnet

The Tenderfoot
    22 February 1904
    Music by Harry Lawson Heartz
    Musical director, Fred J. Eustis
    Music for the Chinese dance, "Hop Lee," composed by Harry Lawson Heartz
    Staging by Richard Carle

The Yankee Consul
    22 February 1904
    Music by Alfred G. Robyn
    Musical director (conductor), Frank N. Darling
    Incidental and dance music arranged by Alfred G. Robyn (uncredited)
    Staging by George Marion

The Royal Chef
    1 April 1904
    Music by Ben M. Jerome
    Musical director, Ben M. Jerome
    Incidental and dance music arranged by Ben M. Jerome (un-

credited)
Staging by Frank Smithson

Piff! Paff!! Pouf!!!
2 April 1904
Music by Jean Schwartz
Musical director (conductor), J. Sebastian Hiller
Orchestrations by Frank Saddler
Music for the "Radium Dance" arranged by Jean Schwarz
Staging by Gerald Coventry
Dances by Augustus Sohlke

The Man from China
2 May 1904
Music by John W. Bratton
Musical director (conductor), Gus Salzer
Incidental and dance music arranged by John W. Bratton (uncredited)
Staging by Barney Fagan

The Southerners
23 May 1904
Music by Will Marion Cook
Music for additional songs composed by Egbert Van Alstyne, Marie Sutherland, William Gould, and Albert Von Tilzer
Musical director, Antonio DeNovellis
Music for "The Ballet of the Squirrels" composed by Will Marion Cook (uncredited)
Staging by George W. Lederer
Dances by Joseph C. Smith

A Little of Everything
6 June 1904
Music composed by George M. Cohan, J. Rosamond Johnson, J. Fred Helf, Paul Dresser, Gus Edwards, Stephen Adams, Frederic Solomon, Arthur Penn, James Reese Europe, Mullen, and Harding and Kennedy
Musical director, Frederic Solomon
Dance music arranged by Frederic Solomon (uncredited)

Staging by Herbert Gresham
Dances by Ned Wayburn

Parsifalia
6 June 1904
Music by Oscar Hammerstein
Incidental and dance music arranged by Oscar Hammerstein (uncredited)

The Maid and the Mummy
25 July 1904
Music by Robert Hood Bowers
Music for additional numbers by Richard Carle
Musical director (conductor), Robert Hood Bowers
Musical arrangements by Richard Carle
Incidental and dance music arranged by Robert Hood Bowers (uncredited)
Staged by Richard Carle
Dances and ensembles by Adolph Neuberger

The Isle of Spice
23 August 1904
Music by Paul Schindler and Ben M. Jerome
Musical director (conductor) Paul Schindler
Dance music arranged by Paul Schindler and Ben M. Jerome (uncredited)
Staging and dances by Augustus Sohlke

A Madcap Princess
5 September 1904
Music by Ludwig Englander
Musical director (conductor), Antonio DeNovellis
Incidental and dance music arranged by Ludwig Englander (uncredited)
Staging by Edward P. Temple

The Rogers Brothers in Paris
5 September 1904
Music by Max Hoffmann

Musical director, Max Hoffman
Dance music arranged by Max Hoffmann (uncredited)
Staging by Herbert Gresham
Musical numbers by Ned Wayburn

The Street Singer
12 September 1904
Music adapted by Victor Colwell
Music for additional numbers composed by Ted S. Barron
Musical director, Victor Colwell
Dance music selected and arranged by Victor Colwell (uncredited)
Dances by Emil Hansel

The Sho-Gun
10 October 1904
Music by Gustav Luders
Musical director (conductor) John McGhie
Incidental and dance music arranged by Gustav Luders (uncredited)
Staging by George Marion
Dances by Samuel Marion

Higgledy-Piggledy
20 October 1904
Music by Maurice Levi
Musical director, Maurice Levi
Dance music arranged by Maurice Levi (uncredited)
Staging by George Marion
Dances by Samuel Marion

Little Johnny Jones
7 November 1904
Libretto and music by George M. Cohan
Musical director (conductor) Charles J. Gebest
Orchestrations by Charles J. Gebest
Dance music arranged by Charles J. Gebest (uncredited)
Staging by George M. Cohan

Humpty Dumpty
> 14 November 1904
> Music by Bob Cole, and J. Rosamond Johnson
> Music for additional numbers composed by J.M. Glover, Frederic Solomon, and William H. Penn
> Musical director (conductor), Frederic Solomon
> Dance music arranged by J.M. Glover and Frederic Solomon (uncredited)
> Staging by Herbert Gresham and Ned Wayburn
> Ballets by Ernest D'Auban

A China Doll
> 19 November 1904
> Music by Alfred E. Aarons
> Musical director, Alfred E. Aarons
> Incidental and dance music arranged by Alfred E. Aarons (uncredited)
> Staging by Max Freeman

Lady Teazle
> 24 December 1904
> Music by A. Baldwin Sloane
> Musical director (conductor), Gustave Kerker
> Orchestrations by Frank Saddler
> Dance music arranged by A. Baldwin Sloane (uncredited)
> Staging by R. H. Burnside

Fantana
> 14 January 1905
> Music by Raymond Hubbell
> Music for additional numbers composed by Gertrude Hoffmann
> Musical director, Albert Krausse
> Incidental and dance music arranged by Raymond Hubbell (uncredited)
> Staging by R.H. Burnside

The Duchess of Dantzic
> 16 January 1905

Music by Ivan Caryll
Musical director (conductor), Barter Johns
Music for dances, "Fricassée" and "Minuet," composed by Ivan Caryll (uncredited)
Staging by Holbrook Blinn
Dances and ensembles by Willie Warde

The School for Husbands
3 April 1905
Play by Stanislaus Stange
Incidental music composed by Julian Edwards

A Yankee Circus on Mars / The Raiders
12 April 1905
Music by Manuel Klein and Jean Schwartz
Additional music composed by Arthur Schwartz
Musical director (conductor), Manuel Klein
Music for "Dance of the Hours" ballet from the opera *La Gioconda* by Amilcare Ponchielli
Incidental music composed by Manuel Klein
Staging by Edward P. Temple
Dances by Samuel Marion
Ballets by Vincenzo Romeo

The Rollicking Girl
1 May 1905
Music by W.T. Francis
Additional music composed by John W. Bratton, W. Aletter, Claire Kummer, Edmund Eysler, Ernest R. Ball, and Seymour Furth
Musical director, Gus Salzer
Incidental and dance music composed by W.T. Francis (uncredited)
Staging by Ben Teal

My Tom-Boy Girl
1 May 1905
Original music for choruses and specialties composed and arranged by Wagner Crosby

Musical director, Wagner Crosby
Incidental music composed by Thomas Cutty
Staging by Priestly Morrison

The Pearl and the Pumpkin
21 August 1905
Music by John W. Bratton
Musical director (conductor), A.M. Langstaff
Incidental and dance music arranged by John W. Bratton (uncredited)
Staging by Herbert Gresham and Ned Wayburn

Easy Dawson
22 August 1905
Music by Harry O. Sutton, Raymond A. Brown, Phil Ray, C.W. Murphy, and William Hargreaves
Musical director (conductor), Harry Braham
Incidental and dance music arranged by Harry Braham
Staging by George Marion

The Belle of the West
1 September 1905
Music by Karl Hoschna
Incidental and dance music arranged by Karl Hoschna (uncredited)
Staging by Edward W. Rose

Miss Dolly Dollars
4 September 1905
Music by Victor Herbert
Musical director (conductor), Antonio DeNovellis
Orchestrations by Victor Herbert
Incidental and dance music composed and arranged by Victor Herbert (uncredited)
Additional dance music, the "Pony Galop," composed by Jean Schwartz
Staging by A.M. Holbrook

The Rogers Brothers in Ireland
    4 September 1905
    Music by Max Hoffmann
    Musical director, Max Hoffmann
    Dance music arranged by Max Hoffmann (uncredited)
    Staging by Herbert Gresham and Ned Wayburn

Bankers and Brokers
    4 September 1905
    Music by Gus Salzer
    Musical director, Gene Salzer
    Incidental and dance music arranged by Gus and Gene Salzer (uncredited)
    Musical numbers and ensembles by John P. Kennedy

The Duke of Duluth
    11 September 1905
    Music by Max S. Witt
    Music for additional numbers composed by Gertrude Hoffmann
    Musical director (conductor), Max S. Witt
    Dance music arranged by Max S. Witt (uncrdited)
    Dances and musical numbers by Samuel Marion

Happyland, or, The King of Elysia
    2 October 1905
    Music by Reginald De Koven
    Musical director (conductor), Herman Perlet
    Orchestrations by Reginald De Koven
    Incidental and dance music composed and arranged by Reginald De Koven (uncredited)
    Staging by R.H. Burnside

Squaw Man
    23 October 1905
    Incidental music composed by Theodore Bendix (uncredited)

Wonderland
    24 October 1905
    Music by Victor Herbert

Musical direction (conductor), Carl Styx
Orchestrations by Victor Herbert
Incidental and dance music composed and arranged by Victor Herbert (uncredited)
Staging by Julian Mitchell

Simple Simon Simple
30 October 1905
Music and lyrics by Charles Puerner, Carlos Curti, Theodore Bendix, Rollin Bond, Henry J. Koenig, Bert Howard, and Arndt Morris
Additional music composed by MacArthur, Albert Von Tilzer, Ernest R. Ball, and Varley
Dance music composed by Theodore Bendix (uncredited)
Staging by Lewis Morton
Dances by Joseph Dawson

The White Cat
2 November 1905
Music by Ludwig Englander
Music for additional numbers by Lester Keith, Jean Schwartz, and Philip Braham
Musical director (conductor), Frederic Solomon
Music for "Dance Nouveau" by Frederic Solomon
Music for "The Ballet of Fruits" by Ludwig Englander
Staging by Herbert Gresham and Ned Wayburn
Ballets by Ernest D'Auban

The Earl and the Girl
4 November 1905
Music by Ivan Caryll
Music for additional songs by E. Ray Goetz, Edward Laska, Max C. Eugene, R.A. Browne, William H. Penn, Nat D. Mann, Albert Von Tilzer, and Jerome Kern
Musical director, Clarence West
Original dance music arranged by Ivan Caryll
Dance music arranged by Melville Ellis (uncredited)
Staging by R.H. Burnside

The Mayor of Tokio
    4 December 1905
    Music by William Frederick Peters
    Musical director, Alfred Moulton
    Music for "La Dance Blanche et Noire" ballet composed by William Frederick Peters (uncredited)
    Dances by Adolph Neuberger

A Society Circus
    13 December 1905
    Music by Manuel Klein and Gustav Luders
    Musical director, Manuel Klein
    Music for the ballet, "Song of the Flowers," by Gustav Luders
    Staging by Edward P. Temple
    Dances by Vincenzo Romeo

Mlle. Modiste
    25 December 1905
    Music by Victor Herbert
    Musical director, John Lund
    Orchestrations by Victor Herbert
    Ballet music composed and arranged by Victor Herbert (uncredited)
    Staging by Fred G. Latham

Forty-Five Minutes from Broadway
    1 January 1906
    Libretto and music by George M. Cohan
    Musical director (conductor), Frederic Solomon
    Dance music arranged by Charles J. Gebest (uncredited)
    Staging by George M. Cohan

Coming Thro' the Rye
    9 January 1906
    Music by A. Baldwin Sloane
    Music for additional songs composed by J. Sebastian Hiller, Bob Adams, Paul Schindler, Ted Snyder, Albert Von Tilzer, and Dave Lewis
    Musical director (conductor) Paul Schindler

Music incidental to the burlesque of "Squaw Man" composed
    by Theodore Bendix
Dance music arranged by A. Baldwin Sloane (uncredited)
Staging by Lewis Hooper
Dances by Joseph C. Smith

The Vanderbilt Cup
16 January 1906
Music by Robert Hood Bowers
Musical director (conductor), Robert Hood Bowers
Dance music arranged by Robert Hood Bowers (uncredited)
Staging by Hugh Ford

Mexicana
29 January 1906
Music by Raymond Hubbell
Musical director (conductor), Herman Perlet
Dance music composed by Raymond Hubbell (uncredited)
Staging by R.H. Burnside

The Filibuster
6 February 1906
Music by William Loraine
Dance music arranged by William Loraine (uncredited)

George Washington, Jr.
12 February 1906
Libretto and music by George M. Cohan
Musical director (conductor), Charles J. Gebest
Music arranged by Charles J. Gebest
Dance music arranged by Charles J. Gebest (uncredited)
Staging by George M. Cohan

Abyssinia
20 February 1906
Music by Will Marion Cook and Bert Williams
Music for additional numbers composed by James J. Vaughn
Vocal director, W.C. Elkins
Musical director (conductor), James J. Vaughn

Ballet music arranged by James J. Vaughn (uncredited)
Staging by Alex Rogers and Jesse A. Shipp
Dances by Aida Overton Walker

Brown of Harvard
26 February 1906
Incidental music composed by Melville Ellis

The Social Whirl
9 April 1906
Music by Gustave Kerker
Additional music composed by Anne Caldwell, George A. Spink, Charles J. Ross, and E. Ray Goetz
Musical director (conductor), Gustave Kerker
Incidental and dance music arranged by Gustave Kerker (uncredited)
Staging by R.H. Burnside

The Free Lance
16 April 1906
Libretto and music by John Philip Sousa
Musical director (conductor), Anton Heindl
Orchestrations by John Philip Sousa
Incidental and dance music composed by John Philip Sousa (uncredited)
Staging by Herbert Gresham

His Honor the Mayor
28 May 1906
Music by Julian Edwards
Music for additional songs composed by Alfred E. Aarons, Gus Edwards, and Ren Shields
Musical director, Daniel Dore
Music for "Fougere Dance" composed by Alfred E. Aarons
Music for the "Skipping Rope Dance," composed by Jean Schwartz
Staging by J.S. Murray

Mam'zelle Champagne
    25 June 1906
    Music by Cassius Freeborn
    Musical director, Cassius Freeborn
    Incidental and dance music arranged by Cassius Freeborn
    Staging by Lionel Lawrence

Panhandle Pete
    16 August 1906
    Music by Samuel Lehman
    Musical director, Oscar Goodfriend
    Incidental and dance music arranged by Samuel Lehman (uncredited)

The Tourists
    25 August 1906
    Music by Gustave Kerker
    Musical director (conductor), Gustave Kerker
    Incidental and dance music arranged by Gustave Kerker (uncredited)
    Staging by R.H. Burnside

About Town
    30 August 1906
    Music by Melville Ellis and Raymond Hubbell
    Music for additional numbers composed by Gus Edwards, A. Baldwin Sloane, and Albert Von Tilzer
    Musical director (conductor), William E. MacQuinn
    Incidental and dance music arranged by Melville Ellis (uncredited)
    Staging by Julian Mitchell

The Man from Now
    3 September 1906
    Music by Manuel Klein
    Music for additional numbers composed by Harry Von Tilzer, Harry Bulger, Bernard Rolt, and Gertrude Hoffman
    Musical director (conductor), John McGhie
    Incidental music arranged by Manuel Klein (uncredited)
    Staging by George Marion

The Red Mill
    24 September 1906
    Music by Victor Herbert
    Musical director (conductor), Max Hirschfeld
    Orchestrations by Victor Herbert
    Incidental and dance music composed and arranged by Victor Herbert (uncredited)
    Staging by Fred G. Latham

Popularity
    1 October 1906
    Incidental music composed by George M. Cohan
    Incidental music arranged by Charles J. Gebest

The Spring Chicken
    8 October 1906
    Music by Ivan Caryll and Lionel Monckton
    Music for additional numbers composed by Richard Carle, Robert Hood Bowers, and Milton W. Lusk
    Musical director, Frank Palma
    Original dance music arranged by Ivan Caryll and Lionel Monckton (uncredited)
    Dances by Adolph Neuberger

The Blue Moon
    3 November 1906
    Music by Howard Talbot and Paul A. Rubens
    Music for additional numbers composed by Gus Edwards
    Musical director, Albert Krausse
    Incidental and dance music arranged by Albert Krausse (uncredited)
    Staging by Frank Smithson

A Parisian Model
    27 November 1906
    Music by Max Hoffmann
    Music for additional songs composed by Will D. Cobb, Gus Edwards, Paul Rubens, Vincent Scotto, Seymour Furth, Herman Avery Wade, P.H. Christine, Vincent Bryan, and

Gertrude Hoffmann
Musical director (conductor), Max Hoffmann
Incidental and ballet music arranged by Max Hoffmann (uncredited)
Staging by Julian Mitchell

Pioneer Days / Neptune's Daughter
28 November 1906
Music by Manuel Klein
Musical director, Manuel Klein
Music for "Under the Sea" (ballet) arranged by Manuel Klein (uncredited)
Staging by Edward P. Temple

The Belle of Mayfair
3 December 1906
Music by Leslie Stuart
Musical director (conductor), Antonio DeNovellis
Original dance music arranged by Leslie Stuart
Staging by Harry B. Burcher

Dream City and The Magic Knight
25 December 1906
Music by Victor Herbert
Musical director, Louis F. Gottschalk
Orchestrations by Victor Herbert
Incidental and dance music composed and arranged by Victor Herbert (uncredited)
Staging by A.M. Holbrook

The Student King
25 December 1906
Music by Reginald De Koven
Musical director (conductor), Arthur Weld
Orchestrations by Reginald De Koven
Incidental and dance music composed and arranged by Reginald De Koven (uncredited)
Staging by George Marion

The Road to Yesterday
 31 December 1906
 Incidental music composed by Melville Ellis

The Princess Beggar
 7 January 1907
 Music by Alfred G. Robyn
 Additional music by Edward Montagu and Leo Friedman
 Musical director, Arthur Pell
 Dance music composed by Alfred G. Robyn (uncredited)
 Staging by Frank Smithson

The Tattooed Man
 18 February 1907
 Music by Victor Herbert
 Musical director (conductor), Arthur Weld
 Orchestrations by Victor Herbert
 Incidental and dance music composed and arranged by Victor Herbert (uncredited)
 Staging by Julian Mitchell

The Grand Mogul
 25 March 1907
 Music by Gustav Luders
 Dance music for "Fete Scene and Drill" composed by Gustav Luders
 Staging by Herbert Gresham

The Orchid
 8 April 1907
 Music by Ivan Caryll and Lionel Monckton
 Music for additional numbers composed by Hugo Frey, Seymour Furth, E. Ray Goetz, Paul Rubens, Jerome Kern, Leslie Stuart, Gus Edwards, Dave Reed, Jr., and Junie McCree
 Musical director (conductor), Alexander Spencer
 Music for "Dance of the Orchid" composed by Hugo Frey
 Staging by Frank Smithson

Azara
> 9 April 1907
> Music by John Knowles Paine
> Musical director (conductor), B.J. Lang
> Orchestrations by John Knowles Paine
> Ballet music composed by John Knowles Paine

Fascinating Flora
> 20 May 1907
> Music by Gustave Kerker
> Music for additional songs composed by Jerome Kern, Fred Fisher, A. Baldwin Sloane, Harry O. Sutton, John Kemble, Lester W. Keith, Kerry Mills, Benjamin Hapgood Burt, and Alfred Solman
> Musical director (conductor), Gustave Kerker
> Dance music arranged by Gustave Kerker (uncredited)
> Staging by R.H. Burnside
> Dances by Jack Mason

The Shoo-Fly Regiment
> 3 June 1907
> Music by J. Rosamond Johnson
> Music for additional songs by Bob Cole, James Reese Europe, and Joe Jordan
> Musical director, James Reese Europe
> Music for "Ballet" by James Reese Europe and J. Rosamond Johnson (uncredited)
> Staging by Bob Cole
> Dances by Siren Nevarro

The Yankee Tourist
> 12 August 1907
> Music by Alfred G. Robyn
> Music for additional numbers composed by Jean Schwartz and Edward Montagu
> Musical director (conductor), John McGhie
> Incidental and dance music arranged by Alfred G. Robyn (uncredited)
> Staging by George Marion

The Dairymaids
    26 August 1907
    Music by Paul Rubens and Frank E. Tours
    Music for additional numbers by William T. Francis, J.J. Montaigne, Jerome Kern, James W. Tate, Harry Von Tilzer, Egbert Van Alstyne, E.G. McLellan and Bernard Rolt, and Charles Wilmot and Herman E. Darewski, Jr.
    Musical director, William T. Francis
    Incidental and dance music arranged by William T. Francis (uncredited)
    Dances by Adolph Neuberger

The Rogers Brothers in Panama
    2 September 1907
    Music by Max Hoffmann
    Musical director, John Harding
    Dance music arranged by Max Hoffmann (uncredited)
    Staging by Ben Teal
    Dances by Pat Rooney

Patsy in Politics
    2 September 1907
    Music by Carl Hand
    Musical director, Carl Hand
    Dance music arranged by Carl Hand (uncredited)
    Dances by Al White

The Black Politician
    14 September 1907
    Music by James Reese Europe
    Musical director, James Reese Europe
    Dance music arranged by James Reese Europe (uncredited)

The Hurdy-Gurdy Girl
    23 September 1907
    Music by Harry Lawson Heartz
    Additional music composed by Richard Carle
    Musical director (conductor), Alfred Dalby
    Orchestrations by Robert Hood Bowers and Alfred Dalby

Dance music arranged by Harry Lawson Heartz
Dances by Richard Carle and Adolph Neuberger

The Girl behind the Counter
1 October 1907
Music by Howard Talbot
Music for additional songs composed by Benjamin Hapgood Burt, Kenneth S. Clarke, Paul Lincke, Paul Rubens, Harry Von Tilzer, Herman Avery Wade, and Bert Fitzgibbons
Musical director (conductor), William E. MacQuinn
Ballet music composed by Howard Talbot (uncredited)
Staging by J.C. Huffman and Julian Mitchell

The Gay White Way
7 October 1907
Music by Ludwig Englander
Music for additional numbers composed by Louis A. Hirsch, John Bratton, Leo Edwards, Seymour Furth, and Jean Schwartz
Musical director, Frank P. Paret
Music for "Le Kic-King" (Dance) by Ludwig Englander (uncredited)
Staging by R.H. Burnside
Dances by Ralph Post

Hip! Hip! Hooray!
10 October 1907
Music by Gus Edwards
Musical director (conductor), Anton Heindl
Dance music arranged by Anton Heindl (uncredited)
Staging by Julian Mitchell

The Hoyden
19 October 1907
Music by Paul Rubens, John L. Golden, and Robert Hood Bowers
Musical director, Robert Hood Bowers
Ballet and dance music composed and arranged by Robert Hood Bowers
Staging by Ben Teal

The Top o' th' World
    19 October 1907
    Music by Manuel Klein and Anne Caldwell
    Musical director, Albert Krauss
    Music for "Eccentric Dance" and "Doll Ballet" by Manuel Klein
    Dance music for "Doll Song," "Little Brown Hen," and "The One Girl" by Anne Caldwell (uncredited)
    Staging by Frank Smithson
    Dances by William Rock and Signor Luigi Albertieri

The Merry Widow
    21 October 1907
    Music by Franz Lehár
    Musical director, Louis F. Gottschalk
    Orchestrations by Franz Lehár
    Original dance music composed by Franz Lehár (uncredited)
    Dance music adapted and arranged by Louis F. Gottschalk
    Staging by George Marion

Miss Pocahontas
    28 October 1907
    Music by Dan J. Sullivan, Augustus Barratt, and Carl Wilmore
    Orchestrations by Albert M. Kanrich
    Ballet music composed by Dan J. Sullivan (uncredited)
    Staging by R.A. Barnet
    Dances by John Coleman

Tom Jones
    11 November 1907
    Music by Edward German
    Musical director (conductor), Herman Perlet
    Original dance music arranged by Edward German
    Dance music adapted and arranged by Herman Perlet (uncredited)
    Dances by Dave Marion

The Auto Race
    25 November 1907
    Music by Manuel Klein
    Musical director, Manuel Klein

Music for "The Four Seasons" (Ballet) by Manuel Klein (uncredited)
Dances by Vincenzo Romeo

The Oyster Man
25 November 1907
Music by Will Vodery and Ernest Hogan
Musical director, Will Vodery
Dance music arranged by Will Vodery (uncredited)
Dances, ensembles, and musical numbers by Ernest Hogan

The Talk of New York
3 December 1907
Libretto and music by George M. Cohan
Musical director (conductor), Gus Kleinecke
Orchestrations by Charles J. Gebest
Dance music arranged by Charles J. Gebest (uncredited)
Staging by George M. Cohan

Polly of the Circus
23 December 1907
Incidental and dance music composed by Frederic Solomon

Lonesome Town
20 January 1908
Music by J.A. Raynes
Music for additional numbers composed by Billy Gaston, Theodore Morse, and Will R. Anderson
Musical director (conductor), J.A. Raynes
Dance music arranged by J.A. Raynes (uncredited)
Dances by C. William Kolb and Max M. Dill

The Soul Kiss
28 January 1908
Music by Maurice Levi
Music for additional numbers composed by Louis A. Hirsch, Fleta Ian Brown, Kenneth S. Clark, and C.M. Chapel
Musical director (conductor), Max Schmidt

Dance music arranged by Maurice Levi (uncredited)
Ballet music for Adeline Genée composed by Cuthbert Clarke
Staging by Herbert Gresham and Julian Mitchell
Ballets by Alexander Genée

Bandanna Land
3 February 1908
Music by Will Marion Cook
Music for additional songs composed by J. Leubrie Hill, Chris Smith, F.H. Williams, Joe Jordan, and Bert Williams
Musical director, Will Marion Cook
Music for "Ethiopia" (Ballet) composed by Al Johns
Music for "The Dancing of Salome" composed and arranged by Joe Jordan
Staging by Jesse A. Shipp and Alex Rogers
Dances by Aida Overton Walker

Fifty Miles from Boston
3 February 1908
Libretto and music by George M. Cohan
Musical director (conductor), Al E. Gaylord
Orchestrations by Charles J. Gebest
Music for dances arranged by Charles J. Gebest (uncredited)
Staging by George M. Cohan

Nearly a Hero
24 February 1908
Music by Seymour Furth
Music for additional numbers composed by Edward B. Claypoole, Louis A. Hirsch, Egbert Van Alstyne, Herman Avery Wade, and Harry Von Tilzer
Musical director (conductor), Oscar Radin
Music for "Waltz and Two-Step" (Minuet) by Seymour Furth (uncredited)
Dance music arranged by Melville Ellis (uncredited)
Staging by George Marion and J.C. Huffman
Dances by William Rock

The Yankee Prince
20 April 1908
Libretto and music by George M. Cohan
Musical director (conductor) Charles J. Gebest
Special drum effects by Samuel Avedon
Orchestrations by Charles J. Gebest
Music for dances arranged by Charles J. Gebest
Staging by George M. Cohan

The Gay Musician
18 May 1908
Music by Julian Edwards
Musical director (conductor), Antonio DeNovellis
Dance music for "D'une Coquete" arranged by Julian Edwards (uncredited)
Staging by Julian Edwards
Dances by Roger Gray

The Hermits in Dixie
25 May 1908
Music by John S. Zamecnik
Additional music composed by Henry L. Sanford, Richard S. Spencer, and Albert Rees Davis
Musical director, Frank B. Meade
Incidental and dance music composed by Henry L Sanford and John S. Zamecnik (uncredited)
Staging by A.M. Holbrook

Three Twins
15 June 1908
Music by Karl Hoschna
Musical director (conductor), C. DeWitt Coolman
Incidental and dance music arranged by Karl Hoschna (uncredited)
Staging by Augustus Sohlke

Follies of 1908
15 June 1908
Music by Maurice Levi
Music for additional numbers composed by Albert Von Tilzer,

    Melville Gideon, and Jean Schwartz
    Musical director (conductor), Frederic Solomon
    Music for "Dance Harlequinette", "Dance du Directoire," and "Pony Ballet," by Maurice Levi (uncredited)
    Principals staging by Herbert Gresham
    Ensembles by Julian Mitchell

Algeria
    31 August 1908
    Music by Victor Herbert
    Musical director (conductor), John McGhie
    Orchestrations by Victor Herbert
    Incidental and dance music composed and arranged by Victor Herbert (uncredited)
    Staging by George Marion

Sporting Days
    5 September 1908
    Music and lyrics by Manuel Klein
    Musical director (conductor), Manuel Klein
    Music for the ballet, *The Three Wishes, or The Land of the Birds*, composed by Manuel Klein
    Songs and incidental music for *The Battle of the Skies* composed by Manuel Klein
    Staging by R.H. Burnside

The American Idea
    5 October 1908
    Libretto and music by George M. Cohan
    Music for additional songs composed by Jean Schwartz, Milton W. Lusk, and Charles J. Gebest
    Musical director (conductor), George A. Nichols
    Orchestrations by Charles J. Gebest
    Dance music arranged by Charles J. Gebest (uncredited)
    Staging by George M. Cohan

The Golden Butterfly
    12 October 1908
    Music by Reginald De Koven

Musical director (conductor), Anton Heindl
Orchestrations by Reginald De Koven
Dance and incidental music composed and arranged by Reginald De Koven (uncredited)
Staging by A.M. Holbrook

Little Nemo
20 October 1908
Music by Victor Herbert
Musical director (conductor), Max Hirschfeld
Orchestrations by Victor Herbert
Dance and incidental music composed and arranged by Victor Herbert (uncredited)
Staging by Herbert Gresham

Too Many Wives
2 November 1908
Music by Frederick V. Bowers
Incidental and dance music selected and arranged by Frederick V. Bowers (uncredited)

Miss Innocence
30 November 1908
Music by Ludwig Englander
Music for additional songs composed by Louis A. Hirsch, Nora Bayes, Jack Norworth, Melville J. Gideon, J. Rosamond Johnson, Jean Schwartz, Egbert Van Alstyne, and Gus Edwards
Musical director, Frank Darling
Dance music arranged by Ludwig Englander and Meville J. Gideon (uncredited)
Staging by Julian Mitchell

The Prima Donna
30 November 1908
Music by Victor Herbert
Musical director (conductor), John Lund
Orchestrations by Victor Herbert
Dance and incidental music composed and arranged by Victor

Herbert (uncredited)
Staging by Fred G. Latham

La Chair
4 December 1908
Ballet music composed by Albert Chantrier

Mr. Hamlet of Broadway
23 December 1908
Music by Ben M. Jerome
Musical director (conductor), Ben M. Jerome
Dance music arranged by Ben M. Jerome (uncredited)
Staging by Ned Wayburn

Stubborn Cinderella
25 January 1909
Music by Joseph E. Howard
Musical director (conductor), Arthur Pell
Ballet music for "The Orange Fête" arranged by Carl Stecker (uncredited)
Staging by George Marion

The Fair Co-Ed
1 February 1909
Music by Gustav Luders
Musical director (conductor), Robert Hood Bowers
Incidental and dance music arranged by Gustav Luders (uncredited)
Staging by Fred G. Latham
Dances by William Rock

Havana
11 February 1909
Music by Leslie Stuart
Music for an additional song composed by Frank Leo
Musical director (conductor), Clarence Rogerson
Original dance music composed by Leslie Stuart (uncredited)
Staging by Ned Wayburn

The Newlyweds and Their Baby
    22 March 1909
    Music by Nat D. Ayer and John W. Bratton
    Musical director, Eugene Salzer
    Dance music arranged by Eugene Salzer
    Staging by Frank Smithson
    Dances by Chris Maxwell

The Beauty Spot
    10 April 1909
    Music by Reginald De Koven
    Additional music composed by Cassius Freeborn, A. Baldwin Sloane, Harry Gifford, Melville Gideon, R. Weston and Paul Barnes
    Musical director, Frank P. Paret
    Orchestrations by Reginald De Koven
    Incidental and dance music arranged by Reginald De Koven (uncredited)
    Dances by Julian Alfred

The Red Moon
    3 May 1909
    Music by J. Rosamond Johnson
    Music for additional numbers composed by James Reese Europe and Bob Cole
    Musical director, James Reese Europe
    Music for "War Dance" composed by J. Rosamond Johnson (uncredited)
    Staging by Bob Cole
    Dances by Benny Jones

The Midnight Sons
    22 May 1909
    Music by Raymond Hubbell
    Music for additional numbers composed by Melville Gideon, Maurice Scott, and Paul Lincke
    Musical director (conductor), George A. Nichols
    Music for "The Harlequin Hoops" and "Parasol Dance" composed by Raymond Hubbell (uncredited)

Staging by Ned Wayburn

Follies of 1909
    14 June 1909
    Music by Maurice Levi
    Music for additional songs composed by Gus Edwards, Nora Bayes and Jack Norworth, and Nat D. Ayer
    Musical director (conductor), Frederic Solomon
    Music for "Dance de Maitre de Ballet" and "The Gaiety Dance" composed by Maurice Levi
    Music for "The Dance of the Widow" composed by Lewis F. Muir
    Staging by Herbert Gresham and Julian Mitchell
    Dances by Julian Mitchell

The Motor Girl
    15 June 1909
    Music by Julian Edwards
    Musical director (conductor), Ben M. Jerome
    Dance and incidental music arranged by Julian Edwards (uncredited)
    Staging by Frank Smithson
    Dances by Wellington Cross

The Dollar Princess
    6 August 1909
    Music by Leo Fall
    Music for additional numbers composed by Frank Tours, George Arthurs, and Jerome Kern
    Musical director, W.T. Francis
    Original dance music arranged by Leo Fall
    Dance music adapted and arranged by W.T. Francis (uncredited)
    Staging by J.A.E. Malone

The Love Cure
    1 September 1909
    Music by Edmund Eysler
    Musical director (conductor), Augustus Barratt

Original incidental and dance music arranged by Edmund Eysler (uncredited)
Dance music adapted by Augustus Barratt (uncredited)
Staging by George Marion

A Trip to Japan
4 September 1909
Music and lyrics by Manuel Klein
Musical director (conductor), Manuel Klein
Music for "Ballet of the Jewels" composed by Manuel Klein
Staging by R.H. Burnside
Dances by Vincenzo Romeo

The Rose of Algeria
20 September 1909
Music by Victor Herbert
Musical director (conductor), Theodore Stearns
Orchestrations by Victor Herbert
Dance and incidental music composed and arranged by Victor Herbert (uncredited)
Staging by Ned Wayburn

The Girl and the Wizard
27 September 1909
Music by Julian Edwards
Additional music composed by Melville Gideon, Louis A. Hirsch, Jerome Kern, George Dougherty, and Seymour Furth
Musical director (conductor), Cassius Freeborn
Dance music under the supervision of Melville Ellis (uncredited)
Staging by Ned Wayburn

The Man Who Owns Broadway
11 October 1909
Libretto and music by George M. Cohan
Musical director (conductor), Karl Weiselbaum
Musical arrangements by Charles J. Gebest
Dance music arranged by Charles J. Gebest (uncredited)
Staging by George M. Cohan

Mr. Load of Koal
   1 November 1909
   Music by J. Rosamond Johnson
   Music for additional numbers composed by Leubrie Hill, Al Johns, and Bert Williams
   Musical director (conductor), James J. Vaughn
   Music for "Hodge Podge" (Dance) composed by J. Rosamond Johnson (uncredited)
   Incidental dance music arranged by James J. Vaughn (uncredited)
   Staging by Jesse A. Shipp and Alex Rogers

The Silver Star
   1 November 1909
   Music by Robert Hood Bowers, Karl Hoschna, Albert Gumble, Jean Schwartz, and Herbert Ingraham
   Musical director, C.J.M. Glaser
   Conductor, Robert Hood Bowers
   Music for "Dancing the Cotillion" by Raymond Hubbell
   Music for "The Cooney Spooney Dance" by Jean Schwartz
   Music for "Fairy Dance," "March Militaire," "Horn Pipe," "The Spirit of Champagne," and "Springtime" (Ballet) composed by C.J.M. Glaser
   Staging by Herbert Gresham
   Dances by Julian Mitchell
   Ballets by Alexander Genée

The Flirting Princess
   1 November 1909
   Music by Joseph E. Howard and Harold Orlob
   Orchestrations by Hilding Anderson
   Incidental and dance music arranged by Harold Orlob (uncredited)

Seven Days
   10 November 1909
   Incidental music composed by Theodore Bendix (uncredited)

Old Dutch
    22 November 1909
    Music by Victor Herbert
    Musical director (conductor), Louis F. Gottschalk
    Orchestrations by Victor Herbert
    Dance and incidental music composed and arranged by Victor Herbert (uncredited)
    Staging by Ned Wayburn

The Jolly Bachelors
    6 January 1910
    Music by Raymond Hubbell
    Additional music composed by Albert Von Tilzer, C.W. Murphy, Will Letters, Ted Snyder, Nora Bayes, and Jack Norworth
    Musical director, Melville Ellis
    Conductor, George A. Nichols
    Orchestrations by Frank Saddler
    Incidental and dance music selected and arranged by Melville Ellis (uncredited)
    Staging by Ned Wayburn

Ragged Robin
    24 January 1910
    Music for musical numbers composed by Chauncey Olcott, Daniel J. Sullivan, Ernest R. Ball, George Spunk, and Manuel Klein
    Musical director, Frederick Knight Logan
    Incidental music for the fairy scenes composed by Frederick Knight Logan
    Staging by Augustus Pitou

Bright Eyes
    28 February 1910
    Music by Karl Hoschna
    Music for additional numbers composed by Florence Holbrook
    Musical director (conductor), Earl Schwartz
    Incidental and dance music arranged by Karl Hoschna (uncredited)
    Staging by Frederick A. Bishop

A Skylark
4 April 1910
Music by Frank G. Dossert
Musical director, Theodore Bendix
Incidental and dance music arranged by Theodore Bendix (uncredited)
Staging by Ben Teal
Dances by David Bennett

A Matinee Idol
25 April 1910
Music by Silvio Hein
Musical director, Albert Krausse
Incidental and dance music composed by Silvio Hein (uncredited)
Staging by Daniel V. Arthur

Tillie's Nightmare
5 May 1910
Music by A. Baldwin Sloane
Additional music composed by John L. Golden
Musical director (conductor), George A. Nichols
Music for "Spook Dance" arranged by Melville Ellis (uncredited)
Staging by Ned Wayburn

The Summer Widowers
4 June 1910
Music by A. Baldwin Sloane
Music for additional numbers composed by Burton Green, Irene Franklin, and Paul Lincke
Musical director (conductor), George A. Nichols
Orchestrations by Frank Saddler
Ballet music supervised by Melville Ellis (uncredited)
Staging and dances by Ned Wayburn

Girlies
13 June 1910
Music by Egbert Van Alstyne

Music for additional songs composed by Benjamin Hapgood Burt,
Musical director (conductor), Charles J. Gebest
Musical arrangements by Charles J. Gebest
Dance music arranged by Charles J. Gebest (uncredited)
Staging by Frederick Thompson
Dances and ensembles by Jack Mason

Follies of 1910
20 June 1910
Music by Gus Edwards, Irving Berlin, Harry Carroll, Ford Dabney, Will Marion Cook, Bert Williams, Lewis F. Muir, Victor Hollander, Joe Jordan, and Harry Von Tilzer
Musical director (conductor), Frank Darling
Incidental musical arrangements for "Our American Colleges" by Maurice Levi
Dance music selected and arranged by Frank Darling (uncredited)
Staging by Julian Mitchell

Up and Down Broadway
18 July 1910
Music by Jean Schwartz
Music for additional numbers composed by Albert Von Tilzer, Ted Snyder, Louis A. Hirsch, and Melville Gideon
Musical director (conductor), Oscar Radin
Music for the duet and dance, "The Dope Fiend," composed by Melville Ellis
Staging by William J. Wilson

The Commuters
15 August 1910
Incidental music composed by Theodore Bendix (uncredited)

The Echo
17 August 1910
Music by Deems Taylor
Music for additional numbers composed by James R. Brewers and Edward B. Claypoole, Nat D. Ayer, George Arthurs, Karl Hoschna, Jerome Kern, and Al Piantadosi

Musical director (conductor), DeWitt C. Coolman
Music for song and dance, "The Newport Glide," by Jean Schwartz
Music for song and dance, "The Yankee Doodle Guards," composed by DeWitt C. Coolman
Staging by Fred G. Latham
Dances by William Rock

Our Miss Gibbs
29 August 1910
Music by Ivan Caryll and Lionel Monckton
Music for additional numbers composed by Jerome Kern, Clarke, Harry Marlowe, George Arthurs, and Harold Lonsdale
Musical director (conductor), W.T. Francis
Original dance music arranged by Ivan Caryll
Dance music adapted and arranged by W.T. Francis (uncredited)
Staging by Thomas Reynolds

Madame Sherry
30 August 1910
Original music by Hugo Felix
New music by Karl Hoschna
Music for additional numbers composed by Phil Schwartz and Harry Von Tilzer
Musical director (conductor), Hans S. Linné
Incidental music composed by Hugo Felix
Dance music arranged by Karl Hoschna (uncredited)
Staging by George W. Lederer

The International Cup
3 September 1910
Music by Manuel Klein
Musical director (conductor), Manuel Klein
Music for the ballet, "Niagara," composed by Manuel Klein
Music for the melodrama, "The Earthquake," composed by Manuel Klein
Staging by R.H. Burnside
Dances by Vincenzo Romeo

He Came from Milwaukee
21 September 1910
Music by Louis A. Hirsch and Ben M. Jerome
Additional music composed by Ted Snyder
Musical director (conductor), Ben M. Jerome
Incidental and dance music arranged by Melville Ellis
Staging by Sydney Ellison

The Silver Bottle
10 October 1910
Music by Samuel Lehman
Musical director, Samuel Lehman
Incidental and dance music arranged by Samuel Lehman (uncredited)

The Bachelor Belles
7 November 1910
Music by Raymond Hubbell
Musical director (conductor) Albert Krausse
Orchestrations by Frank Saddler
Dance music for "Roses and Butterflies" adapted from the music of Charles Gounod, Claude Debussy, and Moritz Moszkowski, and arranged by C.J.M. Glaser
Staging by Julian Mitchell

Naughty Marietta
7 November 1910
Music by Victor Herbert
Musical director (conductor), Gaetano Merola
Orchestrations by Victor Herbert
Incidental and dance music composed and arranged by Victor Herbert (uncredited)
Dances by Pauline Verhoeven

The Spring Maid
26 December 1910
Music by Heinrich Reinhardt
Additional music composed by Robert Hood Bowers
Musical director (conductor), Max Bendix

Ballet and melodramatic music arranged by Robert Hood Bowers
Staging by George Marion

The Hen-Pecks
4 February 1911
Music by A. Baldwin Sloane
Music for additional numbers by Jerome Kern and Herman Finck
Musical director (conductor), George A. Nichols
Orchestrations by Frank Saddler
Dance music arranged by Herman Finck (uncredited)
Staging by Ned Wayburn

The Pink Lady
13 March 1911
Music by Ivan Caryll
Musical director (conductor) Arthur Weld
Original Incidental and dance music arranged by Ivan Caryll
Dance music adapted and arranged by Arthur Weld (uncredited)
Staging by Herbert Gresham
Musical numbers by Julian Mitchell

La Belle Paree
20 March 1911
Music composed by Jerome Kern and Frank Tours
Music for additional numbers composed by Billee Taylor and Aubrey Stauffer
Music for the Chinese Fantasy opera *Bow-Sing* composed by Manuel Klein
Musical director, Manuel Klein
Ballet music for *Bow-Sing* arranged by Manuel Klein (uncredited)
Incidental and dance music for *La Belle Paree* arranged by Frank Tours and Melville Ellis (uncredited)
Staging by J.C. Huffman and William J. Wilson
Dances by William J. Wilson

Hell / Temptations / Gaby
27 April 1911
Music for *Hell* composed by Robert Hood Bowers, Maurice Levi, Irving Berlin, Ted Snyder, and Vincent Bryan
Dance music composed and arranged by Maurice Levi
Music for the ballet *Temptations* composed by Edmond Diet
Musical director (conductor), Charles Berton
Music for *Gaby* composed by Robert Hood Bowers, Irving Berlin, Ted Snyder, Vincent Bryan, and Bernard Rolt and E.G. McLellan
Musical director (conductor), Daniel Dore
Dance music composed and arranged by Robert Hood Bowers
Staging by George Marion
Ballets and ensembles by Alfredo Curti

The Heartbreakers
30 May 1911
Music by Harold Orlob and Melville Gideon
Additional music composed by Sadie Harrison, Phil Schwartz, and Stephen Jones
Musical director, Hilding Anderson
Incidental and dance music arranged by Harold Orlob, Melville Gideon, and Hilding Anderson

The Red Rose
22 June 1911
Music by Robert Hood Bowers
Musical director (conductor), Louis F. Gottschalk
Ballet music composed and arranged by Robert Hood Bowers (uncredited)
Staging by R.H. Burnside
Dances by Jack Mason

Ziegfeld Follies of 1911
26 June 1911
Music by Maurice Levi and Raymond Hubbell
Music for additional numbers composed by James B. Blyler, Sid Brown, Irving Berlin, Vincent Bryan, Jerome Kern, Bert Williams, Seymour Furth, and Ivan Caryll

Musical director (conductor), Joseph Sainton
Dance music composed and arranged by Raymond Hubbell and Maurice Levi (uncredited)
Staging by Julian Mitchell
Dances by Augustus Sohlke and Jack Mason

Hello, Paris
19 August 1911
Music by J. Rosamond Johnson
Music for additional numbers composed by A. Baldwin Sloane and Ned Wayburn Music for burlesque, *A La Broadway*, composed by Harold Orlob
Musical director, Charles Berton
Music for "Dance Grotesque" composed by J. Rosamond Johnson
Music for the dance, "The Frisco Fritz," composed by Ned Wayburn
Music for "The Philadelphia Drag" composed by Harold Orlob
Staging by Ned Wayburn

The Apple of Paris
21 August 1911
Music by Daniel Doré
Musical director, Eugene Salzer
Pantomime and ballet music composed by Daniel Doré

Around the World
2 September 1911
Music and lyrics by Manuel Klein
Musical director, Manuel Klein
Incidental and ballet music composed and arranged by Manuel Klein (uncredited)
Staging by Carroll Fleming
Ensembles by William J. Wilson

Miss Jack
4 September 1911
Music by William Frederick Peters
Musical director, William Frederick Peters

Incidental and ballet music arranged by William Frederick Peters
Staging by Lewis Morton
Musical numbers and ensembles by Bothwell Browne

The Fascinating Widow
11 September 1911
Music by Frederick W. Mills
Music for additional numbers composed by Irving Berlin and Vincent Bryan
Musical director (conductor), August Kleinecke
Orchestrations by William M. Redfield
Dance and incidental music arranged by Frederick W. Mills and August Kleinecke (uncredited)
Staging by George Marion
Dances by Jack Mason

When Sweet Sixteen
14 September 1911
Music by Victor Herbert
Musical director (conductor), Frederick Schwartz
Orchestrations by Victory Herbert
Incidental and dance music composed and arranged by Victor Herbert (uncredited)
Staging by R.H. Burnside

The Little Millionaire
25 September 1911
Libretto and music by George M. Cohan
Musical director, Karl Weixelbaum
Incidental and dance music arranged by Charles J. Gebest (uncredited)
Staging by George M. Cohan
Ensembles by James Gorman

The Revue of Revues
27 September 1911
Music for *In the Limelight* composed by Louis A. Hirsch and Melville Gideon

Musical director (conductor), Silvio Hein
Music for "The Rushing Ballet" composed by Melville Gideon
Music for the Japanese pantomime ballet, "Nel Giappone," composed by Louis Ganne
Incidental music for *Le Débuts de Chichine* arranged by Albert Chantrier
Dances by Augustus Sohlke and William J. Wilson

The Great Name
4 October 1911
Play by James Clarence Harvey
Incidental music composed by Theodore Bendix (uncredited)

The Duchess
16 October 1911
Music by Victor Herbert
Musical director (conductor), John McClure
Orchestrations by Victor Herbert
Incidental and dance music composed and arranged by Victor Herbert (uncredited)
Staging by J.C. Huffman
Dances and musical numbers by William J. Wilson and Augustus Sohlke

The Enchantress
19 October 1911
Music by Victor Herbert
Musical director (conductor), Gus Salzer
Orchestrations by Victor Herbert
Incidental and dance music composed and arranged by Victor Herbert (uncredited)
Staging by Fred G. Latham
Dances and ensembles by Frederic A. Bishop

The Wife Hunters
2 November 1911
Music by Anatole Friedland and Malvin Franklin
Musical director (conductor), Orean Smith
Music for "Specialty Dance," "Pas de Seul," and "The Waltz of

the Wild" composed by Malvin Franklin
Music for "Swinging with Someone" and "Little Dancing Jumping Jigger" composed by Anatole Friedland
Staging and dances by Ned Wayburn

The Red Widow
6 November 1911
Music by Charles J. Gebest
Musical director (conductor), Charles J. Gebest
Incidental and dance music composed and arranged by Charles J. Gebest (uncredited)
Staging by Fred G. Latham
Ballets and marches by James Gorman

Vera Violetta
20 November 1911
Music by Edmund Eysler
Additional music composed by Louis A. Hirsch, Melville Ellis, George M. Cohan, and Jean Schwartz
Musical director (conductor), Samuel Lehman
Original dance music composed by Edmund Eysler (uncredited)
Incidental and dance music adapted and arranged by Melville Ellis (uncredited)
Staging by Lewis Morton
Dances by William J. Wilson and Joseph C. Smith

Undine
20 November 1911
Libretto and music by Manuel Klein
Musical director (conductor), Samuel Lehman
Incidental and dance music composed and arranged by Manuel Klein (uncredited)

The Wedding Trip
25 December 1911
Music by Reginald De Koven
Musical director, Frank E. Tours
Orchestrations by Reginald De Koven

Incidental and dance music composed and arranged by Reginald De Koven (uncredited)
Staging by William J. Wilson

Treemonisha
1911
Music by Scott Joplin
Incidental and dance music arranged by Scott Joplin

Modest Suzanne
1 January 1912
Music by Jean Gilbert
Additional music by Jean Schwartz
Musical director, Louis F. Gottschalk
Original dance music composed by Jean Gilbert
Staging by George Marion

Over the River
9 January 1912
Music (also lyrics) by John L. Golden
Additional music composed by Elsie Janis, Charles Grant, William H. Penn, Jean Schwartz, Egbert Van Alstyne, Charles Eggett, Edward J. Griffin, and Henry B. Murtagh
Musical director, DeWitt Coolman
Dance music composed and arranged by William H. Penn, and DeWitt Coolman (uncredited)
Staging by R.H. Burnside

Hokey-Pokey
8 February 1912
Music by John Stromberg, A. Baldwin Sloane, and W.T. Francis
Music for additional songs composed by Jean Schwartz, Neil Moret and E.C. Jones, Irving Berlin, E. Ray Goetz, and Bert Grant
Musical director (conductor), George A. Nichols
Incidental and dance music arranged by A. Baldwin Sloane and W.T. Francis (uncredited)
Staging by Augustus Sohlke

The Whirl of Society
>5 March 1912
>Music by Louis A. Hirsch, Irving Berlin, Harry Von Tilzer, James V. Monaco, Lewis F. Muir, and Harry Carroll and Arthur Fields
>Music for *Sesostra*, an operatic melodrama, by Henri Hirschmann
>Music for the Oriental fantasy, *The Captive*, composed by Theodore Bendix
>Additional music for *The Captive* composed by Louis A. Hirsch
>Musical director (conductor), Samuel Lehman
>Incidental and dance music supervised by Melville Ellis (uncredited)
>Staging by J.C. Huffman

A Winsome Widow
>11 April 1912
>Music by Raymond Hubbell
>Music for additional numbers composed by Henry I. Marshall, Jean Schwartz, Gus Edwards, and Griffin and Murtagh
>Musical director, Frank N. Darling
>Incidental and dance music arranged by Raymond Hubbell and Frank N. Darling (uncredited)
>Staging by Julian Mitchell

The Wall Street Girl
>15 April 1912
>Music by Karl Hoschna
>Music for additional songs composed by Al Piantadosi, Nathaniel D. Ayer, Benjamin Hapgood Burt, Jean Schwartz, Henry I. Marshall, M.J. Fitzpatrick, and Earl Jones and Charles Daniels
>Musical director (conductor), William Loraine
>Music for "The Indian Rag" composed by Nathaniel D. Ayer
>Dance music arranged by William Loraine (uncredited)
>Staging by Charles Winninger
>Dances by Augustus Sohlke

Let George Do It
>22 April 1912
>Music and lyrics by Paul West and Nathaniel D. Ayer

Music for additional numbers composed by George W. Meyer and William Cahill
Musical director, Eugene Salzer
Music for "The Dramatic Rag" composed by Nathaniel D. Ayer
Dance music arranged by Eugene Salzer (uncredited)
Staging by A.M. Holbrook

Mama's Baby Boy
25 April 1912
Music by Hans S. Linné
Music for additional songs by Will H. Becker
Musical director (conductor), Hans S. Linné
Incidental and dance music composed and arranged by Hans S. Linné (uncredited)
Staging by George W. Lederer
Dances by Julian Alfred

The Passing Show of 1912 / The Ballet of 1830
22 July 1912
Music by Louis A. Hirsch
Music for additional numbers composed by Irving Berlin, Al Piantadosi, and Harold Orlob
Musical director (conductor), Samuel Lehman
Orchestrations by Oscar Radin and Frank Saddler
Ballet music arranged by George Bing from the music of French composers
Dance music for "All the World Is Madly Prancing," "The Spark of Life" (a descriptive dance), "The Bacchanal Rag," and "My Reuben Girlie" composed by Louis A. Hirsch (uncredited)
Staging and dances by Ned Wayburn
Ballets by Theodore Kosloff

The Merry Countess
20 August 1912
Music by Johann Strauss, Jr.
Additional music composed by Melville Ellis, Joseph H. McKeon, Napoleon Laubelet, and Arthur Gutman
Musical director (conductor), Oscar Radin

Dance music selected, composed, and arranged by Melville Ellis
Dances by Emile Agoust

Under Many Flags
31 August 1912
Music and lyrics by Manuel Klein
Musical director (conductor), Manuel Klein
Incidental and ballet music composed by Manuel Klein (uncredited)
Staging by Carroll Fleming
Musical numbers and ensembles by William J. Wilson

My Best Girl
12 September 1912
Music by Augustus Barratt and Clifton Crawford
Additional music composed by Irving Berlin and Jean Schwartz
Musical director (conductor), Augustus Barratt
Incidental and dance music arranged by Augustus Barratt (uncredited)
Staging by Sydney Ellison

An Aztec Romance
16 September 1912
Music by Harold Orlob
Musical director, Harold Orlob
Incidental and dance music composed by Harold Orlob (uncredited)
Staging by Charles B. Hanford

Tantalizing Tommy
2 October 1912
Music by Hugo Felix
Musical director (conductor), Hans S. Linné
Incidental and dance music composed and arranged by Hugo Felix
Staging by George Marion

Ziegfeld Follies of 1912
21 October 1912
Music by Raymond Hubbell

Music for additional numbers composed by James V. Monaco, Bert Grant, Leo Edwards, Bert Williams, and Jean Schwartz
Musical director (conductor), Frank Darling
Orchestrations by Frank Saddler
Dance music arranged by Raymond Hubbell and Frank Darling (uncredited)
Staging by Julian Mitchell

The Lady of the Slipper
28 October 1912
Music by Victor Herbert
Musical director (conductor), William E. McQuinn
Orchestrations by Victor Herbert
Incidental and dance music by Victor Herbert (uncredited)
Staging by R.H. Burnside

The Red Petticoat
13 November 1912
Music by Jerome Kern
Musical director (conductor), Clarence West
Orchestrations by Frank Saddler
Incidental and dance music composed by Jerome Kern (uncredited)
Staging by Joseph W. Herbert

(From) Broadway to Paris
20 November 1912
Music by Max Hoffmann
Music for additional songs by Bobby Jones and Lewis F. Muir
Musical director (conductor), Max Hoffmann
Music for production number, "Everybody Loves a Chicken" composed by Bobby Jones
Music for the production number, "Take Me to That Swanee Shore," composed by Lewis F. Muir
Incidental and dance music composed by Max Hoffmann (uncredited)
Staging and dances by Ned Wayburn

The Firefly
2 December 1912
Music by Rudolf Friml
Musical director (conductor), Gaetano Merola
Incidental and dance music composed by Rudolf Friml (uncredited)
Staging by Fred G. Latham
Dances by Signor Luigi Albertieri

Frivolous Geraldine
22 December 1912
Music by Joseph E. Howard and Herbert Stothart
Musical director, Herbert Stothart
Incidental and dance music arranged by Herbert Stothart (uncredited)

The Sunshine Girl
3 February 1913
Music by Paul Rubens
Additional music by John Golden
Musical director, Augustus Barratt
Dance music composed by Paul Rubens and Dan H. Caslar
Staging by J.A.E. Malone

The Honeymoon Express
6 February 1913
Music by Jean Schwartz
Music for additional numbers composed by Al W. Brown and Al Jolson
Musical director (conductor), Oscar Radin
Orchestrations by Frank Saddler
Ballet music for "The Oriental Bacchanale" adapted from Alexander Borodin under the supervision of Melville Ellis (uncredited)
Staging by Ned Wayburn

The American Maid
3 March 1913
Libretto and music by John Philip Sousa

Musical director (conductor), Herbert Kerr
Orchestrations by John Philip Sousa
Incidental and dance music composed by John Philip Sousa (uncredited)
Staging by George Marion

The Orphan and the Octopus
10 April 1913
Music by Herbert Stothart
Musical director, Dexter R. Mapel
Incidental and dance music composed and arranged by Herbert Stothart (uncredited)
Staging by W.M. Lowrie

All Aboard
5 June 1913
Music by E. Ray Goetz and Malvin Franklin.
Additional music composed by Irving Berlin, Jack Glogau, and Joaquin Valverde
Musical director, DeWitt C. Coolman
Dance music arrangements supervised by Melville Ellis
Staging by William J. Wilson and W.H. Post
Dances by William J. Wilson

Ziegfeld Follies of 1913
16 June 1913
Music by Raymond Hubbell
Music for additional songs composed by Dave Stamper and Leo Edwards
Musical director (conductor), Frank Darling
Dance music for "Cupid's Dart" composed by Louis Dannenberg
Dance music for "Tangoitis," "Turkish Trottishness," and " Classiceccentrique" composed by Raymond Hubbell
Staging by Julian Mitchell

The Passing Show of 1913
24 July 1913
Music by Jean Schwartz and Albert W. Brown
Additional music composed by Harry Von Tilzer

Musical director (conductor), Oscar Radin
Orchestrations by Frank Saddler
Dance music for "(That) Good Old-Fashioned Cakewalk" by Jean Schwartz and Albert W. Brown
Ballet music arranged under the supervision of Melville Ellis (uncredited)
Staging by Ned Wayburn

When Dreams Come True
18 August 1913
Music by Silvio Hein
Additional music composed by Roy Webb
Musical director, Hilding Anderson
Dance music composed by Silvio Hein
Staging by Frank Smithson
Dances by Joseph Santley

America
30 August 1913
Music by Manuel Klein
Musical director, Manuel Klein
Incidental and dance music composed by Manuel Klein (uncredited)
Staging by William J. Wilson

Sweethearts
8 September 1913
Music by Victor Herbert
Musical director (conductor), John McGhie
Orchestrations by Victor Herbert
Incidental and dance music composed by Victor Herbert (uncredited)
Staging by Fred G. Latham
Dances and ensembles by Charles S. Morgan, Jr.

A Broadway Honeymoon
3 October 1913
Music by Joseph E. Howard and Herbert Stothart
Musical director, Herbert Stothart

Incidental and dance music arranged by Herbert Stothart (uncredited)

Her Little Highness
13 October 1913
Music by Reginald De Koven
Musical director (conductor), Max Bendix
Orchestrations by Reginald De Koven
Incidental and dance music composed by Reginald De Koven (uncredited)
Staging by George Marion
Dances by Julian Mitchell

Oh, I Say!
30 October 1913
Music by Jerome Kern
Music for additional numbers composed by Jean Gilbert
Musical director (conductor), Alfred Bendell
Orchestrations by Frank Saddler
Dance music for "The Old Clarinet" composed by Jean Gilbert
Dance and incidental music arranged under the supervision of Melville Ellis (uncredited)
Staging by J.C. Huffman
Dances by Julian Alfred

The Little Café
10 November 1913
Music by Ivan Caryll
Musical director (conductor), Anton Heindl
Original incidental and dance music arranged by Ivan Caryll
Dance music adapted and arranged by Anton Heindl (uncredited)
Staging by Herbert Gresham
Ensembles by Julian Mitchell

The Madcap Duchess
11 November 1913
Music by Victor Herbert
Musical director (conductor), Robert Hood Bowers

Orchestrations by Victor Herbert
Incidental and dance music composed by Victor Herbert (uncredited)
Staging by Fred G. Latham
Dances by Gilbert Clayton

Hop o' My Thumb
26 November 1913
Music by Manuel Klein
Musical direction (conductor), Manuel Klein
Musical arrangements by Manuel Klein
Ballet music composed by J.M. Glover
Staging and dances by Ernest D'Auban
Ballets by Maude Crompton

The Darling of Paris
15 December 1913
Music by Dave Vining
Dance music composed by Melville Ellis

High Jinks
12 January 1914
Music by Rudolf Friml
Music for additional numbers composed by George L. Cobb
Musical director (conductor), Paul Schindler
Incidental and dance music composed by Rudolf Friml (uncredited)
Staging by Frank Smithson

The Whirl of the World
14 January 1914
Music by Sigmund Romberg
Music for additional numbers composed by Edward Laska, Harry Gifford, and Fred Godfrey
Musical director (conductor), Oscar Radin
Music for the dance divertissements, "A Broadway in Paree," "The Dance of the Fortune Wheel," and "Harlequin and Bluebird" composed by Sigmund Romberg
Staging by William J. Wilson

Shameen Dhu
> 2 February 1914
> Music by Chauncey Olcott, Ernest R. Ball, Cassius Freeborn, and James Royce Shannon
> Musical director (conductor), Cassius Freeborn
> Incidental music composed by Cassius Freeborn
> Staging by Henry Miller

The Beauty Shop
> 13 April 1914
> Music by Charles J. Gebest
> Additional music composed by Dave Stamper and Silvio Hein
> Musical director (conductor), Charles J. Gebest
> Incidental and dance music composed by Charles J. Gebest (uncredited)
> Staging by R.H. Burnside

Madam Moselle
> 23 May 1914
> Music by Ludwig Englander
> Additional music composed by William P. Chase
> Musical director (conductor), August Kleinecke
> Dance music arranged by Ludwig Englander and August Kleinecke (uncredited)
> Staging by George W. Lederer
> Dances by Allan K. Foster

Ziegfeld Follies of 1914
> 1 June 1914
> Music by Raymond Hubbell
> Music for additional numbers by Bert Williams, Dave Stamper, A. Seymour Brown, and J. Leubrie Hill
> Musical director (conductor), Frank N. Darling
> Incidental and dance music composed by Raymond Hubbell and Frank N. Darling (uncredited)
> Staging by Leon Errol

The Passing Show of 1914
> 10 June 1914
> Music by Sigmund Romberg and Harry Carroll
> Additional music composed by Gus Edwards and Louis Silvers
> Musical director (conductor), Oscar Radin
> Orchestrations by Frank Saddler, Saul P. Levy, and Hilding Anderson
> Incidental and ballet music selected and arranged by Melville Ellis
> Music for Marilyn Miller's ballet composed by Francis Thomé (uncredited) and arranged by Melville Ellis
> Staging by J.C. Huffman
> Dances and musical numbers by Jack Mason

The Manicure Girl
> 29 June 1914
> Music by Herbert Stothart
> Musical director, Herbert Stothart
> Incidental and dance music arranged by Herbert Stothart (uncredited)

The Dancing Duchess
> 19 August 1914
> Music by Milton Lusk
> Musical director (conductor), John McGhie
> Orchestrations by Otto Meorz and Frank Saddler
> Incidental and dance music arranged by Milton Lusk (uncredited)
> Staging by R.H. Burnside
> Dances by Vera Maxwell

The Girl from Utah
> 24 August 1914
> Music by Paul Rubens
> Music for additional numbers composed by Jerome Kern, Herman Finck, Sidney Jones, Harry Castling, and Worton David
> Musical director (conductor), Gus Salzer
> Dance music composed by Chris Smith
> Staging by J.A.E. Malone

Wars of the World
    5 September 1914
    Music and lyrics by Manuel Klein
    Musical director (conductor), Manuel Klein
    Incidental and dance music composed and arranged by Manuel Klein (uncredited)
    Staging by William J. Wilson

Dancing Around
    10 October 1914
    Music by Sigmund Romberg and Harry Carroll
    Additional music composed by Jean Gilbert, Maurice Abrahams, Harry Robe, Herman Darewski, Grace LeRoy, Irving Berlin, Archie Gottler, and Arthur Lange
    Musical director (conductor), Oscar Radin
    Orchestrations by Oscar Radin and Frank Saddler
    Ballet and dance music selected and arranged by Melville Ellis
    Staging by J.C. Huffman
    Dances by Jack Mason

Experience
    27 October 1914
    Songs and cabaret music by Silvio Hein
    Musical director (conductor), Carlo Edwards
    Incidental music composed by Max Bendix
    Staging by George V. Hobart and J.C. Hufman

The Battle Cry
    31 October 1914
    Incidental music composed by Manuel Klein

The Debutante
    7 December 1914
    Music by Victor Herbert
    Musical director (conductor) Carlo Edwards
    Orchestrations by Victor Herbert
    Incidental and dance music composed by Victor Herbert (uncredited)

Staging by George Marion
Dances by Allan K. Foster

Watch Your Step
8 December 1914
Music and lyrics by Irving Berlin
Music for additional numbers composed by Ted Snyder and E. Ray Goetz
Musical director, DeWitt Coolman
Orchestrations by Frank Saddler
Dance music arranged by DeWitt Coolman (uncredited)
Staging by R.H. Burnside
Dances by Vernon and Irene Castle

The New Henrietta
22 December 1914
Incidental music composed by Thomas W. Hindley

Hello, Broadway!
25 December 1914
Music and lyrics by George M. Cohan
Musical director (conductor), Charles J. Gebest
Dance music arranged by Charles J. Gebest (uncredited)
Staging by George M. Cohan
Dances by James Gorman and Ned Wayburn

90 in the Shade
25 January 1915
Music by Jerome Kern
Music for additional numbers composed by Clare Kummer and P.H. Christine
Musical director (conductor) John McGhie
Music for "Courtship de Dance" composed by Jerome Kern
Staging by Robert Milton
Dances and ensembles by Julian Alfred

Maid in America
18 February 1915
Music by Sigmund Romberg and Harry Carroll

Music for additional numbers composed by Leo Edwards, Nora Bayes, Tom Mellor, Harry Gifford, and Joe Jordan
Musical director (conductor), Oscar Radin
Music for "The Ballet of Color and Motion" composed by Sigmund Romberg
Additional incidental and dance music arranged by Melville Ellis (uncredited)
Staging by J.C. Huffman
Musical numbers by Jack Mason

The Peasant Girl
2 March 1915
Music by Oskar Nedbal
Music for additional numbers composed by Rudolf Friml and Clifton Crawford
Dance music composed by Rudolf Friml (uncredited)
Staging by J.C. Huffman and J.H. Benrimo
Ensembles by Jack Mason

Fads and Fancies
8 March 1915
Music by Raymond Hubbell
Music for additional numbers composed by Jerome Kern
Musical director (conductor), Raymond Hubbell
Incidental and dance music composed by Raymond Hubbell (uncredited)
Staging by Herbert Gresham
Musical numbers by Julian Mitchell

All over Town
26 April 1915
Music by Silvio Hein
Musical director, Robert Hood Bowers
Dance music arranged by Silvio Hein (uncredited)
Staging by J.C. Huffman
Dances by Jack Mason

Nobody Home
20 April 1915

Music by Jerome Kern
Additional music composed by Otto Motzan, C.W. Murphy, and Dan Lipton
Musical director (conductor), Max Hirschfeld
Orchestrations by Frank Saddler
Incidental and dance music composed by Jerome Kern and Otto Motzan (uncredited)
Staging by J.H. Benrimo
Dances by David Bennett

The Passing Show of 1915
29 May 1915
Music by Leo Edwards
Additional numbers composed by William F. Peters, Maurice Abrahams, J. Leubrie Hill, Phil Schwartz, Harold Atteridge, Bobby Jones, and Will Morrissey
Musical director (conductor), Oscar Radin
Music for "The Spring Ballet" composed and performed by Rodion Mendelvitch
Additional dance music arranged by Leo Edwards (uncredited)
Staging by J.C. Huffman
Dances by Jack Mason

Ziegfeld Follies of 1915
21 June 1915
Music by Louis A. Hirsch and Dave Stamper
Music for additional numbers composed by Charles Elbert, Irving Berlin, Will Vodery. and Bert Williams
Musical director (conductor), Frank Darling
Dance music selected and arranged by Frank Darling (uncredited)
Staged by Julian Mitchell and Leon Errol

Hands Up
22 July 1915
Music by E. Ray Goetz and Sigmund Romberg
Music for additional numbers composed by Jean Schwartz, Cole Porter, Bert Grant, and Joe Young
Musical director (conductor), William Daly

Orchestrations by Frank Saddler
Ballet music composed by Sigmund Romberg (uncredited)
Staging by J.H. Benrimo
Dances and ensembles by Jack Mason

The Blue Paradise
5 August 1915
Music by Edmund Eysler
Music for additional numbers composed by Sigmund Romberg, Leo Edwards, and Cecil Lean
Musical director (conductor), Herbert Kerr
Original incidental and dance music composed by Edmund Eysler
Additional incidental and dance music arranged by Sigmund Romberg (uncredited)
Staging by J.H. Benrimo
Dances, ensembles, and musical numbers by Edward Hutchinson

Cousin Lucy
27 August 1915
Music by Jerome Kern
Additional music composed by Percy Wenrich
Musical director (conductor), August Kleinecke
Specialty dance music composed by August Kleinecke
Staging by Robert Milton
Dances by David Bennett

(Ned Wayburn's) Town Topics
23 September 1915
Music by Harold Orlob
Musical director (conductor), Hilding Anderson
Orchestrations by Frank Saddler
Ballet music composed by Harold Orlob (uncredited)
Staging by Ned Wayburn

The Princess Pat
29 September 1915
Music by Victor Herbert
Musical director (conductor), Gus Salzer
Orchestrations by Victor Herbert

Incidental and dance music composed by Victor Herbert (uncredited)
Staging by Fred G. Latham
Dances by Bena Hoffman

Hip-Hip-Hooray
30 September 1915
Music by Raymond Hubbell
Music for additional numbers composed by Benjamin Hapgood Burt, Jean Schwartz, A. Seymour Brown, and John Philip Sousa
Musical director (conductor), Raymond Hubbell
Ballet music composed and arranged by John Philip Sousa and Julius Einödshofer
Staging by R.H. Burnside
Dances by Mariette Lorette

Miss Information
5 October 1915
Music by Jerome Kern
Music for additional numbers composed by Cole Porter, Frank Tours, and Herman Finck
Musical director, Harold Vicars
Dance music composed by Riccardo Drigo, Melville Ellis, and Jerome Kern
Staging by Robert Milton

A World of Pleasure
14 October 1915
Music by Sigmund Romberg
Music for additional songs composed by J. Leubrie Hill and John L. Golden,
Musical director (conductor), Oscar Radin
Music for "Dance Eccentrique," "Japanese Ballet," "Dance of the Square Heads," "The Doll Dance," and "The Dancing Carnival" composed by Sigmund Romberg
Staging by J.C. Huffman
Dances by Jack Mason
Ballets by Theodore Kosloff

The Girl of Tomorrow
    18 October 1915
    Music by Joseph E. Howard and Herbert Stothart
    Musical director, Herbert Stothart
    Incidental and dance music arranged by Herbert Stothart (uncredited)

Around the Map
    1 November 1915
    Music by Herman Finck
    Music for additional numbers composed by Louis A. Hirsch
    Musical director, Charles Previn
    Dance music composed and arranged by Herman Finck
    Staging by Herbert Gresham
    Musical numbers by Julian Mitchell

Katinka
    23 December 1915
    Music by Rudolf Friml
    Musical director (conductor), John McGhie
    Incidental and dance music composed by Rudolf Friml (uncredited)
    Staging by Frank Smithson

Very Good Eddie
    23 December 1915
    Music by Jerome Kern
    Musical director (conductor), Max Hirschfeld
    Orchestrations by Frank Saddler
    Incidental and dance music composed by Jerome Kern (uncredited)
    Staging by Frank McCormack
    Dances by David Bennett

Stop! Look! Listen!
    25 December 1915
    Music and lyrics by Irving Berlin
    Music for additional numbers composed by Henry Kailimai and Jack Alan

Musical director (conductor), Robert Hood Bowers
Orchestrations by Frank Saddler
Dance music arranged by Robert Hood Bowers (uncredited)
Staging by R.H. Burnside
Dances by Joseph Santley

Sybil
10 January 1916
Music by Victor Jacobi
Additional music composed by John Golden
Musical director (conductor), Harold Vicars
Dance music composed by Victor Jacobi (uncredited)
Staging by Fred G. Latham
Musical numbers by Julian Mitchell and Jack Mason

The Pride of Race
11 January 1916
Incidental music composed by George Spink and Silvio Hein

The Cohan Revue of 1916
9 February 1916
Libretto and music by George M. Cohan
Musical director (conductor), Charles J. Gebest
Dance music arranged by Charles J. Gebest (uncredited)
Staging by George M. Cohan

Robinson Crusoe, Jr.
17 February 1916
Music by Sigmund Romberg and James Hanley
Music for additional numbers composed by Albert Von Tilzer, Ted Snyder, John Golden, Pete Wendling, George W. Meyer, James V. Monaco, and Phil Schwartz
Musical director (conductor), Oscar Radin
Orchestrations by Oscar Radin and Frank Saddler
Dance music arranged by Sigmund Romberg (uncredited)
Staging by J.C. Huffman
Musical numbers by Allan K. Foster

Pom-Pom
28 February 1916
Music by Hugo Felix
Additional music by Jean Schwartz
Musical director (conductor), Max Bendix
Incidental and dance music composed by Hugo Felix
Staging by George Marion

See America First
28 March 1916
Music and lyrics by Cole Porter
Musical director (conductor), Clarence West
Incidental and dance music composed by Cole Porter and Melville Ellis (uncredited)
Staging by J.H. Benrimo
Dances by Edward Hutchinson

Step This Way
29 May 1916
Music by E. Ray Goetz and Bert Grant
Music for additional numbers composed by Irving Berlin and Cliff Hess
Musical director (conductor), Frank Tours
Orchestrations by Frank Saddler
Dance music arranged by Frank Tours (uncredited)
Staging by Frank McCormack
Dances and ensembles by Jack Mason

Ziegfeld Follies of 1916
12 June 1916
Music by Louis A. Hirsch, Irving Berlin, Jerome Kern, and Dave Stamper
Music for additional numbers composed by Nat D. Ayer, Will Vodery, Harry Carroll, Franz Lehár, and Leo Edwards
Musical director (conductor), Frank Darling
Ballet music selected and arranged by Frank Darling (uncredited)
Staging by Ned Wayburn

The Passing Show of 1916
    22 June 1916
    Music by Sigmund Romberg and Otto Motzan
    Music for additional numbers composed by Harry Tierney, Egbert Van Alstyne, and Clifton Crawford
    Musical director (conductor), Oscar Radin
    Ballet music selected and arranged by Sigmund Romberg (uncredited)
    Staging by J.C. Huffman
    Dances by Allan K. Foster

The Big Show
    31 August 1916
    Music by Raymond Hubbell
    Music for additional numbers composed by Bert and Frank Leighton, and Max Darewski
    Musical director (conductor), Raymond Hubbell
    Music for the ballet, *The Sleeping Beauty*, composed by Pyotr Ilyich Tchaikovsky
    Music for the aquatic spectacle, *The Queen of the Mermaids*, composed by Raymond Hubbell
    Music for the ice ballet, *The Merry Doll*, composed by Julius Einödshofer and Raymond Hubbell
    Staging by R.H. Burnside
    Sleeping Beauty Ballet by Ivan Clustine
    Ice Ballet by Mariette Loretta

Betty
    3 October 1916
    Music by Paul Rubens
    Additional music by Harry Tierney, Jean Schwartz,, Silvio Hein, Ernest Steffan, and Benjamin Hapgood Burt
    Musical director, William Daly
    Original dance music composed by Paul Rubens
    Dance music adapted and arranged by William Daly
    Staging by Edward Royce

The Century Girl
    6 November 1916

Music by Victor Herbert and Irving berlin
Music for additional numbers composed by Helen Trix, L. Wolfe Gilbert and Carey Morgan, and James Kendis
Musical directors (conductors), Louis Gottschalk and Max Hoffmann
Ballet music composed by Victor Herbert
Dance music selected and arranged by Louis Gottschalk and Max Hoffmann (uncredited)
Staging by Edward Royce and Leon Errol

A Kiss for Cinderella
25 December 1916
Incidental and dance music composed and arranged by Paul Tietjens

Have a Heart
11 January 1917
Music by Jerome Kern
Music for additional numbers by Harry Tierney, James Kendis, and Charles Bayha
Musical director (conductor), Gus Salzer
Orchestrations by Frank Saddler
Incidental and dance music composed and arranged by Jerome Kern and Gus Salzer (uncredited)
Staging by Edward Royce

Love o' Mike
15 January 1917
Music by Jerome Kern
Musical director (conductor) Frank Tours
Orchestrations by Frank Saddler
Incidental and dance music composed and arranged by Jerome Kern and Frank Tours (uncredited)
Staging by J.H. Benrimo

You're in Love
6 February 1917
Music by Rudolf Friml
Musical director (conductor), John McGhie

Incidental and dance music composed by Rudolf Friml (uncredited)
Staging by Edward Clark
Dances and ensembles by Robert Marks

Oh, Boy!
20 February 1917
Music by Jerome Kern
Musical director (conductor), Max Hirschfeld
Orchestrations by Frank Saddler
Incidental and dance music composed and arranged by Jerome Kern (uncredited)
Staging by Edward Royce

Eileen
19 March 1917
Music by Victor Herbert
Musical director (conductor), Arthur Kautzenbach
Orchestrations by Victor Herbert
Incidental and dance music composed by Victor Herbert (uncredited)
Staging by Fred G. Latham
Dances by George Marion

When Johnny Comes Marching Home
7 May 1917
Music by Julian Edwards
Musical director, Antonio DeNovellis
Incidental and dance music arranged by Julian Edwards (uncredited)
Staging by Fred Bishop
Military pageantry by R.H. Burnside

Ziegfeld Follies of 1917
12 June 1917
Music by Raymond Hubbell and Dave Stamper
Music for additional numbers composed by James Hanley, Jack Egan, Jerome Kern, Ring Lardner, Turner Layton, and Leo Edwards

Patriotic Finale composed by Victor Herbert
Musical director (conductor), Frank Darling
Dance music selected and arranged by Frank Darling (uncredited)
Staging by Ned Wayburn

Maytime
16 August 1917
Music by Sigmund Romberg
Musical director (conductor), Frank Tours
Orchestrations by Sandar Harmathy and Carl Kiefert
Incidental and dance music composed by Sigmund Romberg (uncredited)
Staging by Edward P. Temple
Dances by Allan K. Foster

Cheer Up
23 August 1917
Music by Raymond Hubbell
Music for additional numbers composed by Milton Ager and Benjamin Hapgood Burt
Musical director (conductor), Raymond Hubbell
Incidental and ballet music arranged by John Philip Sousa
Staging by R.H. Burnside

Leve It to Jane
28 August 1917
Music by Jerome Kern
Musical director (conductor), John McGhie
Orchestrations by Frank Saddler
Incidental and dance music composed by Jerome Kern (uncredited)
Staging by Edward Royce
Dances and ensembles by David Bennett

Rambler Rose
10 September 1917
Music by Victor Jacobi
Additional music composed by Charles N. Grant and Irving Berlin

Musical director (conductor), Harold Vicars
Incidental and dance music composed by Victor Jacobi (uncredited)
Staging by W.H. Bentley
Dances and ensembles by Jack Mason

Furs and Frills
9 October 1917
Music by Silvio Hein
Music for additional numbers composed by Claude E. MacArthur
Musical director (conductor), Herbert Stothart
Incidental and dance music arranged by Silvio Hein and Herbert Stothart (uncredited)
Staging by Edward Clark

Chu Chin Chow
22 October 1917
Music by Frederick Norton
Music for additional numbers composed by Grace Torrens
Musical director (conductor), Gustave Ferrari
Orchestrations by Percy Fletcher
Incidental and dance music composed by Frederick Norton
Staging by E. Lyall Swete
Dances by Mlle. Guida and Alexis Kosloff

Miss 1917
5 November 1917
Music by Jerome Kern
Music for additional numbers composed by Victor Herbert, Billy Baskette, Gustave Kerker, George Evans, John Stromberg, Bob Cole, J. Rosamond Johnson, Karl Hoschna, Edward Hutchison, Henry I. Marshall, Joseph McCarthy, Gus Van, Joseph Schenck, and Harry Tierney
Musical director (conductor), Robert Hood Bowers
Ballet music composed by Victor Herbert
Staging by Ned Wayburn
Dances by Adolph Bohm

Kitty Darlin'
    7 November 1917
    Music by Rudolf Friml
    Musical director (conductor), William P. Axt
    Incidental and dance music composed by Rudolf Friml (uncredited)
    Staging by Edward Royce

Over the Top
    28 November 1917
    Music by Sigmund Romberg
    Music for additional numbers composed by Herman Tinberg and Frank Carter
    Musical director (conductor), Frank Tours
    Dance music composed and arranged by Sigmund Romberg and Frank Tours (uncredited)
    Staging by J.C. Huffman
    Dances by Allan K. Foster

Azora, the Daughter of Montezuma
    26 December 1917
    Music by Henry Kimball Hadley
    Musical director (conductor), Henry Kimball Hadley
    Music arranged by Henry Kimball Hadley
    Incidental and ballet music composed and arranged by Henry Kimball Hadley

Going Up
    25 December 1917
    Music by Louis A. Hirsch
    Musical director (conductor), Gus Salzer
    Orchestrations by Frank Saddler
    Incidental and dance music arranged by Louis A. Hirsch and Gus Salzer (uncredited)
    Staging by Edward Royce and James Montgomery

The Cohan Revue of 1918
    31 December 1917
    Music and lyrics by Irving Berlin and George M. Cohan

Music for additional numbers composed by David W. Guion, James Brockman, and Cliff Hess
Musical director (conductor), Charles J. Gebest
Orchestrations by Frank Saddler
Incidental and dance music arranged by Charles J. Gebest (uncredited)
Staging by George M. Cohan
Musical numbers by Jack Mason, James Gorman, and George M. Cohan

Oh, Lady! Lady!
1 February 1918
Music by Jerome Kern
Musical director (conductor), Max Hirschfeld
Orchestrations by Frank Saddler
Incidental and dance music composed by Jerome Kern (uncredited)
Staging by Robert Milton and Edward Royce

Sinbad
14 February 1918
Music by Sigmund Romberg
Music for additional numbers composed by Jean Schwartz, Al Jolson, Harry Tierney, Ted Snyder, Edward G. Nelson, Fred Mayo, Buddy DeSylva, and Harold Atteridge
Musical director (conductor) Oscar Radin
Musical arrangements by Jack Mason
Dance music arranged by Sigmund Romberg (uncredited)
Staging by J.C. Huffman and J.J. Shubert
Dances by Jack Mason
Ballets by Alexis Kosloff

Getting Together
18 March 1918
Music and lyrics by Gitz Rice
Additional music composed by Harrison Brockbank, C.W. Murphy, and Worton David
Musical director (conductor), Manuel Klein
Incidental music composed by Roy Webb
Staging by Holbrook Blinn and Frederick Stanhope

The Rainbow Girl
 1 April 1918
 Music by Louis A. Hirsch
 Musical director (conductor), Max Steiner
 Incidental and dance music arranged by Louis A. Hirsch and Max Steiner (uncredited)
 Staging by Julian Mitchell and Herbert Gresham

Fancy Free
 11 April 1918
 Music and lyrics by Augustus Barratt
 Additional music composed by Clifton Crawford
 Musical director (conductor), Augustus Barratt
 Incidental and dance music arranged by Augustus Barratt (uncredited)
 Staging by J.C. Huffman
 Dances and musical numbers by Jack Mason

Yours Truly
 11 April 1918
 Music by Herbert Stothart
 Musical direction by Herbert Stothart
 Incidental and dance music by Herbert Stothart

Hitchy-Koo of 1918
 6 June 1918
 Music by Raymond Hubbell
 Music for additional numbers composed by Percy Wenrich, Henry Marshall, Luigi Arditi, Carl Eckert, and Harold Orlob
 Musical director (conductor), Oscar Radin
 Orchestrations by Maurice DePackh and Frank Saddler
 Dance music arranged by Raymond Hubbell and Harold Orlob (uncredited)
 Staging by Leon Errol

Ziegfeld Follies of 1918
 18 June 1918
 Music by Louis A. Hirsch and Dave Stamper
 Additional music composed by Irving Berlin, Victor Jacobi,

Buddy G. DeSylva, Arthur Jackson, Harry Ruby, Eddie Cantor, Archie Gottler, and Edgar Leslie
Musical director (conductor), Frank Darling
Incidental music composed by Victor Jacobi
Dance music selected and arranged by Frank Darling
Staging by Ned Wayburn

The Passing Show of 1918
25 July 1918
Music by Sigmund Romberg and Jean Schwartz
Music for additional numbers composed by Ray Perkins, Russell Tarbox, Harry DeCosta, Augustus Barratt, and Lee S. Roberts
Musical director (conductor), Charles Previn
Ballet music composed and arranged by Sigmund Romberg and Charles Previn (uncredited)
Staging by J.C. Huffman
Musical numbers and ballets by Jack Mason

Everything
22 August 1918
Music by John Philip Sousa and Irving Berlin
Music for additional numbers composed by William Daly, Percy Wenrich, Harry Tierney, James Tate, J.M. Rumshinsky, Raymond Hubbell, R.P. Weston, Harry Bedford, Max Darewski, John L. Golden, and Bert Lee
Musical director (conductor), William M. Daly
Ballet music arranged by John Philip Sousa
Staging by R.H. Burnside

Fiddlers Three
3 September 1918
Music by Alexander Johnstone
Musical director (conductor), Gene Salzer
Orchestrations by Domenick Sodero
Incidental and dance music arranged by Alexander Johnstone and Gene Salzer (uncredited)
Staging by Clifford Brooke
Dances by Carl Randall

Sometime
    14 October 1918
    Music by Rudolf Friml
    Musical director (conductor), Herbert Stothart
    Incidental and dance music composed by Rudolf Friml (uncredited)
    Staging by Oscar Eagle
    Dances by Allan K. Foster

Little Simplicity
    4 November 1918
    Music by Augustus Barratt
    Musical director (conductor), Augustus Barratt
    Incidental and dance music arranged by Augustus Barratt (uncredited)
    Staging by Edward P. Temple
    Dances by Jack Mason
    Cameron Sisters' dances by Alexis Kosloff

Oh, My Dear!
    27 November 1918
    Music by Louis A. Hirsch
    Music for additional numbers composed by Jerome Kern and Benjamin Hapgood Burt
    Musical director (conductor), Max Hirschfeld
    Dance music arranged by Louis A. Hirsch and Jean Schwartz (uncredited)
    Staging by Robert Milton and Edward Royce

Listen Lester
    23 December 1918
    Music by Harold Orlob
    Musical director (conductor), Gus Salzer
    Dance music arranged by Harold Orlob (uncredited)
    Staging by Robert Marks

The Velvet Lady
    3 February 1919
    Music by Victor Herbert

Musical director (conductor), Frederic Stalberg
Orchestrations by Victor Herbert
Dance music composed and arranged by Victor Herbert (uncredited)
Staging by Edgar MacGregor
Dances by Julian Mitchell

The Royal Vagabond
17 February 1919
Music by Anselm Goetzl and George M. Cohan
Music for additional numbers composed by Harry Tierney and Arthur Sullivan
Musical director (conductor), Gus Salzer
Dance music arranged by Anselm Goetzl (uncredited)
Staging by Julian Mitchell and Sam Forrest

The Legend
12 March 1919
Music by Joseph Carl Breil
Musical director (conductor), Giulio Gatti-Casazza
Incidental music composed by Joseph Carl Breil (uncredited)

The Temple Dancer
12 March 1919
Music by John Adam Hugo
Musical director (conductor), Giulio Gatti-Casazza
Ballet music composed by John Adam Hugo

Tumble In
24 March 1919
Music by Rudolf Friml
Musical director (conductor), Herbert Stothart
Incidental and dance music composed and arranged by Rudolf Friml and Herbert Stothart (uncredited)
Staging by Bertram Harrison
Musical numbers by Bert French

She's a Good Fellow
5 May 1919
Music by Jerome Kern

"Jubilo" based on "Kingdom Comin'" by Henry Clay Work
Musical director (conductor), William Daly
Orchestrations by Frank Saddler
Incidental and dance music composed by Jerome Kern (uncredited)
Staging by Fred G. Latham and Edward Royce

Toot Sweet
7 May 1919
Music by Richard A. Whiting
Music for additional numbers composed by Roy K. Moulton, Camille Robert, and Will Morrissey
Musical director (conductor), Hilding Anderson
Dance music arranged by Hilding Anderson (uncredited)
Staging by Will Morrissey

The Lady in Red
12 May 1919
Music by Robert Winterberg
Additional music composed by Walter Donaldson and George Gershwin
Musical director (conductor), J. Albert Browne
Dance music composed by Otto Motzan (uncredited)
Staging by Frank Smithson

La-La-Lucille!
26 May 1919
Music by George Gershwin
Musical director (conductor), Charles Previn
Specialty dances arranged by George Gershwin and Charles Previn (uncredited)
Staging by Herbert Gresham and Julian Alfred

A Lonely Romeo
10 June 1919
Music by Malvin Franklin and Robert Hood Bowers
Music for additional numbers composed by Richard Rodgers
Musical director (conductor), Robert Hood Bowers
Orchestrations by Charles Grant and Robert Hood Bowers

    Dance music by Malvin Franklyn (uncredited)
    Staging by W.H. Post
    Dances and musical numbers by Jack Mason

Ziegfeld Follies of 1919
    16 June 1919
    Music and lyrics by Irving Berlin
    Music for additional numbers composed by Dave Stamper, Harry Tierney, Walter Donaldson, Harry Akst, Harry Ruby, Robert Hood Bowers, James Hanley, Nat Vincent, Darl MacBoyle, Will E. Skidmore, Marshall Walker, Albert Von Tilzer, Gus Van, Joe Schenck, and Jack Yellen
    Musical director (conductor), Frank Darling
    Orchestrations by Stephen Jones, Victor Herbert, and Robert Hood Bowers
    Ballet music composed by Victor Herbert
    Staging by Ned Wayburn

The Greenwich Village Follies (1919)
    15 July 1919
    Music by A. Baldwin Sloane
    Additional music composed by Bill Munro, Byron Gay, Ted Lewis, Jimmy Morgan, Irving Berlin, A. Behr, Al Herman, Alex Gerber, and Abner Silver
    Musical director, Hilding Anderson
    Orchestrations by Hilding Anderson
    Incidental and dance music arranged by A. Baldwin Sloane and Hilding Anderson (uncredited)
    Staging by John Murray Anderson

Happy Days
    23 August 1919
    Music by Raymond Hubbell
    Musical director, A.J. Garing
    Conductor, Raymond Hubbell
    Orchestrations by Frank Saddler
    Incidental and dance music composed by Raymond Hubbell (uncredited)
    Staging by R.H. Burnside

Declassée
7 October 1919
Musical director, Thomas W. Hindley
Incidental music composed by Thomas W. Hindley (uncredited)

Apple Blossoms
7 October 1919
Music by Fritz Kreisler and Victor Jacobi
Musical director (conductor), William Daly
"Tambourin Chinois" Dance composed by Fritz Kreisler
Incidental and dance music arranged by Victor Jacobi
Staging by Fred G. Latham and Edward Royce

The Little Whopper
13 October 1919
Music by Rudolf Friml
Musical director (conductor), Anton Heindl
Incidental and dance music composed by Rudolf Friml (uncredited)
Staging by Oscar Eagle
Musical numbers by Bert French

The Passing Show of 1919
23 October 1919
Music by Jean Schwartz
Music for additional numbers composed by Chris Schonberg, Benjamin Hapgood Burt, and Sigmund Romberg
Musical director (conductor), Oscar Radin
Orchestrations by J. Bodewalt Lampe, James C. McCabe, Oscar Radin, and Frank Tours
Dance music arranged by Sigmund Romberg (uncredited)
Staging by J.C. Huffman
Dances by Allan K. Foster

Irene
18 November 1919
Music by Harry Tierney
Additional music based on themes composed by Maurice Rich-

mond and Frederic Chopin
Musical director (conductor), Gus Salzer
Dance music arranged by Harry Tierney and Gus Salzer (uncredited)
Staging by Edward Royce

Linger Longer Letty
20 November 1919
Music by Al Goodman
Music for additional numbers composed by Albert Von Tilzer
Musical director (conductor), Al Goodman
Incidental and dance music composed and arranged by Al Goodman (uncredited)
Musical numbers by Will H. Smith

Aphrodite
24 November 1919
Music by Henry Février and Anselm Goetzl
Musical director, William Axt
Ballet music arranged from the music of Modest Mussorgsky and Alexander Glazunov
Incidental music by Anselm Goetz and Henry Février
Staging by E. Lyall Swete
Ballets by Michel Fokine

Angel Face
29 December 1919
Music by Victor Herbert
Musical director (conductor), Harold Vicars
Orchestrations by Victor Herbert
Incidental and dance music arranged by Victor Herbert (uncredit)
Staging by George W. Lederer
Musical numbers by Julian Alfred

Always You
5 January 1920
Music by Herbert Stothart
Musical direction by Herbert Stothart

Incidental and dance music arranged by Herbert Stothart
Staging by Arthur Hammerstein
Dances by Robert Marks

The Night Boat
2 February 1920
Music by Jerome Kern
Music for additional numbers composed by Ivan Caryll, Paul Dresser, J. Rosamond Johnson, James Monaco, George M. Cohan, and Harry Tierney
Musical director (conductor), Victor Baravelle
Orchestrations by Frank Saddler
Incidental and dance music composed by Jerome Kern and Victor Baravelle (uncredited)
Staging by Fred G. Latham
Musical numbers by Ned Wayburn

What's in a Name?
19 March 1920
Music by Milton Ager
Musical director (conductor), Augustus Barratt
Orchestrations by Maurice DePackh and Arthur Lange
Dance music arranged by Augustus Barratt (uncredited)
Staging by John Murray Anderson
Dances by Michio Ito

Honey Girl
3 May 1920
Music by Albert Von Tilzer
Musical director (conductor), Eugene Salzer
Music for the "Bluebird Ballet" arranged by Eugene Salzer (uncredited)
Staging by Bert French and Sam Forrest

George White's Scandals of 1920
7 June 1920
Music by George Gershwin
Additional music composed by Abe Olman, Howard Johnson, and Milton Ager

Musical director (conductor), Alfred Newman
Orchestrations by Frank Saddler
Ballet music arranged by Alfred Newman (uncredited)
Staging by George White

Ziegfeld Follies of 1920
12 June 1920
Music (and lyrics) by Irving Berlin
Additional music composed by Dave Stamper, Gene Buck, Harry Tierney, George Fairman, Gus Van, Joe Schenck, Mac Emery, King Zany, Abner Silver, Eddie Cantor, Abe Olman, Ernie Erdman, and Victor Herbert.
Musical director, Frank Tours
Orchestrations by Maurice DePackh
Dance music composed and arranged by Dave Stamper and Victor Herbert
Staging by Edward Royce

Cinderella on Broadway
24 June 1920
Music by Bert Grant
Music for additional numbers composed by Jean Schwartz, Cliff Friend, and Harry Richman
Musical director (conductor), Oscar Radin
Incidental music by arranged by Al Goodman
Staging by J.C. Huffman
Dances by Allan K. Foster

The Girl in the Spotlight
12 July 1920
Music by Victor Herbert
Musical director, Harold Vicars
Orchestrations by Victor Herbert
Incidental and dance music composed and arranged by Victor Herbert (uncredited)
Staging by George W. Lederer
Musical numbers by Julian Alfred

Poor Little Ritz Girl
 28 July 1920
 Music by Richard Rodgers and Sigmund Romberg
 Musical director, Pierce de Reeder
 Conductor, Charles Previn
 Dance music composed by Sigmund Romberg (uncredited)
 Staging by Ned Wayburn
 Dances by David Bennett

Good Times
 9 August 1920
 Music by Raymond Hubbell
 Musical director, A.J. Garing
 Conductor, Raymond Hubbell
 Orchestrations by Frank Saddler
 Incidental and ballet music for "Shadowland" composed by Max Steiner
 Additional incidental and dance music arranged by Raymond Hubbell (uncredited)
 Staging by R.H. Burnside
 Dances by Cissie Hayden

Spanish Love
 17 August 1920
 Music by H. Maurice Jacquet
 Musical director, Paul Schindler
 Incidental and dance music arranged by H. Maurice Jacquet

The Greenwich Village Follies of 1920
 30 August 1920
 Music by A. Baldwin Sloane
 Music for additional numbers composed by Louis Silvers, Harry Carroll, James Hanley, Albert Von Tilzer, and Johnny Black
 Musical director (conductor), Charles Previn
 Orchestrations by A.C. Columbo and Mornay D. Helm
 Ballet music composed by A. Baldwin Sloane (uncredited)
 Staging by John Murray Anderson

Broadway Brevities of 1920
29 September 1920
Music by Archie Gottler
Additional music composed by Bert Kalmar, Harry Ruby, Irving Berlin, George Gershwin, Robert Hood Bowers, Chris Smith, Charles Bayha, James Hanley, Joseph M. Daly, Walter Donaldson, and Con Conrad
Musical director (conductor), Louis Gress
Orchestrations by Stephen Jones and Will Vodery
Dance music composed by Maurie Rubens
Staging by J.C. Huffman
Dances and musical numbers by Jack Mason

Mecca
4 October 1920
Music by Percy E. Fletcher
Musical director (conductor), Frank Tours
Ballet music composed and arranged by Percy E. Fletcher (uncredited)
Staging by E. Lyall Swete
Dances by Michel Fokine

Kissing Time
11 October 1920
Music by Ivan Caryll
Music for additional numbers by William Daly
Musical director (conductor), Max Steiner
Orchestrations by Ivan Caryll and Claude MacArthur
Original dance music arranged by Ivan Caryll
Dance music adapted and arranged by Max Steiner (uncredited)
Staging by Edward Royce

Mary
18 October 1920
Music by Louis A. Hirsch
Musical director (conductor), Charles J. Gebest
Dance music arranged by Louis A. Hirsch and Charles J, Gebest (uncredited)
Staging by Julian Mitchell and Sam Forrest

The Half Moon
    1 November 1920
    Music by Victor Jacobi
    Musical director (conductor), Harold Vicars
    Incidental and dance music arranged by Victor Jacobi (uncredited)
    Staging by Fred G. Latham
    Dances by Allan K. Foster

Jimmie
    17 November 1920
    Music by Herbert Stothart
    Musical director (conductor), Herbert Stothart
    Incidental and dance music composed and arranged by Herbert Stothart (uncredited)
    Staging by Oscar Eagle
    Dances by Bert French

Sally
    21 December 1920
    Music by Jerome Kern
    Musical director (conductor), Gus Salzer
    Music for "Butterfly Ballet" composed and arranged by Victor Herbert
    Staging by Edward Royce

The Passing Show of 1921
    29 December 1920
    Music by Jean Schwartz
    Music for additional numbers composed by Frank Maguire, Charley Straight, Lew Pollack, Richard Whiting, Malvin Franklin, Ernie Erdman, Abner Silver, and the Howard Brothers
    Musical director (conductor), Al Goodman
    Music for "The Dancing Blues" composed by Lew Pollack
    Incidental and dance music arranged by Al Goodman
    Staging by J.C. Huffman
    Dances by Max Scheck

The Midnight Rounders of 1921
7 February 1921
Music by Jean Schwartz
Music for additional numbers composed by Lew Pollack, Raymond Hubbell, Ernesto DiCapua, Anton Dvorák, Johann Strauss, Jr., Jacques Offenbach, Chauncey Olcott, Ernest E. Ball, and Haydn Wood
Musical director (conductor), Al Goodman
Ballet and dance music composed and arranged by Jean Schwartz and Al Goodman (uncredited)
Staging by Jack Mason

The Rose Girl
11 February 1921
Music by Anselm Goetzl
Additional music composed by Nat Vincent
Musical director, Max Steiner
Ballet music composed by Anselm Goetzl and arranged from a composition by Johannes Brahms
Staging by Hassart Short
Dances by Max Scheck
Ballets by Michel Fokine

You'll Never Know
20 April 1921
Music by Richard Rodgers
Musical director, Richard Rodgers
Incidental and dance music composed and arranged by Richard Rodgers (uncredited)

June Love
25 April 1921
Music by Rudolf Friml
Musical director (conductor), Gene Salzer
Dance music composed by Rudolf Friml (uncredited)
Staging by George Vivian
Dances by David Bennett

Two Little Girls in Blue
  3 May 1921
  Music by Paul Lannin and Vincent Youmans
  Musical director (conductor) Charles Previn
  Orchestrations by Stephen Jones and Paul Lannin
  Ballet and dance music arranged by Paul Lannin (uncredited)
  Staging and dances by Ned Wayburn

The Last Waltz
  10 May 1921
  Music by Oscar Straus
  Music for additional numbers composed by Al Goodman, Ralph Benatzky, and Rudolf Nelson
  Musical director (conductor), Oscar Radin
  Original ballet and dance music composed by Oscar Straus
  Dance music adapted and arranged by Al Goodman (uncredited)
  Staging by J.C. Huffman and Frank Smithson
  Musical numbers by Allan K. Foster and Jack Mason

Shuffle Along
  23 May 1921
  Music by Eubie Blake
  Music for additional numbers composed by Walter Donaldson
  Musical director (conductor), Eubie Blake
  Musical arrangements by Will Vodery
  Dance music arranged by Eubie Blake and Will Vodery (uncredited)
  Staging by Walter Brooks
  Dances by Charles Davis and Lawrence Deas

Snapshots of 1921
  2 June 1921
  Music by George Gershwin, Con Conrad, José Padilla, George Meyer, Malvin Franklin, Harry Ruby, James Monaco, and Leopold Godowsky
  Music for additional numbers composed by Seymour Simons and Harry Brooks
  Musical director (conductor), Herbert Stothart

Music for "Waltz Ballet" composed by Malvin Franklin
Music for "Rendezvous" composed by Leopold Godowsky
Staging by Leon Errol

The Whirl of New York
13 June 1921
Music by Gustave Kerker, Al Goodman, and Lew Pollack
Additional music composed by Leo Edwards, Ed Rose, and Richard Whiting
Musical director (conductor), Al Goodman
Incidental and ballet music arranged by Lew Pollack and Al Goodman (uncredited)
Staging by Lew Morton
Musical numbers by Allan K. Foster

Ziegfeld Follies of 1921
21 June 1921
Music by Victor Herbert, Rudolf Friml, and Dave Stamper
Music for additional numbers composed by Turner Layton, James Hanley, Leo Edwards, Harry Carroll, Maurice Yvain, James V. Monaco, Harry Pease, Ed Nelson, Howard Johnson, Elsie White, Henry Busse, Gus Mueller, Buster Johnson, Harry Von Tilzer, and Richard A. Whiting
Musical director (conductor), Frank Tours
Orchestrations by Maurice DePackh and Stephen Jones
Ballet music composed by Victor Herbert
Staging by Edward Royce

Tangerine
9 August 1921
Music by Monte Carlo and Alma Sanders
Additional music composed by Carle Carlton, Jean Schwartz, Dave Zoob, Frank Crumit, and Benjamin Hapgood Burt
Musical director (conductor), Gus Kleinecke
Dance music arranged by Gus Kleinecke (uncredited)

The Mimic World of 1921
17 August 1921
Music by Jean Schwartz, Lew Pollack, and Owen Murphy

Music for additional numbers composed by Archie Gottler
Musical director (conductor), Al Goodman
Dance music arranged by Al Goodman (uncredited)
Staging by Allan K. Foster

Get Together
3 September 1921
Musical director (conductor), A.J. Garing
Ballet music for "The Thunder Bird" selected from Balakirev, Borodin, Glinka, Rimsky-Korsakov, and Tchaikovsky, conducted by Anselm Goetzl
Ballet music for "The Red Shoes" composed by Raoul Mader, conducted by Anselm Goetzl
Music for additional dance numbers composed by Milton Lusk, and selected from music composed by Amilcare Ponchielli
Staging by R.H. Burnside

Music Box Revue (1921)
22 September 1921
Music and lyrics by Irving Berlin
Musical directors, Anton Heindl and Frank Tours
Orchestrations by Alfred Dalby, Maurice DePackh, Charles Grant, Stephen Jones, Oscar Radin, and Frank Tours
Orchestrations supervised by Harry Akst
Dance music arranged by Frank Tours (uncredited)
Staging by Hassard Short
Dances by Bert French and I. Tarasoff

The O'Brien Girl
3 October 1921
Music by Louis A. Hirsch
Musical director (conductor) Charles J. Gebest
Dance music arranged by Louis A. Hirsch and Charles J. Gebest (uncredited)
Staging by Julian Mitchell

The Love Letter
4 October 1921
Music by Victor Jacobi

Additional music composed by Will West
Musical director (conductor), William Daly
Incidental and dance music arranged by Victor Jacobi (uncredited)
Staging by Edward Royce

Bombo
6 October 1921
Music by Sigmund Romberg
Additional music composed by Pete Wendling, Con Conrad, Walter Donaldson, Vincent Rose, Al Jolson, Billy James, and others
Musical director (conductor), Alfred Goodman
Incidental and dance music by Sigmund Romberg (uncredited)
Staging by J.C. Huffman
Dances by Allan K. Foster

Good Morning, Dearie
1 November 1921
Music by Jerome Kern
Musical director (conductor), Victor Baravelle
Orchestrations by Stephen Jones
Incidental and dance music composed by Jerome Kern and Victor Baravelle (uncredited)
Staging by Edward Royce

Up in the Clouds
2 January 1922
Music by Tom Johnstone
Musical director (conductor), Hilding Anderson
Orchestrations by Hilding Anderson
Incidental and ballet music arranged by Hilding Anderson (uncredited)
Staging by Lawrence Marston
Dances by Allan K. Foster, Max Scheck, and Vaughn Godfrey

The Blue Kitten
13 January 1922
Music by Rudolf Friml

Musical director (conductor), Herbert Stothart
Incidental and dance music composed by Rudolf Friml (uncredited)
Staging by Edgar Selwyn, Leon Errol, and Julian Mitchell

Elsie Janis and Her Gang
16 January 1922
Music by Herman Finck, Ivan Caryll, George S. Hirst, Maurice Yvain, Carey Morgan, and Seymour Simons
Musical director, John L. McManus
Orchestrations by Maurice DePackh
Ballet music arranged by Herman Finck
Staging by Elsie Janis

For Goodness Sake
21 February 1922
Music by William Daly and Paul Lannin
Music for additional numbers composed by George Gershwin
Musical director (conductor), William Daly
Dance music arranged by William Daly and Paul Lannin (uncredited)
Staging by Priestly Morrison
Musical Numbers by Allan K. Foster

Make It Snappy
13 April 1922
Music by Jean Schwartz
Music for additional numbers composed by William Friedlander, Ted Snyder, Harry Ruby, Fred Fisher, Eddie Cantor, Alex Gerber, James F. Hanley, Irving Caesar, Walter Donaldson, Milton Ager, Abner Silver, and J. Russel Robinson
Musical director (conductor), Louis Gress
Orchestrations by J. Dell Lampe
Ballet music selected and arranged by Louis Gress
Staging by J.C. Huffman
Dances by Allan K. Foster
Ballet choreographed by Cleveland Bronner

Some Party
    15 April 1922
    Music by Silvio Hein, Raymond Hubbell, Percy Weinrich, and Gustave Kerker
    Music for additional numbers composed by Albert Solman, Turner Layton, and Mary Earl
    Musical director (conductor), Anton Heindl
    Dance music arranged by Raymond Hubbell
    Dance music in *Burning to Sing, or, Singing to Burn* composed by Gustave Kerker
    Staging by R.H. Burnside
    Dances by Billy Grant

Ziegfeld Follies of 1922
    5 June 1922
    Music by Victor Herbert, Louis A. Hirsch, and Dave Stamper
    Music for additional numbers composed by Jean Schwartz, Ed Gallagher, Al Shean, Ernest Ball, Louis Breau, James F. Hanley, Turner Layton, and Jimmy Duffy
    Musical director (conductor), Oscar Radin
    Ballet music borrowed from Pyotr Ilyich Tchaikovsky and composed by Victor Herbert
    Staging by Ned Wayburn
    Ballets by Michel Fokine

Strut, Miss Lizzie
    18 June 1922
    Music by Henry Creamer
    Music for additional numbers composed by Joe Jordan
    Musical director, Joe Jordan
    Dance music arranged by Joe Jordan (uncredited)
    Staging by Henry Creamer

Daffy Dill
    22 August 1922
    Music by Herbert Stothart
    Musical director (conductor), Herbert Stothart
    Incidental and dance music composed and arranged by Herbert

Stothart (uncredited)
Staging by Julian Mitchell

Better Times
2 September 1922
Music by Raymond Hubbell
Musical director (conductor), A.J. Garing
Orchestrations by Charles Miller, Hilding Anderson, and Frank Saddler
Ballet music composed and arranged by Raymond Hubbell (uncredited)
Staging by R.H. Burnside
Dances by William Holbrook and Mlle. Mantova

The Greenwich Village Follies (1922)
12 September 1922
Music by Louis A. Hirsch
Music for additional numbers composed by Harry Ruby, Irving Caesar, and Ray Henderson
Musical director (conductor), Alfred Newman
Incidental and dance music selected from the music of Rossini and others and arranged by Alfred Newman
Staging by John Murray Anderson
Ballets and dances by Carl Randall and Alexander Yakovleff

The Lady in Ermine
2 October 1922
Music by Jean Gilbert and Al Goodman
Music for additional numbers composed by Sigmund Romberg
Musical director (conductor), Oscar Bradley
Original dance music composed by Jean Gilbert
Dances by Jack Mason
Ballets by Allan K. Foster

Up She Goes
6 November 1922
Music by Harry Tierney
Musical director (conductor), Anton Heindl
Orchestrations by Frank Barry, Lake McCabe, and Alfred Dalby

Dance music arranged by Harry Tierney and Anton Heindl
   (uncredited)
Staging by Frank Craven and Bert French
Dances by Bert French

Little Nellie Kelly
   13 November 1922
   Libretto and music by George M. Cohan
   Musical director (conductor), Charles J. Gebest
   Incidental and dance music arranged by Charles J. Gebest (uncredited)
   Staging by George M. Cohan
   Musical numbers by Julian Mitchell

Our Nell
   4 December 1922
   Music by George Gershwin and William Daly
   Musical director (conductor), Charles Sieger
   Dance music arranged by William Daly and George Gershwin
      (uncredited)
   Staging by W.H. Gilmore and Edgar MacGregor
   Dances by Julian Mitchell

Peaches
   22 January 1923
   Music by Max Steiner
   Musical director, Max Steiner
   Incidental and dance music composed and arranged by Max Steiner
   Staging by George W. Lederer
   Dances by Sammy Lee

The Dancing Girl
   24 January 1923
   Music by Sigmund Romberg
   Music for additional numbers composed by George Gershwin,
      A.J. Carey, Ernest Seitz, and Al Goodman
   Musical director (conductor), Al Goodman
   Dance music arranged by Sigmund Romberg (uncredited)
   Staging by J.C. Huffman

Wildflower
7 February 1923
Music by Herbert Stothart and Vincent Youmans
Musical director (conductor), Herbert Stothart
Orchestrations by Robert Russell Bennett, Stephen Jones, Charles Miller, and Herbert Stothart
Dance music arranged by Herbert Stothart (uncredited)
Staging by Oscar Eagle
Dances and ensembles by David Bennett

Jack and Jill
22 March 1923
Music by Augustus Barratt
Music for additional numbers composed by Alfred Newman, William Daly, Ivor Novello, and Muriel Pollock
Musical director (conductor), Charles Previn
Orchestrations by Maurice DePackh and Stephen Jones
Ballet and dance music arranged by Augustus Barratt and Charles Previn (uncredited)
Dances by Larry Ceballos

If I Were King
25 March 1923
Music by Richard Rodgers
Musical director, Richard Rodgers
Dance music composed and arranged by Richard Rodgers (uncredited)
Staging by Herbert L. Fields

Cinders
3 April 1923
Music by Rudolf Friml
Musical director (conductor), Victor Baravelle
Incidental and dance music composed by Rudolf Friml (uncredited)
Staging by Edward Royce

Dew Drop Inn
17 May 1923
Music by Al Goodman

Music for additional numbers composed by Rudolf Friml, Sigmund Romberg, J. Fred Coots, and Jean Schwartz
Musical director (conductor), Alfred Newman
Dance music arranged by Al Goodman and Alfred Newman (uncredited)
Staging by Fred G. Latham
Dances by M. Francis Weldon

Artists and Models (1923)
20 August 1923
Music by Jean Schwartz
Music for additional numbers composed by Al Goodman
Musical director (conductor), Al Goodman
Dance music composed and arranged by Al Goodman
Staging by Harry Wagstaff Gribble and M. Francis Weldon

Poppy
3 September 1923
Music by Stephen Jones and Arthur Samuels
Music for additional numbers composed by John Egan
Musical director (conductor) Gus Salzer
Orchestrations by Stephen Jones
Dance music arranged by Stephen Jones (uncredited)
Staging by Dorothy Donnelly and Philip Goodman
Musical numbers by Julian Alfred

Music Box Revue (1923)
22 September 1923
Music and lyrics by Irving Berlin
Musical director (conductor), Frank Tours
Orchestrations by Frank Tours, Maurice DePackh, Stephen Jones, and Charles Grant
Ballet music composed and arranged by Frank Tours (uncredited)
Staging by Hassard Short
Dances by Sammy Lee

Runnin' Wild
29 October 1923
Music by James P. Johnson

Musical director, James P. Johnson
Dance music composed and arranged by James P. Johnson (uncredited)
Dances by Lyda Webb

The Stepping Stones
6 November 1923
Music by Jerome Kern
Musical director, Victor Baravelle
Orchestrations by Robert Russell Bennett and Hilding Anderson
Dance music composed and arranged by Jerome Kern and Victor Baravelle (uncredited)
Staging by R.H. Burnside
Dances by Mary Read and John Tiller

Topics of 1923
20 November 1923
Music by Jean Schwartz and Al Goodman
Music for additional numbers composed by Bert Grant
Musical director (conductor), Al Goodman
Dance music arranged by Al Goodman (uncredited)
Staging by J.C. Huffman
Dances by M. Francis Weldon

Mary Jane McKane
25 December 1923
Music by Herbert Stothart and Vincent Youmans
Musical director, Herbert Stothart
Orchestrations by Robert Russell Bennett
Dance music arranged by Herbert Stothart (uncredited)
Staging by Alonzo Price
Dances and ensembles by Sammy Lee

Kid Boots
31 December 1923
Music by Harry Tierney
Music for additional numbers composed by Con Conrad, Billy Rose, George Olson, Edward Kilfeather, Jay Gorney, Ed-

die Cantor, Jerry Benson, J. Russel Robinson, Harry Akst, Joseph Meyer, Fred E. Ahlert, Harry DeCosta, Lew Brown, and Lew Santly
Musical director (conductor), Louis Gress
Orchestrations by Frank Barry
Dance music arranged by Louis Gress (uncredited)
Staging by Edward Royce

Alphabetical Checklist of Choreographers and Stage Managers

THE TERM "STAGE MANAGER" is used in its nineteenth-century sense, in which stage management involved the staging of a production. Until the separation of functions between theatre director and stage manager occurred in the twentieth century, "stage manager" and "director" were interchangeable terms.

Signor Luigi Albertieri, Italian-born choreographer of *In Gotham* (19 September 1898); *The Ladies Paradise* (19 September 1901); *Miss Simplicity* (10 February1902); *The Top o' th' World* (19 October 1907); *The Firefly* (2 December 1912); *Chin Chin* (20 October 1914). In addition, in 1910 Albertieri became the first ballet master of the Chicago Opera Ballet Company; and in 1923 he published *The Art of Terpsichore: an elementary, theoretical, physical, and practical treatise of dancing*.

Julian Alfred, American choreographer, director, and dancer. Choreographic works include *The Beauty Spot* (10 April 1909); *Mama's Baby Boy* (25 May 1912); *Lieber Augustin* (3 September 1913); *Oh, I Say!* (30 October 1913); *90 in the Shade* (25 January 1915); *A Modern Eve* (3 May 1915); *So Long Letty* (23 October 1916); *See-Saw* (23 September 1919); Angel Face (29 December 1919); *My Golden Girl* (2 February 1920); *Lady Billy* (14 December 1920). He also provided musical staging for *The Girl in the Spotlight* (12 June 1920); *The Sweetheart Shop* (31 August 1920); *For Goodness Sake* (21 February 1922); *Letty Pepper* (10 April 1922); *Go Easy Mabel* (8 May 1922); *Poppy* (3 September 1923); *Sitting Pretty* (8 April 1924); *Madame Pompadour* (11 November 1924); *The Vagabond King* (21 September 1925); *Twinkle, Twinkle* (16 November 1926). Directing assignments included *The*

Merry Whirl (30 May 1910); *Odds and Ends of 1917* (19 November 1917); *La, La, Lucille* (26 May 1919); *Love Birds* (15 March 1921); *Poppy* (3 September 1923).

John Murray Anderson, director, writer, designer, producer, born on 20 September 1886 at St. John's Newfoundland, Canada. His musical theatre productions included six editions of *The Greenwich Village Follies* (1919–1924) for which he provided book, lyrics, direction, and/or staging. Other musical staging assignments included *Jack and Jill* (22 Mach 1923); *Music Box Revue* (1924) (1 December 1924); *Ziegfeld Follies* (4 January 1934); *Keep Moving* (23 August 1934); *Life Begins at 8:40* (27 August 1934); *Thumbs Up!* (27 December 1934); *Ziegfeld Follies of 1936* (30 January 1936); *Two for the Show* (8 February 1940); *Ziegfeld Follies of 1943* (1 April 1943); *Laffing Room Only* (23 December 1944); *The Firebrand of Florence* (22 March 1945); *Three to Make Ready* (7 March 1946); *Leonard Sillman's New Faces of 1952* (16 May 1952); *John Murray Anderson's Almanac* (10 December 1950). Directing assignments including *Dearest Enemy* (18 September 1925); *Murray Anderson's Almanac* (14 August 1929); *Jumbo* (16 November 1935); *One for the Money* (4 February 1939); *All in Fun* (27 December 1940); *Heaven on Earth* (16 September 1948). For several of the productions listed, Anderson also provided lighting design. He died on 30 January 1954 in New York City.

Daniel V. Arthur, producer and director, who provided theatrical staging for *A Matinee Idol* (29 April 1910); *The Paradise of Mahomet* (17 January 1911); *Robin Hood* (6 May 1912); *Rob Roy* (15 September 1913). Directing assignments included *Oliver Goldsmith* (19 March 1900); *Judy Forgot* (6 October 1910); *Houses of Sand* (17 February 1925). Producer of *The Gadfly* (18 September 1899); *The Night of the Party* (6 October 1902); *Nancy Brown* (16 February 1903); *Moonshine* (30 October 1905); *Marrying Mary* (27 August 1906); *The Measure of a Man* (20 October 1906); *The Boys and Betty* (2 November 1908); *The Opera Ball* (12 February 1912); *90 in the Shade* (25 January 1915).

James Barnes, actor, producer, writer, director, and stage manager of *Rip Van Winkle* (3 October 1870); *Lucretia Borgia* (13 February 1871); *Little Red Riding-Hood* (15 January 1872); *Dick Whittington and his Cat* (5 February 1872); *Poll and Partner Joe* (19 February 1872); *Luna*

(4 March 1872). Productions directed include *The Golden Butterfly* (5 September 1870); *Paris* (14 November 1870); *Lurline* (1 April 1872); *Ixion* (29 April 1872).

Rose Beckett, choreographer of *The Arabian Nights, or, Aladdin's Wonderful Lamp* (12 September 1887); *Dorothy* (5 November 1887); *The Lady Slavey* (3 February 1896).

David Bennett, dance instructor in Syracuse, New York, who moved to New York City to become a dancer, choreographer, and director. Choreographed productions include *Marcelle* (1 October 1908); *A Skylark* (4 April 1910); *Nobody Home* (20 April 1915); *Cousin Lucy* (27 August 1915); *Very Good Eddie* (23 December 1915); *Go to It* (24 October 1916); *His Little Widows* (30 April 1917); *Leave It to Jane* (28 August 1917); *Oh, Look!* (7 March 1918); *Poor Little Ritz Girl* (28 July 1920); *Pitter Patter* (28 September 1920); *The Right Girl* (15 March 1921); *It's Up to You* (28 March 1921); *June Love* (25 April 1921); *Queen o' Hearts* (10 October 1922); *Wildflower* (7 February 1923); *Adrienne* (28 May 1923); *Battling Buttler* (8 October 1923); *Andre Charlot's Revue of 1924* (9 January 1924); *Vogues of 1924* (27 March 1924); *Majorie* (11 August 1924); *The Dream Girl* (20 August 1924); *Top-Hole* (1 September 1924); *Rose Marie* (2 September 1924); *Dear Sir* (23 September 1924); *Sunny* (22 September 1925); *The City Chap* (26 October 1925); *Florida Girl* (2 November 1925); *Earl Carroll's Vanities* (1926) (24 August 1926); *Criss Cross* (12 October 1926); *Lucky* (22 March 1927); *My Princess* (6 October 1927); *Golden Dawn* (30 November 1927); *Lovely Lady* (29 December 1927); *Three Cheers* (15 October 1928).

Joseph Harry Benrimo, director, writer, stage manager was born circa 1874 in San Francisco, California. Productions staged included *Lady Luxury* (25 December 1914); *The Peasant Girl* (2 March 1915); *Hands Up* (22 July 1915); *The Blue Paradise* (5 August 1915); *Alone at Last* (19 October 1915); *Ruggles of Red Gap* (25 December 1915); *See America First* (28 March 1916); *The Girl from Brazil* (30 August 1916); *Follow Me* (29 November 1916); *Love o' Mike* (15 January 1917); *Good Night, Paul* (3 September 1917); *Creoles* (22 September 1927); *The Yellow Jacket* (7 November 1928); *The Well of Romance* (7 November 1930). Plays directed included *The Yellow Jacket* (4 November 1912); *Nobody Home* (20 April 1915); *Right of Happiness* (2 April 1931). Benrimo died in New York City on 26 March 1942.

R.H. Burnside, director, choreographer, composer, and writer was born in Glasgow, Scotland, on 13 August 1873. The New York City productions he staged included *A Royal Rogue* (24 December 1900); *Winsome Winnie* (1 December 1903); *The Girl from Dixie* (14 December 1903); *Sergeant Kitty* (18 January 1904); *Lady Teazle* (24 December 1904); *Fantana* (14 January 1905); *Happyland* (2 October 1905); *The Earl and the Girl* (4 November 1905); *Mexicana* (29 January 1906); *The Social Whirl* (9 April 1906); *The Tourists* (25 August 1906); *My Lady's Maid* (20 September 1906); *The Belle of London Town* (28 January 1907); *Fascinating Flora* (20 May 1907); *The Gay White Way* (7 October 1907); *Sporting Days* (5 September 1908); *The Pied Piper* (3 December 1908); *The International Cup / The Ballet of Niagra / The Earthquake* (3 September 1910); *The Red Rose* (22 June 1911); *When Sweet Sixteen* (14 September 1911); *The Three Romeos* (13 November 1911); *Over the River* (8 January 1912); *The Lady of the Slipper* (28 October 1912); *The Beauty Shop* (13 April 1914); *The Dancing Duchess* (19 August 1914); *Chin Chin* (20 October 1914); *Watch Your Step* (8 December 1914); *Hip! Hip! Hooray!* (30 September 1915); *Stop! Look! Listen!* (25 December 1915); *The Big Show* (31 August 1916); *When Johnny Comes Marching Home* (7 May 1917); *Cheer Up* (23 August 1917); *Jack O'Lantern* (16 October 1917); *Everything* (22 August 1918); *Miss Millions* (9 December 1917); *The Girl from Home* (3 May 1920); *Good Times* (9 August 1920); *Tip Top* (5 October 1920); *Get Together* (3 September 1921); *Some Party* (15 April 1922); *Better Times* (2 September 1922); *Nifties of 1923* (25 September 1923); *Stepping Stones* (6 November 1923); *China Rose* (19 January 1925); *The City Chap* (26 October 1925); *Criss Cross* (12 October 1926); *Three Cheers* (15 October 1928); *How's Your Health* (26 November 1929); *Smiling Faces* (30 August 1932); *The Only Girl* (21 May 1934); *The Mikado* (15 July 1935); *The Pirates of Penzance* (22 July 1935); *The Gondoliers* (5 August 1935); *Trial by Jury / H.M.S. Pinafore* (12 August 1935); *Robin Hood* (7 November 1944). Productions directed included *The Emerald Isle* (1September 1902); *The Mocking Bird* (10 November 1902); *The Babes and the Baron* (25 December 1905); *The Dove of Peace* (4 November 1912); *Happy Days* (23 August 1919); *Madame Pompadour* (11 November 1924); *Great Day* (17 October

1929); *H.M.S. Pinafore / The Green Table* (21 January 1942); *The Mikado / The Big City / A Ball in Old Vienna* (3 February 1942); *The Pirates of Penzance / The Prodigal Son* (17 February 1942); *Iolanthe* (23 February 1942); *Trial by Jury* (28 February 1942); *Patience* (25 February 1944); *Ruddigore* (2 March 1944); *The Yeomen of the Guard* (3 March 1944). Burnside died on 14 September 1952 in Metuchen, New Jersey.

Davide Costa, ballet dancer and choreographer born in Italy circa 1835, performed in Genoa, Bologna, and Florence where he choreographed a version of *Semiramide sul Trono d'Assiria* at the Teatro Pergola in 1853. Other ballets performed in Italy included *Edmond Dantes, o Il Conte d'Oglaia* (1856); *Pelagio e Loretta l'indovina* (1859); *Folgore, ossia il Demone seduttore* (1861); *Il Conte di Montecristo* (1862); and *Oronos* (1864). He arrived in New York City in 1866 with the Italian ballerina Rita Sangali to choreograph the ballets for the spectacular melodrama *The Black Crook* (12 September 1866) and subsequently designed the dances for *The White Fawn* (17 January 1868); *Barbe-Bleue* (13 July 1868); *Humpty Dumpty* (reconstruction) (25 January 1869); *Hiccory Diccory Dock, or, Harlequin Jack of the Beanstalk!* (18 May 1869); *The Glorious 7* (31 January 1870); *The Twelve Temptations!* (7 February 1870); *Le Petit Faust* (26 September 1870); *The Black Crook* (revival) (12 December 1870); and a second revival of *The Black Crook* (18 December 1871). Costa died of yellow fever in 1873.

Gerald Coventry, American director and stage manager; staged *The Runaways* (11 May 1903); and *Piff! Paff!! Pouff!!!* (26 December 1904). Directed *A Chinese Honeymoon* (2 June 1902); and *Piff! Paff!! Pouff!!!* (2 April 1904).

H.A. Cripps, director, performer, and stage manager; staged productions included *The Begum* (21 September 1887); *The Charlatan* (5 December 1889); *El Capitan* (20 April 1896 and 21 September 1896). Directed *Dr. Syntax* (23 June 1894).

Ernest D'Auban, director and choreographer; choreographed productions included *The Sleeping Beauty and the Beast* (4 November 1901); *Mr. Bluebeard* (21 January 1903); *Mother Goose* (2 December 1903); *Humpty Dumpty* (14 November 1904); *The White Cat* (2 November

1905); *Humpty Dumpty* (12 March 1906); *Hop o' My Thumb* (26 November 1913). Directed *The Sins of Society* (31 August 1909); and *Hop o' My Thumb* (26 November 1913).

John Durang, American dancer and choreographer, born in Lancaster, Pennsylvania, on 6 January 1768. A skilled performer of interlude dances during theatrical performances, Durang was said to have danced the hornpipe blindfolded on thirteen eggs (November 1789); additional interlude dances included the allemande, minuet, fandango, and "Fricassee dance," in addition to the original transformation dance, "Dwarf Dance" advertised in a production of *As You Like It* on 13 July 1786. Productions in which he choreographed dances included *Genii, or, Harlequin's Vagaries* (22 February 1788); *Tammany, or, The Indian Chief* (3 March 1794); *The Children in the Wood* (24 November 1794); *Sophia of Brabant, or, the False Friend* (29 December 1794); *The Country Frolic, or, the Merry Haymakers* (October 1796); *The Magic Tree, or, Neptune's Favor* (4 April 1797); *The Battle of the Kegs* (February 1799); *Harlequin Prisoner, or, the Genii of the Rocks* (March 1803); *Stoffle Rips and Anna Lis, or, Seu Schwarm Wedding* (September 1804); *Spirit of Independence* (October 1807); *Harvest Frolic* (July 1808); *Der Zwergl-Danz* (August 1813). Durang died in Philadelphia on 29 March 1822.

Oscar Eagle, director and stage manager, born 21 January 1861 in Gallipolis, Ohio. Productions staged included *April* (8 April 1918); *The Melting of Molly* (30 December 1918); *The Little Whopper* (13 October 1919); *The Little Blue Devil* (3 November 1919); *Jimmie* (17 November 1920); *Marjolaine* (24 January 1922); *Wildflower* (7 February 1923); *Princess April* (1 December 1924); *Topsy and Eva* (23 December 1924); *Holka Polka* (14 October 1925); *The Matinee Girl* (1 February 1926); *Katy Did* (9 May 1927); *Enchanted Isle* (19 September 1927); *Animal Crackers* (23 October 1928). Productions directed included *Mrs. Wiggs of the Cabbage Patch* (3 September 1904); *Sometime* (4 October 1918); *Three Showers* (5 April 1920); *The Cocoanuts* (8 December 1925); *The Cocoanuts* (16 May 1927); *Houseboat on the Styx* (25 December 1928). Eagle died in New York City on 14 March 1930.

Leon Errol, performer, director, and stage manager, born on 3 July 1881 in Sydney, New South Wales, Australia. First came to America in 1898, managed a theatre company in Portland, Oregon, prior to appearing in five editions of the *Ziegfeld Follies* (1911–1915) and other Broadway revues and musicals including *Sally* (21 December 1920); *Louie the 14th* (3 March 1925); *Yours Truly* (25 January 1927); *Fioretta* (5 February 1929). Staged productions included *Ziegfeld Midnight Frolic* (November 1915); *The Century Girl* (8 November 1916); *Dance and Grow Thin* (18 January 1917); *Hitchy-Koo* (7 June 1917); *Hitchy-Koo* (6 June 1918); *Princess Virtue* (4 May 1921); *Ziegfeld Midnight Frolic* (17 November 1921); *The Blue Kitten* (13 January 1922). Productions directed included *Ziegfeld Follies of 1914* (1 June 1914); *Ziegfeld Follies of 1915* (21 June 1915); *Words and Music* (24 December 1917); *Snapshots of 1921* (2 June 1921). Following a successful film career with RKO, Errol died in Hollywood, California, on 12 October 1951.

Barney Fagan, performer, director, stage manager, choreographer, and composer, born in Boston, Massachusetts, on 12 January 1850. Productions choreographed and staged included *The Passing Show* (12 May 1894); *By the Sad Sea Waves* (28 February 1899); and *The Man from China* (2 May 1904). He also contributed additional music to *The Passing Show*; *By the Sad Sea Waves*; and *Ziegfeld Follies of 1911* (26 June 1911). Fagan died in Bay Shore, New York, on 12 January 1937.

Michel Fokine, ballet dancer and choreographer, born on 23 April 1880 in Saint Petersburg, Russia. He debuted at the age of nine in *The Talisman* choreographed by Marius Petipa and later danced with the Imperial Russian Ballet and became a teacher with the Imperial Ballet School. His choreographic works in Europe included *Acis et Galatée* (1905); *Eunice* (1907); *The Dying Swan* (1907); *Les Sylphides* (1909). Also in 1909, Fokine became resident choreographer with the Ballets Russes in Paris where he choreographed *Scheherazade* (1910); *The Firebird* (1910); *Le Spectre de la Rose* (1911); *Petrushka* (1912); and *Daphnis et Chloé*. After WWI, Fokine moved to New York City where he choreographed ballets in Broadway productions that included *Aphrodite* (24 November 1919); *Mecca* (4 October 1920); *The Rose Girl* (11 February 1921); *Ziegfeld Follies of 1922* (5 June 1922); *Sweet Little Devil* (21 January 1924). In 1921 he established a school of ballet and three years later he organized a ballet company, called the "American Ballet." Fokine died in New York City on 22 August 1942.

Sam Forrest, director, stage manager, born in Richmond, Virginia, circa 1866. Productions staged included *The Royal Vagabond* (17 February 1919); *Honey Girl* (3 May 1920); *Mary* (18 October 1920); *Baby Cyclone* (12 September 1927); *The Merry Malones* (28 September 1927); *My Princess* (6 October 1927); *Billie* (1 October 1928); *The Tavern* (19 May 1930); *The Rhapsody* (15 September 1930); *Pigeons and People* (16 January 1935); *Seven Keys to Baldpate* (27 May 1935); *Dear Old Darling* (2 March 1936); The Cuntry Gentleman (25 May 1936); Fulton of Oak Falls (10 February 1937); The Return of the Vagabond (17 May 1940). Forrest died in New York City on 30 April 1944.

Allan K. Foster, director, stage manager, choreographer. Productions choreographed included *Madam Moselle* (23 May 1914); *The Debutante* (7 December 1914); *Alone at Last* (19 October 1915); *Robinson Crusoe, Jr.* (17 February 1916); *The Passing Show of 1916* (22 June 1916); *The Girl from Brazil* (30 August 1916); *Follow Me* (29 November 1916); *My Lady's Glove* (18 June 1917); *Maytime* (16 August 1917); *Doing Our Bit* (18 October 1917); *Over the Top* (28 November 1917); *Girl o' Mine* (28 January 1918); *The Melting of Molly* (30 December 1918); *Shubert Gaieties of 1919* (17 July 1919); *Hello, Alexander* (7 October 1919); *The Passing Show of 1919* (11 November 1919); *Frivolities of 1920* (8 January 1920); *The Half Moon* (1 November 1920); *Bombo* (6 October 1921); *The Rose of Stamboul* (7 March 1922); *Red Pepper* (29 May 1922); *The Lady in Ermine* (2 October 1922); *Springtime of Youth* (26 October 1922); *The Passing Show of 1923* (14 June 1923); *The Circus Princess* (25 April 1927); *Marching By* (3 March 1932); *Jumbo* (16 November 1935). Productions staged included *The Show of Wonders* (26 October 1916); *The Passing Show of 1917* (26 April 1917); *Sometime* (4 October 1918); *Monte Cristo, Jr.* (12 February 1919); *The Magic Melody* (11 November 1919); *Florodora* (5 April 1920); *Cinderella on Broadway* (24 June 1920); *The Last Waltz* (10 May 1921); *The Whirl of New York* (13 June 1921); *The Mimic World* (17 August 1921); *Up in the Clouds* (2 January 1922); *Make It Snappy* (13 April 1922); *Spice of 1922* (6 July 1922); *The Passing Show of 1922* (20 September 1922); *Sally, Irene and Mary* (23 March 1925).

Augusto Francioli, Italian-born ballet director and choreographer. Productions choreographed included *Princess Nicotine* (25 October 1893); *The Voyage of Suzette* (23 December 1893); *The Passing Show*

(12 May 1894); *Jacinta, or, The Maid of Manzanillo* (26 November 1894); *The 20th Century Girl* (25 January 1895); *Daughter of the Revolution* (27 May 1895); *Marguerite* (10 February 1896); *In Gay New York* (28 May 1896); *Kismet, or, Two Tangled Turks* (4 January 1897); *The Whirl of the Town* (25 May 1897); *The Belle of New York* (28 September 1897); *The Telephone Girl* (27 December 1897); *The Belle of New York* (revival) (22 January 1900).

William Francis, English-born ballet dancer, pantomimist, and choreographer; teacher of John Durang, among others. Productions choreographed included *Caledonian Frolic* (2 November 1793); *Scheming Clown, or, The Sportsman Deceived* (28 February 1794); *La Forêt Noire* (26 April 1794); *Irish Lilt* (9 July 1794); *Rural Revels, or, the Easter Holiday* (10 April 1795); *Sailor's Return* (13 May 1795); *Harlequin Hurry-Scurry* (25 May 1795); *Les Armans d'Arcade* (11 June 1795); *The Miraculous Mill, or, The Old Ground Young* (26 June 1795 and 21 November 1795); *The Warrior's Welcome Home* (10 February 1796); *Shamrock, or St. Patrick's Day* (18 March 1796); *Harlequin's Club* (30 May 1796); *Harlequin Dr. Faustus* (3 June 1796); *American Tar, or, The Press Gang Defeated* (17 June 1796); *The Lucky Escape, or, the Ploughman Turned Sailor* (29 July 1796); *Magician of the Enchanted Castle* (24 April 1797); *Hercules and Omphale* (22 February 1802); *The Corsair* (8 June 1802); *Lady of the Lake* (1 January 1812); *The Bridal Ring* (10 February 1812); *Peasant Boy, or, Innocence Protected* (11 March 1812); *Little Red Riding Hood* (7 December 1812); *Rural Grace* (12 February 1813); *L'Amour vient a bout de tour* (24 February 1813); *The Jovial Crew* (10 March 1813); *La Triomphe de l'Amour* (7 June 1813).

Max Freeman, director and stage manager; productions staged included *Castles in the Air* (5 May 1890); *Claudius Nero* (21 October 1890); *The Fencing Master* (14 November 1892); *Rob Roy* (29 October 1894); *Jacinta, or, The Maid of Manzanillo* (26 November 1894); *The Tzigane* (16 May 1895); *Kismet, or, Two Tangled Turks* (12 August 1895); *The Gold Bug* (21 September 1896); *Santa Maria* (24 September 1896); *The Highwayman* (13 December 1897); *The Little Host* (27 December 1898); *Mother Goose* (1 May 1899); *Erminie* (9 May 1899); *The Rounders* (12 July 1899); *From Broadway to Tokio* (23 January 1900); *Quo Vadis* (9 April 1900); *Sweet Anne Page* (3 December 1900);

Manon Lescaut (19 March 1901); *A Modern Magdalen* (29 March 1902); *The Blonde in Black* (8 June 1903); *Love's Lottery* (3 October 1904); *A China Doll* (19 November 1904); *Mademoiselle Marni* (6 March 1905); *The Girl from Rector's* (1 February 1909); *The Girl in the Taxi* (24 October 1910).

Bert French, American performer, director, stage manager, and choreographer; productions choreographed included *The Maid of the Mountains* (11 September 1918); *Glorianna* (28 October 1918); *The Little Blue Devil* (3 November 1919); *Tickle Me* (17 August 1920); *Jimmie* (17 November 1920); *Blue Eyes* (21 February 1921); *Music Box Revue* (22 September 1921); *Marjolaine* (24 January 1922); *Up She Goes* (6 November 1922); *Elsie* (2 April 1923); *Lollipop* (21 January 1924); *The Chiffon Girl* (19 February 1924). Productions staged included *He Didn't Want to Do It* (20 August 1918); *Tumble In* (24 March 1919); *The Little Whopper* (13 October 1919); *Honey Girl* (3 May 1921); *The Broadway Whirl* (8 June 1921); *Tangerine* (9 August 1921); *Up She Goes* (6 November 1922); *Glory* (25 December 1922).

M.B. Gilbert, choreographer; productions included *My Lady* (11 February 1901); *Miss Simplicity* (10 February 1902).

James Gorman, stage manager, director, and choreographer; staged productions included *Zig-Zag Alley* (19 January 1903); *Running for Office* (27 April 1903); *Flo-Flo* (21 November 1904); *The Grafter* (29 January 1906); *The Yankee Prince* (20 April 1908); *The Little Millionaire* (25 September 1911); *The Red Widow* (6 November 1911); *The Pearl Maiden* (22 January 1912); *The Cohan Revue of 1918* (31 December 1917). Productions choreographed included *Cohan and Harris Minstrels* (3 August 1908); *Hello, Broadway!* (25 December 1914).

Herbert Gresham, performer, director, stage manager, and choreographer, born in London, England, circa 1853. Broadway productions staged included *A Runaway Girl* (25 August 1898); *Sister Mary* (15 September 1899); *Lost River* (3 October 1900); *The Messenger Boy* (16 September 1901); *The Liberty Belles* (30 September 1901); *The Toreador* (6 January 1902); *Maid Marian* (27 January 1902); *The Billionaire* (29 December 1902); *Mr. Bluebeard* (21 January 1903); *The Rogers Brothers in London* (7 September 1903); *Mother Goose* (2

December 1903); *A Little Bit of Everything* (6 June 1904); *The Rogers Brothers in Paris* (5 September 1904); *Humpty Dumpty* (14 November 1904); *Sergeant Brue* (24 April 1905); *Lifting the Lid* (5 June 1905); *The Pearl and the Pumpkin* (21 August 1905); *The Ham Tree* (28 August 1905); *The Rogers Brothers in Ireland* (4 September 1905); *Fritz in Tammany Hall* (16 October 1905); *The White Cat* (2 November 1905); *The Free Lance* (16 April 1906); *The Governor's Son* (4 June 1906); *Barbara's Millions* (8 October 1906); *The Grand Mogul* (25 March 1907); *Follies of 1907* (8 July 1907); *A Waltz Dream* (27 January 1908); *The Soul Kiss* (28 January 1908); *Follies of 1908* (15 June 1908); *Little Nemo* (20 October 1908); *The Mascot* (12 April 1909); *Follies of 1909* (14 June 1909); *The Silver Star* (1 November 1909); *The Young Turk* (31 January 1910); *The Pink Lady* (13 March 1911); *The Count of Luxembourg* (16 September 1912); *Oh! Oh! Delphine* (30 September 1912); *Eva* (30 December 1912); *My Little Friend* (19 May 1913); *The Little Café* (10 November 1913); *The Queen of the Movies* (12 January 1914); *Fads and Fancies* (8 March 1915); *Around the Map* (1 November 1915); *Miss Springtime* (25 September 1916); *The Rainbow Girl* (1 April 1918); *La-La-Lucille* (28 May 1919). Productions directed included *A Midsummer Night's Dream* (26 October 1903); *In Newport* (26 December 1904); *The Prince of India* (24 September 1906); *The Riviera Girl* (24 September 1917). Gresham died in Mount Vernon, New York, on 23 February 1921.

Harry Wagstaff Gribble, performer, writer, and stage manager, born in Seven Oaks, England, on 27 March 1896. Productions staged included *You Know Me Al!* (11 April 1918); *Artists and Models* (20 August 1923); *Artists and Models* (15 October 1924); *Loud Speaker* (7 March 1927); *Revolt* (31 October 1928); *Houseparty* (9 September 1929); *City Haul* (30 December 1929); *The Royal Virgin* (17 March 1930); *The Silent Witness* (23 March 1931); *Cynara* (2 November 1931); *No More Ladies* (23 January 1934); *Mainly for Lovers* (21 February 1936); *Something for Nothing* (9 December 1937); *Johnny Belinda* (18 September 1940); *Anna Lucasta* (30 August 1944). Gribble died in New York City on 28 January 1981.

A. Grossi, Italian-born ballet dancer and choreographer; choreographic works on Broadway included *Mazulm* (11 July 1864); *The Green Monster* (10 July 1865); *The Beauty of Seville* and *Robert and Bertrand*

(31 July 1865); *The Midnight Assault* and *Love among the Bonnets* (7 August 1865); *The Witch of the Black Cavern* (14 August 1865); *Jack and Gill Went Up the Hill* (29 February 1866); *Valiant Valentine* (27 March 1866); *The Sheep's Foot* (18 June 1866); *Cendrillon* (17 December 1866); *A Bird of Paradise* (29 January 1867); *Little Boy Blue, or, Hush-A-Bye Baby* and *Patty and Her Pitcher* (1 April 1867).

Cissie Hayden, dancer and choreographer; Broadway production choreographed: *Good Times* (9 August 1920). Broadway productions in which she danced: *Everything* (22 August 1918); *Happy Days* (23 August 1919).

George V. Hobart, Canadian director, stage manager, and writer, born on 16 January 1867 in Port Hawksbury, Nova Scotia, Canada. Staged productions included *When Sweet Sixteen* (14 September 1911); *Experience* (27 October 1914; 22 January 1918); *Sonny* (16 August 1921); *Lefty Pepper* (10 April 1922). Productions written included *From Broadway to Tokio* (23 January 1900); *A Million Dollars* (27 September 1900); *The Military Maid* (8 October 1900); *Nell-Go-In* (31 October 1900); *The Wild Rose* (5 May 1902); *Sally in Our Alley* (22 August 1902); *The Jersey Lily* (14 September 1903); *Mrs. Black Is Back* (7 November 1904); *A Yankee Circus on Mars* and *The Raiders* (12 April 1905); *The Ham Tree* (28 August 1905); *Moonshine* (30 October 1905); *Coming Thro' the Rye* (9 January 1906); *The Merry Widow Burlesque* (2 January 1908); *The Boys and Betty* (2 November 1908); *The Candy Shop* (27 April 1909); *The Yankee Girl* (10 February 1910); *Ziegfeld Follies of 1911* (26 June 1911); *When Sweet Sixteen* (14 September 1911); *The Woman Haters* (7 October 1912); *Ziegfeld Follies of 1913* (16 June 1913); *Ziegfeld Follies of 1914* (1 June 1914); *Ziegfeld Follies of 1916* (12 June 1916); *Ziegfeld Follies of 1917* (12 June 1917); *Buddies* (27 October 1919); *Kissing Time* (11 October 1920); *Sonny* (16 August 1921); *The Greenwich Village Follies* (12 September 1922). Hobart died in Cumberland, Maryland, on 31 January 1926.

Ernest Hogan, performer, writer, ragtime composer, and stage manager, born in Bowling Green, Kentucky, in 1865. Productions staged included *At Jolly Coon-ey Island* (March 1898); *The Origin of the Cakewalk, or, Clorindy* (18 June 1898); *Rufus Rastus* (29 January 1906); *The Oyster Man* (16 December 1907). Contributed musical numbers to *A Black Sheep* (6 January 1896); *By the Sad Sea Waves* (28 February 1899); *Sons of Ham* (15 October 1900); *Madge Smith, Attorney* (10 December 1900); *Southern Enchantment* (23 February 1903); *Rufus Rastus*; and *The Oyster Man*. Hogan died of tuberculosis in Lakewood, New Jersey, on 20 May 1909.

A.M. Holbrook, performer, stage manager, and choreographer; productions staged included *Cyrano de Bergerac* (18 September 1899); *The Monks of Malabar* (14 September 1900); *The Strollers* (24 June 1901); *Dolly Varden* (27 January 1902); *When Johnny Comes Marching Home* (16 December 1902); *The Office Boy* (2 November 1903); *Babette* (16 November 1903); *A Venetian Romance* (2 May 1904); *The Baroness Fiddlesticks* (21 November 1904); *Miss Dolly Dollars* (4 September 1905); *Twiddle-Twaddle* (1 January 1906); *Marrying Mary* (27 August 1906); *Dream City* (24 December 1906); *Lola from Berlin* (16 September 1907); *The Girls of Holland* (18 November 1907); *Funabashi* (6 January 1908); *The Hermits in Dixie* (25 May 1908); *The Golden Butterfly* (12 October 1908); *The Pearl Maiden* (22 January 1912); *Let George Do It* (22 April 1912); *The Gypsy* (14 November 1912); *Lieber Augustin* (3 September 1913). Productions choreographed included *The Two Roses* (21 November 1904); *The Chocolate Soldier* (13 September 1909); *The Echo* (17 August 1910); *The Girl in the Train* (3 October 1910); *Baron Trenck* (11 March 1912).

William Holbrook, performer, stage manager, and choreographer; productions choreographed included *Better Times* 2 September 1922); *Nifties of 1923* (25 September 1923); *Ripples* (11 February 1930); *Everybody's Welcome* (13 October 1931); *A Connecticut Yankee* (revival) (17 November 1943). Productions staged included *Murray Anderson's Almanac* (14 August 1929); *Who Cares* (8 July 1930).

J.C. Huffman, prolific stage manager for the Shubert Brothers; productions included *The Road to Yesterday* (31 December 1906); *The White Hen* (16 February 1907); *The Girl behind the Counter* (1 October 1907); *Nearly a Hero* (24 February 1908); *The Mimic World* (9 July 1908); *Mlle. Mischief* (28 September 1908); *The Ringmaster* (9 August 1909); *La Belle Paree / Bow-Sing / Tortajada* (20 March 1911); *The Kiss Waltz* (18 September 1911); *The Never Homes* (5 October 1911); *The Duchess* (16 October 1911); *A Night with the Pierrots / Sesostra*

/ *The Whirl of Society* (5 March 1912); *Two Little Brides* (23 April 1912); *The Man with Three Wives* (23 January 1913); *Lieber Augustin* (3 September 1913); *Oh, I Say!* (30 October 1913); *The Passing Show of 1914* (1 June 1914); *Miss Daisy* (9 September 1914); *Dancing Around* (10 October 1914); *Experience* (27 October 1914); *Maid in America* (18 February 1915); *The Peasant Girl* (2 March 1915); *All over Town* (26 April 1915); *The Passing Show of 1915* (29 May 1915); *A World of Pleasure* (14 October 1915); *Robinson Crusoe, Jr.* (17 February 1916); *The Passing Show of 1916* (22 June 1916); *The Show of Wonders* (26 October 1916); *The Passing Show of 1917* (26 April 1917); *My Lady's Glove* (18 June 1917); *Over the Top* (28 November 1917); *Sinbad* (14 February 1918); *Follow the Girl* (2 March 1918); *Fancy Free* (11 April 1918); *The Passing Show of 1918* (28 July 1918); *Monte Cristo, Jr.* (12 February 1919); *Shubert Gaieties of 1919* (17 July 1919); *The Passing Show of 1919* (23 October 1919); *The Magic Melody* (11 November 1919); *Cinderella on Broadway* (24 June 1920); *Broadway Brevities of 1920* (29 September 1920); *The Passing Show of 1921* (29 December 1920); *The Last Waltz* (10 May 1921); *Blossom Time* (29 September 1921); *Bombo* (6 October 1921); *The Rose of Stamboul* (7 March 1922); *Make It Snappy* (13 April 1922); *The Passing Show of 1922* (20 September 1922); *Springtime of Youth* (26 October 1922); *The Dancing Girl* (24 January 1923); *The Passing Show of 1923* (14 June 1923); *Topics of 1923* (20 November 1923); *The Dream Girl* (20 August 1924); *The Passing Show of 1924* (3 September 1924); *The Student Prince* (2 December 1924); *Big Boy* (7 January 1925); *June Days* (6 August 1925); *Princess Flavia* (2 November 1925); *A Night in Paris* (5 January 1926); *The Great Temptations* (18 May 1926); *The Merry World* (8 June 1926); *Katja* (18 October 1926); *Gay Paree* (9 November 1926); *The Circus Princess* (25 April 1927); *My Maryland* (12 September 1927); *The Love Call* (24 October 1927); *Artists and Models* (15 November 1927); *Lovely Lady* (29 December 1927); *Countess Maritza* (9 April 1928); *Marching By* (3 March 1932).

Benny Jones, performer and choreographer, contributed musical staging to *The Red Moon* (3 May 1909).

Alexis Kosloff, ballet dancer and choreographer; productions choreographed included *The Show of Wonders* (26 October 1916); *Chu Chin Chow* (22 October 1917); *Sinbad* (14 February 1918); *Little Simplicity*

(4 November 1918); *The Century Revue* (12 July 1920); *The Love Song* (13 January 1925); *Gay Paree* (18 August 1925); *Sunny* (22 September 1925).

Theodore Kosloff, Russian ballet dancer and choreographer, born in Moscow on 22 January 1882. Productions choreographed included *The Passing Show of 1912* (22 July 1912); *The Passing Show of 1915* (29 May 1915); *Hands Up* (22 July 1915); *A World of Pleasure* (14 October 1915); *See America First* (28 March 1916). Kosloff also choreographed films, including *Manslaughter* (24 September 1922); *The Golden Bed* (25 January 1925); *Sunny* (9 November 1930); *The Raven* (8 July 1935); *Samson and Delilah* (January 1950). Kosloff died in Los Angeles on 22 November 1956.

Fred G. Latham, stage manager, born in England circa 1853. Productions included *Babette* (16 November 1903); *The Two Roses* (21 November 1904); *Mlle. Modiste* (25 December 1906); *The Red Mill* (24 September 1906); *The Prima Donna* (30 November 1908); *The Fair Co-Ed* (1 February 1909); *The Candy Shop* (27 April 1909); *The Echo* (17 August 1910); *The Girl in the Train* (3 October 1916); *The Enchantress* (19 October 1911); *The Red Widow* (6 November 1911); *The Firefly* (2 December 1912); *Sweethearts* (8 September 1913); *The Madcap Duchess* (11 November 1913); *The Only Girl* (2 November 1914); *The Princess Pat* (29 September 1915); *Sybil* (10 January 1916); *Eileen* (19 March 1917); *Her Regiment* (12 November 1917); *The Canary* (4 November 1918); *She's a Good Fellow* (5 May 1919); *Apple Blossoms* (7 October 1919); *The Night Boat* (2 February 1920); *The Half Moon* (1 November 1920); *The Yankee Princess* (2 October 1922); *The Bunch and Judy* (28 November 1922); *Caroline* (31 January 1923); *Dew Drop Inn* (17 May 1923); *One Kiss* (27 November 1923); *Sitting Pretty* (8 April 1924); *The Love Song* (13 January 1925); *Sky High* (2 March 1925); *Happy Go Lucky* (30 September 1926). Latham died in New York City on 31 January 1943.

George W. Lederer, producer and stage manager, born in Wilkes-Barre, Pennsylvania, circa 1862. Staged productions included *The Belle of New York* (28 September 1897); *Yankee Doodle Dandy* (25 July 1898); *The Man in the Moon* (24 April 1899); *The Casino Girl* (19 March 1900); *The Belle of Bohemia* (24 September 1900); *The New Yorkers* (7

October 1901); *The Wild Rose* (5 Mat 1902); *The Chaperons* (5 June 1902); *Sally in Our Alley* (29 August 1902); *The Jewel of Asia* (16 February 1903); *The Blonde in Black* (8 June 1903); *George W. Lederer's Mid-Summer Fancies* (22 June 1903); *The Jersey Lily* (14 September 1903); *The Southerners* (23 May 1904); *Madame Sherry* (30 August 1910); *The Happiest Night of His Life* (20 February 1911); *Mama's Baby Boy* (25 May 1912); *The Charity Girl* (2 October 1912); *Madam Moselle* (23 May 1914); *Angel Face* (29 December 1919); *The Girl in the Spotlight* (12 July 1920); *Peaches* (22 January 1923). Lederer died in Jackson Heights, New York, on 8 October 1938.

Sammy Lee, performer, stage manager, and choreographer, born in New York City on 26 May 1890. Productions choreographed included *The Firefly* (2 December 1912); *Little Miss Charity* (2 September 1920); *The Gingham Girl* (28 August 1922);); *Peaches* (22 January 1923); *Earl Carroll's Vanities* (5 July 1923); *Music Box Revue* (22 September 1923); *Mary Jane McKane* (25 December 1923); *Sweet Little Devil* (21 January 1924); *Lady Be Good!* (1 December 1924); *Tell Me More* (13 April 1925); *Captain Jinks* (8 September 1925); *No, No, Nanette* (16 September 1925); *The Cocoanuts* (8 December 1925); *Tip-Toes* (28 December 1925); *Queen High* (8 September 1926); *Oh, Kay!* (8 November 1926); *Betsy* (28 December 1926); *Rio Rita* (2 February 1927); *Talk About Girls* (14 June 1927); *Ziegfeld Follies of 1927* (18 August 1927); *Yes, Yes, Yvette* (3 October 1927); *Show Boat* (27 December 1927); *Here's Howe* (1 May 1928); *Cross My Heart* (17 September 1928); *Lady Fingers* (31 January 1929); *Ziegfeld Midnight Frolic* (April 1929); *Singin' the Blues* (16 September 1931). Lee died in Woodland Hills, New York, on 30 March 1968.

Filiberto Marchetti, Italian-born ballet choreographer; productions included *Aladdin, Jr.* (8 April 1895); *Monte Carlo* (21 March 1898); *An Arabian Girl and 40 Thieves* (29 April 1899).

Dave Marion, choreographer; productions included *Tom Jones* (11 November 1907); *Somewhere Else* (20 January 1913).

George Marion, performer, stage manager, and choreographer, born on 16 July 1860 in San Francisco. Productions staged included *The Cadet Girl* (25 July 1900); *The Little Duchess* (14 October 1901); *The*

Doings of Mrs. Dooley (22 September 1902); *Mr. Pickwick* (19 January 1903); *The Prince of Pilsen* (17 March 1903); *Peggy from Paris* (10 September 19030; *The Yankee Consul* (22 February 1904); *The Sho-Gun* (10 October 1904); *Higgledy-Piggledy* (20 October 1904); *Woodland* (21 November 1904); *Easy Dawson* (22 August 1905); *The Galloper* (22 January 1906); *The Man from Now* (3 September 1906); *The Student King* (25 December 1906);*The Yankee Tourist* (12 August 1907); *The Merry Widow* (21 October 1907); *Nearly a Hero* (24 February 1908); *The Merry-Go-Round* (25 April 1908); *The Girl Question* (3 August 1908); *Algeria* (31 August 1908); *The Boys and Betty* (2 November 1908); *Stubborn Cinderella* (25 January 1909); *The Gay Hussars* (29 July 1909); *The Love Cure* (1 September 1909); *Madame X* (2 February 1910); *Miss Patsy* (29 August 1910); *The Spring Maid* (26 December 1910); *Everywoman* (27 February 1911); *Hell / Gaby* (27 April 1911); *The Fascinating Widow* (11 September 1911); *Gypsy Love* (17 October 1911); *Modest Suzanne* (1 January 1912); *The Rose Maid* (22 April 1912); *Tantalizing Tommy* (1 October 1912); *The Woman Haters* (3 March 1913); *The Purple Road* (7 April 1913); *Her Little Highness* (13 October 1913); *Sari* (13 January 1914); *Maids of Athens* (18 March 1914); *Suzi* (3 November 1914); *The Debutante* (7 December 1914); *Pom-Pom* (28 February 1916); *Molly O'* (17 May 1916); *The Amber Empress* (19 September 1916); *The Grass Widow* (3 December 1917); *Why Worry?* (23 August 1918); *Head over Heels* (29 August 1918); *Ziegfeld Follies of 1921* (21 June 1921); *Tangerine* (9 August 1921); *White Lilacs* (10 September 1928); *Angela* (3 December 1928); *Boom Boom* (28 January 1929). Additionally, Marion choreographed *Eileen* (19 March 1917). A performer in many Hollywood films, Marion died in Carmel, California, on 30 November 1945.

Samuel Marion, stage manager and choreographer; productions choreographed included *The Mandarin* (2 November 1896); *The Good Mr. Best* (30 August 1897); *The Runaways* (11 May 1903); *The Sho-Gun* (10 October 1904); *Higgledy-Piggledy* (20 October 1904); *Woodland* (21 November 1904); *A Yankee Circus on Mars / The Raiders* (12 April 1905); *The Duke of Duluth* (11 September 1905). Productions staged included *A Son of Rest* (17 August 1903); *The College Widower* (5 January 1905).

Robert Marks, stage manager and choreographer; choreographed productions included *Ski-Hi* (20 June 1908); *You're in Love* (6 February 1917); *Furs and Frills* (9 Octobr 1917); *Toot-Toot!* (11 March 1918); *Rock-a-Bye Baby* (22 May 1918); *Always You* (5 January 1920); *Jim Jam Jems* (4 October 1920). Staged productions included *Listen Lester* (23 December 1918); *Just a Minute* (27 October 1919).

Carl Marwig, choreographer; productions included *The School Girl* (30 December 1895); *The Strange Adventures of Jack and the Beanstalk* (2 November 1896); *The Circus Girl* (23 April 1897); *A Round of Pleasure* (24 May 1897); *The Highwayman* (13 December 1897); *The Bride-Elect* (28 December 1897); *A Reign of Error* (2 March 1899); *In Gay Paree* (20 March 1899); *The Man in the Moon* (24 April 1899); *From Broadway to Tokio* (23 January 1900); *A Million Dollars* (27 September 1900); *Sapho* (12 November 1900); *The Giddy Throng* (24 December 1900); *Beaucaire* (2 December 1901); *The School for Scandal* (31 January 1902); *The Hall of Fame* (5 February 1902); *King Highball* (6 September 1902); *Mary of Magdala* (12 November 1902); *The Blonde in Black* (8 June 1903); *Adrea* (11 January 1905); *Trilby* (8 May 1905).

Jack Mason, performer, stage manager, and choreographer; choreographed works included *The Duke of Duluth* (11 September 1905); *Fascinating Flora* (20 May 1907); *The Young Turk* (31 January 1910); *The Merry Whirl* (30 May 1910); *Girlies* (13 June 1910); *The Red Rose* (22 June 1911); *Ziegfeld Follies of 1911* (26 June 1911);*The Fascinating Widow* (11 September 1911); *Little Boy Blue* (27 November 1911); *The Midnight Girl* (23 February 1914); *The Belle of Bond Street* (30 March 1914); *The Passing Show of 1914* (1 June 1914); *Dancing Around* (10 October 1914); *The Peasant Girl* (2 March 1915); *All over Town* (26 April 1915); *The Passing Show of 1915* (29 May 1915); *Hands Up* (22 July 1915); *A World of Pleasure* (14 October 1915); *Sybil* (10 January 1916); *Step This Way* (29 May 1916); *Follow Me* (29 November 1916); *Her Soldier Boy* (6 December 1916); *Rambler Rose* (10 September 1917); *The Cohan Revue of 1918* (31 December 1917); *Sinbad* (14 February 1918); *Fancy Free* (11 April 1918); *The Passing Show of 1918* (25 July 1918); *Little Simplicity* (4 November 1918); *Good Morning, Judge* (6 February 1919); *Come Along* (8 April 1919); *A Lonely Romeo* (10 June 1919); *Broadway Brevities of 1920* (29 September 1920); *The Last Waltz* (10 May 1921); *The Lady in Ermine* (2 October 1922); *Paradise Alley* (31 March 1924); *Innocent Eyes* (20 May 1924); *Be Yourself* (3 September 1924); *The Merry Malones* (26 September 1927). Productions staged included *The Girl from Brighton* (31 August 1912); *Miss Daisy* (9 September 1914); *Maid in America* (18 February 1915); *Atta Boy* (23 December 1918); *The Midnight Rounders of 1920* (12 July 1920); *The Century Revue* (12 July 1920); *The Midnight Rounders of 1921* (7 February 1921); *The Blushing Bride* (4 February 1922); *Sue, Dear* (10 July 1922); *My Maryland* (12 September 1927); *Swing It* (22 July 1937).

Frank McCormack, performer and stage manager, born in Washington, D.C. in 1876. Productions staged included *Very Good Eddie* (23 December 1915); *Step This Way* (29 May 1916); *The Bonehead* (12 April 1920); *The Bootleggers* (27 November 1922); *The Undercurrent* (3 February 1925); *Easy Terms* (21 September 1925); *The Wasp's Nest* (25 October 1927); *Kidding Kidders* (23 April 1928); *Border-Land* (29 March 1932); *The Web* (27 June 1932); *The Monster* (10 February 1933). McCormack died in Connecticut on 22 May 1941.

Julian Mitchell, stage manager and choreographer, born in New York City in 1854, the son of musical theatre favorite, Maggie Mitchell. Productions staged included *A Hole in the Ground* (12 September 1887); *Paul Kauvar* (24 December 1887); *A Trip to Chinatown* (9 November 1891); *A Milk White Flag* (8 October 1894); *A Black Sheep* (6 January 1896); *At Gay Coney Island* (1 February 1897); *The Idol's Eye* (25 October 1897); *Pousse Café / The Worst Born* (2 December 1897); *The Fortune Teller* (26 September 1898); *The Three Dragoons* (30 January 1899); *Helter Skelter* (6April 1899); *An Arabian Girl and 40 Thieves* (29 May 1899); *The Singing Girl* (23 October 1899); *A Greek Slave* (28 November 1899); *The Princess Chic* (12 February 1900); *Fiddle-Dee-Dee* (6 September 1900); *The Girl from Up There* (7 January 1901); *Hoity Toity* (5 September 1901); *Twirly Whirly* (11 September 1902); *The Wizard of Oz* (20 January 1903); *Babes in Toyland* (13 October 1903); *It Happened in Nordland* (5 December 1904); *Wonderland* (24 October 1905); *About Town* (30 August 1906); *The Great Decade* (15 November 1906); *A Parisian Model* (27 November 1906); *The White Hen* (16 February 1907); *The Tattooed Man* (18February 1907); *Follies of 1907* (8 July 1907); *The Girl behind the Counter* (1 October

1907); *Hip! Hip! Hooray!* (10 October 1907); *The Merry Widow Burlesque* (2 January 1908); *The Soul Kiss* (28 January 1908); *Follies of 1908* (15 June 1908); *The Merry Widow and the Devil* (16 November 1908); *Miss Innocence* (30 November 1908); *Follies of 1910* (20 June 1910); *The Bachelor Belles* (7 November 1910); *Ziegfeld Follies of 1911* (26 June 1911); *A Winsome Widow* (11 April 1912); *The Count of Luxembourg* (16 September 1912); *Oh! Oh! Delphine* (30 September 1912); *Ziegfeld Follies of 1912* (21 October 1912); *Ziegfeld Follies of 1913* (16 June 1913); *Ziegfeld Follies of 1915* (21 June 1915); *Hitchy-Koo* (7 June 1917); *The Rainbow Girl* (1 April 1918); *Head over Heels* (29 August 1918); *The Royal Vagabond* (17 February 1919); *The Rose of China* (25 November 1919); *Morris Gest's Midnight Whirl* (27 December 1919); *Mary* (18 October 1920); *The O'Brien Girl* (3 October 1921); *The Perfect Fool* (7 November 1921); *The Blue Kitten* (13 January 1922); *Pins and Needles* (1 February 1922); *Daffy Dill* (22 August 1922); *Molly Darling* (1 September 1922); *The Yankee Princess* (2 October 1922); *The Rise of Rosie O'Reilly* (25 December 1923); *Ziegfeld Follies of 1924* (24 June 1924); *The Chocolate Dandies* (1 September 1924); *The Grab Bag* (6 October 1924); *Ziegfeld Follies of 1925* (6 July 1925). Productions choreographed included *Follies of 1908* (15 June 1908); *Follies of 1909* (14 June 1909); *The Silver Star* (1 November 1909); *The Pink Lady* (13 March 1911); *Eva* (30 December 1912); *Her Little Highness* (13 October 1913); *The Little Café* (10 November 1913); *The Queen of the Movies* (12 January 1914); *Papa's Darling* (2 November 1914); *Fads and Fancies* (8 March 1915); *Around the Map* (1 November 1915); *Sybil* (10 January 1916); *Miss Springtime* (25 September 1916); *The Riviera Girl* (24 September 1917); *The Girl behind the Gun* (16 September 1918); *Some Night!* (23 September 1918); *The Velvet Lady* (3 February 1919); *Little Nellie Kelly* (13 November 1922); *Our Nell* (4 December 1922); *Sunny* (22 September 1925); *Castles in the Air* (6 September 1926). Mitchell died in Long Branch, New Jersey, on 24 June 1926.

Adolph Neuberger, German-born choreographer; productions included *The Wild Rose* (5 May 1902); *The Maid and the Mummy* (25 July 1904); *The Mayor of Tokio* (4 December 1905); *The Spring Chicken* (8 October 1906); *The Dairymaids* (26 August 1907); *The Hurdy-Gurdy Girl* (23 September 1907).

Alexander Placide, dancer, mime, acrobat, and choreographer. Born in France in 1750. Performed as a tightrope artist at the court of King Louis XVI; performed in Santo Domingo where he became associated with dancer and choreographer Suzanne Theodore Vaillande, with whom he performed the ballet *The Bird Catcher* in New York City (1792). His ballet-pantomimes included *Mirza and Lindor* (8 July 1794); *Jupiter and Europa* (8 March 1795); *Maid of Orleans, or, Joan of Arc* (8 April 1796); *Death of Major André, or, West Point Preserved* (11 May 1796); *Birth, Death, and Renovation of Harlequin* (9 May 1805); *Columbine's Choice, or, Harlequin Statue* (18 April 1808). Ballets performed by the Placide Troupe additionally included *The Blacksmith* (25 March 1793); *The Cooper* (3 April 1793); *Richard Coeur de Lion* (29 May 1793). Placide died in New York City on 26 July 1812.

H. Fletcher Rivers, choreographer; productions included *The Rainmaker of Syria, or, The Woman King* (25 September 1893); *The Girl from Paris* (8 December 1896); *At Gay Coney Island* (1 February 1897); *The Isle of Gold* (26 April 1897); *The Maid in the Moon* (31 July 1899); *(Isham's) Octoroons* (2 October 1899); *The Ameer* (4 December 1899); *Happy Hooligan's Trip around the World* (22 January 1906).

R.A. Roberts, stage manager; productions included *The Widow Jones* (16 September 1895); *The Good Mr. Best* (30 August 1897); *An Irish Gentleman* (29 November 1897); *Hodge, Podge and Co.* (23 October 1900); *Janice Meredith* (10 December 1900); *The Governor's Son* (25 February 1901); *The Widow Jones* (revival) (23 December 1901); *Mrs. Jack* (2 September 1902); *Dorothy Vernon of Haddon Hall* (14 December 1903); *The Lion and the Mouse* (20 November 1905)

William Rock, choreographer, born 1867. Productions included *The Orchid* (8 April 1907); *The Top o' th' World* (19 October 1907); *Nearly a Hero* (24 February 1908); *The Fair Co-Ed* (1 February 1909); *The Echo* (17 August 1910); *The Rose Maid* (22 April 1912). Rock died in Philadelphia on 27 June 1922.

Alex Rogers, performer, writer, composer, and stage manager; productions staged included *Abyssinia* (20 February 1906); *Bandanna Land* (3 February 1908); *Mr. Load of Koal* (1 November 1909); *My Magnolia* (8 July 1926).

Vincenzo Romeo, stage manager and choreographer; choreographed productions included *The Regatta Girl* (14 March 1900); *A Yankee Circus on Mars / The Raiders* (12 April 1905); *A Society Circus* (13 December 1905); *Pioneer Days / Circus Events / Neptune's Daughter* (28 November 1906); *The Auto Race* (25 November 1907); *Sporting Days* (5 September 1908); *A Trip to Japan* (4 September 1909); *The International Cup / The Ballet of Niagara / The Earthquake* (3 September 1910).

Edward Royce, stage manager and choreographer, born on 14 December 1870 in Bath, England. Productions staged included *The Marriage Market* (22 September 1913); *The Laughing Husband* (2 February 1914); *Betty* (3 October 1916); *The Century Girl* (6 November 1916); *Have a Heart* (11 January 1917); *Oh, Boy* (20 February 1917); *Leave It to Jane* (28 August 1917); *Kitty Darlin'* (7 November 1917); *Going Up* (25 December 1917); *Oh, Lady! Lady!* (1 February 1918); *Rock-a-Bye Baby* (22 May 1918); *The Canary* (4 November 1918); *Oh, My Dear!* (27 November 1918); *Come Along* (8 April 1919); *She's a Good Fellow* (5 May 1919); *Apple Blossoms* (7 October 1919); *Irene* (18 November 1919); *Lassie* (6 April 1920); *Ziegfeld Follies of 1920* (22 June 1920); *Kissing Time* (11 October 1920); *Sally* (21 December 1920); *Ziegfeld Midnight Frolic* (8 February 1921); *Ziegfeld Follies of 1921* (21 June 1921); *The Love Letter* (4 October 1921); *Good Morning, Dearie* (1 November 1921); *Orange Blossoms* (19 September 1922); *Cinders* (3 April 1923); *Kid Boots* (31 December 1923); *Annie Dear* (4 November 1924); *Louie the 14th* (3 March 1924); *Princess Ida* (13 April 1925); *No Foolin'* (24 June 1928); *The Merry Malones* (26 September 1927); *She's My Baby* (3 January 1928); *Billie* (1 October 1928). Royce died in London on 15 June 1964.

Joseph Santley, performer, choreographer, and stage manager, born on 10 January 1889 in Salt Lake City. Productions choreographed included *When Dreams Come True* (18 August 1913); *Stop! Look! Listen* (25 December 1915). Productions staged included *Mayflowers* (24 November 1925); *Just Fancy* (11 October 1927); *Life Begins* (28 March 1932). Santley began a film career directing short films for Paramount, where he also co-directed the Marx Brothers in *The Cocoanuts* (3 August 1929). Although he worked for short periods at RKO and Universal, the majority of his film work was spent creating

B-musicals and light comedies for Republic, Monogram, and Mascot Studios. Santley died in West Los Angeles on 8 August 1971.

Max Scheck, stage manager and choreographer; choreographed productions included *The Passing Show of 1921* (29 December 1920); *The Rose Girl* (11 February 1921); *Up in the Clouds* (2 January 1922); *The Hotel Mouse* (13 March 1922); *The Passing Show of 1924* (3 September 1924); *The Love Song* (13 January 1925); *Happy Go Lucky* (30 September 1926); *Katie* (18 October 1926); *Through the Years* (28 January 1932). Productions staged included *Phoebe of Quality Street* (9 May 1921); *Princess Flavia* (2 November 1925); *Say When* (26 June 1926); *Belmont Varieties* (28 September 1932); *Manhattan Varieties* (21 October 1932).

Jesse A. Shipp, performer, writer, and stage manager; staged productions included *A Trip to Coontown* (4 April 1898); *The Policy Players* (16 October 1899); *Sons of Ham* (15 October 1900); *In Dahomey* (18 February 1903); *Abyssinia* (20 February 1906); *Bandanna Land* (3 February 1908); *Mr. Load of Koal* (1 November 1919); *Kilpatrick's Old-Time Minstrels* (19 April 1930).

John C. Slavin, performer and choreographer; choreographed *The Little Host* (26 December 1898), in which he also starred. In addition, Slavin appeared in *1492* (15 May 1893); *The Belle of New York* (28 September 1897); *The Singing Girl* (23 October 1899); *The Liberty Belles* (30 September 1901); *Love's Lottery* (3 October 1904); *Mam'selle Sallie* (26 November 1906); *A Knight for a Day* (16 December 1907); *A Skylark* (4 April 1910); *A Country Girl* (29 May 1911); *Baron Trenck* (11 March 1912); *The Century Girl* (6 November 1916); *Fifty-Fifty, Ltd.* (27 October 1919). Slavin died in New York City on 27 August 1940.

Joseph C. Smith, performer, stage manager, and choreographer; productions choreographed included *The Show Girl, or The Cap of Fortune* (5 May 1902); *The Sultan of Sulu* (29 December 1902); *The Jersey Lily* (14 September 1903); *The Fisher Maiden* (5 October 1903); *Red Feather* (9 November 1903); *The Southerners* (23 May 1904); *When We Were Forty-One* (12 June 1905); *Coming Thro' the Rye* (9 January 1906); *Follies of 1907* (8 July 1907); *The Alaskan* (12 August 1907); *The*

Merry-Go-Round (25 April 1908); *The Queen of the Moulin Rouge* (7 December 1908); *A Certain Party* (24 April 1911); *Vera Violetta* (20 November 1911); *My Little Friend* (19 May 1913); *The Only Girl* (2 November 1914). Staged productions included *Not Yet But Soon* (4 March 1907); *Take It from Me* (31 March 1919).

Frank Smithson, performer and stage manager; productions staged included *The Girl from Paris* (8 December 1896); *Monte Carlo* (21 March 1898); *Hotel Topsy Turvy* (3 October 1898); *Mam'selle 'Awkins* (26 February 1900); *A Million Dollars* (27 September 1900); *The Giddy Throng* (24 December 1900); *The King's Carnival* (13 May 1901); *The Defender* (3 July 1902); *Nancy Brown* (16 February 1903); *Winsome Winnie* (1 December 1903); *The Good Old Summertime* (8 February 1904); *The Royal Chef* (1 September 1904); *The Press Agent* (27 November 1905); *The Blue Moon* (3 November 1906); *Princess Beggar* (7 January 1907); *The Orchid* (8 April 1907); *The Top o' th' World* (19 October 1907); *The Lancers* (5 December 1907); *Lonesome Town* (20 January 1908); *Marcelle* (1 October 1908); *The Queen of the Moulin Rouge* (7 December 1908); *The Newlyweds and Their Baby* (22 March 1909); *The Motor Girl* (15 June 1909); *The Belle of Brittany* (8 November 1909); *Dr. De Luxe* (17 April 1911); *The Girl of My Dreams* (7 August 1911); *Little Boy Blue* (27 November 1911); *The Rose of Panama* (22 January 1912); *Somewhere Else* (20 January 1913); *When Dreams Come True* (18 August 1913); *High Jinks* (10 December 1913); *Katinka* (23 December 1915); *Go to It* (24 October 1916); *Ladies First* (24 Ocober 1918); *The Lady in Red* (12 May 1919); *Love Birds* (15 March 1921); *The Last Waltz* (10 May 1921); *The Blushing Bride* (4 February 1922); *Red Pepper* (29 May 1922); *Sally, Irene and Mary* (4 September 1922); *Vogues of 1924* (27 March 1924); *Innocent Eyes* (20 May 1924); *Honest Liars* (19 July 1926); *Artists and Models* (10 June 1930).

Augustus Sohlke, stage manager and choreographer; productions choreographed included *The French Maid* (27 September 1897); *The Ballet Girl* (21 December 1897); *In Posterland* (23 March 1903); *Spotless Town* (2 April 1903); *Piff! Paff!! Pouf!!!* (2 April 1904); *The Boy and the Girl* (31 May 1909); *Ziegfeld Follies of 1911* (26 June 1911); *The Kiss Waltz* (18 September 1911); *The Revue of Revues* (27 September 1911); *The Duchess* (16 October 1911); *The Wall Street Girl* (15 April 1912). Productions staged included *The Isle of Spice* (23 August

1904); *A Knight for a Day* (16 December 1907); *Three Twins* (15 June 1908); *A Broken Idol* (16 August 1909); *Hokey-Pokey* (8 February 1912); *Hanky Panky* (5 August 1912); *Roly Poly / Without the Law* (21 November 1912).

Frank Tannehill, writer, performer, and stage manager; productions staged included *The Night Clerk* (11 November 1895); *Punch, Judy and Company* (1 June 1903).

I Tarasoff, Russian-born choreographer; co-choreographed *Music Box Revue* (22 September 1921).

Ben Teal, writer and stage manager; staged productions included *The Algerian* (26 October 1893); *The Brownies* (12 November 1894): *The Sunshine of Paradise Alley* (11 May 1896); *The Strange Adventures of Jack and the Beanstalk* (2 November 1896); *A Round of Pleasure* (24 May 1897); *The Bride-Elect* (28 December 1897); *A Reign of Error* (2 March 1899); *In Gay Paree* (20 March 1899); *Ben Hur* (29 November 1899); *Chris and the Wonderful Lamp* (1 January 1900); *The Rogers Brothers in Central Park* (17 September 1900); *Foxy Quiller* (5 November 1900); *Star and Garter* (26 November 1900); *Sweet Nell of Old Drury* (31 December 1900); *The Rogers Brothers in Washington* (2 September 1901); *The Sleeping Beauty and the Beast* (4 November 1901); *The Rogers Brothers in Harvard* (1 September 1902); *Whoop-Dee-Doo* (24 September 1903); *An English Daisy* (18 January 1904); *The Rollicking Girl* (1 May 1905); *The Catch of the Season* (28 August 1905); *The Mountain Climber* (5 March 1906); *The Little Cherub* (6 August 1906); *The Rich Mr. Hoggenheimer* (22 October 1906); *The Rogers Brothers in Panama* (2 September 1907); *The Hoyden* (19 October 1907); *Fluffy Ruffles* (7 September 1908); *The Old Town* (10 January 1910); *A Skylark* (4 April 1910); *The Man from Cook's* (25 March 1912); *Adele* (28 August 1913); *Iole* (29 December 1913); *The Midnight Girl* (23 February 1914); *The Red Canary* (13 April 1914); *The Girl Who Smiles* (9 August 1915); *Broadway and Buttermilk* (15 August 1916).

Edward P. Temple, writer, composer, stage manager, born in New York City in 1861. Staged productions included *Boccaccio* (5 September 1898); *Iolanthe* (12 September 1898); *Dorothy* (19 September 1898); *The Chimes of Normandy* (21 November 1898); *The Bohemian Girl*

(19 December 1898); *The Queen's Lace Handkerchief* (23 January 1899); *H.M.S. Pinafore* (6 February 1899); *The Grand Duchess* (27 February 1899); *Olivette* (13 March 1899); *The Mikado* (27 March 1899); *Trial by Jury* (24 April 1899); *The Magic Melody* (22 January 1900); *A Madcap Princess* (5 September 1904); *A Yankee Circus on Mars / The Raiders* (12 April 1905); *A Society Circus* (13 December 1905); *Pioneer Days / Neptunes Daughter* (28 November 1906); *The Auto Race* (25 November 1907); *Molly May* (8 April 1910); *The Purple Road* (7 April 1913); *The Highwayman* (2 May 1917); *Maytime* (16 August 1917); *The Star Gazer* (26 November 1917); *Girl o' Mine* (28 January 1918); *Little Simplicity* (4 November 1918); *The Kiss Burglar* (17 March 1919); Temple died in New York City on 22 June 1921.

Willie Warde, choreographer; productions included *In Town* (6 September 1897); *San Toy* (1 October 1900); *The Duchess of Dantzic* (16 January 1905); *The Little Michus* (31 January 1907).

Ned Wayburn, performer, composer, writer, stage manager, and choreographer, born on 30 March 1874 in Pittsburgh, Pennsylvania. Productions staged included *By the Sad Sea Waves* (28 February 1899); *Star and Garter* (26 November 1900); *The Night of the Fourth* (21 January 1901); *The Governor's Son* (25 February 1901); *The Hall of Fame* (5 February 1902); *The Belle of Broadway* (15 March 1902); *Mr. Bluebeard* (21 January 1903); *George W. Lederer's Mid-Summer Night Fancies* (22 June 1903); *The Rogers Brothers in London* (7 September 1903); *Mother Goose* (2 December 1903); *Humpty Dumpty* (14 November 1904); *In Newport* (26 December 1904); *The Pearl and the Pumpkin* (21 August 1905); *The Ham Tree* (28 August 1905); *The Rogers Brothers in Ireland* (4 September 1905); *Fritz in Tammany Hall* (16 October 1905); *The White Cat* (2 November 1905); *The Time, the Place and the Girl* (5 August 1907); *School Days* (14 September 1908); *Mr. Hamlet of Broadway* (23 December 1908); *Havana* (11 February 1909); *The Midnight Sons* (22 May 1909); *The Rose of Algeria* (20 September 1909); *The Girl and the Wizard* (27 September 1909); *Old Dutch* (22 November 1909); *The Goddess of Liberty* (22 December 1909); *The Jolly Bachelors* (6 January 1910); *The Prince of Bohemia* (14 January 1910); *The Yankee Girl* (10 February 1910); *Tillie's Nightmare* (5 May 1910); *The Summer Widowers* (4 June 1910); *The Hen-Pecks* (4 February 1911); *Hello, Paris* (19 August 1911); *A la*

Broadway (22 September 1911); *The Never Homes* (5 October 1911); *The Wife Hunters* (2 November 1911); *Penny* (7 December 1911); *The Sun Dodgers* (30 November 1912); *The Honeymoon Express* (6 February 1913); *The Passing Show of 1913* (24 July 1913); *(Ned Wayburn's) Town Topics* (23 September 1915); *Ziegfeld Follies of 1916* (12 June 1916); *Ziegfeld Follies of 1917* (12 June 1917); *Miss 1917* (5 November 1917); *Ziegfeld Follies of 1918* (18 June 1918); *Ziegfeld Midnight Frolic* (July 1918); *Ziegfeld Follies of 1919* (16 June 1919); *The Night Boat* (2 February 1920); *Ed Wynn's Carnival* (5 April 1920); *Poor Little Ritz Girl* (28 July 1920); *Hitchy-Koo* (19 October 1920); *Two Little Girls in Blue* (3 May 1921); *Ziegfeld Follies of 1922* (5 June 1922); *Lady Butterfly* (22 January 1923); *Ziegfeld Follies of 1923* (Summer Edition) (25 June 1923); *Ziegfeld Follies of 1923* (20 October 1923); *Ned Wayburn's Gambols* (15 January 1929). Productions choreographed included *The Billionaire* (29 December 1902); *George W. Lederer's Mid-Summer Night Fancies* (22 June 1903); *A Little Bit of Everything* (6 June 1904); *The Rogers Brothers in Paris* (5 September 1904); *Lifting the Lid* (5 June 1905); *The Flower of the Ranch* (20 April 1908); *The Mimic World* (9 July 1908); *Mlle. Mischief* (28 September 1908); *The Summer Widowers* (4 June 1910); *The Wife Hunters* (2 November 1911); *The Passing Show of 1912* (22 July 1912); *(From) Broadway to Paris* (20 November 1912); *Hello, Broadway!* (25 December 1914); *Smiles* (18 November 1930). Wayburn died in New York City on 2 September 1942.

Francis Weldon, stage manager and choreographer; productions choreographed included *Dew Drop Inn* (17 May 1923); *Topics of 1923* (20 November 1923); *Innocent Eyes* (20 May 1924). In addition, Weldon staged *Artists and Models* (20 August 1923).

George White, performer, writer, composer, stage manager, and choreographer, born circa 1891. White created and staged thirteen editions of *George White's Scandals* (beginning on 28 August 1919), including five editions (1920–1924) with George Gershwin as principal composer. The eighth edition (14 June 1926), with music by Ray Henderson, was the longest running of the series and introduced White's dance sensation, "Black Bottom." In addition to the *Scandals*, White staged *Manhattan Mary* (26 September 1927); *Flying High* (3 March 1930); *George White's Music Hall Varieties* (22 November 1932); *Mel-*

ody (14 February 1933); *Run, Little Chillun* (1 March 1933). In the 1930s and 1940s, White worked in Hollywood, adapting his *Scandals* for the movies. He died in Hollywood on 11 November 1868.

William J. Wilson, performer, stage manager, and choreographer, born circa 1874. Productions choreographed included *La Belle Paree* (20 March 1911); *Around the World* (2 September 1911); *The Kiss Waltz* (18 September 1911); *The Revue of Revues* (27 September 1911); *The Duchess* (16 October 1911); *Vera Violetta* (20 November 1911); *All Aboard* (5 June 1913); *Under Many Flags* (31 August 1912). Productions staged included *Up and Down Broadway* (18 July 1910); *Bow-Sing* (20 March 1911); *The Never Homes* (5 October 1911); *The Wedding Trip* (25 December 1911); *The Dove of Peace* (4 November 1912); *The Man with Three Wives* (23 January 1913); *The Beggar Student* (22 March 1913); *H.M.S. Pinafore* (5 May 1913); *Iolanthe* (12 May 1913); *America* (30 August 1913); *The Pleasure Seekers* (3 November 1913); *The Whirl of the World* (10 January 1914); *Wars of the World* (5 September 1914); *The Road to Mandalay* (1 March 1916); *Mayflowers* (24 November 1925); *The Wild Rose* (20 October 1926); *Oh, Ernest!* (9 May 1927). Wilson died in Cleveland, Ohio, on 2 March 1936.

Dance Music Arrangers Appearing in Upcoming Volumes:

Series 2: 1924–1966 and Series 3: 1967–2015
With a list of representative works

Abbott, James Lynn, *Aida* (23 March 2000); *Wicked* (30 October 2003); *Bombay Dreams* (29 April 2004); *Sweet Charity* (revival) (4 May 2005); *Tarzan* (10 May 2006); *Guys and Dolls* (revival) (1 March 2009).

Abel, Ron, *Blame It on the Movies!* (16 May1989).

Abene, Michael, *A Long Way to Boston* (September 1979).

Abrahamson, Manford, *Dragons* (12 May 1984).

Adams, Roger, *Buttrio Square* (14 October 1952); *Me and Juliet* (28 May1953); *Carnival in Flanders* (8 September 1953); *The Pajama Game* (13 May1954); *Ankles Aweigh* (18 April 1955); *Damn Yankees* (5 May 1955); *Strip for Action* (17 March 1956); *Happy Hunting* (6 December 1956); *New Girl in Town* May 14, 1957); *Redhead* (5 February 1959); *Once Upon a Mattress* (11 April 1959); *Ben Franklin in Paris* (27 October1964); *Mame* (24 May 1966); *Illya Darling* (11 April 1967); *Mata Hari* (18 November 1967); *A Mother's Kisses* (23 September 1968).

Adler, Gary, *Avenue Q* (31 July 2003) (incidental music).

Alchourron, Rodolfo, *Dangerous Games* (19 October 1989).

Alters, Gerald, *John Murray Anderson's Almanac* (10 December 1953); *The Happiest Girl in the World* (3 April 1961); *A Family Affair* (27 January 1962); *That Hat!* (23 September 1964); *Wet Paint* (12 April 1965).

Archer, Nicholas, *Anna Karenina* (26 May 1992).

Aronson, Henry, *Starmites* (27 April 1989); *Prince of Central Park* (9 November 1989); *How It Was Done in Odessa* (10 April 1991).

Atwood, Robert (Bob), *Rumple* (6 November 1957); *13 Daughters* (2 March 1961); *Curley McDimple* (22 November 1967).

Bacon, Glen, *All in Fun* (27 December 1940).

Baker, David, *A Month of Sundays* (25 December 1951); *Of Thee I Sing* (revival) (5 May 1952); *Two's Company* (15 December 1952); *Do Re Mi* (26 January 1960); *Flora, the Red Menace* (11 May 1965); *The Yearling* (10 December 1965); *Cabaret* (20 November 1966); *Androcles and the Lion* (15 November 1967); *Come Summer* (18 February 1969); *Rex* (25 April 1976); *Prince of Grand Street* (7 March 1978); *Cabaret* (revival) (22 October 1987); *Cabaret* (revival) (19 March 1998).

Bargy, Jeanne, also the show's composer; *Greenwich Village U.S.A.* (28 September 1960).

Barnum, H.B., *Your Arms Too Short to Box with God* (22 December 1976); *But Never Jam Today* (31 July 1979); *Your Arms Too Short to Box with God* (revival) (2 June 1980); *Your Arms Too Short to Box with God* (revival) (9 September 1982).

Bauer, George, *Sticks and Stones* (30 June 1957).

Beckett, Hal, *Skating Vanities* (No date).

Bennett, Robert Russell, *Rhapsody* (22 November 1944).

Benskin, Sammy, *Billy Noname* (2 March 1970).

Berg, Tony, *Festival* (16 May 1979).

Berkman, John, *Hellza-Poppin* (1 July 1967); *Come Summer* (18 February 1969); *Jimmy* (23 October 1969); *Follies* (4 April 1971); *W.C.* (15 June

1971); *The Grass Harp* (2 November 1971); *Sugar* (9 April 1972); *Pippin* (23 October 1972); *Smith* (19 May 1973); *Follies* (revival) (5 April 2001); *Follies* (revival) (12 September 2011).

Berkowitz, Sol, *The Unsinkable Molly Brown* (3 November 1960).

Berman, Rob, *Dames at Sea* (22 October 2015).

Bernstein, Elmer, *Peter Pan* (20 October 1954).

Bernstein, Leonard, also the composer of the shows; *On the Town* (28 December 1944); *Wonderful Town* (25 February 1953); *Candide* (1 December 1956); *West Side Story* (26 September 1957); *Mass* (5 September 1971); *1600 Pennsylvania Avenue* (4 May 1976).

Blackton, Jay, *Oh Captain!* (4 February 1958); *I Remember Mama* (31 May 1979).

Blank, Lawrence (Larry) J., *Becoming* (15 June 1976).

Bogin, Abba, *Riverwind* (11 December 1962).

Bowman, Rob, *A Change in the Heir* (29 April 1990).

Brevis, Skip, *Beehive* (30 March 1986).

Bridwell, Thom, *Miss Truth* (5 June 1979) (also co-composer of the show); *Uptown . . . It's Hot!* (29 January 1986).

Broderick, George, *When Hell Freezes Over I'll Skate* (22 July 1983).

Brourman, Michele, *Working* (14 May 1978).

Butcher, George, *Amen Corner* (10 November 1983).

Carroll, Adam, *You'll See Stars* (29 December 1942).

Carroll, Albert, *The Grand Street Follies* (16 June 1923) (also lyricist and member of the cast).

Cashman, Edward, *Belinda!* (3 May 1957).

Chapin, Stephen, *Lies and Legends: The Musical Stories of Harry Chapin* (24 April 1985).

Chapin, Tom, *Lies and Legends: The Musical Stories of Harry Chapin* (24 April 1985).

Charlson, Natalie, *Half-Past Wednesday* (6 April 1962).

Chase, David, *A Funny Thing Happened on the Way to the Forum* (revival) (18 April 1996); *Side Show* (16 October 1997); *The Scarlet Pimpernel* (9 November 1997); *Kiss Me Kate* (revival) (18 November 1999); *Seussical* (30 November 2000); *Follies* (revival) (5 April 2001); *Thoroughly Modern Millie* (18 April 2002); *Flower Drum Song* (revival) (17 October 2002); *The Pajama Game* (revival) (23 February 2006); *The Wedding Singer* (27 April 2006); *Curtains* (22 March 2007); *The Little Mermaid* (10 January 2008); *Cry-Baby* (24 April 2008); *Billy Elliot: The Musical* (13 November 2008); *Bye Bye Birdie* (revival) (15 October 2009); *Promises, Promises* (revival) (25 April 2010); *Elf* (14 November 2010); *How to Succeed in Business Without Really Trying* (revival) (27 March 2011); *Anything Goes* (revival) (7 April 2011); *Evita* (revival) (5 April 2012); *Finding Neverland* (15 April 2015); *Tuck Everlasting* (26 April 2016); *Hello, Dolly!* (20 April 2017); *Anastasia* (24 April 2017).

Cohen, Allen, *The Utter Glory of Morrissey Hall* (13 May1979); *I Remember Mama* (31 May 1979); *Take Me Along* (revival) (14 April 1985).

Cohen, Michael, *Mixed Doubles* (19 October 1966).

Coleman, Charles H., *Timbuktu* (1March 1978 (incidental music and arrangements); *Happy New Year* (27 April 1980).

Coleman, Cy, also the composer of the shows; *Seesaw* (18 March 1973); *I Love My Wife* (17 April 1977); *Home Again, Home Again* (12 March 1979); *Little Me* (revival) (21 January 1982); *The Will Rogers Follies* (1 May 1991).

Collins, Ken, *Jolson* (8 November 1978).

Cox, William, *Music Is* (12 December 1976); *Angel* (10 May 1978).

Cribari, Donna, *Pop* (3 April 1974 (also co-composer of show).

Crigler, Lynn, *Hubba Hubba* (no date).

Cunningham, Bill (Billy) *Rachael Lily Rosenbloom and Don't You Ever Forget It* (26 November 1973); *Let My People Come* (8 January 1974).

Curtis, Norman, *Walk Down Mah Street!* (12 June 1968) (also show's composer).

Cusseaux, Zulema, *Jazzbo Brown* (24 June 1980).

Dallin, Jacques, *Crazy with the Heat* (14 January 1941).

Dansicker, Michael, *On the Swing Shift* (20 May 1983) (also show's composer).

Davis, Buster, *Rodgers and Hart* (13 May 1975).

Davis, Sam, *The Mystery of Edwin Drood* (12 November 2012); *Scandalous* (15 November 2012); *Big Fish* (6 October 2013); *Gigi* (8 April 2015); *An American in Paris* (12 April 2015); *Holiday Inn, The New Irving Berlin Musical* (6 October 2016).

de Benedictis, Richard, *Fade Out—Fade In* (26 May 1964); *Bajour* (23 November 1964); *Do I Hear a Waltz?* (18 March 1965); *Annie Get Your Gun* (revival) (21 September 1966); *A Funny Thing Happened on the Way to the Forum* (revival) (30 March 1972).

Douglass, Jane, also the show's composer; *Bella* (16 November 1961).

Duke, Vernon, *Keep off the Grass* (23 May 1940) (also co-composer).

Edwards, Phil, *Saturday Night Fever* (21 October 1999).

Eljas, Anders, *Chess* (28 April 1988).

Elliott, Jack, *Fiorello!* (23 November 1959); *Tenderloin* (17 October 1960); *Mr. President* (20 October 1962); *She Loves Me* (incidental music) (23 April 1963).

Ellis, Ray, *The Secret Life of Walter Mitty* (26 October 1964).

Eriksmoen, August, *Memphis* (19 October 2009); *The Addams Family* (8 April 2010).

Estey, Robert, *Speed Gets the Poppys* (25 July 1972).

Fallon, Larry, *Changes* (19 February 1980).

Fay, Thomas (Tom), *Merrily We Roll Along* (16 November 1981); *The Rink* (9 March 1984); *Grind* (16 April 1985); *Smile* (1985); *Anything Goes* (revival) (19 October 1987); *Mail* (14 April 1988); *Oh, Kay!* (revival) (1 November 1990); *Damn Yankees* (revival) (3 March 1994); *Once Upon a Mattress* (revival) (19 December 1996); *Anything Goes* (revival) (1 April 2002).

Fenwick, John, *Fauntleroy* (2 July 1981).

Fisher, Harrison, *The Ballad of Johnny Pot* (26 April 1971).

Fisher, Robert, *Little Johnny Jones* (21 March 1982).

Flaherty, Stephen, *Once on This Island* (18 October 1990).

Forrester, Hugh, *Seesaw* (18 March 1973) (original dance arranger, replaced in NYC).

Fraser, Ian, *Say Hello to Harvey!* (14 September 1981).

Freitag, Dorothea, *Windy City* (18 April 1946); *High Time* (17 August 1953); *Mask and Gown* (10 September 1957); *Medium Rare* (6 July 1960); *Tovarich* (18 March 1963); *I'm Solomon* (23 April 1968); *Zorba* (17 November 1968); *Dear World* (6 February 1969); *Gantry* (14 February 1970); *70, Girls, 70* (15 April 1971); *King of Hearts* (22 October 1978).

Friedman, Gary William, *The Me Nobody Knows* (18 May 1971) (also show's composer).

Fuller, Dean, *A Tree Grows in Brooklyn* (10 October 1952); *Maggie* (18 February 1953).

Fuller, Lorenzo, *Look at Us* (5 June 1962).

Fullum, Clay, *The Rothschilds* (19 October 1970).

Gibson, Michael, *Ionescopade* (25 April 1974).

Gillespie, Lee, *Hot and Cold Heros* (9 May 1973).

Goland, Arnold, *The Student Gypsy; or, The Prince of Liederkrantz* (30 September 1963);*What Makes Sammy Run?* (27 February 1964); *Babes in the Wood* (28 December 1964); *Here's Where I Belong* (3 March, 1968).

Goldenberg, William (Billy), *Let It Ride!*(12 October 1961); *110 In the Shade* (24 October 1963); *High Spirits* (7 April 1964); *Henry, Sweet Henry* (23 October 1967).

Goldstein, Jerome, *Bagels and Yox of 1951* (30 March 1951).

Goldstone, Bob, *Dragons* (12 May 1984).

Goodman, Tommy, *Silk Stockings* (24 February 1955).

Gordon, Dan, *Hobo* (10 April 1961).

Graphenreed, Timothy, *The Wiz* (5 January 1975); *Comin' Uptown* (20 December 1979); *The Moony Shapiro Songbook* (3 May 1981); *American Passion* (10 July 1983); *The Wiz* (revival) (24 May 1984); *Leader of the Pack* (8 April 1985); *C'mon and Hear* (22 March 1994).

Greene, Milton, *Not While I'm Eating* (19 December 1961).

Gregory, James, *Streetheat* (27 January 1985).

Gross, Arnold, *Molly* (1 November 1973); *A Matter of Time* (27 April 1975); *Sugar Babies* (9 October 1979); *Merrily We Roll Along* (16 November 1981).

Grundmann, Tim, *Sirocco* (13 August 1976); *The Bride of Sirocco* (31 December 1976) (also show's composer); *Out to Lunch* (7 July 1978); *Eddie's Catchy Tunes* (25 April 1979) (also show's composer).

Gustafson, Bob, *Aida* (23 March 2000).

Haak, Brad, *Lestat* (25 April 2006) (incidental music).

Hague, Albert, also composer of the shows; *Café Crown* (17 April 1964); *Miss Moffat* (7 October 1974).

Hamlisch, Marvin, *Henry, Sweet Henry* (23 October 1967); *Golden Rainbow* (4 February 1968); *Minnie's Boys* (26 March 1970).

Hardwick, Cheryl, *Hang on to the Good Times* (22 January 1985).

Harley, Leslie, *Peg* (1 August 1967); *Who's Who, Baby?* (29 January 1968); *Of Thee I Sing* (revival) (7 March 1969).

Harper, Wally, *Up Eden* (27 November 1968); *Company* (26 April 1970); *Look Where I'm At!* (5 March 1971); *Irene* (13 March 1973); *Music! Music!* (11 April 1974); *So Long, 174th Street* (27 April 1976); *Nefertiti* (20 September 1977); *Spotlight* (11 January 1978); *Peter Pan* (revival) 6 September 1979); *A Day in Hollywood/A Night in the Ukraine* (1 May 1980); *My One and Only* (1 May 1983); *The Three Musketeers* (revival) (11 November 1984); *My Favorite Year* (10 December 1992); *A Grand Night for Singing* (17 November 1993); *The Best Little Whorehouse Goes Public* (10 May 1994); *Company* (revival) (5 October 1995).

Harrell, Gordon (Lowry), *Inner City* (19 December 1971); *Hellzapoppin* (22 November 1976); *Dancin'* (27 March 1978); *La Cage aux Folles*

(21 August 1983); *Grind* (16 April 1985); *Big Deal* (10 April 1986); *The Little Rascals* (7 October 1987); *Teddy and Alice* (12 November 1987); *Nick and Nora* (8 December 1991); *Easter Show* (2 April 1993); *The Red Shoes* (16 December 1993); *Gentlemen Prefer Blondes* (revival) (10 April 1995); *Fosse* (14 January 1999).

Harris, Frederic, *Sky High* (28 June 1979).

Harris, Howard, also show's composer; *Frimbo* (9 November 1980).

Hartley, Richard, *The Rocky Horror Show* (10 March 1975).

Hastings, Harold, *Dear Oscar* (16 November 1972).

Henderson, Luther, *Flower Drum Song* (1 December 1958); *Bravo Giovanni* (19 May 1962); *Funny Girl* (26 March 1964); *I Had a Ball* (15 December 1964); *Hallelujah, Baby!* (26 April 1967); *Golden Rainbow* (4 February 1968); *Purlie* (15 March 1970); *No, No, Nanette* (revival) (19 January 1971); *F. Jasmine Addams* (27 October 1971); *Purlie* (revival) (27December 1972); *Good News* (revival) (23 December 1974); *Doctor Jazz* (19 March 1975); *Rodgers and Hart* (13 May 1975); *Storyville* (27 January 1979); *Jazzbo Brown* (24 June 1980); *The First* (17 November 1981); *Little Ham* (31 August 1987); *Black and Blue* (26 January 1989).

Herbert, Fred, *Carnival in Flanders* (8 September 1953).

Hernández, Oscar, *On Your Feet* (5 November 2015).

Herrmann, Keith, also composer of the show music; *Romance, Romance* (1 May 1988); *Prom Queens Unchained* (30 June 1991).

Hochman, Larry, *Not Tonight, Benvenuto!* (5 June 1979).

Holder, Ray, *Bar Mitzvah Boy* (31 October 1978).

Holdridge, Lee, *A Joyful Noise* (15 December 1966); *The Education of H*Y*M*A*N K*A*P*L*A*N* (4 April 1968).

Holgate, Danny, *Home Sweet Homer* (4 January 1976); *Don't Bother Me, I Can't Cope* (9 April 1974); *Guys and Dolls* (revival) (21 July 1976); *Eubie!* (20 September 1978); *Helen* (22 November 1978); *Suddenly the Music Starts* (3 May 1979); *Daddy Goodness* (19 August 1979).

Hollister, David, *The Tattooed Countess* (3 April 1961).

Holmes, Jack, *Little Mary Sunshine* (18 November 1959); *From A to Z* (20 April 1960); *New Faces of 1962* (1 February 1962); *Frank Merriwell; or, Honor Challenged* (24 April 1971).

Hood, Janet, *Fourtune* (27 April 1980).

Howard, Peter, *Carnival* (13 April 1961); *Subways Are for Sleeping* (27 December 1961); *I Can Get It for You Wholesale* (22 March 1962); *Here's Love* (3 October 1963); *Hello, Dolly!* (16 January 1964); *Wonderworld* (7 April 1964); *The Roar of the Greasepaint—The Smell of the Crowd* (16 May 1965); *How Now, Dow Jones* (7 December 1967); *Her First Roman* (20 October 1968); *1776* (16 March 1969); *La Strada* (14 December 1969); *Minnie's Boys* (26 March 1970); *Ari* (15 January 1971); *Prettybelle* (1 February 1971); *Tricks* (8 January 1973); *Chicago* (3 June 1975); *Annie* (21 April 1977); *Hello, Dolly!* (revival) (5 March 1978); *The Grand Tour* (11 January 1979); *Swing* (25 February 1980); *The Tap Dance Kid* (21 December 1983); *Tatterdemalion* (27 October 1985); *Annie 2: Miss Hannigan's Revenge* (4 January 1990); *Crazy for You* (19 February 1992); *Hello, Dolly!* (revival) (19 October 1995); *Swingin' on a Star* (5 April 1995); *Chicago* (revival) (14 November 1996); *1776* (revival) (14 August 1997); *Minnelli on Minnelli* (8 December 1999).

Hummel, Mark, *Merlin* (13 February 1983); *5,6,7,8 . . . Dance!* (15 June 1983); *The Three Musketeers* (revival) (11 November 1984); *Jerry's Girls* (18 December 1985); *Legs Diamond* (26 December 1988); *Guys and Dolls* (revival) (14 April 1992); *Radio City Christmas Spectacular* (13 November 1992); *The Goodbye Girl* (4 March 1993); *Face Value* (9 March 1993); *Easter Show* (2 April 1993); *Bells Are Ringing* (revival) (12 April 2001).

Hurwitz, Deborah, *Body Shop* (1995).

Ivanoff, Alexandra, *The Club* (14 October 1976).

Janik, Ada, *Musical Chairs* (18 May 1980).

Janusz, Tom, *Wild and Wonderful* (7 December 1971).

Johnson, Louis, *Miss Truth* (5 June 1979) (also co-composer of show).

Johnson, Sy, *Black and Blue* (26 January 1989).

Johnston, Donald, *A Broadway Musical* (21 December 1978); *Joley* (8 March 1979); 42nd Street (25 August 1980); *Onward Victoria* (14 December 1980); *Copperfield* (13 April 1981); *Marilyn: An American Fable* (4 December 1983); *Oh, Kay!* (revival) (1 November 1990).

Jones, Donald G., *The Movie Buff* (14 March 1977).

Jonson, Bill, *Courtin' Time* (13 June 1951).

Jurist, Irma, *Hold It!* (5 May 1948).

Kander, John, *Gypsy* (21 May 1959); *Irma La Douce* (29 September 1960); *Gypsy* (revival) (23 September 1974); *Gypsy* (revival) (16 November 1989).

Katsaros, Doug, *Rockabye Hamlet* (17 February 1976); *Just So* (3 December 1985) (also show's composer); *The Life* (26 April 1997).

Kay, Arthur, *Spring in Brazil* (1 October 1945).

Kayden, Mildred, *Ionescopade* (25 April 1974) (also show's composer).

Kelly, Glen, *Dance a Little Closer* (11 May 1983); *The Tap Dance Kid* (21December 1983); *Rhythm Ranch* (1 November 1989); *Beauty and the Beast* (18 April 1994); *A Christmas Carol* (1 December 1994); *Steel Pier* (24 April 1997); *High Society* (27 April 1998); *The Producers* (19 April 2001); The Frogs (22 July 2004); *The Drowsy Chaperone* (1 May 2006); *The Book of Mormon* (24 March 2011); *A Christmas Story The Musical* (19 November 2012); *Aladdin* (20 March 2014).

Kingsley, Gershon, *Earnest in Love* (4 May 1960); *Put It in Writing* (13 May 1963); *King of the Whole Damn World!* (12 April 1964).

Klein, Randy, *It's Wilde!* (25 May 1980) (also show's composer).

Kosarin, Michael, *Mayor* (13 May 1985); *Das Barbecu* (10 October 1994).

Kosarin, Oscar, *A Tree Grows in Brooklyn* (19 April 1951); *Pal Joey* (revival) (3 January 1952); *Hazel Flagg* (11 February 1953); *The Canterbury Tales* (3 February 1969).

Kowal, James, *Dangerous Games* (19 October 1989).

Krane, David, *Carmelina* (8 April 1979); *Peter Pan* (revival) (6 September 1979); *Colette* (9 February 1982); *Upstairs at O'Neal's* (28 October 1982); *Wind in the Willows* (19 December 1985); *Honky Tonk Nights* (7 August 1986); *Durante* (12 August 1989); *Kiss of the Spider Woman* (3 May 1993); *Damn Yankees* (revival) (3 March 1994); *Show Boat* (revival) (2 October 1994); *Victor/Victoria* (25 October 1995); *Big* (28 April 1996); *Ragtime* (18 January 1998); *Cabaret* (revival) (19 March 1998); *Little Me* (revival) (2 November 1998); *Minnelli on Minnelli* (8 December 1999); *The Music Man* (revival) (27 April 2000); *The Adventures of Tom Sawyer* (26 April 2001); *Oklahoma!* (revival) (21 March 21, 2002); *The Boys from Syracuse* (revival) (18 August 2002); *Man of La Mancha* (revival) (5 December 2002); *La Cage aux Folles* (9 December 2004); *Dr. Seuss' How the Grinch Stole Christmas!* (8 November 2006); *110 in the Shade* (revival) (9 May 2007); *On the Twentieth Century* (revival) (15 March 2015); *She Loves Me* (revival) (17 March 2016).

Kuramoto, Dan, *Zoot Suit* (25 March 1979).

Kyle, Billy, *Alive and Kicking* (17 January 1950).

Lacamoire, Alex, *9 to 5* (30 April 2009); *The People in the Picture* (28 April 2011); *Bring It On The Musical* (1 August 2012); *Annie* (revival) (8 November 2012);

Laird, Marvin, *Skyscraper* (13 November 1965); *Breakfast at Tiffany's* (15 October 1966); *The Happy Time* (18 January 1968); *Georgy* (26 February 1970); *One Night Stand* (20 October 1980); *Broadway Follies* (15 March 1981); *Oh, Brother!* (10 November 1981); *Radio City Christmas Special* (13 November 1992); *Easter Show* (2 April 1993); *Annie Get Your Gun* (revival) (4 March 1999).

Lang, Phil, *Good News* (national tour) (17 December 1973).

Larson, Peter, *Do Black Patent Leather Shows Really Reflect Up?* (27 May 1982); *My One and Only* (1 May 1983).

Lass, Jeff, *Two If By Sea!?* (18 June 1971).

Lawlor, James Reed, *Razzle Dazzle* (19 February 1951); *Tongue in Cheek* (5 April 1958).

Lawn, Sand, *Lunch* (28 June 1994).

Lawrence, Stephen, *Utopia!* (6 May 1963).

Lebowsky, Stanley, *Singin' in the Rain* (2 July 1985).

Lee, Jack, *The Fig Leaves are Falling* (2 January 1969).

Leib, Dick, *Musical Chairs* (18 May 1980).

Leonard, Michael, *We're Civilized?* (8 November 1962).

Lesko, Andrew, *What a Killing* (27 March 1961).

Lessner, George, *Mr. Strauss goes to Boston* (6 September 1945); *Sleepy Hollow* (3 June 1948).

Levenson, Jeanine, *The Secret Garden* (25 April 1991).

Levinsky, Walt, *Boccaccio* (24 November 1975).

Lippa, Andrew, *Good Sports* (5 November 1992).

Loud, David, *And the World Goes 'Round* (18 March 1991); *She Loves Me* (revival) (10 June 1993); *The Visit* (23 April 2015).

MacKay, Harper, *Zenda* (5 August 1963).

Malina, Stuart, *Prom Queens Unchained* (30 June 1991).

Margoshes, Steven (Steve), *Rainbow* (19 December 1972); *More than You Deserve* (21 November 1973); *The Umbrellas of Cherbourg* (2 January 1979); *Hang on to the Good Times* (22 January 1985).

Marks, Robert, *Oh, Johnny* (10 January 1982).

Mark, Zane, *The Full Monty* (26 October 2000); *Never Gonna Dance* (4 December 2003); *Dirty Rotten Scoundrels* (3 March 2005); *All Shook Up* (24 March 2005); *Leap of Faith* (26 April 2012); *Motown The Musical* (14 April 2013).

Martin, Hugh, *As the Girls Go* (13 November 1948).

Marvin, Mel, *Applause* (30 March 1970); *Heathen!* (21 May 1972); *Comedy* (6 November 1972); *Tinypes* (17 April 1980); *What's Wrong with This Picture?* (8 December 1994); *Cymbeline* (2 December 2007) (incidental music).

Masekela, Hugh, *Sarafina!* (28 January 1988).

Matz, Peter, *House of Flowers* (30 December 1954); *Once Over Lightly* (1955); *The Amazing Adele* (26 December 1955); *Jamaica* (31 October 1957); *Whoop-Up* (22 November 1958); *Sail Away* (3 October 1961); *No Strings* (15 March 1962)

Maultsby, Carl, *It's So Nice to be Civilized* (3 June 1980).

Mayers, Lloyd, *Sophisticated Ladies* (1 March 1981).

McClellan, Clark, *Who's Who, Baby?* (29 January 1968).

McDaniel, John, *Grease* (revival) (11 May 1994); *Busker Alley* (1995); *Taboo* (13 November 2003).

McKinney, John, *Mrs. McThing* (12 October 1984); *Harrigan and Hart* (31 January 1985).

McManus, John L., *Rufus Lemaire's Affairs* (28 March 1927).

Meeker, Jesse, *Call Me Madam* (12 October 1950); Seventeen (21 June 1951).

Mello, Al, *Lovely Ladies, Kind Gentlemen* (28 December 1970).

Melrose, Ronald (Ron), *The Act* (29 October 1977); *Perfectly Frank* (30 November 1980); *Woman of the Year* (29 March 1981); *Marilyn: An American Fable* (4 December 1983); *Cabaret* (revival) (22 October 1987); *Ann Reinking . . . Music Moves Me* (23 December 1984); *The Sweet Smell of Success* (14 March 2002); *Imaginary Friends* (12 December 2002); *Jersey Boys* (6 November 2005).

Merkin, Robby, *The Middle of Nowhere* (20 November 1988).

Meyers, Lanny, *O Say Can You See!* (8 October 1962); *Hooray! It's a Glorious Day . . . And All That* (9 March 1966).

Milbank, Stephen, *Hannah . . . 1939* (31 May, 1990).

Miller, Freda, *Flahooley* (14 May 1951).

Mlotek, Zalmen, *The Golden Land* (11 November 1985).

Montero, Gus, *The Lieutenant* (9 March 1975).

Montgomery, Frank, *Hello 1921* (1921) (also co-composer).

Morgenstern, Sam, *O Marry Me!* (17 October 1961).

Morris, John, *Carnival in Flanders* (8 September 1953); *Phoenix '55* (23 April 1955); *Pipe Dream* (30 November 1955); *Shangri-La* (13 June 1956); *Bells Are Ringing* (29 November 1956); *Shinebone Alley* (13

April 1957); *Copper and Brass* (17 October 1957); *Hans Brinker; or, The Silver Skates* (9 February 1958); *First Impressions* (19 March 1959); *The Girls Against the Boys* (2 November 1959); *Bye Bye Birdie* (14 April 1960); *Wildcat* (16 December 1960); *Kwamina* (23 October 1961); *All American* (19 February 1962); *Baker Street* (16 February 1965); *Sherry!* (28 March 1967); *Dear World* (6 February 1969); *Look to the Lilies* (29 March 1970); *Lolita, My Love* (16 February 1971); *Mack and Mabel* (6 October 1974); *The Night that Made America Famous* (26 February 1975).

Neil, Roger, *A Reel American Hero* (25 March 1981).

Ngema, Mbongeni, *Sarafina!* (28 January 1988).

Nightingale, Christopher, *Groundhog Day* (17 April 2017).

Norris, Lee, *Carol Channing with Ten Stouthearted Men* (1970).

Oakley, Scott, *Pal Joey* (revival) (27 June 1976).

Odenz, Leon, *Gambler's Paradise* (1975); *A Mass Murder in the Balcony of the Old Ritz-Rialto* (14 November 1975).

Ott, Horace, *Dude (The Highway Life)* (9 October 1972).

Owens, Frank, *Shades of Harlem* (21 August 1984); *Streetheat* (27 January 1985); *Uptown . . . It's Hot!* (29 January 1986).

Pahl, Mel, *Michael Todd's Peep Show* (28 June 1950).

Palkowsky, Dan, *A Matter of Opinion* (30 September 1980).

Peress, Maurice, *Queenie Pie* (9 October 1986).

Perkinson, Coleridge-Taylor, *Billy* (22 March 1969).

Pfeiffer, Jack, *The Vamp* (10 November 1955).

Pippin, Donald, *Ankles Aweigh* (18 April 1955); *Fashion* (18 February 1974).

Pitot, Genevieve, *Inside U.S.A.* (30 April 1948); *Kiss Me, Kate* (30 December 1948); *Great to be Alive!* (23 March 1950); *Call Me Madam* (12 October 1950); *Two on the Aisle* (19 July 1951); *Two's Company* (15 December 1952); *Can-Can* (7 May 1953); *Shangri-La* (13 June 1956); *Li'l Abner* (15 November 1956); *Livin' the Life* (27 April 1957); *The Body Beautiful* (23 January 1958); *Destry Rides Again* (23 April 1959); *Saratoga* (7 December 1959); *Milk and Honey* (10 October 1961); *La Belle* (13 August 1962); *Sophie* (15 April 1963); *The Girl Who Came to Supper* (8 December 1963); *Cool Off!* (31 March 1964); *Drat! The Cat!* (10 October 1965).

Pomahac, Bruce, *Irving Berlin's White Christmas* (23 November 2008); *Holiday Inn, The New Irving Berlin Musical* (6 October 2016).

Portnoff, Mischa, *Bless You All* (14 December 1950).

Portnoff, Wesley, *Bless You All* (14 December 1950).

Pottle, Sam, *Money* (12 July 1963) (also show's composer).

Pribor, Richard, *Make a Wish* (18 April 1951).

Prince, Robert, *Something More* (10 November 1964); *Half a Sixpence* (25 April 1965); *Hot September* (14 September 1965).

Pruyn, William, *Satchmo: America's Musical Legend* (15 July 1987).

Quigley, Jack, *Barbary Coast* (28 February 1978).

Rago, Joe, *Ballad for a Firing Squad* (11 December 1968).

Raitt, James, *Stardust* (19 February 1987); *Late Nite Comic* (15 October 1987); *Meet Me in St. Louis* (2 November 1989).

Ralston, Alfred, *Oh, What a Lovely War* (30 December 1964).

Redwine, Skip, *The Decline and Fall of the Entire World as Seen through the Eyes of Cole Porter* (30 March 1965).

Reinhardt, Stephen, *The Glorious Age* (11 May 1975).

Reisman, Joe, *Lennon* (5 October 1982).

Rice, Michael, *Gotta Getaway!* (16 June 1984).

Rinehimer, John, *The News* (7 November 1985).

Rittman, Trude, *One Touch of Venus* (7 October 1943); *Carousel* (19 April 1945); *Brigadoon* (13 March 1947); *Allegro* (10 October 1947); *Look Ma, I'm Dancin'!* (29 January 1948); *Gentlemen Prefer Blondes* (8 December 1949); *Peter Pan* (Bernstein) (24 April 1950); *The King and I* (29 March 1951); *Paint Your Wagon* (12 November 1951); *Wish You Were Here* (25 June 1952); *The Girl in Pink Tights* (5 March 1954); *Peter Pan* (Charlap) (20 October 1954); *Fanny* (4 November 1954); *My Fair Lady* (15 March 1956); *At the Grand* (7 July 1958); *Christine* (7 May 1960); *Camelot* (3 December 1960); *Hot Spot* (19 April 1963); *Jennie* (17 October 1963); *Darling of the Day* (27 January 1968); *Maggie Flynn* (23 October 1968); *Two By Two* (10 November 1970); *Ambassador* (19 November 1972); *Gone With the Wind* (28 August 1973); *Gigi* (13 November 1973); *A Musical Jubilee* (13 November 1975).

Roberts, Jimmy, *God Bess You, Mr. Rosewater* (14 October 1979); *Trixie True Teen Detective* (7 December 1980).

Roffman, Frederick, *Ape Over Broadway* (12 March 1975).

Rogers, Robert, *Miss Moffat* (7 October 1974).

Romoff, Colin, *A Mother's Kisses* (23 September 1968).

Rosemont, Walter L., *Battling Buttler* (8 October 1923) (also show's composer).

Rosenthal, Laurence, *The Music Man* (19 December 1957); *Goldilocks* (11 October 1958); *Take Me Along* (22 October 1959); *Saratoga* (7 December 1959) (pre-Broadway arranger); *Donnybrook* (18 May 1961).

Roven, Glen, *Double Feature* (8 October 1981).

Salvador, Dom, *Sarava* (23 February 1979).

Sandberg, Steve, *Chronicle of a Death Foretold* (15 June 1995).

Saunders, Merl, *Buck White* (2 December 1969).

Savino, Domenico, *Sons o' Fun* (1 December 1941).

Schaefer, Hal, *Kismet* (3 December 1953); *The Ziegfeld Follies* (16 April 1956); *A Funny Thing Happened on the Way to the Forum* (8 May 1962); *Foxy* (16 February 1964); *Royal Flush* (31 December 1964); *A Funny Thing Happened on the Way to the Forum* (revival) (30 March 1972).

Schechtman, Saul, *Fallout* (20 May 1959).

Schierhorn, Paul, *The News* (7 November 1985) (also show's composer).

Schlein, Irving, *Love Life* (7 October 1948) (assistant to Kurt Weill on ballet music).

Schneider, Charles, *Your Own Thing* (13 January 1968).

Schutz, Herb, *Cape Cod Follies* (18 September 1929).

Scott, Ed, *Walking Happy* (26 November 1966).

Scott, Nathan, *3 for Tonight* (6 April 1955).

Sheets, Walter, *Foolin' Ourselves* (16 January 1957).

Sheinkman, Mordecai, *We Take the Town* (17 February 1962).

Sherman, Milt, *Paradise Island* (22 June 1961); *Mardi Gras* (26 June 1965).

Shire, David, *The Sap of Life* (2 October 1961); *Graham Crackers* (23 January 1963) (also show's composer); *Love Match* (3 November 1968) (also show's composer); *Company* (26 April 1970).

Siegmeister, Elie (also Elie Siegmaster), *Carnival in Flanders* (8 September 1953); *Kean* (2 November 1961).

Silberman, Joel, *Really Rosie* (30 September 1980).

Simon, John, *Rock and Roll! The First 5,000 Years* (24 October 1982).

Simons, Ted, *That 5 A.M. Jazz* (19 October 1964).

Skloff, Michael, *Jokers* (14 October 1986); *Arthur, the Musical* (1 November 1990) (also show's composer).

Smith, Steven, *Movie Star* (1982).

Sommer, Kathy, *Romance, Romance* (1 May 1988).

Spangler, David Sheridan, *The Magic Show* (28 May 1974).

St. Louis, Louis, *Grease* (14 February 1972); *Over Here!* (6 March 1974); *El Bravo* (16 June 1981); *Raggedy Ann* (16 October 1986); *Roza* (1 October 1987); *Bring in the Morning* (23 April 1994).

Starer, Robert, *The Gay Life* (18 November 1961).

Starobin, Michael, *Double Feature* (8 October 1981)

Stecko, Bob, *Babes in Toyland* (updated revival) (21 December 1979).

Stegmeyer, William, *After You, Mr. Hyde* (25 June 1968).

Stein, Julian, *The Sap of Life* (2 October 1961); *Half-Past Wednesday* (6 April 1962); *1491* (2 September 1969).

Sternberg, Ann, *All in Love* (10 November 1961).

Still, Frank, *Lady Lily* (28 November 1978).

Stolz, Robert, *The Merry Widow* (revival) (4 August 1943); *Mr. Strauss goes to Boston* (6 September 1945) (also so-composer).

Strayhorn, Billy, *Beggar's Holiday* (26 December 1946).

Sturiale, Grant, *The Little Prince and the Aviator* (December 1982); *Durante* (12 August 1989).

Styne, Jule, *High Button Shoes* (9 October 1947); *Miss Lonelyhearts* (3 October 1957) (incidental music).

Tartaglia, Bob, *Smile, Smile, Smile* (4 April 1973).

Terry, Mike, *Buck White* (2 December 1969).

Tesori, Jeanine, *How to Succeed in Business Without Really Trying* (revival) (23 March 1995); *Dream* (3April 1997); *The Sound of Music* (revival) (12 March 1998); *Swing!* (9 December 1999).

Thaler, Fred, *Platinum* (12 November 1978).

Thompson, Aaron, *Hi-De-Ho* (6 May 1933).

Thompson, Jay, *Lorelei* (27 January 1974).

Troob, Daniel, *Goodtime Charley* (3 March 1975); *Pacific Overtures* (11 January 1976); *The Baker's Wife* (11 May 1976); *Bring Back Birdie* (5 March 1981)

Urbont, Jacques, *Stag Movie* (3 January 1971).

Wade, Uel, *I Remember Mama* (31 May 1979); *Love* (15 April 1984)

Wahler, David, *Twanger* (15 November 1972).

Walberg, Betty, *West Side Story* (26 September 1957); *Gypsy* (21 May 1959); *Anyone Can Whistle* (4 April 1964); *Fiddler on the Roof* (22 September 1964); *Kelly* (6 February 1965); *On A Clear Day You Can See Forever* (17 October 1965); *It's a Bird . . . It's a Plane . . . It's Superman* (29 March 1966).

Waldman, Robert, *The Robber Bridegroom* (9 October 1979) (also show's composer).

Walker, Chris, *Me and My Girl* (10 August 1986).

Walker, Don, *Bless You All* (14 December 1950); *The Beauty Part* (26 December 1962) (incidental music); *The Bronx Express* (date unknown).

Warner, Neil, *Man of La Mancha* (22 November 1965); *Man of La Mancha* (revival) (22 June 1972); *Man of La Mancha* (revival) (24 April 1992).

Warner, Russell, *Shenandoah* (7 January 1975); *The Red Blue-Grass Western Flyer Show* (16 August 1977); *Whoopee!* (revival) (14 February 1979); *A Long Way to Boston* (September 1979); *Zapata* (17 September 1980); *The Five O'Clock Girl* (28 January 1981); *Little Johnny Jones* (21 March 1982); *The Great American Backstage Musical* (15 September 1982).

Warnick, Clay, *Park Avenue* (4 November 1946).

Webb, Robert, *Seven Brides for Seven Brothers* (8 July 1982).

Weigert, Rene, *Ziegfeld Follies* (1 March 1957).

Weill, Kurt, also composer of the shows; *Lady in the Dark* (23 January 1941); *One Touch of Venus* (7 October 1943); *Firebrand of Florence* (22 March 1945); *Street Scene* (9 January 1947); *Love Life* (7 October 1948); *Lost in the Stars* (30 October 1949).

Weiner, Mark, *Hot and Cold Heros* (9 May 1973).

Weissman, Bernard, *You'll See Stars* (29 December 1942).

Werner, Fred, *The Conquering Hero* (16 January 1961); *Little Me* (17 November 1962); *Sweet Charity* (29 January 1966); *Noël Coward's Sweet Potato* (29 September 1968).

Wheeler, Harold, *Promises, Promises* (1 December 1968); *Coco* (18

December 1969); *A Chorus Line* (19 October 1975) (uncredited); *Dreamgirls* (9 December 1981); *Leader of the Pack* (8 April 1985) (opening dance sequence).

Will, Ethyl, *Easter Show* (2 April 1993).

Wilson, Art, *Meet the People* (25 December 1940).

Woldin, Judd, *The Beast in Me* (14 May 1963); *Raisin* (18 October 1973) (also show's composer).

Wooley, Scott, *Ain't Broadway Grand* (18 April 1993); *State Fair* (27 March 1996).

York, Donald (Don), *Can-Can* (revival) (30 April 1981); *A Christmas Carol* (30 October 1981); *5, 6, 7, 8 . . . Dance!* (15 June 1983).

Bibliography

Musical Scores

Aarons, Alfred E., Harry B. Smith, and Robert B. Smith. *A China Doll*. New York: M. Witmark, 1904.

Aronson, Rudolph. "Marche Triomphale." New York: C.H. Ditson, 1875.

——. "Mazurka Melodique." New York: C.H. Ditson, 1874.

Aronson, Rudolph, and Sydney Rosenfeld. *The Rainmaker of Syria*. Comic Opera in Two Acts. New York: T.B. Harms, 1893.

Baker, Thomas. "The Emperor's March." Performed at Barnum's Museum, in the Grand Spectacle, *The Christian Martyrs*. New York: William A. Pond, 1867.

——. *Gems from* The Black Crook. New York: William A. Pond, 1866.

——. "The Laura Keene Schottisch." New York: Firth, Pond, 1856.

——. "The Rachel Schottisch." New York: Horace Waters, 1855.

——. "The Seven Sons Galop." New York: Horace Waters, 1861.

——. *Thomas Baker's Operatic Quadrilles composed on themes selected from the most Celebrated Operas, Performed at the Academy of Music*. New York: Horace Waters, 1855.

——. "Transformation Polka." From *The Black Crook*. New York: William A. Pond, 1867.

Baker, Thomas, arr. *Overture to Auber's Opera* The Syren, *as performed at Niblo's Garden*. Arranged for the pianoforte. New York: Horace Waters, 1854.

Barratt, W. Augustus. *The Death of Cuthullin*. London: Paterson and Sons, [1897].

——. *Little Simplicity: Selections*. New York: Shapiro, Bernstein, 1918.

Barratt, W. Augustus, Howard Talbot, and Adrian Ross. *Kitty Grey*. Adapted from *Les Fétards* by J.S. Pigott. With additional numbers by Lionel Monckton, Paul Rubens, and Bernard Rolt. London: E. Ascherberg, 1901.

Batchelor, W.H. "March of the Forty Thieves." Cincinnati: John Church, 1892.

Batchelor, W.H., and Harry B. Smith. *Selections from the Operatic Extravaganza* Sinbad. Cincinnati: John Church, 1891.

Batchelor, W.H., Willard Thompson, and H.T. Vynne. *Musical Selections from "Ali Baba," or, Morgiana and the Forty Thieves*. Cincinnati: John Church, 1892.

Bendix, Theo. *The Commuters*: "A Suburban Scramble." New York: Leo Feist, 1910.

———. *The Great Name* "Waltzes." New York: Leo Feist, 1911.

———. "Nat-u-ritch. An Indian Idyll." Intermezzo from *The Squaw Man*. New York: Jos. W. Stern, 1906.

———. *Seven Days* "Waltzes." New York: Leo Feist, 1910.

Bendix, Theo, and George H. Jessop. "I Am So Shy." As sung by Miss Minnie Palmer, With great success in the Musical Comedy *My Sweetheart*. New York: C.H. Ditson, 1882.

Berlin, Irving, and Harry B. Smith. *Watch Your Step*. New York: Irving Berlin, 1914.

Blake, Eubie, Noble Sissle, Flournoy Miller, and Aubrey Lyle. *Shuffle Along*. New York: M. Witmark, 1921.

Böteführ, W.D.C. "Pas de Demons." As performed at the Varieties Theatre in The Black Crook. St. Louis: R.J. Compton, 1867.

Bowers, Robert Hood. "Cute an' Cunnin'." Slow Fox Trot. From *A Lonely Romeo*. New York: Jerome H. Remick, 1919.

———. "Galop." From *The Vanderbilt Cup*. New York: Jerome H. Remick, 1906.

———. "Melodrama." From *The Spring Maid*. New York: Joseph W. Stern, 1911.

Bowers, Robert Hood, and Richard Carle. *The Maid and the Mummy*. New York: M. Witmark, 1904.

Bowers, Robert Hood, Harry B. Smith, and Robert B. Smith. *The Red Rose*. New York: Jerome H. Remick, 1911.

Braham, David, and Edward Harrigan. *Collected Songs*. Edited with an introduction by Jon W. Finson. Recent Researches in American Music, vol. 27. Music of the United States of America, vol. 7. Madison, WI: A-R Editions, 1997.

Braham, George. *Selection from Ed. Harrigan's Musical Play "Under Cover."* Arr. By Karl L. Hoschna. New York: M. Witmark, 1903.
Braham, John, and Edward Harrigan. "Steady Company." Boston: White and Goullaud, 1872.
Braham, John, and Edward Righton. "Young Village Beauty." Boston: White, Smith and Perry, 1869.
Braham, John, and J. Cheever Goodwin. "A Long Time Ago." Song (Mock Sentimental). Boston: Miles and Thompson, 1891.
Braham, John, and J. Cohan. "Rowing on the Lake." Song and Dance. Boston: White and Goullaud, 1870.
Braham, John, and William Cavanah. "Kaloolah," Song and Dance. Boston: John P. Perry, 1875.
Bratton, John W., and Paul West. *The Man from China*. New York: M. Witmark, 1904.
——. *The Pearl and the Pumpkin*. New York: M. Witmark, 1905.
Bray, John, and James Nelson Barker. *The Indian Princess*. Earlier American Music, vol. 11. New introduction by H. Wiley Hitchcock. New York: Da Capo Press, 1972.
Breil, Joseph, and Jacques Byrne. *The Legend*. London: Chappell, 1919.
Brinkworth, W.H., and James Barnes. "Happy Little Flip-Flaps." Double Song and Dance. New York: William A. Pond, 1875.
Bristow, George F. *Rip Van Winkle*. Earlier American Music, vol. 25. Edited with a new introduction by Steven Ledbetter. New York: Da Capo Press, 1991.
Brode, Herman. "March." In *Choice Selections from* The Silver King. Played Nightly at Wallack's Theatre. New York: Williams, 1883.
Carr, Benjamin. *Musical Miscellany in Occasional Numbers*. Earlier American Music, vol. 21. Compiled and with a new introduction by Eve R. Meyer. New York: Da Capo Press, 1982.
——. *Selected Secular and Sacred Songs*. Recent Researches in American Music, vol. 15. Edited by Eve R. Meyer. Madison, WI: A-R Editions, 1986.
Carr, F. Osmond, and W.S. Gilbert. *His Excellency*. London: Joseph Williams, 1894.
Caryll, Ivan, and C.M.S. McLellan. *The Little Café*. New York: Chappell, 1913.
——. *The Pink Lady*. New York: Chappell, 1911.
Caryll, Ivan, and Harry B. Smith. *Papa's Darling*. Based on *Le Fils Surnaturel* by Grenet D'Ancourt and Maurice Vaucaire. New York: Chappell, 1904.

Caryll, Ivan, and Henry Hamilton. *The Duchess of Dantzic*. London: Chappell, 1903.

Caryll, Ivan, and H.J.W. Dam. *The Shop Girl*. Additional numbers by Adrian Ross and Lionel Monckton. London: Hopwood and Crew, n.d.

Caryll, Ivan, Cecil Cook, Owen Hall, Adrian Ross, and Claude Aveling. *The Girl from Kay's*. London: Chappell, 1903.

Caryll, Ivan, George Grossman, Jr., Adrian Ross, Percy Greenbank, and Lionel Monckton. *The Spring Chicken*. London: Chappell, 1905.

Caryll, Ivan, Owen Hall, and Adrian Ross. *The Little Cherub*. London: Chappell, 1906.

Caryll, Ivan, Seymour Hicks, and Percy Greenbank. *The Earl and the Girl*. London: Chappell, 1904.

Caryll, Ivan, Seymour Hicks, Harry Nicholls, Aubrey Hopwood, Harry Greenbank, and Lionel Monckton. *A Runaway Girl*. London: Chappell, 1898.

Catlin, E[dward] N[oble], and Edward Harrigan. "Sweet Louisa." From *The Little Frauds*. Boston: White and Goullaud, 1871.

Cellier, Alfred, and Albert Jarret. *The Sultan of Mocha*. London: Enoch, [1874].

Cellier, Alfred, and B.C. Stephenson. *Doris*. Arranged from the full score by Ivan Caryll. London: Chappell, [1889].

———. *Dorothy*. London: Chappell, [1886].

Cellier, Alfred, and James Albery. *The Spectre Knight*. London: Metzler, [1878].

Cellier, Alfred, and W.S. Gilbert. *The Mountebanks*. London: Chappell, 1892.

Chadwick, George W., and R.A. Barnet. *Tabasco*. Boston: B.F. Wood, 1894.

Chadwick, George W., and Robert Grant. *The Peer and the Pauper*. Ms., 1884.

Chadwick, George W., and William Chauncy Langdon. *Judith*. New York: G. Schirmer, 1901.

Chassaigne, Francis, and A. de Leuven. *Actéon et le centaure Chiron*. Paris: Ph. Feuchot, 1878.

Chassaigne, Francis, Eugène Leterrier, and Albert Vanloo. *Falka*. English version by H.B. Farnie. Boston: White-Smith, 1884.

Chassaigne, Francis, Louis Péricaud, and Lucien Delormel. *Deux Mauvaises Bonnes*. Paris: Ph. Feuchot, 1876.

———. *Les Enfants de la balle*. Paris: Ph. Feuchot, 1877.
Chilvers, Thomas H. "Beautiful Ivy Leaf." *The Ivy Leaf*. Arranged by J.C. Mayseder. Boston: Oliver Ditson, 1891.
———. "Detroit Light Infantry Grand March." Detroit: C.J. Whitney, 1884.
———. "I ove You All." *The Head Waiters*. Detroit: Whitney Warner, 1901.
Chilvers, Thomas H., and Edgar Smith. "If This Were the Age of Romance." *The Little Host*. New York: Edward Schuberth, 1898.
———. "I'm a Shy Little Innocent Thing." The Little Host. New York: Edward Schuberth, 1898.
Chilvers, Thomas H., and William J. Dawson. "Maureen Mavourneen." *The Ivy Leaf*. Detroit: C.J. Whitney, 1885.
Chipman, J.S. "Three Bears." Song. In *Cinderella and the Prince, or, Castle of Heart's Desire*. Book by R.A. Barnet. Lyrics by D.K. Stevens and R.A. Barnet. Music by Louis F. Gottschalk and Edward W. Corliss. Boston: White-Smith, 1904.
Chubb, T. Youres. "Fifth Washington Greys." Grand March. New York: Firth and Hall, 1846.
———. "I'd Marry Him Tomorrow." From *A Loan of a Lover*. With an Arrangement for the Piano Forte, Arranged by T. Youres Chubb. New York: Gier and Walker, 1836.
———. "The Music of Balfe's Celebrated Opera *The Bohemian Girl*." New York: Atwill, 1844.
Clifton, Arthur, and Colonel W.H. Hamilton. *The Enterprise*. Baltimore: Arthur Clifton, [1823].
Comer, Thomas, and S.S. Steele. *Favourite Melodies from the Grand Chinese Spectacle of Aladdin or the Wonderful Lamp*. Boston: Prentiss and Clark, 1847.
Connelly, Michael. "Galop." In *The Forty Thieves*. New York: William A. Pond, 1869.
Cook, Will Marion, J.A. Shipp, Alex Rogers, and Bert A. Williams. *Bandana Land*. New York: Gotham-Attucks, 1908.
Corliss, Edward W. and R.A. Barnet. *Queen of the Ballet*. With additional numbers by Alfred Norman, George Lowell Tracy, Henry Lawson Heartz, Walter Gould, and Hastings Weblyn. Lyrical assistance by Frederic W. Arnold, Jr. Boston: White-Smith, 1893.
Darley, Francis T.S., and James Robinson Planché. *Fortunio and His Seven Gifted Servants*. Philadelphia: J.M. Stoddart, 1883.

Debillemont, Jean-Jacques. *Le Tour du Monde* de Dennery et Jules Verne. Transcrits pour Piano par Jean-Jacques Debillemont. Paris: Léon Grus, [1875].

Debillemont, Jean-Jacques, and H. Boisseaux. *Astaroth*. Paris: E. Girod, [1861].

De Koven, Reginald. *Ballet Music.* "Fireflies, Ballet." "Japanese Ballet." As Performed in *From Broadway to Tokio*. New York: G. Schirmer, 1900.

———. *Ballet Music from* The Man in the Moon. Cincinnati: John Church, 1899.

———. "Pantomime Dance." From *The Little Duchess*. New York: Edward Schuberth, 1901.

DeKoven, Reginald, and Frederic Ranken. *Happyland, or, The King of Elysia*. New York: Jos. W. Stern, 1905.

De Koven, Reginald, and Harry B. Smith. *Foxy Quiller*. New York: Edward Schuberth, 1900.

———. *The Highwayman*. New York: T.B. Harms, 1898.

———. *Maid Marian*. New York: Edward Schuberth, 1901.

———. *Robin Hood*. New York: G. Schirmer, 1891.

———. *Rob Roy*. New York: G. Schirmer, 1894.

De Koven, Reginald, and Joseph W. Herbert. *The Beauty Spot*. New York: Jos. W. Stern, 1909.

De Koven, Reginald, Charles Klein, and Charles Emerson Cook. *Red Feather*. New York: Jos. W. Stern, 1903.

DeKoven, Reginald, Fred DeGresac, and Harry B. Smith. *The Wedding Trip*. New York: Jerome H. Remick, 1911.

De Koven, Reginald, Frederic Ranken, and Stanislaus Stange. *The Student King*. New York: Jos. W. Stern, 1906.

Devin, William. "Ballet." In *The Casino Girl*. Book by Harry B. Smith. Music by Ludwig Englander. Interpolated numbers by Harry T. MacConnell and Arthur Nevin. New York: E. Schuberth, 1900.

Diet, Edmund, and A. Curti. *Temptations*. Paris: Edmund Diet, 1911.

Drigo, Richard (Riccardo). *Les Millions d'Arlequin*. Ballet en 2 actes de Marius Petipa. Leipzig: Zimmermann, 1901.

Dumont, Frank. *Africanus Blue Beard*. Music arranged for the piano by Alfred B. Sedgwick. New York: De Witt, 1876.

———. *Gambrinus, King of Lager Beer*. Music arranged for the piano by Alfred B. Sedgwick. New York: De Witt, 1876.

Early Melodrama in America. The Voice of Nature (1803). Edited by Karl Kroeger. *The Aethiop* (1813). Orchestral Restoration by Victor Fell Yellin. New York: Garland, 1994.

Edwards, Julian, and Harry B. Smith. *Jupiter, or, The Cobbler and the King*. Cincinnati: John Church, 1893.
Edwards, Julian, and Stanislaus Stangé. *Brian Boru*. Cincinnati, OH: John Church, 1896.
——— . *Dolly Varden*. New York: M. Witmark, 1901.
——— . *The Jolly Musketeer*. New York: M. Witmark, 1898.
——— . *Love's Lottery*. New York: M. Witmark, 1904.
——— . *When Johnny Comes Marching Home*. New York: M. Witmark, 1902.
Edwards, Leo, and Harold Atteridge. *The Passing Show of 1915*. Additional numbers by William F. Peters and J. Leubrie Hill. New York: G. Schirmer, 1915.
Eichberg, Julius, and Benjamin E. Woolf. *The Doctor of Alcantara*. New enlarged and revised edition. Boston: Oliver Ditson, 1879.
Einödshofer, Julius. "Flirt Waltz." From the ballet, *Flirting in St. Moritz*. Berlin: C.M. Roehr, 1913; New York: Jerome H. Remick, 1913.
Ellis, Melville. "Malena." Intermezzo from *The Road to Yesterday*. New York: M. Witmark, 1907.
——— . "School-Boy and Girl: Dance." New York: M. Witmark, 1905.
——— . "The Tango Dance." From *The Merry Countess*. New York: M. Witmark, 1912.
Emmet, J. K. "Emmet's Baby Song." As sung in *Fritz in Bohemia*. Cincinnati: John Church, 1884.
. "Emmet's Swell Song." From *Fritz in Ireland*. Cincinnati: John Church, 1881.
. "I Know What Love Is." As sung in *Fritz in Ireland*. Cincinnati: John Church. 1879.
Englander, Ludwig. *Selections from the Romantic Comic Opera 1776*. New York: Wm. A. Pond, 1884.
Englander, Ludwig, and Harry B. Smith. *The Casino Girl*. Interpolated numbers by Harry T. MacConnell and Arthur Nevin. New York: E. Schuberth, 1900A.
——— . *The Little Corporal*. New York: Breitkopf and Härtel, 1898.
——— . *A Madcap Princess*. New York: Jos. W. Stern, 1904.
——— . *The Office Boy*. New York: Jos. W. Stern, 1903.
——— . *The Rounders*. New York: Edward Schuberth, 1899.
——— . *The Strollers*. New York: Edward Schuberth, 1901.
Englander, Ludwig, and J. Cheever Goodwin. *The Monks of Malabar*. New York: Edward Schuberth, 1900B.

Englander, Ludwig, and Stanislaus Stange. *The Two Roses*. New York: Jos. W. Stern, 1904.

Englander, Ludwig, Frederic Ranken, and Harry B. Smith. *The Jewel of Asia*. New York: Jos. W. Stern, 1903.

Europe, James Reese. "The Castle Doggy Fox Trot." New York: Joseph W. Stern, [1913].

Eysler, Edmund, and Leo Stein. *Vera Violetta*. Leipzig: Josef Weinberger, 1908.

Eysler, Edmund, Leo Stein, and Carl Lindau. *The Love-Cure*. English version and adaptation for the American stage by Oliver Herford. New York: G. Schirmer, 1909.

Eysler, Edmund, Sigmund Romberg, Edgar Smith, and Herbert Reynolds. *The Blue Paradise*. Based on the original libretto by Leo Stein and Bela Jenbasch. New York: G. Schirmer, 1915.

Fall, Leo, A.M. Willner, and F. Grünbaum. *The Dollar Princess*. American version by George Grossmith, Jr. New York: T.B. Harms and Francis, Day and Hunter, 1909.

Felix, Hugo, and Anne Caldwell. *Pom-Pom*. New York: T.B. Harms, 1916.

Felix, Hugo, and Victorien Sardou. *The Merveilleuses*. Adapted for the English stage by Basil Hood. Lyrics by Adrian Ross. London: Chappell, 1906.

Felix, Hugo, Basil Hood, and Howard Talbot. *The Pearl Girl*. London: Chappell, 1913.

Felix, Hugo, C.E. Hands, and Adrian Ross. *Madame Sherry*. London: Chappell, 1904.

Felix, Hugo, Michael Morton, Paul Gavault, and Adrian Ross. *Tantalizing Tommy*. London: Chappell, 1912.

Fletcher, Percy, and Oscar Asche. *Cairo, a Mosaic in Music and Mime*. London: Ascherberg, Hopwood and Crew, 1920.

Francis, W.T. "Dance of the Angeles." New Orleans: Junius Hart, 1885.

———. "La Media Noche." Arranged for Piano by W.T. Francis. Played at the World's Exposition at New Orleans, by the Celebrated Mexican Military Band. New Orleans: Junius Hart, 1885.

———. "Les Petites Blondes. Gavotte." New Orleans: Louis Grunewald, 1885.

———. "Priscilla: Dance Characteristique." New York: M. Witmark, 1902.

Francis, W.T., and Edgar Smith. "Golf-Song. In *The Little Host*. New York: Edward Schuberth, 1898.

Francis, W.T., and Sydney Rosenfeld. *The Rollicking Girl*. New York: M. Witmark, 1905.

Franklin, Malvin. *Modern Dances: Society's Latest Dance Folio.* New York: Knickerbocker Music, 1914.

Franklin, Malvin M., Robert Hood Bowers, Harry B. Smith, Lew Fields, and Robert B. Smith. *A Lonely Romeo.* Chicago: Jerome H. Remick, 1919.

Freeborn, Cass. "The Stop-Trot Rag." New York: M. Witmark, 1914.

Friml, Rudolf. "A Garden Matinee: Entr'Acte." Chicago: Lyon and Healy, 1906.

——. "Three Dances for Piano." From the Japanese Ballet, *O Mitake San.* New York: G. Schirmer, 1911.

Friml, Rudolf, and Otto Hauerbach (Harbach). *Katinka.* New York: G. Schirmer, 1916.

Friml, Rudolf, and Rida Johnson Young. *Some Time.* New York: G. Schirmer, 1919.

Friml, Rudolf, Leo Dietrichstein, and Otto Hauerbach (Harbach). *High Jinks.* New York: G. Schirmer, 1913.

Furst, William. *Selections from* The Darling of the Gods. Chicago: Howley, Haviland, and Dresser, 1903.

——. *David Harum:* "March." Chicago: Howley, Haviland, and Dresser, 1900.

Gabriel, Max. *In Gotham:* "Waltzes." New York: M. Witmark, 1898.

Gabriel, Max, and Georg Okonkowski. *Stolze Thea.* Berlin: Kollo-Verlag, 1917.

Ganne, Louis, and Maurice Ordonneau. *Les Saltimbanques.* Partition Chant et Piano. Paris: Choudens, 1900.

Ganne, Louis, Maurice Vaucaire, and Georges Mitchell. *Hans, Le Joueur de Flûte.* Partition Complète pour Chant et Piano. Paris: G. Ricordi, 1906.

Gaunt, Percy. *Songs from Hoyt's* A Trip to Chinatown. New York: T.B. Harms, 1892.

Gebest, Charles J. *The American Idea:* "March." New York: Cohan and Harris, 1908.

Gebest, Charles J., Channing Pollock, and Rennold Wolf. *The Red Widow.* New York: M. Witmark, 1911.

Giorza, Paolo. "Skirt Dance." London: Hopwood and Crew, 1896.

Glaser, C.J.M. *The Silver Star: Ballet Music.* New York: C.J.M. Glaser, 1910.

Glover, Howard. *Palomita; or, the Veiled Songstress.* New York: J.L. Peters, 1875.

Glover, Howard, and Robert Burns. *Tam O'Shanter.* London: Chappell, [1855].

Gottschalk, Louis F., Edward W. Corliss, R.A. Barnet, and D.K. Stevens. *Cinderella and the Prince, or, Castle of Heart's Desire*. Additional musical numbers by D.J. Sullivan and J.S. Chipman. New York: White-Smith, 1904.

Grant, John B., and Sydney Rosenfeld. *The Mystic Isle*. Philadelphia: Lee and Walker, 1886.

Graziano, John, ed. *Italian Opera in English*. Nineteenth-Century American Musical Theater, vol. 3. New York: Garland, 1994.

Hadley, Henry K., and David Stevens. *Azora, the Daughter of Montezuma*. New York: G. Schirmer, 1917.

Hadley, Henry K., and Frederic Ranken. *Nancy Brown*. New York: Jos. W. Stern, 1903.

Heartz, Harry Lawson "Hop Lee." Chinese Dance from *The Tenderfoot*. New York: M. Witmark, 1903.

Heartz, Harry Lawson, and R.A. Barnet. *Miladi and the Musketeer*. Boston: White-Smith, 1900.

———. *Miss Simplicity*. With additional numbers by Edward W. Corliss and Clifton Crawford. Lyrical assistance by Edward A. Church and D.K. Stevens. Boston: White-Smith, 1901.

Heartz, Harry Lawson, and Richard Carle. *The Hurdy Gurdy Girl*. Boston: White-Smith, 1907.

———. *The Tenderfoot*. New York: M. Witmark, 1903.

Hein, Silvio. *When Dreams Come True*: "The Santley Tango." New York: T.B. Harms and Francis, Day and Hunter, 1913.

Hein, Silvio, and George V. Hobart. *The Boys and Betty*. New York: Marie Cahill, 1908.

———. *The Yankee Girl*. New York: Blanche Ring, 1909.

Hein, Silvio, Armand Barnard, E. Ray Goetz, and Seymour Brown. *A Matinée Idol*. New York: Shapiro, 1909.

Hein, Silvio, Edwin Milton Royle, and Benjamin Hapgood Burt. *Marrying Mary*. New York: Jos. W. Stern, 1906.

Hein, Silvio, Joseph Santley, and Harry B. Smith. *All Over Town*. New York: T.B. Harms and Francis, Day, and Hunter, 1915.

Herbert, Victor, and Harry B. Smith. *Babette*. New York: M. Witmark, 1903.

———. *The Idol's Eye*. New York: Edward Schuberth, 1897.

———. *Little Nemo*. Based on Winsor McCay's cartoons. New York: Cohan and Harris, 1908.

———. *The Wizard of the Nile*. New York: Edward Schuberth, 1895.

Herbert, Victor, and Henry Blossom. *Eileen*. New York: M. Witmark, 1917.
——— ———. *Mlle. Modiste*. New York: M. Witmark, 1905.
——— ———. *The Prima Donna*. New York: M. Witmark, 1908.
——— ———. *The Princess Pat*. New York: M. Witmark, 1915.
——— ———. *The Velvet Lady*. New York: M. Witmark, 1919.
Herbert, Victor, and Rida Johnson Young. *Naughty Marietta*. New York: M. Witmark, 1910.
Herbert, Victor, Anna Caldwell, Laurence McCarty, and James O'Dea. *The Lady of the Slipper*. New York: M. Witmark, 1912.
Herbert, Victor, David Stevens, and Justin Huntly McCarthy. *The Madcap Duchess*. New York: G. Schirmer, 1913.
Herbert, Victor, and Glen MacDonough. *Algeria*. Chicago: Chas. K. Harris, 1908.
Herbert, Victor, Harry B. Smith, and A.N.C. Fowler. *The Tattooed Man*. New York: M. Witmark, 1907.
Herbert, Victor, Harry B. Smith, and Robert B. Smith. *The Débutante*. New York: G. Schirmer, 1914.
Herbert, Victor, Harry B. Smith, Fred De Grésac, and Robert B. Smith. *Sweethearts*. New York: G. Schirmer, 1913.
Hewitt, James. *Selected Compositions*. Recent Researches in American Music, vol 7. Edited by John W. Wagner. Madison, WI: A-R Editions, 1980.
Hewitt, John Hill. *The Collected Works of John Hill Hewitt*. Edited by N. Lee Orr and Lynn Wood Bertrand. Nineteenth-Century American Musical Theater vol. 6. New York: Garland, 1994.
Hill, J. Leubrie. "Rag-time Drummer." London: Keith, Prowse, 1903.
Hirsch, Louis A., and Rennold Wolf. *The Rainbow Girl*. New York: M. Witmark, 1917.
Hirsch, Louis A., Ben M. Jerome, Mark Swan, Edgar Smith, and Edward Madden. *He Came from Milwaukee*. New York: Chas. K. Harris, 1910.
Hirsch, Louis A., Otto Harbach, and Frank Mandel. *Mary*. New York: Victoria, 1921.
Hirsch, Louis A., Otto Harbach, and James Montgomery. *Going Up*. New York: M. Witmark, 1918.
Hoffmann, Max. *Broadway to Paris*. New York: T.B. Harms and Francis, Day and Hunter, 1912.
——— ———. *The Rogers Bros. in Ireland*: "Killarney." New York: Rogers Bros. Music, 1905.

Hoffmann, Max, Edward Madden, Sylvester Maguire, and Aaron Hoffman. *The Rogers Bros in Panama*. New York:Rogers Bros, 1907.

Hoffmaster, William. "Durang's Horn-Pipe." Boston: Oliver Ditson, 1823.

Howson, Frank A. "Fireman's Song and Chorus." New York: Frank A. Howson, 1887.

——— ———. *The King's Musketeer*: "March and Two Step." New York: Jos. W. Stern, 1899.

Hubbell, Raymond. "The Rooster Dance." From *The Runaways*. New York: Chas. K. Harris, 1903.

Hubbell, Raymond, and Addison Burkhardt. *The Runaways*. New York: Chas. K. Harris, 1903.

Hubbell, Raymond, Robert B. Smith, and Clara Driscoll. *Mexicana*. New York: Chas. K. Harris, 1906.

Hubbell, Raymond, Robert B. Smith, and Sam S. Shubert. *Fantana*. New York: M. Wimark, 1904.

Jacobi, Victor, and Harry B. Smith. *Rambler Rose*. New York: T.B. Harms and Francis, Day and Hunter, 1917.

Jacobi, Victor, and William Le Baron. *The Half Moon*. New York: T.B. Harms and Francis, Day and Hunter, 1920.

Jacobi, Victor, M[iksa] Bródy, and F[erenc] Martos. *The Marriage Market*. Adapted for the English stage by Gladys Unger. Lyrics by Arthur Anderson and Adrian Ross. Arranged by H.M. Higgs. London: Chappell, 1913.

——— ———. *Sybill*. Leipzig: W. Karczag, 1919.

Jacobi, Victor, M[iksa] Bródy, and F[erenc] Martos. *Sybil*. English version and lyrics by Harry Graham. Additional lyrics by Harry B. Smith. London: Chappell, 1915 and 1916.

Jakobowski, Edward, Claxton Bellamy, and Harry Paulton. *Erminie*. Boston: White-Smith, [1886].

Jerome, Ben M., George E. Stoddard, and Charles S. Taylor. *The Royal Chef*. New York: F.B. Haviland, 1904.

Johnstone, Alexander, and William Cary Duncan. *Fiddlers Three*. New York: M. Witmark, 1918.

Jones, Sidney, Edward Morton, Harry Greenbank, and Adrian Ross. *San Toy, or, The Emperor's Own*. London: Keith, Prowse, 1899.

Jones, Sidney, Owen Hall, and C.H. Taylor. *The Medal and the Maid*. London: Keith, Prowse, 1903.

Jones, Sidney, Owen Hall, and Harry Greenbank. *An Artist's Model*. London: Hopwood and Crew, 1895.

―――. *A Gaiety Girl*. London: Hopwood and Crew, n.d.
―――. *The Geisha*. London: Hopwood and Crew, 1896.
Joplin, Scott. *Treemonisha*. New York: Scott Joplin, 1911.
Kelley, Edgar Stillman. *Aladdin. A Chinese Suite for Orchestra*. New York: G. Schirmer, 1915.
―――. *Ben-Hur*. Edited by Charles Feleky. New York: Towers and Curran, 1902.
Kelley, Edgar Stillman, and C. M. S. McLellan. *Puritania*. Cincinnati: John Church, 1892.
Kelley, Edgar Stillman, and Elizabeth Hodgkinson. *The Pilgrim's Progress*. Text based on the Allegory of John Bunyan. Boston: Oliver Ditson, 1917.
Kelly, Michael. "Dance" in *Cinderella*. Massachusetts: n.p. [1812].
―――. "Dance of Naiads" in the *Forty Thieves*. Philadelphia: G.R. Blake, n.d.
―――. "Tambarine [sic] Dance" in the *Forty Thieves*. Philadelphia: A. Bacon, [1817].
―――. *The Music of* Cinderella. Arranged for the pianoforte by G. Woodham. Philadelphia: G. R.Blake, 1806.
Kelly, Michael, and George Coleman the Younger. *The Grand Dramatic Romance of Blue-Beard, or Female Curiosity*. London: Longman and Broderip, 1798.
Kelly, Michael, and Richard Brinsley Sheridan. *The Music of* Pizarro, *A Play*. London: Published for Mr. Kelly, 1799.
Kerker, Gustave, and Frederic Ranken. *Winsome Winnie*. New York: Jos. W. Stern, 1903.
Kerker, Gustave, and Hugh Morton. *The Belle of New York*. New York: T.B. Harms, 1897-8.
Kerker, Gustave, and Joseph Herbert. *The Social Whirl*. New York: T.B. Harms, 1906.
Kerker, Gustave, and R.H. Burnside. *Burning to Sing, or Singing to Burn*. New York: T.B. Harms, 1904.
―――. *The Tourists*. New York: T.B. Harms, 1906.
Kern, Jerome, and Anne Caldwell. *Good Morning, Dearie*. New York: T.B. Harms, 1921.
Kern, Jerome, Guy Bolton, and Clifford Grey. *Sally*. New York: T.B. Harms, 1921.
Kern, Jerome, Guy Bolton, and P.G. Wodehouse. *Have a Heart*. New York: T.B. Harms, 1917.

———. *Oh, Lady! Lady!!* New York: T.B. Harms, 1918.
Kern, Jerome, Philip Bartholmae, Guy Bolton, Schuyler Greene, and Herbert Reynolds. *Very Good Eddie*. New York: T.B. Harms, 1916.
Kiefert, Carl, James T. Tanner, and Adrian Ross. *The Ballet Girl*. London: Enoch and Sons, 1897.
Klein, Manuel. *The International Cup*: "Seaside Frolics: Skipping Rope Dance." New York: M. Witmark, 1910.
———. *Neptune's Daughter: Selection*. New York: M. Witmark, 1907.
———. *The Proud Prince*: "Triumphal March." New York: M. Witmark, 1903.
———. *A Society Circus*: "March of the Flowers." New York: M. Witmark, 1906.
Klein, Manuel, and R.H. Burnside. *Ballet. Music by Manuel Klein*. New York Hippodrome, Season 1910–1911. Copyist's MS. NYPL, *MSP.
Klein, Manuel, Anna Caldwell, Mark E. Swan, and James O'Dea. *The Top o' the World*. New York: M. Witmark, 1907.
Klein, Manuel, John Kendrick Bangs, and Vincent Bryan. *The Man from Now*. New York: M. Witmark, 1906.
Klein, Manuel, R.H. Burnside, and Austin Strong. *The Pied Piper*. New York: M. Witmark, 1909.
Koppitz, Charles. *Incidental Music to Shakespeare's* Henry VIII. MS parts [c. 1872]. Library of Congress M1510/.K83H4/Case.
Kreisler, Fritz. "Tambourin Chinois." London: Schott, 1911.
Kreisler, Fritz, Victor Jacobi, and William Le Baron. *Apple Blossoms*. New York: T.B. Harms and Francis, Day and Hunter, 1919.
Lachaume, Aimé and Gerhart Hauptmann. *The Sunken Bell*. Translated by Charles Henry Meltzer. New York: Doubleday, Page, 1911.
Levi, Maurice. "Gay Coney Island March and Two-Step." From *At Gay Coney Island*. New York: M. Witmark, 1896.
Levi, Maurice, and Harry B. Smith. *The Soul Kiss*. New York: M. Witmark, 1908.
Levi, Maurice, Grant Stewart, and John J. McNally. *The Rogers Bros.: A Reign of Error*. New York: Howley, Haviland, 1899.
Lewis, Walter H., and Bert Leston Taylor. *The Explorers*. New York: M. Witmark, 1902.
Lingard, William Horace. "The Grecian Bend." New York: Wm. A. Pond, 1898.
Linné, Hans S. "Rose Waltz." From *Mama's Baby Boy*. New York: M. Witmark, 1911.

Linné, Hans S., and Junie McCree. *Mama's Baby Boy*. New York: M. Witmark, 1911.
Loraine, William. "Franco-American Dance." From *Peggy from Paris*. New York: M. Witmark, 1903.
Loraine, William, and George Ade. *Peggy from Paris*. New York: M. Witmark, 1903.
Loraine, William, and John P. Wilson. *The Filibuster*. New York: M. Witmark, 1905.
Luders, Gustav, and Frank Pixley. *The Burgomaster*. New York: M. Witmark, 1900.
———. *The Grand Mogul*. New York: M. Witmark, 1906.
———. *Marcelle*. New York: M. Witmark, 1908.
———. *The Prince of Pilsen*. New York: M. Witmark, 1902.
———. *Woodland*. New York: M. Witmark, 1904.
Luders, Gustav, and George Ade. *The Fair Co-Ed*. New York: M. Witmark, 1908.
———. *The Sho-Gun*. New York: M. Witmark, 1904.
Lutz, W. Meyer, A.C.Torr, and Horace Mills. *Miss Esmeralda*. With incidental songs by Robert Martin. London: C. Jefferys, n.d.
Lutz, W. Meyer, George R. Sims, and Henry Pettitt. *Faust Up To Date*. Edited by Howard Paul. Pianoforte accompaniment arranged by Martyn Van Lennep. New York: William A. Pond, 1889.
Lyons, Julius J., and Adolph Nowak, and Sidney Rosenfeld. *The Lady or The Tiger?* Potpourri. Arranged by Adolph Nowak. New York: Willis Woodward, 1888.
Maeder, J. Gaspard, and S.J. Burr. *The Peri, or, the Enchanted Fountain*. New York: William Hall, 1852.
Mallet, Francis D. *Mons. Labasses's Quadrilles*. Boston: G. Graupner, n.d.
Mann, Nat D. *The Second Fiddle*: "Waltzes." New York: M. Witmark, 1904.
Marenco, Romualdo, and Luigi Manzotti. *Excelsior*. Milan: Ricordi, [1881].
Maretzek, Max. "Knickerbocker Dance." From *Sleepy Hollow*. New York: Edward Schuberth, 1880.
Mazzinghi, Joseph, and William Reeve. *Paul and Virginia*. London: Goulding, Phipps and D'Almaine, [1800].
McKever, J. Hood. "Fire-Fly Waltz." From *The White Fawn*. New York: C.H. Ditson, [1868].
[Mollenhauer, Edward]. "Marche d'Aika Amazonian." New York: Dodworth, 1868.

———. "White Fawn Galop. Introducing The Building Chorus." In *The White Fawn*. New York: J. Schuberth, 1868.

Mollenhauer, Edward, and Charles Barnard. *The Wager, or, the Masked Ball*. Vocal selections. New York: Edward Schuberth, 1879.

Monckton, Lionel, Howard Talbot, Mark Ambient, A.M. Thompson, and Arthur Wimperis. *The Arcadians*. London: Chappell, 1909.

Monckton, Lionel, James T. Tanner, Adrian Ross, and Percy Greenbank. *The Quaker Girl*. London: Chappell, 1910.

Monckton, Lionel, James T. Tanner, and Adrian Ross. *A Country Girl*. Additional lyrics and numbers by Paul A. Rubens. Additional lyrics by Percy Greenbank. London: Chappell, 1902

Morse, Woolson. "Madam Piper March." From *Madam Piper*. New York: T.B. Harms, 1884.

Morse, Woolson, and J. Cheever Goodwin. *Songs from the Comic Opera* Panjandrum. New York: T.B. Harms, 1893.

———. *Vocal Gems from* Dr. Syntax. New York: T.B. Harms, 1894.

———. *Vocal Gems from* Lost, Strayed or Stolen. New York: T.B. Harms, 1896.

———. *Vocal Gems from* Wang. New York: T.B. Harms, 1891.

Mullaly, W[illiam] S. "The Big Sunflower." Sung with Immense Success by W. Sheppard, of the Original Christy Minstrels. London: Hopwood and Crew, 1869.

Mullaly, W[illiam] S., and Clay M. Greene. "The Hebrew Fancy Ball." In *Bluebeard, Jr*. New York: Richard A. Saalfield, 1889.

Neuendorff, Adolf, and H. Italiener. *The Rat-Charmer of Hamelin*. New York: Edward Schuberth, 1881.

Nevin, Arthur, and Randolph Hartley. *A Daughter of the Forest*. Cincinnati: John Church, 1912.

———. *Poia*. Founded on legends collected by Walter McClintock. Berlin: Adolph Fürstner, 1909.

Norton, Frederick, and Oscar Ashe. *Chu Chin Chow*. New York: Edward B. Marks, 1916.

Operti, Giuseppe. *Aladdin*. Boston: G.D. Russell, 1874.

———. *Selections from* The Black Crook. New York: J.L. Peters, 1871.

Operti, Giuseppe, and Philip Lawrence. *Selections from* The Blacksmith's Treasure. Cincinnati: Geo. D. Newhall, 1879.

Operti, Giuseppe, and David Belasco. *The Stranglers of Paris: Music Selected and Composed by G. Operti*. MS orchestra parts. American Music Collection. NYPL, JPB 83–138.

Orlob, Harold, Harry B. Smith, Thomas J. Gray, and Robert B. Smith. *Ned Wayburn's Town Topics*. New York: G. Schirmer, 1915.
Pelissier, Victor. *Pelissier's Columbian Melodies*. Recent Researches in American Music, vols. 13 and 14. Edited by Karl Kroeger. Madison, WI: A-R Editions, 1984.
Peters, William Frederick, and Richard Carle. *The Mayor of Tokyo*. New York: M. Witmark, 1905.
Peters, William, Frederick, Heinrich Reinhardt, Fred de Gressac, and William Cary Duncan. *The Purple Road*. New York: T.B. Harms, 1903.
Pflueger, Carl, and R.A. Barnet. *1492*. Boston: White-Smith, 1892.
Planquette, Robert, and Henri Blondeau. *Le Paradis de Mahomet*. Completée par Louis Ganne. Partition Chant et Piano. Paris: Choudens, 1906.
Pons, Signor G. "Cotillions from *Cinderella*." The most favorite airs in *Cinderella*, Arranged as Cotillions by G. Pons. With new figures, by Mr. Parker. And danced with great Success at his Academy, Tammany Hall. New York: Bourne, 1831A.
——. "He Loved as Few Love Ever." Lyrics by John Thomas. New York: Hewitt, 1831B.
——. "Grand March." As Performed in the new and admired Opera of *Cinderella*. New York: Bourne, 1831C.
——. "Swift as the Flash!" With the variations as sung by Mrs. Austin. In the new and highly successful Opera of *Cinderella*. The Air from Rossini's Opera, *Guillaume Tell*. Arranged and the variations composed by Signor G. Pons. New York: Bourne, 1831D.
Porter, Susan L., ed. *British Opera in America*. Nineteenth-Century American Musical Theater, vol. 1. New York: Garland, 1994.
Puerner, Charles. *The Diamond Arrow*. Holograph MS. American Music Collection. NYPL, JPG 78-45.
——. *Mary of Magdala*: "Egyptian Dance." New York: M. Witmark, 1903.
Reinagle, Alexander. "Country Dance" from *Speed the Plough*. No. 1[b] in *Francis's Ball Room Assistant*. Philadelphia: G. Willig, 180–.
——. "Grand March" from *Alexander the Great*. No. 2[a] in *Francis's Ball Room Assistant*. Philadelphia: G. Willig, 180–.
——. *The Music in the Historical Play of* Columbus. Lyrics to movement 6 by Alexander Martin. Philadelphia: A. Reinagle, [1797].
——. *The Philadelphia Sonatas*. Recent Researches in American Music, vol. 5. Edited by Robert Hopkins. Madison, WI: A-R Editions, 1978.
Rice, Edward E. *Adonis Gavotte*. New York: Wm. A. Pond, 1885.

——— ———. *Heifer Dance*. Boston: Oliver Ditson, 1875.
Rice, Edward E., and J. Cheever Goodwin. *Evangeline*. Boston: Louis P. Goullaud, 1877.
Riis, Thomas L., ed. *The Music and Scripts of* In Dahomey. Music of the United States of America. Vol. 5. Madison, WI: A-R Editions, 1996.
Robyn, Alfred G., and Edward Paulton. *Princess Beggar*. New York: M. Witmark, 1906.
Robyn, Alfred G., and Henry M. Blossom, Jr. *The Yankee Consul*. New York: M. Witmark, 1903.
Romberg, Sigmund, and Harold Atteridge. *A World of Pleasure*. Additional numbers by J. Leubrie Hill. New York: G. Schirmer, 1915.
Romberg, Sigmund, Jean Schwartz, and Harold Atteridge. "Jazzamarimba Dance." New York: Jerome H. Remick, 1919.
——— ———. *Monte Cristo Jr*. New York: Jerome H. Remick, 1919.
Romberg, Sigmund, Rida Johnson Young, and Cyrus Wood. *Maytime*. New York: G. Schirmer, 1917.
Rooke, W.M., and I.T. Haines. *Amilie, or, The Love Test*. London: Duff and Hodgson, n.d.
Root, George F. *The Haymakers*. Recent Researches in American Music, vols. 9 and 10. Edited by Dennis R. Martin. Madison, WI: A-R Editions, 1984.
Rubens, Paul A. *Three Little Maids*. Additional numbers by Percy Greenbank and Howard Talbot. London: Chappell, 1902.
Schindler, Paul, Ben M. Jerome, Allen Lowe, and George E. Stoddard. *The Isle of Spice, or, His Majesty of Nicobar!* New York: Jos. W. Stern, 1903.
Schleiffarth, George, and Harry B. Smith. *Rosita, or, Cupid and Cupidity*. Chicago: Geo. Schleiffarth, 1885.
Schwartz, Jean. "Pony Galop: Skipping Rope Dance." New York: Francis, Day and Hunter, 1906.
Schwartz, Jean, Stanislaus Stange, and William Jerome. *Piff! Paff! Pouf!* New York: Shapiro, Remick, 1904.
Sedgwick, Alfred B. *The Collected Works of Alfred B. Sedgwick*. Edited by Michael Meckna. Nineteenth-Century American Musical Theater, vol. 7. New York: Garland, 1994.
Shook, Benjamin L. "Dat Gal of Mine." Cleveland, OH: H.N. White, 1902.
Skelly, Joseph P. *The Charge of the Hash Brigade*. Music arranged for the pianoforte by Alfred B. Sedgwick. New York: De Witt, 1876.
Slaughter, Walter, and Basil Hood. *The French Maid*. London: E. Ascherberg, 1896.

Sloane, A. Baldwin, and R.A. Barnet. *The Strange Adventures of Jack and the Bean-stalk*. Boston: White-Smith, 1896.

Sloane, A. Baldwin, and Sydney Rosenfeld. *The Mocking Bird*. New York: Jos. W. Stern, 1902.

Solomon, Edward, and H.P. Stephens. *The Red Hussar*. London: Metzler, 1889.

Solomon, Frederic. *Polly of the Circus*: "March." New York: Maurice Shapiro, 1908.

Sousa, John Philip, and Charles Klein. *El Capitan*. New York: G. Schirmer, n.d.

Spenser, Willard. *The Little Tycoon*. New York: Willard Spenser, 1882.

Spink, George, and Silvio Hein. "Melody" from *The Pride of Race*. New York: T.B. Harms, 1916.

Stahl, Richard. "Hot Stuff: March." New York: Carl Fisher, 1895.

——— ———. *Shing Ching* "Potpourri." Cincinnati: John Church, 1894.

Stanford, Charles Villiers, and George H. Jessop. *Shamus O'Brien*. Based on the poem by Joseph Sheridan Le Fanu. Pianoforte arrangement by Myles B. Foster. London: Boosey, 1896.

Stöpel, R[obert], arr. *The Corsican Brothers*: "The Ghost Melody." London: Chappell, n.d.

Stothart, Herbert P., and George B. Hill. *The Orphan and the Octopus*. Madison, WI: University of Wisconsin, 1913.

Stromberg, John, W.T. Francis, Edgar Smith, and Robert B. Smith. *Twirly Whirly*. New York: M. Witmark, 1902.

Stuart, Leslie, Charles H.E. Brookfield, and Cosmo Hamilton. *The Belle of Mayfair*. London: Francis, Day, and Hunter, 1906.

Stuart, Leslie, Owen Hall, and W.H. Risque. *The Silver Slipper*. New York: T.B. Harms, 1901.

Sullivan, Dan J., R.A. Barnet, and R.M. Baker. *Miss Pocahontas: An Indian War-Whoop in Two Whoops*. Boston: White-Smith, 1906.

Talbot, Howard, and George Dance. *A Chinese Honeymoon*. London: Hopwood and Crew, 1901.

Talbot, Howard, Fred Thompson, C.H. Bovill, and Ralph Roberts. *Mr. Manhattan*. Additional numbers by Silvio Hein and Philip Braham. New York: Leo Feist, 1916.

Taylor, Raynor, and William Diamond. *The Ethiop*. Philadelphia: G.E. Blake, n.d.

Tierney, Harry, James Montgomery, and Joseph McCarthy. *Irene*. New York: Leo Feist, 1920.

Tietjens, Paul. "Dance of the Beauties." New York: G. Schirmer, 1917.
Tietjens, Paul, and L. Frank Baum. *The Wizard of Oz*. New York: M. Witmark, 1902.
Trajetta, Phil. *Six Sacred Hymns, with an Accompaniment for the Organ, to which are added an Overture and Five Ricercarios, making a Cantata entitled The Day of Rest*. Philadelphia: Phil. Trajetta, 1845.
Vaughan, James. "Happy Jim." London: Keith, Prowse, 1903.
Venanzi, Angelo, and Imre Kiralfy. *America: Grand Spectacle*. Copyist's MS, 3–18 December 1893. American Music Collection. NYPL, JPB 84-353.
Vodery, Will H., Henry Creamer, Ben Harris, and Eddie Hunter. *How Come?* New York: Goodman and Rose, 1923.
Von Tilzer, Harry. "Chocolate Drops." New York: Harry Von Tilzer Music, 1902.
Ware, William. *A Selection of the most Admired Airs in the New Pantomime of* Harlequin and Mother Goose. London: W. Hodsoll, n.d.
——. *The much admired Overture to the New Pantomime call'd* Harlequin and Mother Goose. London: W. Hodsoll, n.d.
Wathall, Alfred G. *Pasquita: A Romance of the Philippines*. Cincinnati: Fillmore Music, 1910. Reprint, Delhi: Facsimile, 2015.
——. *Singbad the Sailor*. Cincinnati, OH: Fillmore Music, 1911.
Wathall, Alfred G., and George Ade. *The Sultan of Sulu*. New York: M. Witmark, 1902.
Williams, Bert. "Jig." London: Keith, Prowse, 1903.
Williams, Jesse. "All among the Hay." Lyrics by Wallace Markham. London: Hopwood and Crew, 1969.
——. "All among the Hay." Lyrics by Wallace Markham. Boston: White and Goullaud, 1870.
——. "Eulalie Schottische." New York: Hitchcock, 1894.
——. "Golden Dreams." Gavotte. Lyrics by J. Cheever Goodwin. New York: Carl Fischer, 1892.
Witmark, Isidore. "Schottische (Barn Dance)" from *The Chaperons*. New York: M. Witmark, 1901.
——. "The Witmark Minstrel Overture." New York: M. Witmark, 1909.
Witmark, Isidore, and Frederic Ranken. *The Chaperons*. New York: M. Witmark, 1901.
Witt, Max S. *Henry V*: "Danse Antique." New York: Jos. W. Stern, 1900.

Books, Dissertations, and Articles

Able, E. Lawrence. "John Hill Hewitt: Dixie's Original One-Man Band." *Civil War Times* October 2003. http://www.historynet.com/john-hill-hewitt-dixies-original-one-man-band.htm.

Alden, John. "A Season in Federal Street: J.B. Williamson and the Boston Theatre 1796–1797." *Proceedings of the American Antiquarian Society* 65no.1 (1955): 9–74.

Anderson, Gillian R. "'The Temple of Minerva' and Francis Hopkinson: A Reappraisal of America's First Poet-Composer." *Proceedings of the American Philosophical Society* 120 no. 3 (June 1976): 166–177.

Appletons' Annual Cyclopaedia and Register of Important Events of the Year 1891. New series, vol. 16. New York: D. Appleton, 1892.

Aronson, Rudolph. *Theatrical and Musical Memoirs*. New York: McBride, Nast and Co., 1913.

Badger, Reid. *A Life in Ragtime*. New York: Oxford University Press, 1995.

Baker's Biographical Dictionary of Musicians. 3rd ed. Revised and enlarged by Alfred Remy, M.A. New York: G. Schirmer, 1919.

Banfield, Stephen. *Jerome Kern*. Yale Broadway Masters series, with a foreword by Geoffrey Block, general editor. New Haven: Yale University Press, 2006.

Barker, James Nelson. *The Indian Princess, or, La Belle Sauvage*. Philadelphia: T. and G. Palmer, 1808.

Barnard, Charles, and Frank A. Howson. *The Dreamland Tree*. New York: Charles Barnard, 1883.

Barnet, Anne Alison. *Extravaganza King: Robert Barnet and Boston Musical Theater*. Boston: Northeastern University Press, 2004.

Barras, Charles M. *The Black Crook*. Harvard University, Houghton Library, 1866. MS Thr 271 (2).

Benjamin, Rick. *Black Manhattan*. "Liner Notes." New York: Recorded Anthology of American Music, 2003.

———. "From Barrelhouse to Broadway: The Musical Odyssey of Joe Jordan." http://www.dramonline.org/albums/from barrelhouse to broadway-the-musical-odyssey-of-joe-jordan/notes.

Bennett, Robert Russell. *The Broadway Sound: The Autobiography and selected Essays of Robert Russell Bennett*. Edited by George J. Ferencz. Rochester, NY: University of Rochester Press, 1999.

Bierley, Paul E. *John Philip Sousa: A Descriptive Catalog of His Works*. Music in American Life series. Urbana: University of Illinois Press, 1973.

Bloom, Ken. *American Song: The Complete Musical Theatre Companion.* Second edition, 1877–1995. 2 vols. New York: Schirmer Books, 1996.

Bordman, Gerald. *American Musical Theatre: A Chronicle.* Expanded edition. New York: Oxford University Press, 1986.

——. *Days to Be Happy, Years to Be Sad: The Life and Music of Vincent Youmans.* New York: Oxford University Press, 1982.

——. *Jerome Kern: His Life and Music.* New York: Oxford University Press, 1980.

Boucicault, Dion. *Plays by Dion Boucicault.* British and American Playwrights series. Edited with an introduction and notes by Peter Thomson. Cambridge: Cambridge University Press, 1984.

Breil, Joseph Carl. "Making the Musical Adaptation." *Opportunities in the Motion Picture Industry—and How to Qualify for Positions in its Many Branches* 2 (1922): 85–87.

Brooks, Lynn Matluck. *John Durang.* Amherst, NY: Cambria Press, 2011.

Brooks, Tim, *Lost Sounds: Blacks and the Birth of the Recording Industry, 1890-1919.* Urbana-Champaign: University of Illinois Press, 2004.

Brown, Mary Ellen. "*Il Pesceballo* and Francis James Child." https://scholarworks.iu.edu/dspace/bitstream/handle/2022/3738/002_Il_Pesceballo_and_Francis_James_Child_essay.pdf .

Brown, Scott E. *James P. Johnson.* With a James P.Johnson Discography 1917–1950 by Robert Hilbert. Metuchen, NJ: Scarecrow Press, 1986.

Brown, T. Allston. *A History of the New York Stage from the First Performance in 1732 to 1901.* Three vols. New York: n.p., 1903. Reissue, New York: Benjamin Blom, 1964.

Cantor, Eddie. *My Life Is in Your Hands and Take My Life: The Autobiographies of Eddie Cantor.* Foreword by Will Rogers. New introduction by Leonard Maltin. New preface and addendum by Brian Gari. New York: Cooper Square Press, 2000.

Charters, Ann. *Nobody: The Story of Bert Williams.* London: Macmillan, 1970.

"A Chat with Mr. Ivan Caryll." *Musical Opinion and Music Trade Review* 21 no. 251 (August 1897): 756.

Daly, Joseph Francis. *The Life of Augustin Daly.* New York: Macmillan, 1917.

Durang, John. *The Memoir of John Durang.* Edited by Alan S. Downer. Pittsburgh: Historical Society of York County, 1966.

Edwards, Bill. "Ford Dabney." http://ragpiano.com/comps/fdabney.shtml.

———. "Harry Von Tilzer." http://ragpiano.com/comps/hvntizr.shtml.
———. "Jean Schwartz." http://ragpiano.com/comps/schwartz.shtml.
———. "John Stepan Zamecnik." http://ragpiano.com/comps/zamecnik.shtml.
———. "Joseph Zachariah Taylor Jordan." http://ragpiano.com/comps/jjordan.shtml.
———. "Otto Motzan." http://ragpiano.com/comps/omotzan.shtml.
Encyclopédie multimedia de la comédie musicale théâtrale en France. Website: http://194.254.96.55/cm/?for=lis&compalp=0&init=o
The Euterpeiad, or, Musical Intelligencer and Ladies' Gazette. Vol. 2. Boston: Thomas Badger Jr., 1822. Reprint, New York: DaCapo, 1977.
Everett, William A. *Rudolf Friml*. American Composers series. Urbana: University of Illinois Press, 2008.
———. *Sigmund Romberg*. Yale Broadway Masters series. With a Foreword by Geoffrey Block. New Haven: Yale University Press, 2007.
Ewen, David. *Great Men of American Popular Song*. Englewood Cliffs, N.J.: Prentice-Hall, 1970.
Fiske, Harrison Grey. *The New York Mirror Annual and Directory of the Theatrical Profession for 1888*. New York: New York Mirror, 1888.
Fiske, Roger. *English Theatre Music in the Eighteenth Century*. London: Oxford University Press, 1973.
Franceschina, John. *David Braham: The American Offenbach*. New York: Routledge, 2003A.
———. *Duke Ellington's Music for the Theatre*. Jefferson, NC: McFarland, 2001.
———. *Harry B. Smith: Dean of American Librettists*. New York: Routledge, 2003B.
———. *Music Theory through Musical Theatre: Putting It Together*. New York: Oxford University Press, 2015.
Furst, William, George C. Hazelton, and [Joseph Henry] Benrimo. *The Yellow Jacket*. New York: Samuel French, 1912–1913.
Furst, William, William B. Hazelton, and Edward Spencer. *Electric Light*. Baltimore: Sun, 1879.
Gailey, Meredith. *Arthur Nevin*. http://www.allmusic.com/artist/arthur-nevin-mn0002199444/biography.
Gänzl, Kurt. *The Encyclopedia of The Musical Theatre*. 2 vols. New York: Schirmer, 1994.
———. *The Encyclopedia of the Musical Theatre*. Second edition. 3 vols. New York: Schirmer, 2001.

———. *Lydia Thompson: Queen of Burlesque*. New York: Routledge, 2002A.

———. *William B. Gill: From the Goldfields to Broadway*. New York: Routledge, 2002B.

Gasbarro, Norman. "Testimony of William Withers Jr.—Lincoln Assassination Witness (2012). http://civilwar.gratzpa.org/2012/05/testimony-of-william-withers-jr-lincoln-assassination-witness/.

———. "William Withers Jr.—Lincoln Assassination Witness (2012). http://civilwar.gratzpa.org/2012/05/william-withers-jr-lincoln-assassination-witness/.

"George Schleiffarth." *Musical World* no.317, vol.27 (May 1890), 208.

Glover, James M. *Jimmy Glover His Book*. London: Methuen, 1911.

Gold, Sylviane. "Tailoring the music: choreographers' secret collaborators: dance arrangers." *Dance Magazine* 1 January 2010.

Gould, Neil. *Victor Herbert*. New York: Fordham University Press, 2008.

Griffel, Margaret Ross. *Operas in German: A Dictionary*. Adrienne Fried Block, Advisory Ed. Westport, CT: Greenwood, 1990.

Guest, Ivor. *Adeline Genée*. London: Adam and Charles Black, 1958.

Hall, Ann P. "Celebrating John Knowles Paine's Legacy." *The Harvard University Gazette* (4 May 2000) http://news.harvard.edu/gazette/2000/05.04/paine.html.

Hamm, Charles. Yesterdays: Popular Song in America. New York: W.W. Norton, 1979.

Hanaford, Harry Prescott, and Dixie Hines, eds. *Who's Who in Music and Drama: An Encyclopedia of Biography of Notable Men and Women in Music and the Drama*. New York: H.P. Hanaford, [1914].

Hanley, Peter. "James Hubert Blake's WWI Draft Registration Card" http://www.doctorjazz.co.uk/draftcards3.html#ragdcjhb.

Highfill, Philip H., Jr., Kalman A. Burnim, and Edward A. Langhans. *A Biographical Dictionary of Actors, Actresses, Musicians, Dancers, Managers, and Other Stage Personnel in London 1660–1800*. Vol. 6. Carbondale, Illinois: Southern Illinois University Press, 1978.

Henneke, Ben Graf. *Laura Keene*. Tulsa, OK: Council Oak Books, 1990.

The Horn Family. http://freepages.genealogy.rootsweb.ancestry.com/~hartsman/Horn/HornPage2/horn%20family%20page2.html#charlesedwardhorn.

Howard, Joe. *Gay Nineties Troubadour*. Miami Beach: Joe Howard Music, 1956.

Howard, John Tasker. *Our American Music: Three Hundred Years of It*. 3rd ed. New York: Thomas Y. Crowell, 1946.

Huggins, Coy Elliott. "John Hill Hewitt: Bard of the Confederacy." Ph.D. diss., Florida State University, 1964.
Ives, E., Jr., ed. *The Musical Review and Record of Musical Science, Literature, and Intelligence*. New York: William Osborn, 1839.
James, Reese D. *Old Drury of Philadelphia: A History of the Philadelphia Stage 1800–1835*. New York: Greenwood Press, 1968.
Jannotta Family Papers, 1809–1972. Abraham Lincoln Presidential Library and Museum, Springfield, IL.
"John Elliot Mallandaine." http://members.shaw.ca/mallandaine/john.billing.html.
Johnson, H, Earle. *Musical Interludes in Boston 1795–1830*. New York: Columbia University Press, 1943. Reprint, New York: AMS Press, 1967.
Kattwinkel, Susan. *Tony Pastor Presents: Afterpieces from the Vaudeville Stage*. Westport, CT: Greenwood Press, 1998.
Kelly, Michael. *Reminiscences of Michael Kelly of the King's Theatre, and Theatre Royal Drury Lane, including A Period of Nearly Half a Century; with Original Anecdotes of Many Distinguished Persons, Political, Literary, and Musical..* 2 vols. London: Henry Colburn, 1826.
Kilgarriff, Michael. *Sing Us One of the Old Songs: A Guide to Popular Song 1860–1920*. New York: Oxford University Press, 1998.
Kimball, Robert, ed. *Cole*. With a biographical essay by Brendan Gill. New York: Holt, Rinehart and Winston, 1971.
Kiralfy, Bolossy. *Bolossy Kiralfy, Creator of Great Musical Spectacles: An Autobiography*. Barbara M. Barker, ed. Ann Arbor: UMI Research Press, 1988.
Kiralfy, Imre. *America: A Grand Historical Spectacle*. Chicago: Imre Kiralfy, 1893.
Kirstein, Lincoln. *Dance: A Short History of Classical Theatrical Dancing*. With an appreciation by Nancy Reynolds. Anniversary edition. Princeton: Princeton Book Company, 1987.
Klein, Herman. *Herman Klein and the Gramophone*. Edited and with a Biographical Sketch by William R. Moran. Portland, Oregon: Amadeus Press, 1990.
Knowles, Mark. *Tap Roots: The Early History of Tap Dancing*. Jefferson, NC: McFarland, 2002.
Krasner, Orly Leah. "Reginald De Koven (1859–1920) and American Comic Opera at the Turn of the Century." Ph.D. diss., CUNY, 1995.

Lefferts, Peter M. *Chronology and Itinerary of the Career of Will Vodery: Materials for a Biography*. Lincoln, Nebraska: Faculty Publications: School of Music, 2016.

LoBianco, Lorraine. "Alfred Newman Biography." http://www.tcm.com/this-month/article/133240%7C0/Alfred-Newman-Biography.html.

Loney, Glenn, ed. *Musical Theatre in America*. Westport, CT: Greenwood, 1984.

Lowens, Irving. *Music and Musicians in Early America*. New York: W.W. Norton, 1964.

Macqueen-Pope, W. *Gaiety: Theatre of Enchantment*. London: W.H. Allen, 1949.

Magriel, Paul, ed. *Chronicles of the American Dance: From the Shakers to Martha Graham*. New York: Dance Index, 1948. Reprint, New York: Da Capo Paperback, 1978.

Mandell, Jonathan. "What Is a Dance Arranger?" *TDF Stages: A Theatre Magazine*, July 2011. http://wp.tdf.org/index.php/2011/07/what-is-a-dance-arranger/.

Maretzek, Max. *Revelations of an Opera Manager in 19th Century America*. With a new introduction by Charles Haywood. New York: Dover, 1968.

——. *Further Revelations of an Opera Manager in 19th Century America*. Edited and annotated by Ruth Henderson. Sterling Heights, MI: Harmonie Park Press, 2006.

Marrocco, W. Thomas, and Harold Gleason. *Music in America: An Anthology from the Landing of the Pilgrims to the Close of the Civil War, 1620–1865*. New York: W.W. Norton, 1964.

Mates, Julian. *The American Musical Stage before 1800*. New Brunswick, NJ: Rutgers University Press, 1962.

Mazzulli, Teresa F. "Boston's 'Conservatorio'—The First." *The Boston Musical Intelligencer*, 30 September 2011. http://www.classical-scene.com/2011/09/30/boston%E2%80%99s-%E2%80%9Cconservatorio%E2%80%9D-%E2%80%94-the-first/.

——. "Where Did Trajetta Go?" *The Boston Musical Intelligencer*, 20 March 2012. http://www.classical-scene.com/2012/03/20/where-did-trajetta-go/.

McCabe, John. *George M. Cohan: The Man Who Owned Broadway*. Garden City, NY: Doubleday, 1973.

Metcalf, Frank J. "Philip Anthony Corri and Arthur Clifton." *Journal of the Presbyterian Historical Society (1901-1930)*, vol. 11 no. 7 (April 1923): 268–272. Retrieved from http://www.jstor.org/stable/23323600

Morell, Parker. *Lillian Russell: The Era of Plush*. New York: Random House, 1940.

"Musical Items." *The Etude* 15:6 (June, 1897), 145.

Nathan, Hans. *Dan Emmett and the Rise of Early Negro Minstrelsy*. Norman: University of Oklahoma Press, 1962.

Nettl, Paul. *The Story of Dance Music*. New York: Philosophical Library, 1947.

Norton, Richard C. *A Chronology of American Musical Theater*. 3 vols. New York: Oxford University Press, 2002.

Odell, George C.D. *Annals of the New York Stage*. 15 vols. New York: Columbia University Press, 1927–1949.

O'Neill, Rosetta. "The Dodworth Family and Ballroom Dancing in New York." In . *Chronicles of the American Dance: From the Shakers to Martha Graham*. Paul Magriel, ed. New York: Dance Index, 1948. Reprint, New York: Da Capo Paperback, 1978.

Paterek, Josephine D. "A Survey of Costuming on the New York Commercial Stage: 1914–1934." 2 vols. Ph.D. diss., University of Minnesota, 1961.

Peck, Russell A. *A Cinderella Bibliography*. http://d.lib.rochester.edu/cinderella/text/pantomime-burlesque-and-childrens-drama#scripts

Peterson, Bernard L., Jr. *A Century of Musicals in Black and White*. Westport, CT: Greenwood Press, 1993.

Pflueger, Carl, and R.A. Barnet. *Injured Innocents*. Boston: White-Smith, 1890.

Pincus-Roth, Zachary. "The Dance Arranger." *Ask Playbill.Com* 8 May 2008.

Pisani, Michael V. *Music for the Melodramatic Theatre in Nineteenth-Century London and New York*. Iowa City: University of Iowa Press, 2014.

Planché, James Robinson. *Plays by James Robinson Planché*. British and American Playwrights series. Edited with an introduction and notes by Donald Roy. Cambridge: Cambridge University Press, 1986.

Porter, Cole. *The Complete Lyrics of Cole Porter*. Edited by Robert Kimball. With a foreword by John Updike. New York: Alfred A. Knopf, 1983.

Porter, Susan L. *With an Air Debonair: Musical Theatre in America: 1785–1815*. Washington, D.C.: Smithsonian Institution Press, 1991.

Preston, Katherine K. "Introduction: From Nineteenth-Century Stage Melodrama to Twenty-First-Century Film Scoring." *Journal of Film Music* 5.1–2 (2012) 7–14.

Reiff, Anthony, Jr. *Anthony Reiff Papers*. Special Collections Research Center, Swem Library, College of William and Mary.

Riis, Thomas L. *Just Before Jazz: Black Musical Theater in New York, 1890 to 1915*. Washington, DC: Smithsonian Institution Press, 1989.

Rogers, Katharine M. *L. Frank Baum, Creator of Oz*. New York: St. Martin's Press, 2002; New York: Da Capo Press, 2003.

Root, Deane L. *American Popular Stage Music 1860–1880*. Ann Arbor: UMI Research Press, 1981.

Sadie, Stanley, ed. *The New Grove Dictionary of Music and Musicians*. 20 vols. London: Macmillan, 1980; reprint, New York: Grove, 1995.

Sampson, Henry T. *Blacks in Blackface: A Source Book on Early Black Musical Shows*. Metuchen, NJ: Scarecrow, 1980.

Sanjek, Russell. *American Popular Music and its Business: The First Four Hundred Years*. Volume 2: From 1790 to 1909. New York: Oxford University Press, 1988.

Schleifer, Martha Furman. *American Opera and Music for the Stage Eighteenth and Nineteenth Centuries. Three Centuries of American Music: A Collection of American Sacred and Secular Music*. Vols. 5 and 6. N.p.: G.K. Hall, 1990.

Sciannameo, Franco. *Phil Trajetta (1777–1854), Patriot, Musician, Immigrant*. Hillsdale, NY: Pendragon Press, 2010.

Skinner, Dr. Graeme. "George Loder and Emma Neville." *Australharmony* (an online resource toward the history of music and musicians in colonial and early Federation Australia), 2016. http://sydney.edu.au/paradisec/australharmony/loder-george.php.

Smith, Harry B. *First Nights and First Editions*. Boston: Little, Brown, and Company, 1931.

Sonneck, Oscar George Theodore. *A Bibliography of Early Secular American Music*. Washington, D.C.: H.L. McQueen, 1905. Reprint, Lexington, KY: Ulan Press, 2014.

———. *Early Opera in America*. New York: G. Schirmer, 1915.

Southern, Eileen. *Biographical Dictionary of Afro-American and African Musicians*. Westport, CT: Greenwood, 1982.

———. *The Music of Black Americans: A History*. Third edition. New York: W.W. Norton, 1997.

Spitzer, John, ed. *American Orchestras in the Nineteenth Century*. Chicago: University of Chicago Press, 2012.

Stephen, Sir Leslie, ed. *Dictionary of National Biography*. Vol. 22. New York: Macmillan, 1890.

Stratyner, Barbara. *Ned Wayburn and the Dance Routine: From Vaudeville to the Ziegfeld Follies*. Studies in Dance History, No. 13. Madison, Wisconsin: A-R Editions, 1996.
Stubblebine, Donald J. *Early Broadway Sheet Music*. Jefferson, NC: McFarland, 2002; reprint, 2010.
Suskin, Steven. *The Sound of Broadway Music: A Book of Orchestrators and Orchestrations*. New York: Oxford University Press, 2009
Swartz, Mark Evan. *Before the Rainbow*. Baltimore: Johns Hopkins University Press, 2000.
Temperley, Nicholas, ed. *Musicians of Bath and Beyond: Edward Loder (1809–1865) and His Family*. Music in Britain, 1600–2000. Woodbridge, Suffolk: Boydell, 2016.
The Theatrical Censor. Philadelphia, 1805–1806.
Tompkins, Eugene, and Quincy Kilby. *The History of the Boston Theatre 1854–1901*. 1908. Reissue. New York: Benjamin Blom, 1969.
Thompson, Brian C. "Henri Drayton, English Opera and Anglo-American Relations, 1850–72." *Journal of the Royal Musical Association* 136:2, 247–303.
——. "Journeys of an Immigrant Violinist: Jacques Oliveira in Civil War-Era New York and New Orleans." *Journal of the Society for American Music* 6:1 (2012), 51–82.
Verne, Jules and Adolphe d'Ennery. *Around the World in 80 Days: The 1874 Play*. Contributors: Philippe Burgaud, Jean-Louis Trudel, Jean-Michel Margot, and Brian Taves. Edited by Brian Taves for the North American Jules Verne Society. The Palik Series. Albany, GA: BearManor Fiction, 2012.
Wagner, John Waldorf. "James Hewitt: His Life and Works." Ph.D. diss., Indiana University, 1969.
Waters, Edward N. *Victor Herbert*. New York: Macmillan, 1955.
Weinert-Kendt, Rob. "A Tailor of Music, Skilled in Alterations: The Arranger Glen Kelly Knows the Broadway Score." *The New York Times* 26 June 2014.
Westover, Jonas. "A Study and Reconstruction of *The Passing Show of 1914*: The American Musical Revue and Its Development in the Early Twentieth Century." 2 vols. Ph.D. diss., CUNY, 2010.
White, Eric Walter. *A History of English Opera*. London: Faber and Faber, 1983.
Whitton, Joseph. *"The Naked Truth!" An Inside History of* The Black Crook. Philadelphia: H.W. Shaw, 1897.

Will Accooe. http://africlassical.blogspot.com/2012/12/will-accooe-1874-1904-composed-black.html

Winden, William Craig. "The Life and Music Theater Works of John Hill Hewitt." D. Mus. A. diss., University of Illinois at Urbana-Champaign, 1972.

Wolfe, Richard J. *Secular Music in America 1801–1825*. 3 vols. New York: New York Public Library, 1964.

Woll, Allen. *Black Musical Theatre*. Baton Rouge: Louisiana State University Press, 1989. Reprint, New York: Da Capo, n.d.

Ziegfeld, Richard and Paulette. *The Ziegfeld Touch: The Life and Times of Florenz Ziegfeld, Jr.* Foreword by Patricia Ziegfeld Stephenson. New York: Harry N. Abrams, 1993.

Index

A

Aarons, Alfred E., 145, 158, 176, 183
Abbott, James Lynn, xix, 295
Abel, Ron, 295
Abene, Michael, 295
About Town, 122, 184, 285
Abrahamson, Manford, 295
Abyssinia, 182–183, 287, 289
Accooe, Will (William J.), 150, 154, 155, 157, 158, 165
Adams, Bob, 164, 181
Adams, J.K., 145
Adams, Roger, xiv, xv, 295
Adams, Stephen, 173
Adelmorn, the Outlaw, 35
Adler, Gary, 295
Adler, Richard, xv
Adonis, 15, 97
Africa, 121
Agoust, Emile, 216
Ahmed!, 73
Ahmed al Kamel, 41
Aladdin, 72, 305
Aladdin, Jr., 127, 282
Aladdin, or, The Wonderful Lamp, 10, 42, 52
Aladdin the Second, xii, 69
Albertieri, Luigi, 145, 159, 191, 218, 267
Alchourron, Rodolfo, 295
Alfred, Julian, 198, 215, 221, 226, 245, 248, 250, 264, 267–268
Algeria, 195, 283
The Algerian, 120, 291

Alhambra, 80
Alhambra Theatre (London), 13
Ali Baba, or, Morgiana and the Forty Thieves, 116
All Aboard, 219, 294
All over Town, 17, 18, 227, 280, 284
Almost a Life, 81
Alters, Gerald, 295
Always You, 248–249, 284
The Ameer, 151, 287
America, 16, 18, 120, 220, 294
The American Idea, 195
The American Maid, 218–219
American Tar, or, The Press Gang Defeated, 30, 275
Amilie, or, The Love Test, 40–41
Amour, or, The Arabian Nights, 76
The Andalusian, or, The Young Guard, 43
Anderson, Hilding, 201, 208, 220, 224, 229, 245, 246, 258, 261, 265
Anderson, John Murray, 246, 249, 251, 261, 268
Angel Face, 248, 267, 282
Antiope, 13, 107
Aphrodite, 248, 273,
Apollo in New York, 45
Apple Blossoms, 247, 281, 288
The Apple of Paris, 209
An Arabian Girl and 40 Thieves, 148, 282, 285
The Arabian Nights, or, Aladdin's Wonderful Lamp, 103, 269

Arcadia, 100
Archer, Nicholas, 296
The Archers, or, The Mountaineers of Switzerland, 30
Are You Insured?, 98–99
Arnold, Richard, 62, 63
Arnold, Samuel, 26, 32, 33
Aronson, Henry, xviii, 296
Aronson, Rudolph, 20, 119
Around the Map, 231, 277, 286
Around the World, 209, 294
Around the World in 80 Days, 13, 14, 73, 74
Arrah-Na-Brogue!, 71
Arrah-Na-Pogue, or, The Wicklow Wedding, 53
Arthur, Daniel V., 203, 268
Artists and Models, 264, 277, 280, 290, 293
An Artist's Model, 131
The Art of Maryland, 134
Arundel, Frederick, 142
At Gay Coney Island, 16, 138, 285, 287
Atwood, Robert (Bob), xv, 296
Auber, Daniel, 43, 47, 49, 55
The Auto Race, 191–192, 288, 292
Axt, William (P.), 239, 248
Ayer, Nat(haniel) D., 198, 199, 204, 214, 215, 233
Azael, the Prodigal, 43
Azara, 188
Azora, the Daughter of Montezuma, 239
Azrael, or The Magic Charm, 70
An Aztec Romance, 216
Azurine, or, A Voyage to the Earth, 77

B

Baba!, 77
The Babes in the Wood, 70
Babes in the Wood and The Good Little Fairy Birds; or, Who Killed Cock Robin?, 81
Babes in the Wood, or, Who Killed Cock Robin?, 79
The Babes in the Wood, Robin Hood and His Merry, Merry Men, and Harlequin, Who Killed Cock Robin?, 111
Babes in Toyland, 18, 169, 285, 314
Babette, 170, 279, 281
The Bachelor Belles, 206, 286
Bacon, Glen, 296
Bad Dickey, 63
Baker, Benjamin A., 55, 61
Baker, David, 296
Baker, R. Melville, 160
Baker, Thomas, xii, 4, 10, 13, 45, 46, 47, 48, 49, 50, 51, 52, 54, 56, 57, 59, 65, 72, 80, 81, 100, 119
The Ballet Girl, 18, 141, 290
The Ballet of 1830, 215
Bandanna Land, 193, 287, 289
Bankers and Brokers, 179
The Banker's Daughter, 81
Baravelle, Victor, 249, 258, 263, 265
Bargy, Jeanne, 296
Barker, Richard, 109, 110, 111, 113, 115, 116, 117, 123, 126, 127, 128, 129, 131, 132, 133, 134, 136, 146,
Barnes, Harry, 126
Barnes, James, 64, 67, 68, 69, 70, 73, 268–269
Barnet, Robert. A., 172, 191
Barnum, H.B., xvii, 296
Barratt, Augustus, 191, 199–200, 216, 218, 241, 242, 243, 249, 263
Barrett, Oscar, 86
Batchelor, W.H., 109, 112, 116, 117, 127, 148, 160
The Battle Cry, 225
Bauer, Adolph, 123
Bauer, George, 296
Bauer, Henry, 143
Baumgarten, Karl, 25
Beane, George A., 155
Beautiful Stars, 113
The Beauty Shop, 223, 270
The Beauty Spot, 18, 198, 267
Beckett, Hal, 296
Beckett, Harry, 12, 66

Beckett, Rose, 103, 132, 269
Bee Hive, or, Industry Must Prosper, 38
The Begum, 104, 271
Beissenherz, Henry D., 48, 50, 54, 55
The Belle of Bridgeport, 155
The Belle of Mayfair, 186
The Belle of New York, 140, 275, 281, 289
The Belle of the West, 16, 178
La Belle Paree, 207, 279, 294
Bendix, Max, 206, 221, 225, 233
Bendix, Theodore, 90, 101. 102, 179, 180, 182, 201, 203, 204, 211, 214
Bennett, David, 203, 228, 229, 231, 237, 251, 254, 263, 269
Bennett, Michael, xvi, xvii
Bennett, Robert Russell, 263, 265, 296
Benrimo, Joseph Harry, 227, 228, 229, 233, 235, 269–270
Benskin, Sammy, 296
Bentley, W.H., 238
Beppo, 62
Berg, Tony, 296
Berkman, John, ix, xvii, 296–297
Berkowitz, Sol, 297
Berlin, Irving, 204, 208, 210, 213, 214, 215, 216, 219, 225, 226, 228, 231, 233, 235, 237, 239, 241, 242, 246, 250, 252, 257, 264, 299, 311
Berman, Rob, 297
Bernard, G.P., 92
Bernstein, Elmer, 297
Bernstein, Leonard, xiv, 297, 312
Bertrand, A., 111, 119
Better Times, 261, 270, 279
Betty, 234, 288
Between You and Me and the Post, 54
Bibeyran, Mamert, 89, 99, 105, 109, 110, 117, 118
Biddle, Nicholas, 128
Big Pony, The Gentlemanly Savage, 102
The Big Show, 234, 270
The Billionaire, 163, 276, 293
A Bird of Paradise, 57, 278
Bishop, Frederic(k) A., 202, 211, 236
Bishop, Henry (Rowley), 38, 39, 43, 50

Black Beard, or, The Genovese Pirate, 36
The Blackbird, 91
Black Castle, or, Specter of the Forest, 37
The Black Crook, xi, xii, xix, 4, 6, 7–9, 10, 13, 14, 56, 57, 65, 67, 81, 84, 100, 119, 271
The Black Domino, 54
The Black Politician, 189
A Black Sheep, 131, 279, 285
Blackton, Jay, 297
Black Venus, 13, 88
The Black Venus!, 92
Blake, Eubie, 255
Blake, Louis, 112
Blake, Micah, 112
Blandowski, A., 77
Blank, Lawrence (Larry) J., 297
Blinn, Holbrook, 177, 240
The Blonde in Black, 166, 276, 282, 284
Blondette, or, The Naughty Prince and the Pretty Peasant, 49
The Blue and the Gray, 76
Blue Beard, 33
Bluebeard, Jr., or, Fatima and the Fairy, 108–109
Blue Beard, or, the Mormon, the Maiden, and the Little Militaire, 66
Blue Beard, or, The Punishment of Curiosity, 47
The Blue Kitten, 258–259, 273, 286
The Blue Moon, 185, 290
The Blue Paradise, 229, 269
Bogin, Abba, 297
The Bohea-man's Girl, 41
Bohm, Adolph, 238
Bombo, 258, 274, 280
Böteführ, W.D.C., 57
Boullay, Louis, 28
Bourville Castle, or, The Gallic Orphans, 31
Bowers, Frederick V., 162, 196
Bowers, Robert Hood, 174, 182, 185, 189, 190, 197, 201, 206, 207, 208, 221, 227, 232, 238, 245, 246, 252
Bowman, Rob, 297
Bowron, George, 86, 114

Bowron, William Lloyd, 89, 110
Boyce, William, 28
A Boy Wanted, 137
Brady, Leo, ix
Brady, William A., 151
Braham, David, xii, xiii, 60, 69, 71, 72, 73, 74, 75, 76, 77, 78, 79, 80, 81, 82, 83, 84, 85, 86, 88, 90, 91, 92, 93, 94, 95, 96, 97, 98, 99, 100, 102, 104, 105, 106, 107, 111, 113, 114, 120, 125, 133, 135, 138
Braham, George F., 98, 99, 133, 168
Braham, Harry, 95, 96, 117, 178
Braham, John J., 66, 82, 100, 103, 104, 108, 109, 111, 131, 148, 151, 152
Braham, Philip, 180
A Brass Monkey, 105
Bratton, John W., 121, 132, 133, 139, 158, 160, 163, 169, 173, 177, 178, 190, 198
Bray, John, 6, 37
The Brazilian, 109
Breil, Joseph Carl, 244
Brevis, Skip, 297
Brian Boru, 135
The Bridal Ring, 38, 275
The Bride-Elect, 16, 142, 284, 291
The Bride of Abydos, or, The Pirate of the Isles, 72
Bridwell, Thom, 297
Bright Eyes, 202
Brinkworth, William H., 64, 67, 68, 69, 70, 73
Bristow, George F., 45
Broadway Brevities of 1920, 252, 280, 284
A Broadway Honeymoon, 220
Brode, Herman, 86, 92, 96
Broderick, George, 297
The Brook, 82
Brooke, Clifford, 242
Brooks, Harry, 255
Brooks, Mel, xviii
Brooks, Walter, 255
Brooks, William, 3
Broschi, Karl, 110

Brother and Sister, 50
Brourman, Michele, 297
Brown, Albert W., 218, 219, 220
Brown, A. Seymour, 223, 230
Brown, Fleta Ian, 192
Brown, Lew, 266
Brown, Raymond A., 159, 178
Brown, Sid, 208
Brown, William Potter, 135
Browne, Bothwell, 210
Browne, J. Albert, 245
Browne, J.H., 80
Browne, R.A., 180
The Brownies, 125, 291
Brown of Harvard, 183
Brymn, James T., 154
The Buccaneers, 127
Buimi, Adele, 76
Buisseret, Mons., 74
Burcher, Harry B., 162, 186
The Burgomaster, 155
Burnside, R.H., 128, 162, 170, 172, 176, 179, 180, 182, 183, 184, 188, 190, 195, 200, 205, 208, 210, 213, 217, 223, 224, 226, 230, 232, 234, 236, 237, 242, 246, 251, 257, 260, 261, 265, 270–271
Burns, Thomas H., 101
Burt, Benjamin Hapgood, 159, 171, 188, 190, 204, 214, 230, 234, 237, 243, 247, 256
Butcher, George, 297
By the Sad Sea Waves, 147, 273, 279, 292

C

The Cadet Girl, 153, 282
The Cadi, 113
Caldwell, Anne, 183, 191
Caledonian Frolic, 24, 275
The Caliph, 133
Candy, 117
The Candy Shop, 278, 281
El Capitan, 132–133, 271
Capocchio and Dorinna, 24
Carle, Carlo, 60

Carle, Richard, 139, 145, 149, 172, 174, 185, 189, 190
Carl, The Fiddler, 67
Carmen, or, Soldiers and Seville-ians, 86–87
Carr, Benjamin, 6, 24, 25, 26, 27, 28, 30, 31,
Carr, (F.) Osmond, 126, 129, 130, 139, 140
Carroll, Adam, 297
Carroll, Albert, 297
Carroll, Harry, 204, 214, 224, 225, 226, 233, 251, 256
Carroll, Vinnette, xvii
Caryll, Ivan, 101, 104, 111, 113, 114, 124, 126, 130, 134, 136, 138, 143, 157, 158, 161, 162, 169, 177, 180, 185, 187, 205, 207, 208, 221, 249, 252, 259
Cashman, Edward, 298
The Casino Girl, 18, 152, 281
Caslar, Dan H., 218
Castle, Irene, 226
The Castle of Otranto, 34
Castles in Spain, 89
Castles in the Air, 109, 275, 286
Castle, Vernon, 226
Catlin, E.N., 66, 67
The Cat's in the Larder, or, The Maid with a Parasol, 41
Ceballos, Larry, 263
A Celebrated Hard Case, 79
Cellier, Alfred, 101, 102, 111, 114, 118
Cendrillon, 57, 278
The Century Girl, 234–235, 273, 288, 289
Chadwick, George W., 91, 123
La Chair, 197
Chantrier, Albert, 197, 211
The Chaperons, 16, 161, 282
Chapin, Stephen, 298
Chapin, Tom, 298
The Charlatan, 16, 144, 271
Charlson, Natalie, 298
Chase, David, xviii, 1–2, 298
Chassaigne, Francis, 105, 106, 107, 109

Cheer Up, 237, 270
The Children in the Wood, 26, 71, 272
Chilvers, Thomas, 146
A China Doll, 178, 276
A Chinese Honeymoon, 161, 271
Chipman, J.S., 172
Chitten, Vincenzina, 114
Chow Chow, or, A Tale of Pekin, 69
Chris and the Wonderful Lamp, 151, 291
Christiani, E., 110, 117
The Christian Martyrs, 10, 57
Christmas Joys and Sorrows, 79
Christrup, Charles, 79, 92
Chu Chin Chow, 238, 280
La Cigale, 113
Cinderella, 16, 36, 40, 46, 48, 114
Cinderella and the Prince, or, The Castle of Heart's Desire, 18, 172
Cinderella at School, 89
Cinderella e la Comare, or, The Lover, The Lackey, and the Little Glass Slipper, 54
Cinderella on Broadway, 250, 274, 280
Cinderella, or, The Little Glass Slipper, 87
Cinderella, or, The Lover, the Lackey, and the Little Glass Slipper, 56
Cinders, 263, 288
The Circus Girl, 138, 284
A Circus in Town, 103
Clarke, Cuthbert, 193
Clark, Edward, 236, 238
Claudius Nero, 110, 275
Clayton, Gilbert, 222
Clifton, Arthur, 39
Clio, 99
Clorinda! The Girl of the Period / Peter Gray, or, Ding Dong Din, 62
Clustine, Ivan, 234
Cohan, George M., xiii, xviii, 119, 129, 136, 137, 156, 166, 171, 173, 175, 181, 182, 185, 192, 193, 194, 195, 200, 210, 212, 226, 232, 239, 240, 244, 249, 262
The Cohan Revue of 1916, 232

The Cohan Revue of 1918, 239, 276, 284
Cohen, Allen, 298
Cohen, Michael, 298
Cole, Bob, 164, 169, 170, 176, 188, 198, 238
Coleman, Charles H., 298
Coleman, Cy, xvi, 298
Coleman, John, 143, 191
Collins, Ken, 299
Columbus, or, The Discovery of America, 31, 33
Columbus Reconstructed, 55–56
Colville, Charles, 82
Colwell, Victor, 175
Comer, Thomas, 42, 44
Coming Thro' the Rye, 181–182, 278, 289
The Commuters, 204
Condell, Henry, 38
Connelly, Michael, xii, 10, 13, 59, 60, 63, 65, 66, 69, 70, 71, 78, 79, 96
A Contented Woman, 137
Cooke, John (Jonathan) (P.), 44, 45, 47, 52, 53, 54
Cook, Cecil, 169
Cook, Frederick, 47, 48
Cook, Will Marion, 143, 150, 152, 160, 165, 173, 182, 193, 204
Coolman, C. DeWitt, 194, 205, 213, 219, 226
Coppe, Carlo, 127
Coppini, Ettore, 13, 96, 103
Cordelia's Aspirations, 94–95, 98
Corliss, Edward W., 142, 143, 156, 159, 160, 172
The Corsair, 103–104, 275
The Corsican Brothers, 44
Costa, Davide, xii, 9, 10, 56, 58, 62, 63, 64, 65, 67, 271
Cousin Lucy, 229, 269
A Country Girl, 162, 289
Coventry, Gerald, 161, 166, 173, 271
Cox, William, 299
Craven, Frank, 262
Crawford, Clifton, 156, 158, 159, 160, 170, 216, 227, 234, 241

Creamer, Henry, 260
Cribari, Donna, 299
Crigler, Lynn, 299
Cripps, H.A., 104, 105, 112, 118, 123, 133, 144, 271
Crosby, Wagner, 177, 178
Cross, Wellington, 199
Cruger, Randolph, 121
The Crystal Slipper, 15, 109
Cunningham, Bill (Billy), 299
Curti, Alfredo, 208
Curti, Carlos, 180
Curtis, Norman, 299
Cushman, Asa, 61
Cusseaux, Zulema, 299
Cutty, Thomas, 178
Cyrano de Bergerac, 149, 279
Cyranose De Bric-a-Brac, 144

D

Daffy Dill, 260–261, 286
The Dairymaids, 189, 286
Dallin, Jacques, 299
Daly, Augustin, 83, 112, 115, 134, 162
Daly, Lucy, 120
Daly, William H., 100, 110, 113
Daly, William (M.), 228, 234, 242, 245, 247, 252, 258, 259, 262, 263
Dancing Around, 225, 280, 284
The Dancing Duchess, 224, 270
The Dancing Girl, 262, 280
The Danicheffs, 78
Dannenberg, Louis, 219
Dansicker, Michael, 299
Dan's Tribulations, 95
Darley, Francis T.S., 93
Darling, Edward Irving, 102, 127
Darling, Frank (N.), 172, 196, 204, 214, 217, 219, 223, 228, 233, 237, 242, 246
The Darling of Paris, 222
The Darling of the Gods, 163
D'Auban, Ernest, 158, 165, 171, 176, 180, 222
D'Auban, John, 130, 131
The Daughter of the Regiment, or, The 800 Fathers, 64

Index | 355

Daughter of the Revolution, 128, 275
Davenport, George C., 85
David Harum, 154
Davis, Buster, 299
Davis, Charles, 255
Davis, Joseph, 119
Davis, Sam, 299
Davy Jones, 123
Dawson, Joseph, 180
A Day and a Night in New York, 144
Day, John B., 113
Deane, Benjamin (J)., 3, 53, 56, 67, 73
Deas, Lawrence, 255
De Benedictis, Richard, 299
Debillemont, Jean-Jacques, 13, 74, 89
The Debutante, 225–226, 274, 283
Declassée, 247
The Deep, Deep Sea, or, The Sea Serpent, 40
De Koven, Reginald, 16, 17, 18, 19, 104, 113, 117, 118, 119, 120, 124, 125, 127, 129, 131, 136, 141, 147, 148, 152, 155, 158, 159, 168, 170, 179, 186, 195, 196, 198, 212, 213, 221
The Deluge, or, Paradise Lost, 13, 72
DeMarque, M., 26, 28
Dennée, Charles, 151, 152
DeNovellis, Antonio, 94, 110, 124, 136, 141, 147, 149, 152, 155, 157, 163, 173, 174, 178, 186, 194, 236
Deulin, Mlle., 48
The Devil in the Bowery, 50
The Devil's Auction, or, The Golden Branch, 58, 93
Dew Drop Inn, 263–264, 281, 293
Dibdin, Charles, 28, 29, 31
Dick Whittington and His Cat, 67, 268
Diet, Edmond, 18, 21, 208
Dill, Max M., 192
Diplomacy, 80
Dixey, Henry E., 97, 104, 108
The Doctor of Alcantara, 49
Dodson, A.E., 130
Dodworth, Harvey B.,
The Dollar Princess, 199
Dolly Varden, 159, 279

Dombey and Son, 10, 42
Donnelly, Dorothy, 264
Donnelly, Henry V., 121
The Donovans, 74
Doré, Daniel, 168, 183, 208, 209
Douglass, Jane, 299
Down Broadway, 77
Dream City and The Magic Knight, 186
Drigo, Riccardo, 230
Dr. Syntax, 123, 271
Druessa, 86
The Duchess, 211, 279, 290, 294
The Duchess of Dantzic, 176–177, 292
Duff, James C., 130
The Duke of Duluth, 179, 283, 284
The Duke's Motto, 50
Duke, Vernon, 299
Durang, John, xxi, 5, 24, 25, 26, 272, 275
"Durang's Horn-Pipe," xxi, 5, 24
"Dwarf Dance" 5, 24, 272
Dyring, H.T., 90

E

Eagle, Oscar, 243, 247, 253, 263, 272
The Earl and the Girl, 17, 180, 270
Easy Dawson, 178, 283
The Echo, 204–205, 279, 281, 287
Edgewood Folks, 86
Edouin, Willie, 78, 79, 82, 85, 155
Edwardes, George, 124
Edwards, Carlo, 225
Edwards, Gus, 149, 156, 164, 165, 170, 171, 173, 184, 185, 187, 190, 196, 199, 204, 214, 224
Edwards, Harry B., 112
Edwards, Julian, 107, 109, 115, 126, 135, 146, 152, 153, 155, 159, 163, 177, 183, 194, 199, 200, 236
Edwards, Leo, 161, 190, 217, 219, 227, 228, 229, 233, 236, 256
Edwards, Phil, xviii, 299
Edwards, Sherman, xvi
Edwin and Angelina, or, The Banditti, 31
Eichberg, Julius, 49, 55, 56, 59

Eileen, 236, 281, 283
Einödshofer, Julius, 169, 230, 234
Eljas, Anders, 300
Elliott, Jack, 300
Ellis, Melville, xix, 20, 149, 160, 161, 167, 180, 183, 184, 187, 193, 200, 202, 203, 204, 206, 207, 212, 214, 215, 216, 218, 219, 220, 221, 222, 224, 225, 227, 230, 233
Ellison, Sydney, 206, 216
Ellis, Ray, 300
Ellis, Sydney R., 147
Elsie Janis and Her Gang, 259
The Elves, or, The Statue Bride, 46, 54
Elysium, 116
Emmet, Joseph K(line), 80, 83
The Enchanted Beauty, or, the Dream of 100 Years, 42
Enchantment, 13, 15, 83
The Enchantress, 211, 281
Englander, Ludwig, 20, 122, 123, 126, 128, 133, 134, 139, 148, 149, 152, 153, 156, 157, 160, 161, 165, 169, 174, 180, 190, 196, 223
An English Daisy, 171, 291
The Enterprise, or, Love and Pleasure, 39
Eriksmoen, August, 300
Erminie, 101, 275
Ernani, or, The Horn of a Dilemma, 59
Errol, Leon, 223, 228, 235, 241, 256, 259, 272–273
Estey, Robert, 300
The Ethiop, or, Child of the Desert, 39
Europe, James Reese, 17, 173, 188, 189, 198
Eustis, Fred J., 93, 96, 97, 98, 108, 109, 120, 126, 129, 133, 151, 152, 159, 172
Evangeline, or The Belle of Arcadie, 72
Evans, Thomas, 144
Everything, 242, 270, 278
The Evil Eye, or the Many Merry Mishaps of Nid and the Weird Wonderful Wanderings of Nod, 146–147
Excelsior, 13, 15, 94

Excelsior, Jr., 131
Experience, 225, 278, 280
The Explorers, 157
Eysler, Edmund, 177, 199, 200, 212, 229

F
Fad and Folly, 163
Fads and Fancies, 227, 277, 286
Fagan, Barney, 122, 123, 147, 173, 273
The Fair Co-Ed, 197, 281, 287
Fair Luna, 24
The Fair One with Blonde Wig, 63
The Fair One with the Golden Locks, 49
The Fairy Prince O'Donoughue, or, the White Horse of Killarney, 53
Fall, Leo, 199
Fallon, Larry, 300
Fancy Free, 241, 280, 284
Fantana, 176, 270
Fascinating Flora, 188, 270, 284
The Fascinating Widow, 210, 283, 284
Faust on Time, 107
Faust, or, The Demon, the Doctor and the Devil's Draught, 57–58
Faust Up to Date, 108
Faustus, or, The Demon of the Drachenfels, 42–43
Fay, Thomas (Tom), 300
Fee-G!, 73
Felix, Hugo, 205, 216, 233
The Fencing Master, xiii, 117, 275
Fenwick, John, 300
Feudal Times, or, The Banquet Gallery, 37
Février, Henry, 248
Fiddlers Three, 242
The Field of the Cloth of Gold, 60
Fields, Arthur, 240
Fields, Herbert L., 263
Fifty Miles from Boston, 193
Figman, Max, 170
The Filibuster, 183
La Fille du Tambour Major, 87
Finck, Herman, 207, 224, 230, 231, 259
The Firefly, 17, 218, 267, 281, 282
Fire-Fly!, 63

Fire Fly, or, The Friend of the Flag, 59
Fisher, Harrison, 300
The Fisher Maiden, 168–169, 289
Fisher, Robert, 300
Fitzgerald, William H., 93, 138, 153
Flaherty, Stephen, 300
Fleming, Carroll, 209, 216
Fleron, William, 116
Fletcher, Percy (E.), 238, 252
Fleur-De-Lis, 129
Flick Flock, 62
The Flirting Princess, 201
A Flitch of Bacon, or, the Matrimonial Prize, 29
Florio, Caryl, 102, 127
Florodora, 155, 274
Floyd, W.R., 86
Fokine, Michel, 248, 252, 254, 260, 273
Follies of 1908, 194–195, 277, 286
Follies of 1909, 17, 199, 277, 286
Follies of 1910, 204, 286
Ford, Hugh, 182
La Forêt Noire, 25, 27, 275
The Foresters, 115
For Freedom Ho, 39
For Goodness Sake, 259, 267
Formosa, or, The Railroad to Ruin, 62
Forrester, Hugh, 300
Forrest, Sam, 244, 249, 252, 274
Fortuna, or, The Princess Tough, 129
The Fortune Teller, xiii, 145, 285
Fortunio and His Gifted Servants!, 68
Fortunio and His Seven Gifted Servants, 93
Forty-Five Minutes from Broadway, 181
The Forty Thieves, 39
The Forty Thieves, or Striking Oil in Family Jars!, 14, 60
Foster, Allan K., 223, 226, 232, 234, 237, 239, 243, 247, 250, 253, 255, 256, 257, 258, 259, 261, 274
4-11-14, 107
1492, Up to Date or Very Near It, 16, 18, 118
Fourth of July, or, Temple of American Independence, 33

Fowler, John, 107
Fox, George L., 13, 48, 51, 53, 65
Foxy Grandpa, 160
Foxy Quiller, 155, 291
Fra Diavolo (Auber), 55
Fra Diavolo, or, The Beauty and the Brigands / Thrice Married, 52
Franchi, Leon, 134
Francioli, Augusto, 120, 121, 123, 125, 126, 128, 132, 133, 137, 139, 140, 142, 274–275
Francis, James, 162
Francis, W. T., 122, 128, 142, 148, 162, 168, 177, 199, 205, 213
Franklin, Malvin, 17, 211, 212, 219, 245, 246, 253, 255, 256
Fraser, Ian, 300
Freeborn, Cassius, 184, 198, 200, 223
The Free Lance, 183, 277
Freeman, Max, 109, 110, 117, 125, 127, 129, 134, 135, 141, 146, 149, 152, 176, 275–276
Frehrmann, Max, 118
Freitag, Dorothea, 300–301
French, Bert, 244, 247, 249, 253, 257, 262, 276
The French Maid, 16, 140, 290
Frey, Hugo, 187
Friedland, Anatole, 211, 212
Friedman, Gary William, 301
Friedman, Leo, 166, 187
Friml, Rudolf, xviii, 20, 218, 222, 227, 231, 235, 236, 239, 243, 244, 247, 254, 256, 258, 259, 263, 264
Fritz in Ireland, or, The Bellringer of the Rhine, 83
Frivolous Geraldine, 218
(From) Broadway to Paris, 217, 293
From Broadway to Tokio, 16, 152, 275, 278, 284
Frow-Frow, 76
Fry, William Henry, 42
Fuller, Dean, 301
Fuller, Larry, xvii
Fuller, Lorenzo, 301
Fullum, Clay, 301

Fun on the Bristol, or, A Night on Long Island Sound, 91
Fun on the Bristol, or A Night on the Sound, 86
Furs and Frills, 238, 284
Furst, William, 117, 118, 120, 123, 129, 131, 154, 163
Furth, Seymour, 177, 185, 187, 190, 193, 200, 208

G

Gabriel Grub; or, The Story of the Goblins Who Stole the Sexton!, 72
Gabriel, Max, 145
Gaby, 208, 283
A Gaiety Girl, 124
Galloway, James T., 135
Gambrinus, King of Lager Beer, 15, 74
Ganne, Louis, 211
Gardiner, Jack, 135
Garrett O'Magh, 155–156
Gaunt, Percy, 106, 107, 114, 124
The Gay Musician, 194
The Gay White Way, 190, 270
Gebest, Charles J., xiii, 147, 156, 166, 175, 181, 182, 185, 192, 193, 194, 195, 200, 204, 210, 212, 223, 226, 232, 240, 252, 257, 262
The Geisha, 134
Genée, Adeline, 193
Genée, Alexander, 193, 201
Genée, Richard, 88
Gentleman Joe, the Hansom Cabby, 132
George Washington, Jr., xiii, 182
George White's Scandals of 1920, 249–250
George W. Lederer's Mid-Summer Night Fancies, 167, 292, 293
German, Edward, 191
Gershwin, George, xviii, 20, 21, 245, 249, 252, 255, 259, 262, 293
Getting Together, 240
Get Together, 257, 270
Gibson, Michael, 301
Gideon, Melville (J.), 195, 196, 198, 200, 204, 208, 210, 211

Gilbert, Jean, 213, 221, 225, 261
Gilbert, M.B., 156, 159, 276
Gil Blas, or, The Cavern, 35
Gilfert, Charles, 37, 38, 39
Gilles, Napoleon, 58
Gillespie, Lee, 301
Gillingham, George, 28
Gill, William, 81, 85, 100
Gilmore, W.H., 262
Giorza, Paolo, 62, 143
The Girl and the Wizard, 200, 292
The Girl behind the Counter, 190, 279, 285
The Girl from Kay's, 169
The Girl from Paris, 136, 287, 290
The Girl from Utah, 224
Girlies, 203–204, 284
The Girl in the Spotlight, 250, 267, 282
The Girl of Tomorrow, 231
A Glance at New York in 1848, 42
Glaser, C.J.M., 21, 201, 206
The Glorious 7, 63, 271
Glover, Howard, xii, 58, 60, 61, 75
Glover, J.M., 158, 171, 176, 222
Gloves, W.F., 127
The Goats, 78
Godfrey, D.S., 117
Godfrey, Fred, 222
Godfrey, Vaughn, 258
Godowsky, Leopold, 255, 256
Goetz, E. Ray, 180, 183, 187, 213, 219, 226, 228, 233
Goetzl, Anselm, 244, 248, 254, 257
Going Up, 239, 288
Goland, Arnold, 301
The Gold Bug, 134, 275
Goldenberg, William (Billy), xv, 301
The Golden Butterfly, 64, 195, 269, 279
Goldstein, Jerome, 301
Goldstone, Bob, 301
Goodman, Al(fred), 248, 250, 253, 254, 255, 256, 257, 258, 261, 262, 263, 264, 265
Goodman, Philip, 264
Goodman, Tommy, 301
Good Morning, Dearie, 258, 288

The Good Mr. Best, 139, 283, 287
Good Times, 251, 270, 278
Gordon, Dan, 301
Gorman, James, 164, 166, 210, 212, 236, 240, 276
Gottschalk, L(ouis) F., 131, 151, 157, 158, 159, 170, 172, 186, 191, 202, 208, 213, 235
Goula, Juan, 89
The Governor's Son, 156, 277, 287, 292
The Grand Mogul, 187, 277
Granger, Frederick, 35, 37
Grant, Bert, 213, 217, 228, 233, 250, 265
Grant, Billy, 260
Grant, Charles (N.), 213, 237, 245, 257, 264
Grant, John B., 101, 102
Grant, Micky, xvii
Graphenreed, Timothy, xvii, 301
Graupner, Gottlieb, 35, 39
Gray, Roger, 194
The Great Name, 211
A Greek Slave, 151, 285
Greene, Milton, 302
The Green Monster, or, The White Knight and the Giant Warrior, 53
The Greenwich Village Follies (1919), 246, 268
The Greenwich Village Follies of 1920, 251, 268
The Greenwich Village Follies (1922), 261, 268, 278
Gregory, James, 302
Gresham, Herbert, 144, 149, 157, 158, 159, 163, 165, 167, 171, 174, 175, 176, 178, 179, 180, 183, 187, 193, 195, 196, 199, 201, 207, 221, 227, 231, 241, 245, 276–277
Gress, Louis, 252, 259, 266
Grétry, A.E.M., 26, 32
Gribble, Harry Wagstaff, 264, 277
The Grim Goblin, 86
The Grip, 99–100
Gross, Arnold, 302
Grossi, A(ntonio), xii, 53, 54, 55, 57, 277–278

Grundmann, Tim, 302
Guida, Mlle., 238
Gunn, John, 130
Gustafson, Bob, 302

H

Haak, Brad, 302
Hadley, Henry K., 165, 239
Hague, Albert, 302
Hahn, Henry, 60
Haig, Alexander, 122
Half a King, 134
The Half Moon, 253, 274, 281
The Hall of Fame, 159, 284, 292
Hamlet II, 127–128
Hamlisch, Marvin, xvi, xviii, 302
Hammerstein, Arthur, 249
Hammerstein, Oscar, 20, 132, 135, 174
Hand, Carl, 189
Hands Up, 228–229, 269, 281, 284
Hanford, Charles B., 216
Hanlon Brothers, 118
Hansel, Emil, 175
Happy Days, 246, 270, 278
Happyland, or, The King of Elysia, 179
Hardwick, Cheryl, 302
Harlequin Bluebeard, or, The Good Fairy Preciosa and the Bad Demon Rustifusti, 52
Harlequin! Demon Statue, The Enchanted Pills and Magic Apple Tree; or High Diddle Diddle, the Cat's in the Fiddle, the Cow Jumped over the Moon!, 75
Harlequin Jack, The Giant Killer, 48
Harlequin Pastry Cook, 25–26
Harlequin's Almanac, or, The Four Seasons, 36
Harlequin Shipwreck'd, or, the Grateful Lion, 26
Harlequin's Invasion, 28
Harlequin's Triumph in War and in Love, 37–38
Harley, Leslie, 302
Harper, Wally, 302
Harrell, Gordon (Lowry), 302–303

Harrigan, Edward, xiii, 66, 78, 79, 80, 81, 82, 84, 85, 86, 88, 90, 91, 92, 93, 94, 95, 97, 98, 99, 100, 102, 104, 105, 106, 107, 111, 114, 120, 125, 133, 168
Harris, Frederic, 303
Harris, Howard, 303
Harrison, Bertram, 244
Harrison, E., 74
Harrison, Louis, 114
Sadie, Harrison, 208
Hartley, Richard, 303
Hastings, Harold, 303
The Haunted Tower, 26–27
Havana, 197, 292
Have a Heart, 235, 288
Hayden, Cissie, 251, 278
Hayden, Martin, 116
The Heartbreakers, 208
Heartz, Harry Lawson, 142, 143, 156, 159, 160, 172, 189, 190
The Heathen, 144
He Came from Milwaukee, 206
Heindl, Anton, 164, 183, 190, 196, 221, 247, 257, 260, 261, 262
Hein, Silvio, 203, 211, 220, 223, 225, 227, 232, 234, 238, 260
Hell, 208, 283
Hello, Broadway!, 226, 276, 293
Hello, Paris, 209, 292
Henderson, Alexander, 71
Henderson, Clayton W., 7
Henderson, Luther, xvii, xviii, 303
Henderson, Ray, 261, 293
Hendrik Hudson, or, The Discovery of Columbus, 110
The Hen-Pecks, 207, 292
Henry V, 15, 154
Henry VIII, 14, 69
Herbert, Fred, 303
Herbert, Joseph W., 170, 171, 217
Herbert, Victor, 17, 19, 125, 130, 134, 138, 140, 141, 145, 149, 150, 151, 153, 169, 170, 178, 179, 180, 181, 185, 186, 187, 195, 196, 197, 200, 202, 206, 207, 210, 211, 217, 220, 221, 222, 225, 229, 230, 235, 236, 237, 238, 243, 244, 246, 248, 250, 253, 256, 260
Her Little Highness, 221, 283, 286
The Hermits in Dixie, 17, 194, 279
Hernandez, Arthur, 90
Hernández, Oscar, 303
Herrmann, Keith, 303
Hewitt, James, 6, 25, 30, 33, 34, 36, 37, 40
Hewitt, John Hill, 50
Hiawatha, 85
Hiawatha, or, Ardent Spirits and Laughing Waters, 45
Hiccory Diccory Dock, or, Harlequin Jack of the Beanstalk!, 62, 271
Higgledy-Piggledy, 175, 283
High Jinks, 222, 290
The Highwayman, 16, 141, 275, 284, 292
Hiller, J. Sebastian, 112, 118, 123, 133, 143, 156, 162, 173, 181
Hill, J. Leubrie, 165, 193, 223, 228, 230
Hindley, Thomas W., 91, 133, 226, 247
Hip-Hip-Hooray, 230
Hip! Hip! Hooray!, 190, 270, 286
A Hired Girl, 142
Hirschfeld, Max, 161, 165, 169, 185, 196, 228, 231, 236, 240, 243
Hirsch, Louis A., 190, 192, 193, 196, 200, 204, 206, 210, 212, 214, 215, 228, 231, 233, 239, 241, 243, 252, 257, 260, 261
Hirschmann, Henri, 214
His Excellency, 129–130
His Honor the Mayor, 183
Hitchy-Koo of 1918, 241
Hobart, George V., 225, 278
Hochman, Larry, 303
Hoffman, A.W., 13, 94, 100, 103, 114, 119,
Hoffman, Bena, 230
Hoffman(n), Gertrude, 176, 179, 184, 186
Hoffman(n), Max, 140, 167, 168, 174, 175, 179, 185, 186, 189, 217, 235

Hoffmann, W.H., 99
Hoffmaster, William, 5, 24,
Hogan, Ernest, 192, 278–279
Hogan's Alley, 135
Hokey-Pokey, 213, 291
Holbrook, A.M., 149, 157, 159, 163, 170, 178, 186, 194, 196, 215, 279
Holbrook, Florence, 202
Holbrook, William, 261, 279
Holder, Ray, 303
Holdridge, Lee, 303
A Hole in the Ground, 103, 285
Holgate, Danny, 304
Hollister, David, 304
Holmes, Jack, 304
Honey Girl, 249, 274, 276
The Honeymoon Express, 218, 293
Hood, Janet, 304
Hooper, Lewis, 155, 163, 182
Hop o' My Thumb, 222, 272
Hop O' My Thumb, or, The Ogre and the Dwarf!, 48
Horn, Charles E., 20, 38, 39, 41
Horner, Sidney H., 108
Horrors, or, The Marajah of Zogobad, 82
The Horse Marines / Nicodemus, 60–61
Hoschna, Karl L., 152, 178, 194, 201, 202, 204, 205, 214, 238
Hotel Topsy Turvy, 145, 290
The Hottest Coon in Dixie, 157
The House that Jack Built, 11, 51
The House that Jack Built, or, Harlequin and the Fairy Generous, 51
The House-Warming, 87–88
Howard, Joseph E., 145, 197, 201, 218, 220, 231
Howard, Peter, 304
Howe, Junius, 142
Howson, Frank A., 68, 147
Howson, John, 87
The Hoyden, 190, 291
Hoyt, Charles H., 96, 101, 105, 107, 110, 131, 137, 140, 144
Hubbell, Raymond, 166, 176, 182, 184, 198, 201, 202, 206, 208, 209, 214, 216, 217, 219, 223, 227, 230, 236, 237, 241, 242, 246, 251, 254, 260, 261
Huffman, J.C., 190, 193, 207, 211, 214, 221, 224, 225, 227, 228, 230, 232, 234, 239, 240, 241, 242, 247, 250, 252, 253, 255, 258, 259, 262, 265, 279–280
Hugo, John Adam, 244
Hummel, Mark, 304
Humphrey, Fred W., 61
Humphreys, H.W., 61
Humphreys, Joseph, 123
Humpty Dumpty, xii, 59, 67, 75–76, 84, 90, 176, 271, 272, 277, 292
Humpty Dumpty Abroad!, 71
Humpty Dumpty in Every Clime, 74
Humpty Dumpty Junior, or, The Fairy of the Diamond Mines and the Giant's Festival, 64
Humpty Dumpty's Dream, 80
The Hurdy-Gurdy Girl, 189–190, 286
Hurly-Burly, 144
Hurwitz, Deborah, 304
The Hustler, 114
Hutchinson, Edward, 229, 233
Hydes, Watty, 115, 122, 146, 149, 155, 169

I

Iascaire, 77
The Idea, 122
The Idol's Eye, 140–141, 285
If I Were King, 263
Ill Treated Il Travadatore!, or, The Mother, The Maiden and the Musicianer, 51
In a Balcony, 154–155
In Dahomey, 17, 20, 165–166, 289
The Indian Princess, or, La Belle Sauvage, 37
In Gay New York, 133, 275
In Gay Paree, 148, 284, 291
In Gotham, 145, 267
The International Cup, 18, 205, 270, 288
In Town, 139–140, 292

Investigation, 97
The Invisible Prince, or, The Island of Tranquil Delights, 47
Irene, 247–248, 274, 288, 302
The Irish Artist, 124
An Irish Gentleman, 141, 287
The Irish Tailor, or, the Humours of the Thimble, 29
The Iron Chest, 32
Irwin, May, 121, 146
Isham, John W., 136
(Isham's) Octoroons, 150, 287
The Isle of Champagne, 16, 117–118
The Isle of Gold, 138–139, 287
The Isle of Spice, 174, 290
The Italian Monk, 33
Ito, Michio, 249
Itzel, Adam, Jr., 99, 112, 118
Ivanhoe, 61
Ivanoff, Alexandra, 305
The Ivy Leaf, 100
Ixion!, or, The Man at the Wheel, 10, 59

J

Jacinta, or, The Maid of Manzanillo, 125, 275
Jack and Gill Went Up the Hill, 54, 278
Jack and Jill, 73, 263, 268
Jack Sheppard, 15, 99
Jack, the Giant Killer, 70
Jacobi, Georges, 13, 106, 107, 119, 127, 150
Jacobi, Victor, 232, 237, 238, 241, 242, 247, 253, 257, 258
Jacquet, H. Maurice, 251
Jakobowski, Edward, 101, 107, 170
Jalma, 94
Jambone, Michele, xii, 59
James, Harry, 137, 142
Janik, Ada, 305
Janis, Elsie, 213, 259
Jannota, A., 58
Janusz, Tom, 305
Jarrett, Henry C., 87
Jefferson, William, 155

Jerome, Ben (M.), 160, 161, 165, 167, 170, 172, 174, 197, 199, 206
The Jersey Lily, 168, 278, 282, 289
The Jewel of Asia, 165, 282
Jimmie, 253, 272, 276
John Murray Anderson's Almanac, 268, 295
Johns, Al, 165, 193, 201
Johnson, James P., 264, 265
Johnson, J. Rosamond, 149, 155, 158, 161, 164, 165, 168, 171, 173, 176, 188, 196, 198, 201, 209, 238, 249
Johnson, Louis, xvii
Johnson, Sy, 305
Johnston, Donald, 305
Johnstone, Alexander, 242
Johnstone, Tom, 258
Johnston, Robert, 74
The Jolly Bachelors, 202, 292
The Jolly Musketeer, 146
A Jolly Surprise, 115
Jones, Benny, 198, 280
Jones, Donald G., 305
Jones, Edward, 111
Jones, Sidney, 123, 124, 126, 131, 134, 151, 154, 171, 224
Jones, Stephen, 208, 246, 252, 255, 256, 257, 258, 263, 264
Jonson, Bill, 305
Joplin, Scott, 213
Jordan, Joe, 188, 193, 204, 227, 260
Josef, Carl, 110, 117
Joshua Whitcomb, 82
June Love, 254, 269
Jupiter, or, The King and the Cobbler, 115
Jurist, Irma, 305

K

Kajanka, 108
Kander, John, 305
Kate Kip, Buyer, 146
Katinka, 231, 290
Katsaros, Doug, xvii, 305
Kay, Arthur, 305
Kayden, Mildred, 305

Kelley, Edgar Stillman, 108, 116
Kelly, Edwin, 76
Kelly, Glen, 305
Kelly, James T., 142
Kelly, John T., 128, 131, 134, 146, 162
Kelly, Michael, 6, 33, 34, 35, 36, 37, 38, 39
Kelly, Robert A., 157
Kenilworth, or, Ye Queen, Ye Knight and Ye Maiden, 69
Kennedy, Harry, 124
Kennedy, John P., 179
Kerker, Gustave, 19–20, 101, 102, 103, 104, 109, 117, 119, 120, 121, 124, 128, 130, 132, 133, 134, 136, 137, 139, 140, 142, 143, 148, 161, 163, 166, 170, 176, 183, 184, 188, 238, 256, 260
Kern, Jerome, 20, 171, 180, 187, 188, 189, 199, 200, 204, 205, 207, 208, 217, 221, 224, 226, 227, 228, 229, 230, 231, 233, 235, 236, 237, 238, 240, 243, 244, 245, 249, 253, 258, 265
Kerr, C. Herbert, 165
Key, James Barton, 128
The Khedive, 112
Kid Boots, xxi, 265–266, 288
Kiefert, Carl, 141, 237
King Charming, or, The Blue Bird of Paradise, 45
King Cotton, or, The Exiled Prince, 49
King Highball, 162, 284
King Kaliko, 116
King Linkum the First, 50
The King of Coney Island, 46
The King's Carnival, 156, 290
Kingsley, Gershon, 306
The King's Musketeer, 16, 147
Kiralfy, Bolossy, 13, 64, 74, 77, 82, 83, 84, 88, 94, 96, 99, 100, 106, 107
Kiralfy, Imre, 13, 64, 67, 71, 72, 74, 77, 82, 83, 84, 88, 94, 96, 99, 100, 103, 120
Kismet, or, Two Tangled Turks, 128–129, 137, 275

A Kiss for Cinderella, 16, 235
Kissing Time, 252, 278, 288
The Kitty, 106
Kitty Darlin', 239, 288
Kleinecke, August (Gus), 192, 210, 223, 229, 256
Klein, Manuel, 164, 169, 177, 181, 184, 186, 191, 192, 195, 200, 202, 205, 207, 209, 212, 216, 220, 222, 225, 240
Klein, Randy, 306
The Knickerbockers, 118–119
Kolb, C. William, 192
Koppitz, Charles, 48, 56, 58, 69
Kosarin, Michael, 306
Kosarin, Oscar, 306
Kosloff, Alexis, 238, 240, 243, 280–281
Kosloff, Theodore, 215, 230, 281
Kowal, James, 306
Krakaner, Prof., 58
Krane, David, 306
Krause, Christian, 85, 91
Krause, Fritz, 119
Krausse, Albert, 112, 122, 124, 132, 138, 146, 151, 176, 185, 203, 206
Kreisler, Fritz, 247
Kruger, Eloise, 128
Kuramoto, Dan, 306
Kuttner, Alfred J., 146, 147
Kyle, Billy, 306

L

Labarre, Trille, 32
Lacamoire, Alex, 306
Lachaume, Aimé, 153, 158
Lacy, Rophino, 40
Lady Audley's Secret, 56
The Lady in Ermine, 261, 274, 285
The Lady in Red, 245, 290
Lady of the Lake, 38, 275
The Lady of the Slipper, 217, 270
The Lady or the Tiger?, 105
The Lady Slavey, 132, 269
Lady Teazle, 176, 270
Lagardère; or, the Hunchback of Paris, 103

Laird, Marvin, 307
La-La-Lucille!, 245, 277
Lalla Rookh, or, The Fire Worshippers, 47
Lalla Rookh, or The Pearl of India, 68
Lambelet, Napoléon, 134, 145, 149
La Manna, Signor, 45, 50
Lanergan, J.W., 86
Lang, Phil, 307
Lanner, Kathi, 73
Lannin, Paul, 255, 259
Larson, Peter, 307
Lass, Jeff, 307
The Last of the Hogans, 114
The Last Waltz, 255, 274, 280, 285, 290
Latham, Fred G., 170, 181, 185, 197, 205, 211, 212, 218, 220, 222, 230, 232, 236, 245, 247, 249, 253, 264, 281
The Launch, or, Huzza for the Constellation, 32
Lauri, John, 62, 70
Lawlor, James Reed, 307
Lawn, Sand, 307
Lawn Tennis, 87
Lawrence, Lionel, 184
Lawrence, Stephen, 307
Lawton, Frank, 124
The Leather Patch, 100
Leave It to Jane, 269, 288
Lebowsky, Stanley, 307
Lederer, George W., 140, 143, 148, 153, 157, 161, 165, 166, 167, 168, 173, 205, 215, 223, 248, 250, 262, 281–282
Lee, Jack, 307
Lee, Sammy, xiii, 262, 264, 265, 282
Lefranc, Mr., 131
The Legend, 244
Lehár, Franz, 191, 233
Lehman, Samuel, 184, 206, 212, 214, 215
Leib, Dick, 307
LeMack, Thomas, 114, 121
Leo and Lotos, 70
Leonard, Michael, 307
Leonardo, 130

Leoni, Mr., 110
Leonora, 42
Lepri, Giovanni, 89
Lesko, Andrew, 307
Lessner, George, 307
Let George Do It, 214–215, 279
Levenson, Jeanine, 307
Levi, Maurice, 120, 126, 138, 139, 147, 149, 150, 157, 158, 161, 175, 192, 193, 194, 195, 199, 204, 208, 209
Levinsky, Walt, 307
Lewis, Walter H., 157
The Liberty Belles, 158, 276, 289
Linger Longer Letty, 248
Linné, Hans S., 205, 215, 216
The Lion Tamer, 16, 115
Lippa, Andrew, 307
Listen Lester, 243, 284
Little Boy Blue, or, Hush-A-Bye Baby and Patty and Her Pitcher, 57, 278
The Little Café, 221, 277, 286
Little Christopher Columbus, 124
Little Dew Drop, or, The Fairies' Home in the Palace of Neptune, 58
The Little Duchess, 158, 282
The Little Frauds, 14, 66
The Little Host, 16, 146, 275, 289
Little Jack Sheppard, 15, 101
Little Johnny Jones, xiii, xviii, 175, 300, 316
The Little Millionaire, 210, 276
Little Nellie Kelly, 262, 286
Little Nemo, xiii, 196, 277
A Little of Everything, 173–174
The Little Primrose, 96–97
Little Red Riding Hood, 151–152, 268, 275
Little Simplicity, 243, 280, 284, 292
The Little Trooper, 123
The Little Tycoon, 100
The Little Whopper, 247, 272, 276
The Little Yankee Sailor, 28
The Loan of a Lover, 49
The Lock and Key, 32
Locke, E.A., 77
Locke, Matthew, 27, 35
Loder, Edward, 43

Loder, George, 41, 42, 43
Lodoiska, or, The Rescue of the Princess of Poland, 36–37
Loesch, George, 76, 78, 85, 86, 113, 122
Loftus, Cissie, 146, 149, 155
Logan, Frederick Knight, 202
A Lonely Romeo, 245–246, 284
Lonesome Town, 192, 290
Loraine, William, 160, 168, 182, 214
Lorette, Mariette, 230
The Lorgaire (!), 81, 106
Lothian, Napier, 56, 60, 68, 94, 95, 96, 97
Lothian, Napier, Jr., 112, 115, 121, 130
Loud, David, 308
The Love Cure, 199–200, 283
Love in a Camp, or Patrick in Prussia, 24
The Love Letter, 257–258, 288
Love o' Mike, 235, 269
Love's Young Dream, 83
Lowitz, William W., 115
Lowrie, W.M., 219
Loyalina, or, Brigadier-General Fortunio, and His Seven Gifted Aides-de-Camp, 51–52
The Lucky Escape, or, the Ploughman Turned Sailor, 31, 275
Lucretia Borgia, M.D., La Grande Doctresse, 60
Luders, Gustav, 20, 147, 149, 155, 166, 171, 175, 181, 187, 197
Luna, the Little Boy who cried for the Moon, 68
Lund, John, 170, 181, 196
Lurline, 65, 269
Lusk, Milton (W.), 185, 195, 224, 257
Lutz, W. Meyer, 83, 101, 104, 106, 108, 148, 169
Lynne, Harry, 43

M

Macbeth, 27, 35, 39
MacConnell, Harry T., 152, 153, 156
MacDonough, Thomas B., 90
MacGregor, Edgar, 244, 262
MacKay, Harper, 308
Mack, Cecil, 150, 154
Madame Sherry, 205, 282
Madam Moselle, 223, 274. 282
Madam Piper, 96
The Madcap Duchess, 221–222, 281
A Madcap Princess, 174, 292
Maddern, Richard, 108
Madeleine, or, The Magic Kiss, 126–127
Mader, Raoul, 257
Maeder, Frank, 82
Maeder, James Gaspard, 44, 45, 49, 55
Maffit, James S., 70, 73
Maflin, A.W., 20, 66, 96
Maggie, the Midget, 104
The Magic Slipper, 82
The Maid and the Mummy, 174, 286
Maid in America, 226–227, 280, 285
The Maid in the Moon, 149, 287
Maid Marian, 159, 276
The Maid of Plymouth, 121
The Major, 90, 98
Make It Snappy, 259, 274, 280
Malina, Stuart, 308
Mallandaine, John Elliot, 70, 71
Malone, J.E.A., 140, 199, 218, 224
Malvina, Mme., 89, 95, 151, 155
Mama's Baby Boy, 215, 267, 282
Mam'selle Napoleon, 171
Mam'zelle Champagne, 184
The Mandarin, 136, 283
The Man from China, 173, 273
The Man from Now, 184, 283
Manhattan Mary, 293
The Manicure Girl, 224
The Man in the Moon, 17, 148, 281, 284
Manning, James H., 119
Mann, Nat. D., 136, 164, 180
Manola, Marion, 109
Mantova, Mlle., 261
The Man Who Owns Broadway, 200
Manzotti, Luigi, 13, 94, 152
Marchetti, Filiberto, 127, 143, 148, 282
Marchetti, Henry, 143
Marenco, Romualdo, 13, 21, 94, 96, 152
Maretzek, Max, 20, 77, 83, 127

Margoshes, Steven (Steve), 308
Marguerite, 132, 275
Marion, Dave, 191, 282
Marion, George, 153, 158, 164, 166, 168, 172, 175, 178, 184, 186, 188, 191, 193, 195, 197, 200, 207, 208, 210, 213, 216, 219, 221, 226, 233, 236, 282–283
Marion, Samuel, 136, 139, 166, 167, 175, 177, 179, 283
Marita, 101
Marius, C.D., 123
Marks, Robert (choreographer), 236, 243, 249, 284
Marks, Robert (dance music arranger), 308
Marks, Walter, xv
Mark, Zane, 308
The Marquis of Michigan, 145
Marrying Mary, 268, 279
Martinetti, Ignacio, 146
Martinetti, Julien, 76
Martin, Hugh, 308
Marty Malone, 133
Marvin, Mel, 308
Marwig, Carl, 125, 131, 136, 138, 139, 141, 142, 147, 148, 152, 154, 159, 162, 163, 166, 284
Mary, 252, 274, 286
Mary Jane McKane, 265, 282
Mary of Magdala, 163, 284
Masekela, Hugh, 308
The Masked Ball, 84
Mason, Jack, 188, 204, 208, 209, 210, 224, 225, 227, 228, 229, 230, 232, 233, 238, 240, 241, 242, 243, 246, 252, 254, 255, 261, 284–285
Massaniello, Hero and Martyr of Italian Liberty, 47
A Matinée Idol, 203, 268
Mattei, Tito, 104, 105
Matz, Peter, xv, 308
Maultsby, Carl, 308
Maurice, Louie, 141, 145
Mavourneen, 113, 122
Maxwell, Chris, 198

Maxwell, Vera, 224
Mayers, Lloyd, 308
The Mayor, 84
The Mayor of Tokio, 181, 286
Maytime, xiii, 237, 274, 292
Mazeppa and the Wild Horse, 40
Mazeppa, or, the Untamed Rocking Horse, 51
Mazzinghi, Joseph, 34
McAllister's Legacy, 98
McClellan, Clark, 308
McCormack, Frank, 231, 233, 285
McCormick, Will A., 156
McDaniel, John, 309
McGhie, John, 149, 175, 184, 188, 195, 220, 224, 226, 231, 235, 237
McKinney, John, 309
McManus, John L., 309
McNooney's Visit, 102
McSorley's Inflation, 92
Mecca, 18, 252, 273
The Medal and the Maid, 171
Medea!, or, The Best of Mothers with a Brute of a Husband, 58
Meeker, Jesse, 309
Meinrath, Joseph, 109
Mello, Al, 309
Melrose, Ronald (Ron), 309
Mendelvitch, Rodion, 228
Mephisto and the Four Sensations, 70–71
Merkin, Robby, 309
The Merry Countess, 16, 215–216
The Merry Monarch, 109–110
The Merry Tramps, 135
The Merry Widow, 191, 283
The Merry Widow and the Devil, 286
The Merry Widow Burlesque, 278, 286
The Merry World, 128, 280
The Messenger Boy, 157, 276
Mestayer, William A., 106
Mexicana, 182, 270
Meyers, Lanny, 309
Michael Strogoff, 13, 90
A Midnight Bell, 106–107
The Midnight Rounders of 1921, 254, 285

The Midnight Sons, 198–199, 292
Miladi and the Musketeer, see *My Lady*
Milbank, Stephen, 309
A Milk White Flag, and Its Battle-Scarred Followers on the Field of Mars and in the Court of Venus, 124
Miller, Charles, 261, 263
Miller, Freda, 309
Miller, Fred (R.), (Jr.), 87, 88, 96, 97, 111, 123
Miller, Henry, 223
The Milliners, or, The Wooden Block, 30
A Million Dollars, 153–154, 278, 284, 290
Mills, Frederick W., 84, 127, 133, 210
Milton, Robert, 226, 229, 230, 240, 243
The Mimic World of 1921, 256–257
Minnie Palmer's Boarding School, 85
The Minstrel of Clare, 132
The Miraculous Mill, or, The Old Ground Young, 28, 275
Miss Blythe of Duluth, 117
Miss Dolly Dollars, 18, 178, 279
Miss Esmeralda, 106
Miss Information, 230
Miss Innocence, 196, 286
Miss Jack, 209–210
Miss 1917, 238, 293
Miss Philadelphia, 142
Miss Pocahontas, 16, 191
Miss Simplicity, 159, 267, 276
Mitchell, Jerry, xix
Mitchell, Julian, 103, 114, 124, 132, 138, 141, 145, 147, 148, 150, 151, 152, 162, 164, 169, 180, 184, 186, 187, 190, 193, 195, 196, 199, 201, 204, 206, 207, 209, 214, 217, 219, 221, 227, 228, 231, 232, 241, 244, 252, 257, 259, 261, 262, 285–286
Mitchell, William, 41, 42
M'Liss, Child of the Sierras, 92
Mlle. Modiste, 181, 281
Mlotek, Zalmen, 309
The Mocking Bird, 162, 270
Modest Suzanne, 213, 283

Mollenhauer, Edward (R.), 10, 49, 53, 58, 83, 84, 88, 89,
Monckton, Lionel, 130, 134, 138, 143, 144, 145, 149, 150, 151, 154, 157, 158, 162, 185, 187, 205
Monplaisir, Mons., 45, 46
Monte Carlo, 16, 143, 282, 290
Monte Cristo, Jr., 104–105, 274, 280
Montero, Gus, 309
Montgomery, Frank, 309
Montgomery, James, 239
Moore, John, 44, 83
Moore, Marshall, 158
Moragas, Ricardo, 89
Mordecai Lyons, 91–92
Morgan, Charles S., Jr., 220
Morgenstern, Sam, 309
Morris, John, 309–310
Morrison, Priestly, 178, 259
Morrissey, Will, 228, 245
Morse, (Henry) Woolson, 80, 82, 89, 96, 109, 110, 112, 118, 123
Morse, Robert G., 156
Morse, Theodore F., 164, 165, 166, 167, 169, 192
Morton, Lew(is), 180, 210, 212, 256
Mother Goose, 170–171, 271, 275, 276, 292
Mother Goose! And the Fairy Legend of the Golden Egg, 52–53
Mother Goose, or, The Golden Egg, 37
The Motor Girl, 199, 290
Motzan, Otto, 228, 234, 245
The Mountebanks, 118
Mr. Bluebeard, xii, 165, 271, 276, 292
Mr. Hamlet of Broadway, 197, 292
Mr. Load of Koal, 201, 287, 289
Mr. Pickwick, 164, 283
The Muddy Day, 92–93
Muir, Lewis F., 199, 204, 214, 217
Mullaly, John, 111
Mullaly, W.S., 94, 108, 114
Müller-Norden, Alfred, 168, 171
The Mulligan Guard Ball (!), 81, 93
The Mulligan Guard Pic-Nic, 80, 86. 94
The Mulligan Guard's Chowder, 82

The Mulligan Guard's Christmas, 84
The Mulligan Guard's Nominee, 88
The Mulligan Guard's Surprise, 85
Mulligan's Silver Wedding, 88
Murphy, C.W., 178, 202, 228, 240,
Murphy, Edward, 137
Murphy, Owen, 256
Murray, J.S., 183
Murtagh, Henry B., 213, 214
Musette, or, The Secret of Guilde Court, 77
Musgrave, Frank, 86, 87, 89
Music Box Revue (1921), 257, 276, 291
Music Box Revue (1923), 264, 282
Music Box Revue (1924), 268
La Musquitoe, 41
My Best Girl, 216
My Lady, 17, 156, 276
The Mysterious Marriage, or, the Heirship of Roselva, 33
The Mysterious Monk, 31
Mystic Isle, 101–102
My Sweetheart, 90
My Tom-Boy Girl, 177–178

N
Nadjy, 105
"The 'Nadjy' Dance," 106
The Naiad Queen (Pearson), 42
The Naiad Queen, or, The Mysteries of the Lurlie Berg!, 41
Nancy Brown, 17, 165, 268, 290
Nash, John (E.), 107, 109, 119, 121, 122, 135, 145
Naughty Marietta, 206
Nearly a Hero, 193, 279, 283, 287
Nedbal, Oskar, 227
(Ned Wayburn's) Town Topics, 229, 293
Neil, Roger, 310
Neptune's Daughter, 186, 288
Neuberger, Adolph, 160, 174, 181, 185, 189, 190, 286
Neuendorff, Adolph, 116
Nevarro, Siren, 188
Nevin, Arthur, 152, 153
The New Fritz, Our Cousin German, 80

The New Henrietta, 226
The Newlyweds and Their Baby, 198, 290
Newman, Alfred, 148, 250, 261, 263, 264
Newport, or, The Swimmer, the Singer and the Cypher, 83
New York City Directory, 114
Neyer, Ernest, 80, 81
Ngema, Mbongeni, 310
Nia-For-Lica, In the Halls of Montezuma, 80
Nichols, George A., 147, 195, 198, 202, 203, 207, 213
The Night Boat, 249, 281, 293
The Night Clerk, 130, 291
Nightingale, Christopher, 310
A Night in Rome, 55
Nimble Nip!, or, Ogre Ugliphiz, Fairy Silvereyes and the Princess with the Strawberry Mark, 75
90 in the Shade, 226, 267, 268
Nixon, James M., 52
Nobody Home, 17, 227–228, 269, 270
Norcross, I.W., Jr., 111
Norman, Alfred (pseudonym of Minnie Graves Watson), 142, 143
Norman Leslie, 40
Norris, Lee, 310
Norton, Frederick, 238
Notoriety, 125
Novelty, 45
Novissimo, Arthur, 87, 104
Nowak, Adolph, 104, 105, 109,

O
Oakley, Scott, 310
The O'Brien Girl, 257, 286,
The Ocallallas, 121–122
Odenz, Leon, 310
Oedipus Tyrannus, 91
The Office Boy, 169–170, 279
Off the Earth, 126
Oh, Boy!, xiii, 236, 288
Oh, I Say!, 221, 267, 280
Oh, Lady! Lady!, 240, 288

Oh, My Dear!, 243, 288
Olcott, Chauncey, 122, 124, 132, 137, 146, 155, 202, 223, 254
Old Dutch, 202, 292
Old Lavender, 78, 99
Olio, 25
Olympiana, or, A Night with Mitchell, 46
Ondina!, or, The Spirit of the Waters, 48
On the Track, 67
On the Yellowstone, 95
Operti, Giuseppe, xii, 59, 60, 61, 62, 63, 65, 66, 67, 72, 74, 76, 95, 99
The Orchid, 187, 287, 290
The O'Reagans, 102
Oriental America, or, In the Isle of San Domingo, 136
The Origin of the Cakewalk, or, Clorindy, 143, 278
Orlob, Harold, 19, 201, 208, 209, 215, 216, 229, 241, 243,
The Orphan and the Octopus, 219
Ott, Horace, 310
Our Goblins, or, Fun on the Rhine in Germany, 85
Our Miss Gibbs, 205
Our Nell, 262, 286
Over the Garden Wall, 102
Over the River, 213, 270
Over the Top, 239, 274, 280
Owens, Frank, 310
Oxygen!, or, Gas in Burlesque Metre, 78
The Oyster Man, 192, 278, 279

P

The Page's Revel, or, the Summer Night's Bivouac/Nicodemus, 59–60
Pahl, Mel, 310
Paine, John Knowles, 91, 188
The Palace of Truth, 14, 68
"The Palace of Truth Polka-Mazurka," 14
Palkowsky, Dan, 310
Palomita, 75
Panhandle Pete, 184
Panjandrum, 118

Paola, or, The First of the Vendettas, 107
Paret, Frank P., 190, 198
A Parisian Model, 185–186, 285
Paris, or, The Apple of Discord, 65
Paris, or, The Judgement, 61
A Parlor Match, 134–135
Parsifalia, 174
Parsloe, Charles T., 113,
Pascal, Florian, 101
The Passing Show (1894), 122–123, 273, 274–275
The Passing Show of 1912, 215, 281, 293
The Passing Show of 1913, 219–220, 293
The Passing Show of 1914, 18, 20, 224, 280, 284
The Passing Show of 1915, 228, 280, 281, 284
The Passing Show of 1916, 234, 274, 280
The Passing Show of 1918, 242, 280, 284
The Passing Show of 1919, 247, 274, 280
The Passing Show of 1921, 253, 280, 289
The Patriot, or, Liberty Asserted, 25
Patsy in Politics, 189
Paul and Virginia, 34
Paul Clifford, 43–44, 66
Paulton, Edward, 101
Paulton, Harry, 170
Paxton, George, 144
Peaches, 262, 282
The Pearl and the Pumpkin, 178, 277, 292
The Pearl of Pekin, 104
Peasant Boy, or Innocence Protected, 38, 275
The Peasant Girl, 227, 269, 280, 284
Peggy from Paris, 168, 283
Peiper, Ted, 108
Pelissier, Victor, 6, 25, 26, 27, 29, 30, 31, 32, 33, 34, 35, 36, 37, 38
Penelope, 106
Pennoyer, A.S., 66
Penn, Arthur, 173
Penn, William H., 160, 161, 171, 176, 180, 213
Penny-Ante, or, The Last of the Fairies, 96

Penson, William, 40
Peress, Maurice, 310
The Peri, or, The Enchanted Fountain, 44
Perkins, Fred, 75, 77, 84, 89, 100, 110, 121, 122, 125, 127, 131, 169
Perkins, Ray, 242
Perkinson, Coleridge-Taylor, 310
Perlet, Herman, 118, 125, 128, 131, 132, 135, 136, 138, 139, 140, 142, 143, 145, 146, 148, 151, 158, 171, 179, 182, 191
Perot, Mons., 43
Pete, 104
Peterschen, Frank, 80
Peterschen, W.T., 43, 48, 52, 53
Peters, William F(rederick), 154, 161, 163, 181, 209, 210, 228
Le Petit Faust, xix, 64, 271
The Pet of the Petticoats!, 49
Petroliamania, or, Oil on the Brain, 53
Pfeiffer, Jack, 310
Pflueger, Carl, 118
Piantadosi, Al, 204, 214, 215
Pierre de Province and La Belle Magulone, 30
Pierrette, 98
"Pierrette Dances," 18
Piff-Paff, or, The Magic Armory, 79
Piff! Paff!! Pouf!!!, 17, 173, 290
Pike, Maurice, 73
The Pink Lady, 207, 277, 286
Pioneer Days, 186, 288, 292
Pippin, Donald, 310
Pippin, or, The King of the Gold Mines, 63
Pippins, 110–111
The Pique Family!, a Play on the Da-ly, 75
Pitot, Genevieve, 311
Pitou, Augustus, 113, 122, 124, 132, 138, 146, 156, 202
Pizarro, or, The Spaniards in Peru, 34
Placide, Alexander, 5, 287
Pleininger, Carl, 135
Pluto, 60

Po-Ca-Hon-Tas, 55
Po-Ca-Hon-Tas, or, The Gentle Savage, 45
Po-Ca-Hon-Tas, or, Ye Gentle Savage, 50–51
The Policy Players, 150, 289
Pollack, Lew, 253, 254, 256
Poll and Partner Joe, 67–68, 268
Polly of the Circus, 192
Polly Middles, 115
Pomahac, Bruce, 311
Pom-Pom, 18, 233, 283
Pons, Mons. (Signor G.), 40
Poor Jack, or, the Sailor's Landlady, 27–28
Poor Little Ritz Girl, 251, 269, 293
Poor Vulcan, 29
Pop, 93
Poppy, 264, 267, 268
Popularity, 185
Porter, Cole, 20, 21, 228, 230, 233
Portnoff, Mischa, 311
Portnoff, Wesley, 311
Post, Ralph, 190
Post, W.H., 219, 246
Pottle, Sam, 311
Pousse Café / The Worst Born, 141, 285
Pratt, Charles E., 71
Pratt, S(ilas) G., 94
Predigan, Auguste, 58
Previn, Charles, 231, 242, 245, 251, 255, 263
Pribor, Richard, 311
Price, Alonzo, 265
The Pride of Race, 232
The Prima Donna, 196–197, 281
Prince Achmet!, 88
Prince Ananias, 125
Prince Kam, or, A Trip to Venus, 121
The Prince of Pilsen, 17, 166, 283
Prince, Robert, 311
The Princess Beggar, 187
Princess Bonnie, 129
The Princess Chic, 152, 285
Princess Nicotine, 120, 274
The Princess Pat, 229–230, 281

The Prodigal Son, 15, 112, 271
The Proud Prince, 169
Pruyn, William, 311
Puerner, Charles, 13, 20, 80, 81, 82, 83, 84, 88, 89, 90, 93, 96, 102, 103, 113, 115, 116, 118, 120, 121, 128, 163, 180
The Pupil in Magic, 110
Puritania, or, The Earl and the Maid of Salem, 116
The Purse, or, Benevolent Tar, 27
Pygmalion, or, The Peerless and Beautiful Statue, 61
The Pyramid, 102–103

Q

The Quaker, 31
The Queen of Hearts, or, Harlequin, the Knave of Hearts, who stole the Tarts, and the Old Woman that Lived in a Shoe, 62
Queen of the Ballet, 17, 142–143
Quigley, Jack, 311
Quo Vadis, 153, 275

R

Radin, Oscar, 193, 204, 215, 218, 220, 222, 224, 225, 227, 228, 230, 232, 234, 240, 241, 247, 250, 255, 257, 260,
A Rag Baby, 95–96
Ragged Robin, 202
Rago, Joe, 311
The Raiders, 177, 278, 283, 288, 292
The Rainbow Girl, 241, 277, 286
The Rainmaker of Syria, or, The Woman King, 119, 287
The Rainmakers, 121
Raitt, James, 311
Ralston, Alfred, 311
Rambler Rose, 237–238, 284
Randall, Carl, 242, 261
The Ratcatcher, or, The Pied Piper of Hamelin, 13, 99
Raymond and Agnes, or, The Bleeding Nun, 35

Raynes, J.A., 192
Raynham, Walter, 108
Read, Mary, 265
The Rebel, 153
Red Feather, 170, 289
The Red Hussar, 109
Red Letter Nights!, or, Catching a Croesus, 95
The Red Mill, 185, 281
The Red Moon, 198, 280
The Red Petticoat, 217
The Red Rose, 208, 270, 284
The Red Widow, 212, 276, 281
Redwine, Skip, 311
Reeve, William, 6, 26, 27, 30, 34, 35, 36
The Regatta Girl, 152, 288
Reiff, Anthony, xii, 46, 59, 87, 103
A Reign of Error, 147, 284, 291
Reilly and the 400, 111
Reinagle, Alexander, 6, 24, 25, 26, 27, 28, 29, 30, 31, 33, 34, 35, 36, 37, 39
Reinhardt, Heinrich, 206
Reinhardt, Stephen, 312
Reisman, Joe, 312
Revels, or Bon-Ton George, Jr., 87
The Revue of Revues, 210–211, 290, 294
Reynolds, Thomas, 205
Rial, Jay, 106
Rice, Edward E(verett), 72, 82, 85, 87, 93, 97, 103, 104, 108, 118, 124, 131, 140, 141, 143, 145, 149, 151, 160, 162
Rice, Gitz, 240
Rice, Michael, 312
Richard Coeur de Lion, or, The Triumph of Love, 32
Richelieu of the Period!, 65–66
Ricketts, Thomas, 155
Rinehimer, John, 312
The Ring of Fate, or, Fire, Air, Earth and Water, 52
Rip Van Winkle, 45, 268
The Rising Generation, 119
Rittman, Trude, 312
Rivers, H. Fletcher, 119, 136, 138, 139, 149, 150, 151, 287

The Road to Yesterday, 187. 279
The Robber of the Rhine, 116
Roberts, Jimmy, 312
Roberts, Mister, 43, 44
Roberts, R.A., 129, 139, 141, 156, 287
Robespierre, 150
Robin Hood, xiii, 113, 268, 270
Robin Hood, or, Sherwood Forest, 25, 34
Robin Hood; or, The Maid That Was Arch, and the Youth That Was Archer, 69
Robinson Crusoe, 61, 79
Robinson Crusoe, and His Man Friday!, 61
Robinson Crusoe, Esq. and His Man Friday, 85
Robinson Crusoe, His Man Friday, Monkey, and the King of Caribee Islands, 74
Robinson Crusoe, Jr., 232, 274, 280
Robinson Crusoe, or, the Genius of Columbia, 30
Rob Roy, 124–125, 268, 275
Robyn, Alfred G., 125, 172, 187, 188
Rock, William, 191, 193, 197, 205, 287
Rodgers, Richard, xii, xiv, xv, xvii, 20, 21, 245, 251, 254, 263
Roffman, Frederick, 312
Rogers, Alex, 165, 183, 193, 201, 287
The Rogers Brothers in Central Park, 291
The Rogers Brothers in Harvard, 161, 291
The Rogers Brothers in Ireland, 16, 179, 277, 292
The Rogers Brothers in London, 167, 276, 292
The Rogers Brothers in Panama, 189, 291
The Rogers Brothers in Paris, 174, 277, 293
(The Rogers Brothers) In Wall Street, 149–150
The Rogers Brothers in Washington, 157, 291
Rogers, Eugene, 160

Rogers, Gus, 167
Rogers, Max, 167
Rogers, Robert, 312
Roger, Victor, 123, 145
The Rollicking Girl, 177, 291
A Romance of Athlone, 146
Romberg, Sigmund, 222, 224, 225, 226, 227, 228, 229, 230, 232, 234, 237, 239, 240, 242, 247, 251, 258, 261, 262, 264
Romeo and Juliet, 20, 93
Romeo, Vincenzo, 152, 177, 181, 192, 200, 205, 288
Romoff, Colin, 312
Ronzani, Signor, 53, 58
Rooke, William Michael, 40, 41
Rooney, Pat, 167, 189
Rose, Edward W., 178
Rosemi-Shell!, or, My Daughter! Oh, My Daughter!, 75
Rosemont, Walter L., 312
Rosenfeld, Carl (Charles), 110, 117, 119, 135
Rosenthal, Laurence, 312
The Rose Girl, 254, 273, 289
The Rose of Algeria, 200, 292
Rosina, 29
Rosita, or, Cupid and Cupidity, 95
Rothstein, Fred. A., 105
Roughing It!!, 70
The Rounders, 149, 275
'Round New York in 80 Minutes, 150–151
A Round of Pleasure, 139, 284, 291
Round the Clock; or, New York by Dark, 72–73
Roven, Glen, 312
The Royal Chef, 17, 172–173, 290
The Royal Vagabond, 244, 274, 286
Royce, Edward, xiii, 234, 235, 236, 237, 239, 240, 243, 245, 247, 248, 250, 252, 253, 256, 258, 263, 266, 288
Rubens, Maurie, 252
Rubens, Paul (A.), 155, 157, 158, 162, 167, 169, 171, 185, 187, 189, 190, 218, 224, 234

Rubens, Walter, 167
A Runaway Girl, 143–144, 276
The Runaways, 166, 271, 283
Running for Office, 166, 276
Runnin' Wild, 17, 264–265
A Run on the Bank, 126
Rural Revels, or, the Easter Holiday, 28, 275

S

Sadak and Kalasgrade!, or, The Waters of Oblivion, 48
Sadler, Frank, 152
Sally, xiii, 18, 253, 273, 274, 288
Sally in Our Alley, 161, 278, 282
Sally, Irene and Mary, 274, 290
Salsbury, Nate, 82
Salvador, Dom, 313
Salzer, Eugene ("Gene"), 179, 198, 209, 215, 242, 249, 254
Salzer, Gus, 146, 156, 169, 173, 177, 179, 211, 224, 229, 235, 239, 243, 244, 248, 253, 264
Sandberg, Steve, 313
Sanderson, James, 6, 36, 38,
Sanford, Henry L, 194
Santa Claus; or, Harlequin Bob Cratchet and Ding Dong Dell!, 78
Santa Maria, 16, 135, 275
Santley, Joseph, 220, 232, 288–289
San Toy, 154, 292
Sardanapalus, 76
Sardine-Apples!, King of Ninnyvah and Astoria, L.I., 77
Sator, Henry, 81, 82, 85, 87, 88, 97
Saunders, Merl, 313
Savino, Domenico, 313
The Saw Mill, or, A Yankee Trick, 40
Schaefer, Hal, 313
Schechtman, Saul, 313
Scheck, Max, 253, 254, 258, 289
Schierhorn, Paul, 313
Schilling, Carl, 144, 150
Schindler, Paul, 139, 156, 174, 181, 222, 251
Schleiffarth, George, 95

Schlein, Irving, 313
Schmidt, Max, 192
Schmidt, Mons., 43
Schneider, Charles, 313
Schonberg, Chris, 247
Schonberg, James, 69
The School for Husbands, 177
The School Girl, 131, 284
Schultz, Charles, 54, 55, 68
Schutz, Herb, 313
Schwartz, Frederick, 210
Schwartz, Jean, 156, 158, 160, 161, 165, 168, 171, 173, 177, 178, 180, 183, 188, 190, 195, 196, 201, 202, 204, 205, 212, 213, 214, 216, 217, 218, 219, 220, 228, 230, 233, 234, 240, 242, 243, 247, 250, 253, 254, 256, 259, 260, 264, 265
Schwartz, Phil, 205, 208, 228, 232
Scott, Cyril, 171
Scott, Ed, 313
Scott, Nathan, 313
The Secret, or, Partnership Dissolved, 33–34
Sedgwick, Alfred B., 74
See America First, 233, 269, 281
Selwyn, Edgar, 259
Selwyn, J.H., 52
The Serenade, 138
Sergeant Kitty, 172, 270
The Seven Ages, 108
"The Seven Ages" ballet, 103
Seven Days, 201
The Seven Sisters!, 47
The Seven Sons!, 10, 48
Seymour, William, 152
Shameen Dhu, 223
Shamus O'Brien, 137
The Shaughraun, 72
The Sheep's Foot(!), 54–55, 278
Sheets, Walter, 313
Sheinkman, Mordecai, 313
Sheridan, John F., 86
Sherman, Milt, 313
She's a Good Fellow, 244–245, 281, 288

Shield, William, 24, 25, 26, 28, 29, 32
Ship Ahoy!, 111
Shipp, Jesse A., 150, 154, 166, 183, 193, 201, 289
Shire, David, 313
The Sho-Gun, 175, 283
The Shoo-Fly Regiment, 188
Shook, Benjamin L., 165
The Shop Girl, 130
Short, Hassard, 257, 264
The Show Girl, or The Cap of Fortune, 160, 289
Shuffle Along, 255
Shylock: A Jerusalem Hearty Joke, 44
Shylock, or, The Merchant of Venice Preserved, 58
The Sicilian Romance, or, The Spectre of the Cliffs, 30
Sieba and the Seven Ravens, 13, 96
Siegmeister, Elie, 314
Silberman, Joel, 314
The Silver Bottle, 206
The Silver King, 92
The Silver Slipper, 162
The Silver Star, 18, 201, 277, 286
Simon, John, 314
Simonson, Selli, 13, 99, 126, 128, 162
Simons, Ted, 314
Simple Simon Simple, 180
Sinbad, 53, 240, 280, 284
Sinbad, or, The Maid of Balsora, 112, 117
Sinbad the Sailor, 71
The Singing Girl, 150, 285, 289
Sir Dan O'Pallas, Chief of the Assyrian Jim Jams, 76
Sister Mary, 17, 18, 149, 276
Skloff, Michael, 314
A Skylark, 203, 269, 289, 291
Slaughter, Walter, 108, 111, 132, 140, 171
Slavin, John C., 146, 289
The Sleeping Beauty and the Beast, 17, 158, 271, 291
Sleepy Hollow, or, The Headless Horseman, 83

Sloane, A. Baldwin, 131, 135, 136, 140, 145, 146, 147, 152, 153, 154, 156, 158, 159, 162, 164, 167, 170, 172, 176, 181, 182, 184, 188, 198, 203, 207, 209, 213, 246, 251
Smiff, 89
Smith, Chris, 193, 224, 252
Smith, Edgar, 128
Smith, Joseph C., 160, 164, 168, 169, 170, 173, 182, 212, 289–290
Smith, Orean, 211
Smith, Will H., 248
Smithson, Frank, 143, 145, 154, 156, 165, 173, 185, 187, 191, 198, 199, 220, 222, 231, 245, 255, 290
Smith, Steven, 314
Snapshots of 1921, 17, 18, 255–256, 273
The Social Whirl, 183, 270
A Society Circus, 181, 288, 292
Sohlke, Augusta, 105
Sohlke, Augustus, 140, 141, 173, 174, 194, 209, 211, 213, 214, 290–291
Solomon, Edward, 105, 106, 108, 109, 111, 114
Solomon, Frederic, 17, 101, 107, 116, 123, 148, 149, 153, 158, 160, 165, 170, 171, 173, 176, 180, 181, 192, 195, 199
Some Party, 17, 260, 270
Sometime, 243, 272, 274
Sommer, Kathy, 314
The Son in Law, 32
A Son of Rest, 167, 283
Sons of Ham, 154, 279, 289
Sophia of Brabant, or, the False Friend, 26, 272
Sorg, John C., 129, 153
The Soul Kiss, xii, 192–193, 277, 286
Sousa, John Philip, 19, 110, 111, 115, 133, 142, 144, 151, 183, 218, 219, 230, 237, 242
The Southerners, 173, 282, 289
Spangler, David Sheridan, 314
Spanish Love, 251
The Spanish Patriots, or, Royal Restoration, 37

Speed the Plough, 34
Spencer, Alexander, 105, 164, 187
Spenser, Willard, 100, 129
Spiel, Prof., 100
Spink, George, 164, 183, 232
The Spirit of the Air, or, The Enchanted Star, 43
Sporting Days, 195, 270, 288
Sprake, J., 40
The Spring Chicken, 185, 286
The Spring Maid, 206–207, 283
Squatter Sovereignty, 91
Squaw Man, 179, 182
Stag Party, or, A Hero In Spite of Himself, 131
Stahl, Richard, 103, 106, 107, 111, 115, 118, 121, 131, 132, 137, 140, 144
Stair, E.D., 126
Stamford, John Villers, 136
Stamper, Dave, 219, 223, 228, 233, 236, 241, 246, 250, 256, 260
Stanhope, Frederick, 240
Stanton, W., 56
Starer, Robert, 314
Starobin, Michael, 314
Stecker, Carl, 197
Stecko, Bob, 314
Stegmeyer, William, 314
Steindorff, Paul, 117, 127, 138, 142, 144, 145, 150
Steiner, Max, 241, 251, 252, 254, 262
Stein, Julian, 314
The Stepping Stones, 265
Step This Way, 233, 284, 285
Sternberg, Ann, 314
Stevens, D.K., 156, 172
St. George and the Dragon, or The 7 Champions of Christendom, 65
Still, Frank, 314
St. Louis, Louis, 314
Stoepel, Robert, 44, 55, 56, 98
Stolz, Robert, 314
Stop! Look! Listen!, 231–232, 270, 288
Storace, Stephen, 26, 27, 32, 36, 37

Storey, Fred, 106
Stothart, Herbert, x, 218, 219, 220, 221, 224, 231, 238, 241, 243, 244, 248, 249, 253, 255, 259, 260, 261, 263, 265
Stout, G.L., 71, 73
A Straight Tip, 111
The Strange Adventures of Jack and the Beanstalk, 135–136, 284, 291
A Stranger in New York, 140
The Stranglers of Paris, 15, 95
Straus, Oscar, 255
Strayhorn, Billy, 315
Strebinger, Frederic, 13, 62, 64, 65, 66, 67, 71
The Street Singer, 175
Stretti, Rene, 130
The Strollers, 156–157, 279
Stromberg, John, 129, 134, 141, 144, 162, 213, 238
Strut, Miss Lizzie, 260
Stuart, Leslie, 147, 155, 162, 186, 187, 197
Stubborn Cinderella, 197, 283
The Student King, 186, 283
Studley, Samuel L., 113, 119, 121, 122, 125, 138, 153, 159
Sturiale, Grant, 315
Styne, Jule, 315
Sullivan, Arthur, xx, 13, 21, 67, 83, 96, 103, 115, 134, 244
Sullivan, Dan(iel) J., 172, 191, 202
The Sultan of Sulu, 164, 289
The Summer Widowers, 203, 292, 293
The Sunken Bell, 153
The Sunshine Girl, 218
The Sunshine of Paradise Alley, 133, 291
Superba, 118
Sutherland, Lillie, 137
Sweethearts, 220, 281
Sweet Inniscarra, 137–138
Swete, E. Lyall, 238, 248, 252
Sybil, 232, 281, 284, 286
Sykes, Jerome, 113, 125

T

Tabasco, 123
Talbot, Howard, 143, 161, 167, 169, 185, 190
A Tale of Mystery, or, The Dumb Man of Arpenay, 35–36
The Talk of New York, 192
Tammany, or, The Indian Chief, 25, 272
Tamponi, Francis, 93
Tangerine, 256, 276, 283
Tannehill, Frank, 291
Tannehill, Frank, Jr., 130
Tantalizing Tommy, 216, 283
The Tar and the Tartar, 112
Tarasoff, I., 257, 291
Tarr, E.S., 66
The Tars from Tripoli, 36
Tartaglia, Bob, 315
The Tattooed Man, 187, 285
Taylor, Raynor, 6, 24, 25, 28, 29, 30, 31, 32, 34, 39
Teal, Ben, 120, 125, 133, 136, 139, 142, 147, 148, 151, 155, 157, 158, 161, 168, 171, 177, 189, 190, 203, 291
The Telephone Girl, 142, 275
The Tempest, 39
The Temple Dancer, 18, 244
Temple, Edward P., 174, 177, 181, 186, 237, 243, 291–292
Temptations, 18, 208
The Tenderfoot, 172
Terriss, Thomas ("Tom"), 124, 171
Terry, Mike, 315
Tesori, Jeanine, 315
A Texas Steer, or, Money Makes the Mare Go, 110
Thaler, Fred, 315
Thomé, Francis, 20, 224
Thompson, Aaron, 315
Thompson, Frederick, 204
Thompson, Jay, 315
Thompson, Lydia, 10, 11, 12, 65
Thorne, Thomas Pearsall, 121, 130
Three Blind Mice!, or, Harlequin Tell-Tale Tit, 66
The Three Dragoons, 147, 285
The Three Hunchbacks!, 66
Three Little Maids, 167
The Three Mus-Ke-Teers, 69
The Three Sisters!, 55
Three Twins, 194, 291
Thrilby, 128
Tib, or, The Cat in Crinoline, 50
Tierney, Harry, 234, 235, 238, 240, 242, 244, 246, 247, 248, 249, 250, 261, 262, 265
Tietjens, Paul, 164, 235
Tiller, John, 265
Tillie's Nightmare, 203, 292
A Tin Soldier, 101
Tissington, Henry, xii, xix, 54, 56, 57, 58, 63, 64, 66, 68, 73, 78, 81
Tom Jones, 191, 282
Tom-Tom, The Piper's Son Stole a Pig and Away He Run, 56
Too Many Wives, 196
Toot Sweet, 245
Topics of 1923, 265, 280, 293
The Top o' th' World, 191, 267, 287, 290
The Toreador, 158–159, 276
The Tourists, 184, 270
The Tourists in a Pullman Palace Car, 83–84
Tourjée, Homer, 127
Tours, Frank (E.), 134, 167, 189, 199, 207, 212, 230, 233, 235, 237, 239, 247, 250, 252, 256, 257, 264
Towle, George P., 154, 165
Tracy, George Lowell, 131, 142
Trajetta, Phil, 37, 38
Treemonisha, 17, 213
A Trip to Buffalo, 160
A Trip to Chinatown, 114, 285
A Trip to Japan, 200, 288
A Trip to Mars, 119
A Trip to Niagara, or, Travelers in America, 39
Troob, Daniel, 315
Tumble In, 244, 276
The Twelve Temptations!, xii, 63, 271
The 20th Century Girl, 126, 275
Twirly-Whirly, 162

The Two Cadis, 59
Two Little Girls in Blue, 255, 293
The Two Orphans, 73
The Tycoon, or, Young American in Japan, 47
Tyte, Alexander, 51, 53, 54, 57
The Tzigane, 127, 275

U

Uncle Tom's Cabin, 44
Under Cover, 168
Under Many Flags, 216, 294
Undine, 212
Up and Down Broadway, 204, 294
Up in the Clouds, 258, 274, 289
Up She Goes, 261–262, 276
Urbont, Jacques, 315

V

Valeria, 44
Valiant Valentine, 54, 278
Van Den Berg, Joseph, 141, 154
The Vanderbilt Cup, 182
Van Hamme, Mons., 68
Variety, or, The Picture Gallery, 46
Varney, Louis, 153
Varney, Pierre Joseph Alphonse, 44
Vassar Girls, 97
Vaughn, James (J.), 165, 182, 183, 201
Vera Violetta, 212, 290, 294
Verhoeven, Pauline, 206
Veron, Paul, 101
Very Good Eddie, 231, 269, 285
The Velvet Lady, 17, 243–244, 286
Venanzi, Angelo, 21, 120
Venus, 91
Vicars, Harold, 139, 230, 232, 238, 248, 250, 253
The Viceroy, 153
The Viking, 127
Vincent, L.J., 70
Vincent, Nat, 246, 254
Vining, Dave, 222
Virgin of the Sun, 38
Vivian, George, 254
Vodery, Will, 192, 228, 233, 252, 255

Vogel, Prof., 76
The Voice of Nature, 35
Vokes, Frederick, 71
Vokes, (Walter) Fawdon, 71
The Volunteers, 27
Von Olker, Ferdinand, 51, 82, 86
Von Suppé, Franz, 115
Von Tilzer, Albert, 173, 180, 181, 184, 194, 202, 204, 232, 246, 249, 251
Von Tilzer, Harry, 20, 147, 158, 160, 161, 165, 168, 169, 184, 189, 190, 193, 204, 205, 214, 219, 256
Le Voyage en Suisse, 90
The Voyage of Suzette, 120–121, 274
Voyagers in Southern Seas, or The Children of Captain Grant, 89

W

Waddy Coogan, 105
Wade, Herman Avery, 185, 190, 193
Wade, Uel, 315
Wagner, John, 146
Wahler, David, 315
Walberg, Betty, 315
Walcot, Charles M., 50, 51
Waldman, Robert, 316
Walker, Aida Overton, 183, 193
Walker, Chris, 316
Walker, Don, 316
Waller, Henry, 121, 122, 159, 163
Wall, Harry, 60, 61
The Wall Street Girl, 214, 290
Walton, George, 124
Wang, 112
Wannemacher, Henry, 77, 78, 84
Warde, Willie, 140, 154, 177, 292
Ward, F.T., 111
Ware, William (Henry), 6, 36, 37, 39
Warner, Neil, 316
Warner, Russell, 316
Warnick, Clay, 316
The Warrior's Welcome Home, 29, 275
Wars of the World, 225, 294
Watch Your Step, 226, 270
The Water Queen, 13, 106
Wathall, Alfred G., 164

Wayburn, Ned, 20, 146, 147, 156, 159, 163, 165, 167, 171, 174, 175, 176, 178, 179, 180, 197, 199, 200, 202, 203, 207, 209, 212, 215, 217, 218, 220, 226, 229, 233, 237, 238, 242, 246, 249, 251, 255, 260, 292–293
Wayrauch, H., 52, 53
Webb, Lyda, 265
Webb, Robert, 316
Webb, Roy, 220, 240
The Wedding Trip, 212–213, 294
Wee Willie Winkie, 64–65
Weigert, Rene, 316
Weill, Kurt, 316
Weiner, Mark, 316
Weissman, Bernard, 316
Weixelbaum, Karl, 164, 210
Weld, Arthur, 152, 153, 155, 162, 166, 171, 186, 187, 207
Weldon, (M.) Francis, 264, 265, 293
Well-Fed Dora, 96
Werner, Fred, 316
West, (J.) Clarence, 107, 180, 217, 233
West, Paul, 214
Westward Ho, 126
We, Us and Company at Mud Springs, 97–98
What's in a Name?, 249
Wheeler, Harold, 316–317
When Dreams Come True, 16, 220, 288, 290
When Johnny Comes Marching Home, 16, 163, 236, 270, 279
When Sweet Sixteen, 210, 270, 278
The Whirl of New York, 256, 274
The Whirl of Society, 214, 280
The Whirl of the Town, 139, 275
The Whirl of the World, 222, 294
White, Al, 189
The White Cat, xii, 180, 271, 277, 292
The White Elephant, 107
The White Fawn, xii, 10, 14, 58, 271,
White, George, 250, 293–294
Whoop-Dee-Doo, 168, 291
Widmer, Henry, 89, 90, 95, 112, 115
The Widow Jones, 129, 287

The Wife Hunters, 211–212, 293
Wildflower, 263, 269, 272
The Wild Rose, 160, 278, 282, 286, 294
Will, Ethyl, 317
Williams, Bert, 150, 154, 161, 165, 182, 193, 201, 204, 208, 217, 223, 228
Williams, Fred, 83
Williams, Jesse, 82, 87, 97, 98, 101, 105, 113, 115, 116, 117, 120, 127, 128, 139, 148
Wilson, Art, 317
Wilson, William J., 204, 207, 209, 211, 212, 213, 216, 219, 220, 222, 225, 294
Wine, Women and Song, 144
Winninger, Charles, 214
A Winsome Widow, 214, 286
Winsome Winnie, 170, 270, 290
Withers, William, (Jr.), 13, 71, 72, 73, 77, 90
Witmark, Isidore, 114, 119, 161
Witt, Max S., 154, 167, 179
The Wizard of Oz, 17, 164, 285
The Wizard of the Nile, 130
Woldin, Judd, 317
Wolff, Emil O., 119
The Wonder Child, or, The Follies of Earth, Air and Sea, 78
Wonderland, 179–180, 285
The Woolen Stocking, 120
Wooley, Scott, 317
Woolf, Benjamin E(dward), 53, 87, 126
Woolf, Edward, 41, 42
A World of Pleasure, 18, 230, 280, 281, 284
The World's Fair, or, Columbia in the Clouds, 43
Wormser, André, 112

Y

Yakovleff, Alexander, 261
A Yankee Circus on Mars, xii, 177, 278, 283, 288, 292
The Yankee Consul, 172, 283
Yankee Doodle Dandy, 143, 281
The Yankee Prince, 194, 276

The Yankee Tourist, 188, 283
Yates, B., 45, 46
York, Donald (Don), 317
You'll Never Know, 254
Youmans, Vincent, xviii, 255, 263, 265
Young Baccus, or, Spirits and Water, 46
You're in Love, xiii, 235–236, 284
Yours Truly, 241, 273

Z

Zamecnik, John S., 194
Zanfretta, Alexander, 62
Zanina, or, The Rover of Cambaye, 88
Zanita, 15, 97
Zara!, 92
Zaulig, Fred W., 60, 75, 76
Zaza, 154
Zenobia, Queen of Palmyra, 94
Ziegfeld Follies of 1911, 17, 208–209, 273, 278, 284, 286, 290
Ziegfeld Follies of 1912, 216–217, 286
Ziegfeld Follies of 1913, 219, 278, 286
Ziegfeld Follies of 1914, 223, 273, 278
Ziegfeld Follies of 1915, 228, 273, 286
Ziegfeld Follies of 1916, 233, 278, 293
Ziegfeld Follies of 1917, 236–237, 278, 293
Ziegfeld Follies of 1918, 241–242, 293
Ziegfeld Follies of 1919, 246, 293
Ziegfeld Follies of 1920, 250, 288
Ziegfeld Follies of 1921, 256, 283, 288
Ziegfeld Follies of 1922, 260, 273, 293
Zig-Zag Alley, 164, 276
Zimmerman, Charles, 101, 103, 105, 144, 164
Z-Seltzer!, 94

www.ingramcontent.com/pod-product-compliance
Lightning Source LLC
Chambersburg PA
CBHW071948220426
43662CB00009B/1046